ANNUAL EDITIONS

AMERICAN FOREIGN POLICY 99/00

Fifth Edition

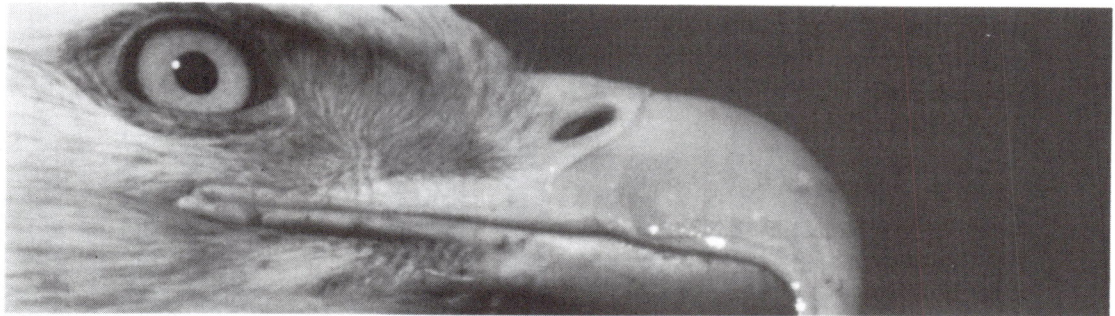

EDITOR

Glenn P. Hastedt
James Madison University

Glenn Hastedt received his Ph.D. from Indiana University. He is professor of political science at James Madison University, where he teaches courses on U.S. foreign policy, national security policy, and international relations. His special area of interest is on the workings of the intelligence community and the problems of strategic surprise and learning from intelligence failures. In addition to having published articles on these topics, he is the author of *American Foreign Policy: Past, Present, Future,* Second Edition; coauthor of *Dimensions of World Politics;* and editor and contributor to *Controlling Intelligence.* He is currently working on two volumes of readings, *Toward the Twenty-First Century* and *One World; Many Voices.*

Dushkin/McGraw-Hill
Sluice Dock, Guilford, Connecticut 06437

Visit us on the Internet
http://www.dushkin.com/annualeditions/

Credits

1. The United States and the World: Strategic Choices
Facing overview—The White House Official Photograph. 13—AP/Wide World photo by Amel Emric.
2. The United States and the World: Regional and Bilateral Relations
Facing overview—AP Photo/David Brauchli.
3. The Domestic Side of American Foreign Policy
Facing overview—UN/DPI Photo by Evan Schneider.
4. The Institutional Context of American Foreign Policy
Facing overview—Congressional News Photo.
5. The Foreign Policy-Making Process
Facing overview—UN Photo/M. Grant.
6. U.S. International Economic Strategy
Facing overview—© 1998 by PhotoDisc, Inc.
7. U.S. Post–Cold War Military Strategy
Facing overview—© 1998 by PhotoDisc, Inc.
8. Historical Perspectives on American Foreign Policy
Facing overview—AP/Wide World photo by Diether Endlicher.

Copyright

Cataloging in Publication Data
Main entry under title: Annual Editions: American Foreign Policy. 1999/2000.
  1. U.S. Foreign Relations—Periodicals. I. Hastedt, Glenn P., *comp.*
II. Title: American foreign policy.
327.73'05   ISBN 0-07-041437-8   ISSN 1075-5225

© 1999 by Dushkin/McGraw-Hill, Guilford, CT 06437, A Division of The McGraw-Hill Companies.

Copyright law prohibits the reproduction, storage, or transmission in any form by any means of any portion of this publication without the express written permission of Dushkin/McGraw-Hill, and of the copyright holder (if different) of the part of the publication to be reproduced. The Guidelines for Classroom Copying endorsed by Congress explicitly state that unauthorized copying may not be used to create, to replace, or to substitute for anthologies, compilations, or collective works.

Annual Editions® is a Registered Trademark of Dushkin/McGraw-Hill, A Division of The McGraw-Hill Companies.

Fifth Edition

Cover image © 1999 PhotoDisc, Inc.

Printed in the United States of America   234567890BAHBAH5432109   Printed on Recycled Paper

Members of the Advisory Board are instrumental in the final selection of articles for each edition of ANNUAL EDITIONS. Their review of articles for content, level, currentness, and appropriateness provides critical direction to the editor and staff. We think that you will find their careful consideration well reflected in this volume.

EDITOR

Glenn P. Hastedt
James Madison University

ADVISORY BOARD

Linda S. Adams
Baylor University

Kirsten Bookmiller
Millersville University

Phillip Brenner
American University

Ralph G. Carter
Texas Christian University

Alistair D. Edgar
Wilfrid Laurier University

Nader Entessar
Spring Hill College

Will Hazelton
Miami University

Christopher M. Jones
Northern Illinois University

James A. Klemstine
North Carolina State University

Donald Mayer
Shippensburg University

Steve Newlin
California State University
Chico

James W. Peterson
Valdosta State University

George Poteat
Troy State University

Helen E. Purkitt
U.S. Naval Academy

Nathaniel Richmond
Utica College

J. Philip Rogers
Central European University

John T. Rourke
University of Connecticut
Storrs

Douglas W. Simon
Drew University

Elizabeth Spalding
George Mason University

James C. Sperling
University of Akron

Joseph E. Thompson
Villanova University

Kristine Thompson
Concordia College

B. Thomas Trout
University of New Hampshire

Caroline S. Westerhof
University of South Florida

Shelton Williams
Austin College

Stephen D. Wrage
U.S. Naval Academy

EDITORIAL STAFF

Ian A. Nielsen, Publisher
Roberta Monaco, Senior Developmental Editor
Dorothy Fink, Associate Developmental Editor
Addie Raucci, Senior Administrative Editor
Cheryl Greenleaf, Permissions Editor
Joseph Offredi, Permissions/Editorial Assistant
Diane Barker, Proofreader
Lisa Holmes-Doebrick, Program Coordinator

PRODUCTION STAFF

Brenda S. Filley, Production Manager
Charles Vitelli, Designer
Lara M. Johnson, Design/Advertising Coordinator
Laura Levine, Graphics
Mike Campbell, Graphics
Tom Goddard, Graphics
Juliana Arbo, Typesetting Supervisor
Jane Jaegersen, Typesetter
Marie Lazauskas, Word Processor
Kathleen D'Amico, Word Processor
Larry Killian, Copier Coordinator

To the Reader

In publishing ANNUAL EDITIONS we recognize the enormous role played by the magazines, newspapers, and journals of the public press in providing current, first-rate educational information in a broad spectrum of interest areas. Many of these articles are appropriate for students, researchers, and professionals seeking accurate, current material to help bridge the gap between principles and theories and the real world. These articles, however, become more useful for study when those of lasting value are carefully collected, organized, indexed, and reproduced in a low-cost format, which provides easy and permanent access when the material is needed. That is the role played by ANNUAL EDITIONS.

New to ANNUAL EDITIONS is the inclusion of related World Wide Web sites. These sites have been selected by our editorial staff to represent some of the best resources found on the World Wide Web today. Through our carefully developed topic guide, we have linked these Web resources to the articles covered in this ANNUAL EDITIONS reader. We think that you will find this volume useful, and we hope that you will take a moment to visit us on the Web at **http://www.dushkin.com/** to tell us what you think.

This fifth volume of *Annual Editions: American Foreign Policy* presents an overview of American foreign policy in transition. It is a transition that is proceeding unevenly and at several different levels. At the broadest level, American foreign policy is in a transition from relying upon the grand strategies that shaped definitions of the national interests and mobilized America's resources during the cold war era to developing a new set of fundamental principles and guiding concepts. This transition is evident in the reworking of American relations with other states and in efforts to establish international mechanisms for preserving the peace.

It is uncertain how well prepared the policymakers, American political institutions, and the American public are for this transition. The rush of events in such places as Bosnia, Rwanda, Cuba, China, India, Pakistan, the Middle East, and North Korea has outpaced the ability of the policymakers to develop a coherent strategy. There is also uncertainty in Congress, the bureaucracy, and the American public over how best to respond to events abroad. The contradictory signals sent out by these political forces point to a potentially long and difficult transition to a post–cold war era.

Annual Editions: American Foreign Policy 99/00 examines the many issues and problems involved in making this transition from a cold war–centered American foreign policy to one firmly rooted in the international politics of the 1990s. It is divided into eight units. The first addresses questions of grand strategy. The second unit focuses on selected regional and bilateral relations. In the third unit, our attention shifts inward to the ways in which domestic forces affect the content of American foreign policy. The fourth unit looks at the institutions that make American foreign policy. In the fifth unit, the process by which American foreign policy is made is illustrated by accounts of recent foreign policy decisions. The sixth and seventh units provide an overview of the economic and military issues confronting the United States today. The final unit provides students with a sampling of recent writings by authors whose goal it is to reflect on the past so that American foreign policy in the present and future might be improved.

I would like to thank Ian Nielsen for supporting the concept of an *Annual Editions: American Foreign Policy* and for helping to oversee the process of putting this volume together. Also deserving of thanks are the many people at Dushkin/McGraw-Hill who worked to make the project a success and those faculty on the Advisory Board who provided input on the selection of articles. In the end, the success of *Annual Editions: American Foreign Policy* depends upon the views of the faculty and students who use it. I encourage you to let me know what worked and what did not so that each successive volume will be better than its predecessor. Please complete and return the postage-paid article rating form at the end of this book.

Glenn Hastedt
Editor

Contents

To the Reader	iv
Topic Guide	2
⊚ Selected World Wide Web Sites	4
Overview	6

1. **The Benevolent Empire,** Robert Kagan, *Foreign Policy,* Summer 1998. — 8
   Robert Kagan maintains that **American hegemony** is better for the world than any of the realistic alternatives. He contends that no state really wants **multipolarity** and that **Bosnia** proves that if multilateralism is to succeed it must be preceded by **unilateralism.**

2. **The Perils of (and for) an Imperial America,** Charles William Maynes, *Foreign Policy,* Summer 1998. — 14
   Charles Maynes presents *a rejoinder to Kagan's argument.* He argues *that we are at a point of no return in constructing* a truly new type of *post–cold war international system.* Maynes builds a case against American hegemony by examining its impact on the American character, the domestic costs it would entail, the backlash it would provoke in other states, and the opportunities that would be lost by pursuing such a strategy.

3. **A New Realism,** Ronald Steel, *World Policy Journal,* Summer 1997. — 21
   Focusing on the concept of **national security,** Ronald Steel calls for a reexamination of the **concepts** we use to think about American foreign policy and international relations. He argues that security is not a condition but a feeling and a process. It is neither an absolute nor an end in itself.

4. **Democracy at Risk: American Culture in a Global Culture,** Benjamin R. Barber, *World Policy Journal,* Summer 1998. — 30
   One of the primary goals of American foreign policy has been to promote democracy. Yet, Benjamin Barber maintains that *the emerging global culture,* which is a product of American pop culture and is producing a consumer society, is *indifferent to democracy* and threatens our civil liberties.

UNIT 1

The United States and the World: Strategic Choices

Four articles review some of the foreign policy choices the United States has today.

The concepts in bold italics are developed in the article. For further expansion please refer to the Topic Guide and the Index.

UNIT 2

The United States and the World: Regional and Bilateral Relations

Nine selections consider U.S. relations with Russia, Asia, Europe, and the developing world.

Overview   42

A. RUSSIA

5. **The United States and the New Russia: The First Five Years,** Raymond L. Garthoff, *Current History*, October 1997.   44

    Raymond Garthoff presents an overview of U.S.–Russian relations over the past 5 years. He argues that by the end of 1993 the honeymoon period had ended. Garthoff maintains that the ***greatest failure in U.S. foreign policy*** has been that of not effectively bringing Russia into a new security architecture for Europe.

6. **Is Russia Still an Enemy?** Richard Pipes, *Foreign Affairs*, September/October 1997.   52

    Richard Pipes asserts that Russia is not an enemy but that it might become one because ***a battle for Russia's soul*** is in progress between anti-Western and pro-Western forces. Which view will triumph will be determined by the Russians themselves, and the West can only marginally influence the decision. He calls for the U.S. to adopt ***a subtle policy*** that mixes toughness with understanding.

B. ASIA

7. **Testing the United States–Japan Security Alliance,** James Shinn, *Current History*, December 1997.   57

    Some in Japan maintain that the U.S.–Japan security alliance is really a patron-client relationship. This feeling is only one of many circumstances that are placing a great deal of stress on ***U.S.–Japanese relations.*** James Shinn examines which forces are pulling it apart, which are holding it together, how the alliance might be tested, and what the consequences of failure are.

8. **South Asian Arms Race: Reviving Dormant Fears of Nuclear War,** Barbara Crossette, *New York Times*, May 29, 1998.   63

    The ***detonation of nuclear devices*** by India and Pakistan in 1998 shocked the world. Barbara Crossette discusses the consequences of these tests both for the Indian subcontinent and the world. Experts fear that India and Pakistan could be drawn into a nuclear war over Kashmir.

C. EUROPE

9. **America and Europe: Is the Break Inevitable?** Werner Weidenfeld, *The Washington Quarterly*, Summer 1997.   65

    Perceptions on both sides of the Atlantic regarding the proper nature of the ***American-European relationship*** are undergoing radical change. Werner Weidenfeld argues that for a new era of cooperation to emerge, political elites in both the United States and Europe will need to fashion a ***new sense of transatlantic community.***

10. **Why Are We in Bosnia?** Richard Holbrooke, *The New Yorker*, May 18, 1998.   72

    Ambassador Richard Holbrooke, a key figure in engineering the Dayton Accords, recounts the key steps in the Clinton ***administration's decision to involve itself in Bosnia.*** He concludes with a call for American leadership if future Bosnias are to be avoided.

The concepts in bold italics are developed in the article. For further expansion please refer to the Topic Guide and the Index.

D. THE DEVELOPING WORLD

11. Pivotal States and U.S. Strategy, Robert S. Chase, Emily B. Hill, and Paul Kennedy, *Foreign Affairs*, January/February 1996.
Pivotal states are defined as those "whose fate is uncertain and whose future will profoundly affect their surrounding regions." The great danger that they face is not external aggression but that they will become **victims of internal disorder.** The authors identify and discuss the contemporary situation in nine pivotal states. — 77

12. The Middle East Peace Process: A Crisis of Partnership, Madeleine Albright, *Vital Speeches of the Day*, June 1, 1998.
In her speech, Secretary of State Madeleine Albright reaffirms America's commitment to the **Arab-Israeli peace process** even though it is not a party to those negotiations. Albright explains the logic behind the **U.S. foreign policy position.** She also explains what the United States has been doing to overcome the impasse in the peace talks. — 85

13. Africa, the 'Invisible Land,' Is Gaining Visibility, Salih Booker, *Washington Post National Weekly Edition*, April 6, 1998.
Salih Booker outlines the ingredients of the **United States' first real Africa policy.** It will promote great private business ventures and promote democracy but lacks additional funds for development, relieving debt, or using U.S. forces for peacekeeping purposes. Booker asserts that refinements are still necessary if the United States is to take advantage of the opportunities that now exist. — 88

Overview — 90

A. THE PUBLIC, PUBLIC OPINION, AND THE MEDIA

14. The Common Sense, John Mueller, *The National Interest*, Spring 1997.
John Mueller argues that, when looked at over time, the public's views on American foreign policy are consistent and reasonable. He presents 10 propositions about how American public opinion will influence **foreign policy in the post–cold war era.** — 92

15. Netanyahu and American Jews, Jonathan Broder, *World Policy Journal*, Spring 1998.
Jonathan Broder asserts that **Israel's most powerful political constituency** in the United States is deeply alienated from Israeli prime minister Benjamin Netanyahu. He states that the stage is set for a major confrontation between the United States and Israel, and Netanyahu is counting on Congress to act as a counterweight to the Clinton administration. — 99

UNIT 3

The Domestic Side of American Foreign Policy

Four selections examine the domestic impact of American foreign policy.

The concepts in bold italics are developed in the article. For further expansion please refer to the Topic Guide and the Index.

B. THE ROLE OF AMERICAN VALUES

16. On American Principles, George F. Kennan, *Foreign Affairs,* March/April 1995. — **108**
George Kennan calls a principle *"a general rule of conduct"* that defines the limits within which foreign policy ought to operate. Building on a position argued by President John Quincy Adams when Adams was secretary of state, Kennan says that the best way for a big country such as the United States to help smaller ones is by the *power of example.*

17. Globalization: The Great American Non-Debate, Alan Tonelson, *Current History,* November 1997. — **113**
In his essay, Alan Tonelson states that the failure to fully incorporate globalization into American foreign and domestic policy has had serious consequences. Using **NAFTA** as an example, he fears that *the globalization of production* will threaten America's future as a cohesive and successful society.

Overview — 120

UNIT 4
The Institutional Context of American Foreign Policy

Six articles examine how the courts, state and local governments, Congress, and bureaucracy impact on U.S. foreign policy.

A. LAW AND THE COURTS

18. Against an International Criminal Court, Lee A. Casey and David B. Rivkin Jr., *Commentary,* May 1998. — **122**
Both authors have served in the Justice Department. They argue that *the UN-sponsored treaty* to establish an International Criminal Court is flawed. Fears also exist that it will be a rogue institution. They contend that international mechanisms already exist to bring outlaws to justice.

B. STATE AND LOCAL GOVERNMENTS

19. Paying Something for Nothing, Kimberly Ann Elliott, *State Government News,* May 1998. — **125**
At least 25 different *state and local jurisdictions* have imposed *economic sanctions against foreign countries.* Principal targets include Nigeria, Myanmar, and Cuba. Kimberly Elliott argues that such sanctions are counterproductive and may be unconstitutional.

C. CONGRESS

20. The Senate's Strange Bedfellows, John Isaacs, *The Bulletin of the Atomic Scientists,* January/February 1998. — **128**
John Isaacs writes prior to the Senate's support of NATO expansion. In his article he comments on the political alignment of forces that is shaping up. Isaacs notes that the *ideological battle lines* normally present in Senate foreign policy debates are totally blurred on the question of NATO enlargement.

D. BUREAUCRACY

21. **Racing toward the Future: The Revolution in Military Affairs,** Steven Metz, *Current History,* April 1997. — 131

    Desert Storm was seen by many in the military as the prologue to **a fundamental shift in warfare**—a revolution in military affairs. These new ideas now serve as the blueprint for most **long-term thinking in the Defense Department.** Steven Metz questions the value of this change in thinking.

22. **Why Spy? The Uses and Misuses of Intelligence,** Stanley Kober, *USA Today Magazine (Society for the Advancement of Education),* March 1998. — 136

    Stanley Kober asserts that two steps are needed to improve the effectiveness of the intelligence community. First, it must **concentrate on genuine threats** to American national security, such as terrorism, and not on economic espionage. Second, at a political level the intelligence community should be used to bring into **focus the assumptions behind policy initiatives.**

23. **Tin Cup Diplomacy,** Hans Binnendijk, *The National Interest,* Fall 1997. — 141

    Reductions in the post–cold war international affairs budget have been deep. Hans Binnendijk is concerned that these cuts are affecting the ability of the United States to influence events abroad and to practice preventive diplomacy. Only the continued presence of a large military allows the United States to retain global influence.

Overview — 144

24. **Inside the White House Situation Room,** Michael Donley, Cornelius O'Leary, and John Montgomery, *Studies in Intelligence,* Number 1, 1997. — 146

    Established after the Bay of Pigs disaster in 1960, the White House Situation Room provides current intelligence and crisis support to the **National Security Council.** The authors of this report describe the role of the council in the policy-making process in an era of 24-hour-a-day television news. They pay particular attention to its intelligence support role and its relationship with other Washington decision-making centers.

25. **NATO Expansion: The Anatomy of a Decision,** James Goldgeier, *The Washington Quarterly,* Winter 1998. — 152

    Relying on interviews with major players in the Clinton administration, James Goldgeier recounts the three key phases in the decision-making process that led to support for **NATO expansion.** He finds that this decision was made because a few key people supported it and that it was taken over **widespread bureaucratic opposition.**

26. **The White House Dismissed Warnings on China Satellite Deal,** Jeff Gerth and John M. Broder, *New York Times,* June 1, 1998. — 161

    One of the most controversial foreign policy decisions of the Clinton administration was that of **approving a license for Loral Space & Communications to export a satellite to China.** The authors examine this decision and note that the White House **ignored bureaucratic warnings** because the company was facing heavy fines for delay.

UNIT 5

The Foreign Policy-Making Process

Three selections review some of the elements that affect the process of American foreign policy.

The concepts in bold italics are developed in the article. For further expansion please refer to the Topic Guide and the Index.

UNIT 6

U.S. International Economic Strategy

Four selections discuss how economics and trade strategies affect American foreign policy choices.

Overview   **164**

27. **Globalization and Its Discontents: Navigating the Dangers of a Tangled World,** Richard N. Haass and Robert E. Litan, *Foreign Affairs*, May/June 1998.   **166**
The authors identify three **fundamentally different approaches** to addressing the problem of the **globalization of America's economy.** The first embraces free markets and rejects IMF-bailouts of troubled currencies. The second calls for creating new institutions to direct the global marketplace. The third calls merely for remodeling some existing international institutions.

28. **For a New, Progressive IMF,** Robert Borosage, *Foreign Service Journal*, April 1998.   **170**
Over the past year the **International Monetary Fund (IMF)** has moved into the spotlight as a central player in managing the global economy with its bailouts of the stumbling Asian currencies. A great deal of controversy has surrounded these activities. Borosage turns a critical eye to its actions and calls for a **new internationalism** as the basis for reform.

29. **Foreign Aid,** Carol Graham, *The Brookings Review*, Spring 1997.   **176**
Carol Graham argues that the reluctance of the United States to provide foreign aid is seen by other nations as evidence of Washington's unwillingness to pay its global dues. Graham examines **three issues central to the debate over the future of foreign aid:** Would states have performed worse without aid? How are we allocating aid? Do policies promote growth?

30. **Bogotá Aid: To Fight Drugs or Rebels?** Diana Jean Schemo and Tim Golden, *New York Times*, June 2, 1998.   **178**
Focusing on **Colombia,** this article examines the problems encountered in using foreign aid, particularly **military aid,** to stop **drug trafficking** in a country beset by internal conflict. One of the fears that the Clinton administration has is that the drug traffickers and **guerrillas** will bond more closely and create a strategic threat to the United States.

UNIT 7

U.S. Post–Cold War Military Strategy

Four articles examine U.S. military planning in the context of the post–cold war era.

Overview   **182**

A. THE USE OF MILITARY POWER

31. **Inventing Threats,** Carl Conetta and Charles Knight, *The Bulletin of the Atomic Scientists*, March/April 1998.   **184**
The authors use the Pentagon's recent **"Quadrennial Defense Review"** as the basis for evaluating American national security policy. They contend that the military has begun inventing threats by moving from **threat-based analysis to capability-based analysis.** In the process, "wild card" scenarios are gaining credibility.

32. **Responding to Terrorism,** David Tucker, *The Washington Quarterly*, Winter 1998.   **189**
David Tucker is a staff member of the assistant secretary of defense for special operations and low-intensity conflict. He reviews and evaluates the **effectiveness of three current and six past U.S. policies designed to combat terrorism.** Tucker recommends a combination of elements from many of these strategies.

The concepts in bold italics are developed in the article. For further expansion please refer to the Topic Guide and the Index.

B. ARMS CONTROL

33. Paring Down the Arsenal, Frank von Hippel, *The Bulletin of the Atomic Scientists,* May/June 1997.   **197**
In March 1997, Bill Clinton and Boris Yeltsin met in Helsinki and pledged themselves to begin **START III negotiations.** Frank von Hippel calls for moving rapidly in this direction by pulling missiles off hair-trigger alert and making deep cuts in nuclear stockpiles. He presents a three-stage strategy for bringing this about.

34. The New Arms Race: Light Weapons and International Security, Michael T. Klare, *Current History,* April 1997.   **204**
During the cold war the major nonnuclear arms control problem involved the sale of large and expensive weapons systems. This is no longer the case. Michael Klare argues that **the key weapons affecting the outcome of ethnic and sectarian conflicts** are light weapons such as assault rifles, antitank weapons, and shoulder-fired antiaircraft missiles. His strategy addresses the sale of these weapons by governments and black market sales.

Overview   210

35. Closing the Gate: The Persian Gulf War Revisited, Michael Sterner, *Current History,* January 1997.   **212**
The Persian Gulf War is perhaps the most written-about military operation of the post–cold war era. Much has been made over the manner in which the war ended and the failure to remove Saddam Hussein from power. Michael Sterner examines the question of what coalition forces might have done differently at the war's end and what the impact of those actions might have been.

36. Rethinking N+1, Brad Roberts, *The National Interest,* Spring 1998.   **220**
In 1961 **Albert Wohlstetter** wrote a famous article on **nuclear proliferation,** something he termed the N+1 problem. Brad Roberts reexamines Wohlstetter's arguments in light of developments in the post–cold war international system. Roberts maintains that **the old answer of providing security guarantees to would-be proliferators in order to stop them no longer works.**

Index   225
Article Review Form   228
Article Rating Form   229

UNIT 8

Historical Retrospectives on American Foreign Policy

Two articles examine some of the history of American foreign policy.

The concepts in bold italics are developed in the article. For further expansion please refer to the Topic Guide and the Index.

1

Topic Guide

This topic guide suggests how the selections and World Wide Web sites found in the next section of this book relate to topics of traditional concern to American foreign policy students and professionals. It is useful for locating interrelated articles and Web sites for reading and research. The guide is arranged alphabetically according to topic.

The relevant Web sites, which are numbered and annotated on pages 4 and 5, are easily identified by the Web icon (☼) under the topic articles. By linking the articles and the Web sites by topic, this ANNUAL EDITIONS reader becomes a powerful learning and research tool.

TOPIC AREA	TREATED IN	TOPIC AREA	TREATED IN
Africa	13. Africa, the 'Invisible Land' ☼ **4, 9, 22, 28**	Developing World	11. Pivotal States and U.S. Strategy 29. Foreign Aid ☼ **4, 9, 19, 20, 21, 22, 23, 24**
Arms Control	5. United States and the New Russia 33. Paring Down the Arsenal 34. New Arms Race 36. Rethinking N+1 ☼ **7, 9, 29**	Domestic and Foreign Policy Linkages	4. Democracy at Risk 15. Netanyahu and American Jews 27. Globalization and Its Discontents ☼ **1, 3, 4, 10, 11, 16**
Arms Trade	26. White House Dismissed Warnings 34. New Arms Race ☼ **18, 20, 29**	Drugs	30. Bogatá Aid ☼ **8, 13**
Asia	7. Testing the United States–Japan Security Alliance 8. South Asian Arms Race 26. White House Dismissed Warnings 28. For a New, Progressive IMF ☼ **7, 9, 18, 20, 21**	Economic Sanctions	8. South Asian Arms Race 19. Paying Something for Nothing 32. Responding to Terrorism ☼ **7, 8, 9, 26**
Bosnia	1. Benevolent Empire 10. Why Are We in Bosnia? ☼ **5, 6, 7, 25, 26, 28, 31**	Elections	26. White House Dismissed Warnings ☼ **20**
Central Intelligence Agency (CIA)	22. Why Spy? 32. Responding to Terrorism ☼ **12, 26**	Europe	1. Benevolent Empire 5. United States and the New Russia 9. America and Europe 10. Why Are We in Bosnia? 25. NATO Expansion ☼ **1, 3, 5, 6, 7, 10, 11, 14, 16, 18, 31**
Congress	15. Netanyahu and American Jews 20. Senate's Strange Bedfellows 26. White House Dismissed Warnings 28. For a New, Progressive IMF ☼ **2, 4, 9, 32**	Foreign Aid	11. Pivotal States and U.S. Strategy 29. Foreign Aid 30. Bogatá Aid ☼ **13, 15, 19, 20, 22, 23, 28**
Courts and Law	18. Against an International Criminal Court 32. Responding to Terrorism ☼ **16, 26**	Globalization	4. Democracy at Risk 17. Globalization 27. Globalization and Its Discontents 28. For a New, Progressive IMF ☼ **3, 7, 8, 9, 13, 14, 16, 17, 19, 20, 21, 22, 23, 24**
Democracy	4. Democracy at Risk 13. Africa, the 'Invisible Land' ☼ **1, 3, 4, 9, 22, 28**		

TOPIC AREA	TREATED IN	TOPIC AREA	TREATED IN
Human Rights	13. Africa, the 'Invisible Land' 18. Against an International Criminal Court 30. Bogotá Aid ○ *4, 9, 19, 28*	**(NATO)**	25. NATO Expansion ○ *7, 14, 31*
International Trade	4. Democracy at Risk 17. Globalization 19. Paying Something for Nothing 22. Why Spy? 27. Globalization and Its Discontents 28. For a New, Progressive IMF ○ *7, 8, 9, 13, 14, 15, 16, 17, 19, 20, 21, 22, 24, 25*	**Nuclear Weapons**	8. South Asian Arms Race 33. Paring Down the Arsenal 36. Rethinking N+1 ○ *6, 7, 25, 26, 27, 29, 30, 31*
		Peacekeeping	18. Against an International Criminal Court ○ *14, 25*
		Policy Making	10. Why Are We in Bosnia? 15. Netanyahu and American Jews 24. Inside the White House Situation Room 25. NATO Expansion 26. White House Dismissed Warnings ○ *3, 5, 6, 14, 16, 20, 31, 32*
Middle East	11. Pivotal States and U.S. Strategy 12. Middle East Peace Process 15. Netanyahu and American Jews 35. Closing the Gate ○ *1, 9, 10, 11, 16, 17, 18, 20, 25, 26, 32*	**Presidency**	10. Why Are We in Bosnia? 15. Netanyahu and American Jews 25. NATO Expansion 26. White House Dismissed Warnings ○ *14, 20, 31*
Military Power	1. Benevolent Empire 2. Perils of (and for) an Imperial America 14. Common Sense 21. Racing toward the Future 25. NATO Expansion 31. Inventing Threats 35. Closing the Gate ○ *5, 6, 10, 11, 14, 16, 25, 26, 27, 29, 30, 31*	**Public Opinion and the Media**	14. Common Sense
		Russia	5. United States and the New Russia 6. Is Russia Still an Enemy? 25. NATO Expansion ○ *7, 14*
Multilateralism	1. Benevolent Empire 2. Perils of (and for) an Imperial America ○ *1, 3, 5, 6, 16, 17, 18, 19, 29, 31, 32*	**State Department and Diplomacy**	12. Middle East Peace Process 23. Tin Cup Diplomacy 25. NATO Expansion ○ *7, 14*
National Interest and American Values	2. Perils of (and for) an Imperial America 3. New Realism 4. Democracy at Risk 16. On American Principles 17. Globalization ○ *5, 6, 10, 11, 16, 17, 19*	**Terrorism**	22. Why Spy? 32. Responding to Terrorism 34. New Arms Race ○ *26, 29*
North Atlantic Treaty Organization	5. United States and the New Russia 10. Why Are We in Bosnia? 20. Senate's Strange Bedfellows		

AE: American Foreign Policy

The following World Wide Web sites have been carefully researched and selected to support the articles found in this reader. If you are interested in learning more about specific topics found in this book, these Web sites are a good place to start. The sites are cross-referenced by number and appear in the topic guide on the previous two pages. Also, you can link to these Web sites through our DUSHKIN ONLINE support site at http://www.dushkin.com/online/.

The following sites were available at the time of publication. Visit our Web site—we update DUSHKIN ONLINE regularly to reflect any changes.

General Sources

1. American Diplomacy
http://www.unc.edu/depts/diplomat/
American Diplomacy is an intriguing online journal of commentary, analysis, and research on U.S. foreign policy and its results around the world.

2. The Federal Web Locator
http://www.law.vill.edu/Fed-Agency/fedwebloc.html
Use this handy site as a launching pad for the Web sites of federal U.S. agencies, departments, and organizations. It is well organized and easy to use.

3. Foreign Affairs
http://www.foreignaffairs.org/
This site of the well-respected magazine *Foreign Affairs* is a valuable research tool. It allows users to search the magazine's archives and provides access to the field's leading journals, documents, online resources, and so on.

4. United States Information Agency (USIA)
http://www.usia.gov/usis.html
An interesting and wide-ranging home page of the USIA, it provides definition, related documentation, and a discussion of topics of concern to students of foreign policy and foreign affairs. It addresses today's "Hot Topics" as well as ongoing issues that form the foundation of the field.

The United States and the World: Strategic Choices

5. The Henry L. Stimson Center
http://www.stimson.org/
Stimson, a nonprofit and (self-described) nonpartisan organization, focuses on issues where policy, technology, and politics intersect. Use this site to find assessments of U.S. foreign policy in the post–cold war world.

6. ISN International Relations and Security Network
http://www.isn.ethz.ch/
This site, maintained by the Center for Security Studies and Conflict Research, is a clearinghouse for information on international relations and security policy. The many topics are listed by category (Traditional Dimensions of Security and New Dimensions of Security), and by major world region.

The United States and the World: Regional and Bilateral Relations

7. Center for Russian, East European, and Eurasian Studies
http://reenic.utexas.edu/reenic.html
This site has exhaustive information—from women's issues to foreign relations—regarding more than two dozen countries in Central/Eastern Europe and Eurasia. Also check out University of Texas/Austin's site on Broader Asia (http://asnic.utexas.edu/asnic/index.html).

8. Inter-American Dialogue (IAD)
http://www.iadialog.org/
This is the Web site for IAD, a premier U.S. center for policy analysis, communication, and exchange in Western Hemisphere affairs. The organization has helped to shape the agenda of issues and choices in hemispheric relations.

9. World Wide Web Virtual Library: International Affairs Resources
http://info.pitt.edu/~ian/index.htm
Surf this site and its extensive links to learn about specific countries and regions; to research various think tanks and to study such vital topics as international law, development, the international economy, human rights, and peacekeeping.

The Domestic Side of American Foreign Policy

10. Carnegie Endowment for International Peace
http://www.ceip.org/
One of the most important goals of this organization is to stimulate discussion and learning among both experts and the public on a range of international issues. The site provides links to the well-respected magazine *Foreign Policy*, to the Moscow Center, and to descriptions of various programs.

11. RAND
http://www.rand.org/
RAND is a nonprofit institution that works to improve public policy through research and analysis. Links offered on this home page provide for keyword searches of certain topics and descriptions of RAND activities and major research areas (such as international relations and strategic defense policy).

The Institutional Context of American Foreign Policy

12. Central Intelligence Agency (CIA)
http://www.odci.gov/cia/ciahome.html
Use this official CIA page to learn about many facets of the agency and to connect to other sites and resources.

13. NAFTA Border Home Page
http://www.iep.doc.gov/border/nafta.htm
This site offers extensive information on the North American Free Trade Agreement, including the full text of NAFTA documents and access to the National Trade Data Bank file. It provides Web links to a variety of NAFTA-related statistics.

14. The NATO Integrated Data Service (NIDS)
http://www.nato.int/structur/nids/nids.htm
NIDS was created to bring information on security-related matters to within easy reach of the widest possible audience. Check out this Web site to review North Atlantic Treaty Organization documentation of all kinds, to read *NATO Review* magazine, and to explore key issues in the field of European security and transatlantic cooperation.

15. The North American Institute (NAMI)
http://www.santafe.edu/~naminet/index.html
NAMI, a trinational public-affairs organization, is concerned with the emerging "regional space" of Canada, the United

States, and Mexico and the development of a North American community. It provides links for study of trade, the environment, institutional developments, and other topics.

16. United States Department of State
http://www.state.gov/
The State Department page is a must for any student of foreign affairs. Explore this site to find out what the Department does, what services it provides, what it says about U.S. interests around the world, and much more.

The Foreign Policy-Making Process

17. Belfer Center for Science and International Affairs (BCSIA)
http://ksgwww.harvard.edu/csia/
BCSIA is the hub of the John F. Kennedy School of Government's research, teaching, and training in international affairs and provides insight into the development of leadership in policy making.

18. DiploNet
http://www.clark.net/pub/diplonet/DiploNet.html
DiploNet is concerned with the needs of diplomats in the post–cold war era. It provides avenues of research into negotiation and diplomacy. It also addresses conflict management and resolution, peace making, and multilateral diplomacy.

19. InterAction
http://www.interaction.org/
InterAction encourages grassroots action and engages government bodies and policymakers on various advocacy issues, including initiatives to expand international humanitarian relief, refugee, and development assistance programs.

20. Welcome to the White House
http://www.whitehouse.gov/WH/Welcome.html
This official site provides background information for students interested in the policy-making process. It includes a tour of the White House, a search of federal documents and speeches, and "virtual" access to the Briefing Room.

U.S. International Economic Strategy

21. International Monetary Fund (IMF)
http://www.imf.org/
This Web site is essential reading for anyone wishing to learn more about this important body's effects on foreign policy and the global economy. It provides information about the IMF, directs readers to various publications and current issues, and suggests links to other organizations.

22. United States Agency for International Development
http://www.info.usaid.gov/
This Web site covers such broad and overlapping issues as Democracy, Population and Health, Economic Growth, Development, and Regions and Countries.

23. United States Trade Representative
http://www.ustr.gov/
This home page explains the important mission of the U.S. Trade Representative and provides background information, access to international trade agreements, and links to other sites.

24. World Bank
http://www.worldbank.org/
News (i.e., press releases, summaries of new projects, speeches); publications; and coverage of numerous topics regarding development, countries, and regions are provided at this Web site. It also contains links to other important global financial organizations.

U.S. Post–Cold War Military Strategy

25. The Commission on Global Governance
http://www.cgg.ch/
This site provides access to *The Report of the Commission on Global Governance*, produced by an international group of leaders who want to find ways in which the global community can better manage its affairs. It pays particular attention to reform of the United Nations.

26. Counter-Terrorism Page
http://counterterrorism.com/
Site contains a summary of worldwide terrorism events, groups, and terrorism strategies and tactics, including articles from 1989 to the present of American and international origin, plus links to related Web sites and graphs.

27. Federation of American Scientists (FAS)
http://www.fas.org/
FAS, a nonprofit policy organization, maintains this site to provide coverage of and links to such topics as Global Security, Peace and Security, and Governance in the post–cold war world, and notes a variety of valuable resources.

28. Human Rights Web
http://www.hrweb.org/
The history of the human-rights movement, text on seminal figures, landmark legal and political documents, and ideas on how individuals can get involved in helping to protect human rights around the world can be found on this valuable site.

29. U. S. Arms Control and Disarmament Agency (ACDA)
http://www.acda.gov/
This official home page of the ACDA provides links to extensive information on the topic of arms control and disarmament. Researchers can examine texts of various speeches, treaties, and historical documents. Also connects to CTBT (Comprehensive Test-Ban Treaty) page.

Historical Retrospectives on American Foreign Policy

30. The Bulletin of the Atomic Scientists
http://www.bullatomsci.org/
This site allows you to read more about the Doomsday Clock and other issues as well as topics related to nuclear weaponry, arms control, and disarmament.

31. DefenseLINK
http://www.defenselink.mil/
Learn about the Department of Defense at this site. News, publications, and other related sites of interest are noted. BosniaLINK and GulfLINK can also be found here.

32. United States Institute of Peace (USIP)
http://www.usip.org/
The USIP, which was created by Congress to promote peaceful resolution of international conflicts, seeks to educate people and disseminate information on how to achieve peace.

We highly recommend that you review our Web site for expanded information and our other product lines. We are continually updating and adding links to our Web site in order to offer you the most usable and useful information that will support and expand the value of your Annual Editions. You can reach us at: *http://www.dushkin.com/annualeditions/*.

www.dushkin.com/online/

Unit Selections

1. **The Benevolent Empire,** Robert Kagan
2. **The Perils of (and for) an Imperial America,** Charles William Maynes
3. **A New Realism,** Ronald Steel
4. **Democracy at Risk: American Culture in a Global Culture,** Benjamin R. Barber

Key Points to Consider

❖ How much freedom does the United States have in choosing a foreign policy?

❖ What countries are "poisonous snakes" and which are (or could become) "dragons"?

❖ Are Benjamin Barber's concerns about the future of democracy valid? If so, what type of foreign policy should the United States adopt?

❖ Who makes the most convincing case regarding the merits of a foreign policy of primacy, Kagan or Maynes?

❖ If "national security" is an attitude, what should our attitude be to the challenges facing the United States? Is there a need to rethink our basic ideas about security? How do we move from "attitudes" to "policy" in the arena of world politics?

 **Links**   www.dushkin.com/online/

5. **The Henry L. Stimson Center**
   http://www.stimson.org/
6. **ISN International Relations and Security Network**
   http://www.isn.ethz.ch/

These sites are annotated on pages 4 and 5.

The United States and the World: Strategic Choices

For much of the cold war there was little debate about the proper direction of American foreign policy. A consensus had formed around the policy of containment. It was a policy that identified communism and the Soviet Union as the primary threat to American national interests and prescribed a strategy of constant vigilance, global competition, and unparalleled military strength. That world is no longer with us. We have entered a period that has yet to develop its own identity. It is a world that offers more choices to American foreign policy but also sends contradictory signals as to which of these choices will best protect American national interests in the last years of this century and the first years of the next century.

In speaking about the foreign policy challenges of the post–cold war era, R. James Woolsey, President Clinton's first director of the Central Intelligence Agency, suggested that rather than having to contend with a single menacing dragon, the United States now faces a jungle filled with many poisonous snakes. Instead of containing the dragon, the test for any U.S. foreign policy would be how well it handles these snakes.

Not all strategists were convinced that this characterization of the post–cold war international system is correct. For neoidealists, the 1990s represent a moment to be seized. It is a time in which the strategies of conflict and confrontation of the cold war can be replaced by strategies designed to foster cooperation among states and to lift the human condition. For neoisolationists, the 1990s provide the United States with the long-awaited opportunity to walk away from the distracting and corrupting influence of international affairs. Now, they say, is the time to focus on domestic concerns and embrace traditional American values. Finally, some realists maintain that dragons are still very much with us and that instead of worrying about snakes the United States ought to focus its energy on containing the dragons.

Metaphors alone cannot guide foreign policy. They only provide a point of departure for thinking about problems. What is also needed is the articulation of a strategic perspective in which goals, threats and opportunities, and tactics are linked together by an overall vision and sense of purpose. In September 1993 the Clinton administration sought to put forward such a grand strategy.

The administration argued that the United States must remain actively engaged in world politics, not out of altruism but because of "real American interests that will suffer if we are seduced by the isolationist myth." It asserted that the successor doctrine to containment should be that of enlargement, which involves (1) strengthening the community of major market democracies, (2) fostering and consolidating new democracies and market economies, (3) countering aggression by "backlash" states hostile to democracy and markets, as well as supporting their liberalization, and (4) working to help democracy and market economics take root in regions of greatest humanitarian concern.

In carrying out this doctrine, administration spokespersons asserted that the United States must be patient and pragmatic, view democracy broadly, and respect diversity. Diplomacy was identified as America's first choice as a means for solving problems, but because there will always be times when words and sanctions are not enough, modern military forces were called a continued necessity. Finally, it was asserted that the choice between unilateralism and multilateralism was a false dichotomy and that elements of each could coexist within the broader strategic framework of American foreign policy.

The articulation of a Clinton Doctrine did little to silence the administration's foreign policy critics. Today, doubts are still expressed by strategists over the wisdom and feasibility of a strategy of enlargement. The readings in this section are designed to introduce us to the scope of this debate and the range of strategic options now before the United States.

The first reading, "The Benevolent Empire" by Robert Kagan, asserts that few states really want true multipolarity. He maintains that continued American dominance is a better international arrangement than all realistic alternatives, and it is important for international security and prosperity. Charles William Maynes, "The Perils of (and for) an Imperial America," presents a rebuttal to Kagan and others who call for the United States to adopt a hegemonic foreign policy. His arguments center on the domestic costs of such a strategy, its impact on the American character, the international backlash it would provoke, and the opportunities that would be lost by embracing such a strategy.

The last two readings in this section take a slightly different approach to the problem of selecting a grand strategy for the United States as it enters the next century. Ronald Steel, in "A New Realism" uses the concept of national security as a point of departure for evaluating the threats and challenges facing the United States. He notes that national security is not a condition but a feeling and a process and warns against seeking "absolutes" in U.S. foreign policy. Benjamin Barber, in "Democracy at Risk: American Culture in a Global Culture," is less concerned with advancing a specific grand strategy than he is with warning Americans about the consequences of America's growing economic involvement in world affairs.

The Benevolent Empire

by Robert Kagan

Not so long ago, when the Monica Lewinsky scandal first broke in the global media, an involuntary and therefore unusually revealing gasp of concern could be heard in the capitals of many of the world's most prominent nations. Ever so briefly, prime ministers and pundits watched to see if the drivewheel of the international economic, security, and political systems was about to misalign or lose its power, with all that this breakdown would imply for the rest of the world. Would the Middle East peace process stall? Would Asia's financial crisis spiral out of control? Would the Korean peninsula become unsettled? Would pressing issues of European security go unresolved? "In all the world's trouble spots," the *Times* of London noted, leaders were "calculating what will happen when Washington's gaze is distracted."

Temporarily interrupting their steady grumbling about American arrogance and hegemonic pretensions, Asian, European, and Middle Eastern editorial pages paused to contemplate the consequences of a crippled American presidency. The liberal German newspaper *Frankfurter Rundschau*, which a few months earlier had been accusing Americans of arrogant zealotry and a "camouflaged neocolonialism," suddenly fretted that the "problems in the Middle East, in the Balkans or in Asia" will not be solved "without U.S. assistance and a president who enjoys respect" and demanded that, in the interests of the entire world, the president's accusers quickly produce the goods or shut up. In Hong Kong, the *South China Morning Post* warned that the "humbling" of an American president had "implications of great gravity" for international affairs; in Saudi Arabia, the *Arab News* declared that this was "not the time that America or the world needs an inward-looking or wounded president. It needs one unencumbered by private concerns who can make tough decisions."

The irony of these pleas for vigorous American leadership did not escape notice, even in Paris, the intellectual and spiritual capital of antihegemony and "multipolarity." As one pundit (Jacques Amalric) noted wickedly in the left-leaning *Liberation*, "Those who accused the United States of being overbearing are today praying for a quick end to the storm." Indeed, they were and with good reason. As Aldo Rizzo observed, part in lament and part in tribute, in Italy's powerful *La Stampa:* "It is in times like these that we feel the absence of a power, certainly not [an] alternative, but at least complementary, to America, something which Europe could be. Could be, but is not. Therefore, good luck to Clinton and, most of all, to America."

This brief moment of international concern passed, of course, as did the flash of candor about the true state of world affairs and America's essential role in preserving a semblance of global order. The president appeared to regain his balance, the drivewheel kept spinning, and in the world's great capitals talk resumed of American arrogance and bullying and the need for a more genuinely multipolar system to manage international affairs. But the almost universally expressed fear of a weakened U.S. presidency provides a useful antidote to the pervasive handwringing, in Washington as well as in foreign capitals, over the "problem" of American hegemony. There is much less to this problem than meets the eye.

The commingled feelings of reliance on and resentment toward America's international dominance these days are neither strange nor new. The resentment of power, even when it is in the hands of one's friends, is a normal, indeed, timeless human emotion—no less so than the arrogance of power. And perhaps only Americans, with their rather short memory, could imagine that the current resentment is the unique product of the expansion of American

---

ROBERT KAGAN *is a senior associate at the Carnegie Endowment for International Peace and is director of its U.S. Leadership Project, which examines America's role in the post–Cold War world and the challenge of providing effective global leadership.*

dominance in the post–Cold War era. During the confrontation with the Soviet Union, now recalled in the United States as a time of Edenic harmony among the Western allies, not just French but also British leaders chafed under the leadership of a sometimes overbearing America. As political scientist A.W. DePorte noted some 20 years ago, the schemes of European unity advanced by French financial planner Jean Monnet and French foreign minister Robert Schuman in 1950 aimed "not only to strengthen Western Europe in the face of the Russian threat but also—though this was less talked about—to strengthen it vis-à-vis its indispensable but overpowering American ally." Today's call for "multipolarity" in international affairs, in short, has a history, as do European yearnings for unity as a counterweight to American power. Neither of these professed desires is a new response to the particular American hegemony of the last nine years.

And neither of them, one suspects, is very seriously intended. For the truth about America's dominant role in the world is known to most clear-eyed international observers. And the truth is that the benevolent hegemony exercised by the United States is good for a vast portion of the world's population. It is certainly a better international arrangement than all realistic alternatives. To undermine it would cost many others around the world far more than it would cost Americans—and far sooner. As Samuel Huntington wrote five years ago, before he joined the plethora of scholars disturbed by the "arrogance" of American hegemony: "A world without U.S. primacy will be a world with more violence and disorder and less democracy and economic growth than a world where the United States continues to have more influence than any other country shaping global affairs."

The unique qualities of American global dominance have never been a mystery, but these days they are more and more forgotten or, for convenience' sake, ignored. There was a time when the world clearly saw how different the American superpower was from all the previous aspiring hegemons. The difference lay in the exercise of power. The strength acquired by the United States in the aftermath of World War II was far greater than any single nation had ever possessed, at least since the Roman Empire. America's share of the world economy, the overwhelming superiority of its military capacity—augmented for a time by a monopoly of nuclear weapons and the capacity to deliver them—gave it the choice of pursuing any number of global ambitions. That the American people "might have set the crown of world empire on their brows," as one British statesman put it in 1951, but chose not to, was a decision of singular importance in world history and recognized as such. America's self-abnegation was unusual, and its uniqueness was not lost on peoples who had just suffered the horrors of wars brought

In truth, the benevolent hegemony exercised by the United States is good for a vast portion of the world's population.

on by powerful nations with overweening ambitions to empire of the most coercive type. Nor was it lost on those who saw what the Soviet Union planned to do with *its* newfound power after World War II.

The uniqueness persisted. During the Cold War, America's style of hegemony reflected its democratic form of government as much as Soviet hegemony reflected Stalin's approach to governance. The "habits of democracy," as Cold War historian John Lewis Gaddis has noted, made compromise and mutual accommodation the norm in U.S.–Allied relations. This approach to international affairs was not an example of selfless behavior. The Americans had an instinctive sense, based on their own experience growing up in a uniquely open system of democratic capitalism, that their power and influence would be enhanced by allowing subordinate allies a great measure of internal and even external freedom of maneuver. But in practice, as Gaddis points out, "Americans so often deferred to the wishes of allies during the early Cold War that some historians have seen the Europeans—especially the British—as having managed *them.*"

Beyond the style of American hegemony, which, even if unevenly applied, undoubtedly did more to attract than repel other peoples and nations, American grand strategy in the Cold War consistently entailed providing far more to friends and allies than was expected from them in return. Thus, it was American *strategy* to raise up from the ruins powerful economic competitors in Europe and Asia, a strategy so successful that by the 1980s the United States was thought to be in a state of irreversible "relative" economic decline—relative, that is, to those very nations whose economies it had restored after World War II.

And it was American *strategy* to risk nuclear annihilation on its otherwise unthreatened homeland in order to deter attack, either nuclear or conventional, on a European or Asian ally. This strategy also came to be taken for granted. But when one considers the absence of similarly reliable guarantees among the various European powers in the past (between, say, Great Britain and France in the 1920s and 1930s), the willingness of the United States, standing in relative safety behind two oceans, to link its survival to that of other nations was extraordinary.

Even more remarkable may be that the United States has attempted not only to preserve these guarantees but to expand them in the post–Cold War era. Much is made these days, not least in Washington, of the American defense budget now being several times higher than that of every other major power. But on what is that defense budget spent? Very little funding goes to protect national territory. Most of it is devoted to making good on what Americans call their international "commitments."

Even in the absence of the Soviet threat, America continues, much to the chagrin of some of its politicians, to define its "national security" broadly, as encompassing the security of friends and allies, and even of abstract principles, far from American shores. In the Gulf War, more than 90 percent of the military forces sent to expel Iraq's army from Kuwait were American. Were 90 percent of the interests threatened American? In almost any imaginable scenario in which the United States might deploy troops abroad, the primary purpose would be the defense of interests of more immediate concern to America's allies—as it has been in Bosnia. This can be said about no other power.

Ever since the United States emerged as a great power, the identification of the interests of others with its own has been the most striking quality of American foreign and defense policy. Americans seem to have internalized and made second nature a conviction held only since World War II: Namely, that their own well-being depends fundamentally on the well-being of others; that American prosperity cannot occur in the absence of global prosperity; that American freedom depends on the survival and spread of freedom elsewhere; that aggression anywhere threatens the danger of aggression everywhere; and that American national security is impossible without a broad measure of international security.

Let us not call this conviction selfless: Americans are as self-interested as any other people. But for at least 50 years they have been guided by the kind of enlightened self-interest that, in practice, comes dangerously close to resembling generosity. If that generosity seems to be fading today (and this is still a premature judgment), it is not because America has grown too fond of power. Quite the opposite. It is because some Americans have grown tired of power, tired of leadership, and, consequently, less inclined to demonstrate the sort of generosity that has long characterized their nation's foreign policy. What many in Europe and elsewhere see as arrogance and bullying may be just irritability born of weariness.

If fatigue is setting in, then those nations and peoples who have long benefited, and still benefit, from the international order created and upheld by American power have a stake in bolstering rather than denigrating American hegemony. After all, what, in truth, are the alternatives?

Whatever America's failings, were any other nation to take its place, the rest of the world would find the situation less congenial. America may be arrogant; Americans may at times be selfish; they may occasionally be ham-handed in their exercise of power. But, *excusez-moi*, compared with whom? Can anyone believe that were France to possess the power the United States now has, the French would be less arrogant, less selfish, and less prone to making mistakes? Little in France's history as a great power, or even as a medium power, justifies such optimism. Nor can one easily imagine power on an American scale being employed in a more enlightened fashion by China, Germany, Japan, or Russia. And even the leaders of that least benighted of empires, the British, were more arrogant, more bloody-minded, and, in the end, less capable managers of world affairs than the inept Americans have so far proved to be. If there is to be a sole superpower, the world is better off if that power is the United States.

What, then, of a multipolar world? There are those, even in the United States, who believe a semblance of international justice can be achieved only in a world characterized by a balance among relative equals. In such circumstances, national arrogance must theoretically be tempered, national aspirations limited, and at-

1. Benevolent Empire

tempts at hegemony, either benevolent or malevolent, checked. A more evenly balanced world, they assume, with the United States cut down a peg (or two, or three) would be freer, fairer, and safer.

A distant, though unacknowledged cousin of this realist, balance-of-power theory is the global parliamentarianism, or world federalism, that animates so many Europeans today, particularly the French apostles of European union. (It is little recalled, especially by modern proponents of foreign policy "realism," that Hans Morgenthau's seminal work, *Politics Among Nations*, builds slowly and methodically to the conclusion that what is needed to maintain international peace is a "world state.") In fact, many of today's calls for multipolarity seem to spring from the view, popular in some Washington circles but downright pervasive in European capitals, that traditional measures of national power, and even the nation-state itself, are passé. If Europe is erasing borders, what need is there for an overbearing America to keep the peace? America's military power is archaic in a world where finance is transnational and the modem is king.

We need not enter here into the endless and so far unproductive debate among international-relations theorists over the relative merits of multipolar, bipolar, and unipolar international "systems" for keeping the peace. It is sufficient to note that during the supposed heyday of multipolarity—the eighteenth century, when the first "Concert of Europe" operated—war among the great powers was a regular feature, with major and minor, and global and local, conflicts erupting throughout almost every decade.

We should also not forget that utopian fancies about the obsolescence of military power and national governments in a transnational, "economic" era have blossomed before, only to be crushed by the next "war to end all wars." The success of the European Union, such as it is, and, moreover, the whole dream of erasing boundaries, has been made possible only because the more fundamental and enduring issues of European security have been addressed by the United States through its leadership of NATO, that most archaic and least utopian of institutions. Were American hegemony really to disappear, the old European questions—chiefly, what to do about Germany—would quickly rear their hoary heads.

But let's return to the real world. For all the bleating about hegemony, no nation really wants genuine multipolarity. No nation has shown a willingness to take on equal responsibilities for managing global crises. No nation has been willing to make the same kinds

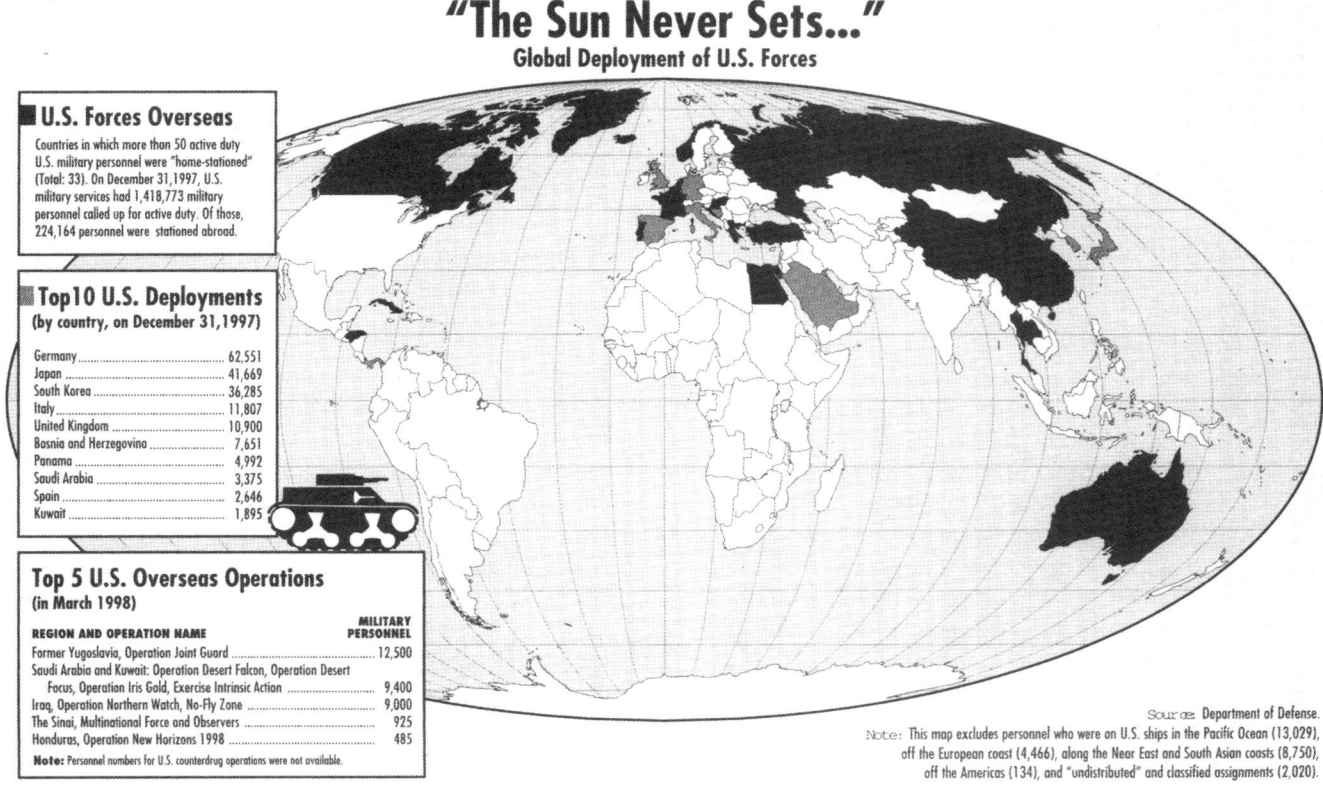

"The Sun Never Sets..."
Global Deployment of U.S. Forces

U.S. Forces Overseas
Countries in which more than 50 active duty U.S. military personnel were "home-stationed" (Total: 33). On December 31, 1997, U.S. military services had 1,418,773 military personnel called up for active duty. Of those, 224,164 personnel were stationed abroad.

Top 10 U.S. Deployments
(by country, on December 31, 1997)

Germany	62,551
Japan	41,669
South Korea	36,285
Italy	11,807
United Kingdom	10,900
Bosnia and Herzegovina	7,651
Panama	4,992
Saudi Arabia	3,375
Spain	2,646
Kuwait	1,895

Top 5 U.S. Overseas Operations
(in March 1998)

REGION AND OPERATION NAME	MILITARY PERSONNEL
Former Yugoslavia, Operation Joint Guard	12,500
Saudi Arabia and Kuwait: Operation Desert Focus, Operation Iris Gold, Exercise Intrinsic Action	9,400
Iraq, Operation Northern Watch, No-Fly Zone	9,000
The Sinai, Multinational Force and Observers	925
Honduras, Operation New Horizons 1998	485

Note: Personnel numbers for U.S. counterdrug operations were not available.

Source: Department of Defense.
Note: This map excludes personnel who were on U.S. ships in the Pacific Ocean (13,029), off the European coast (4,466), along the Near East and South Asian coasts (8,750), off the Americas (134), and "undistributed" and classified assignments (2,020).

> *For all the bleating about hegemony, no nation really wants genuine multipolarity.*

of short-term sacrifices that the United States has been willing to make in the long-term interest of preserving the global order. No nation, except China, has been willing to spend the money to acquire the military power necessary for playing a greater role relative to the United States—and China's military buildup has not exactly been viewed by its neighbors as creating a more harmonious environment.

If Europeans genuinely sought multipolarity, they would increase their defense budgets considerably, instead of slashing them. They would take the lead in the Balkans, instead of insisting that their participation depends on America's participation. But neither the French, other Europeans, nor even the Russians are prepared to pay the price for a genuinely multipolar world. Not only do they shy away from the expense of creating and preserving such a world; they rightly fear the geopolitical consequences of destroying American hegemony. Genuine multipolarity would inevitably mean a return to the complex of strategic issues that plagued the world before World War II: in Asia, the competition for regional preeminence among China, Japan, and Russia; in Europe, the competition among France, Germany, Great Britain, and Russia.

Kenneth Waltz once made the seemingly obvious point that "in international politics, overwhelming power repels and leads other states to balance against it"—a banal truism, and yet, as it happens, so untrue in this era of American hegemony. What France, Russia, and some others really seek today is not genuine multipolarity but a false multipolarity, an honorary multipolarity. They want the pretense of equal partnership in a multipolar world without the price or responsibility that equal partnership requires. They want equal say on the major decisions in global crises (as with Iraq and Kosovo) without having to possess or wield anything like equal power. They want to increase their own prestige at the expense of American power but without the strain of having to fill the gap left by a diminution of the American role. And at the same time, they want to make short-term, mostly financial, gains, by taking advantage of the continuing U.S. focus on long-term support of the international order.

The problem is not merely that some of these nations are giving themselves a "free ride" on the back of American power, benefiting from the international order that American hegemony undergirds, while at the same time puncturing little holes in it for short-term advantage. The more serious danger is that this behavior will gradually, or perhaps not so gradually, erode the sum total of power that can be applied to protecting the international order altogether. The false multipolarity sought by France, Russia, and others would reduce America's ability to defend common interests without increasing anyone else's ability to do so.

In fact, this erosion may already be happening. In the recent case of Iraq, America's ability to pursue the long-term goal of defending the international order against President Saddam Hussein was undermined by the efforts of France and Russia to attain short-term economic gains and enhanced prestige. Both these powers achieved their goal of a "multipolar" solution: They took a slice out of American hegemony. But they did so at the price of leaving in place a long-term threat to an international system from which they continue to draw immense benefits but which they by themselves have no ability to defend. They did not possess the means to solve the Iraq problem, only the means to prevent the United States from solving it.

This insufficiency is the fatal flaw of multilateralism, as the Clinton administration learned in the case of Bosnia. In a world that is not genuinely multipolar—where there is instead a widely recognized hierarchy of power—multilateralism, if rigorously pursued, guarantees failure in meeting international crises. Those nations that lack the power to solve an international problem cannot be expected to take the lead in demanding the problem be solved. They may even eschew the exercise of power altogether, both because they do not have it and because the effective exercise of it by someone else, such as the United States, only serves to widen the gap between the hegemon and the rest. The lesson President Bill Clinton was supposed to have learned in the case of Bosnia is that to be effective, multilateralism must be preceded by unilateralism. In the toughest situations, the most effective multilateral response comes when the strongest power decides to act, with or without the others, and then asks its partners whether they will join. Giving equal say over international decisions to nations with vastly unequal power often means that the full measure of power that can be deployed in defense of the international community's interests will, in fact, not be deployed.

Those contributing to the growing chorus of antihegemony and multipolarity may know they are playing a dangerous game, one that needs to be conducted with the utmost care, as French leaders did during the Cold War, lest the entire international system come crashing down around them. What they may not have adequately calculated, however, is the possibility that Americans will not respond as wisely as they generally did during the Cold War.

Americans and their leaders should not take all this sophisticated whining about U.S. hegemony too seriously. They certainly should not take it more seriously than the whiners themselves do. But, of course, Americans are taking it seriously. In the United States these days, the lugubrious guilt trip of post–Vietnam liberalism is echoed even by conservatives, with William Buckley, Samuel Huntington, and James Schlesinger all decrying American "hubris," "arrogance," and "imperialism." Clinton administration officials, in between speeches exalting America as the "indispensable" nation, increasingly behave as if what is truly indispensable is the prior approval of China, France, and Russia for every military action. Moreover, at another level, there is a stirring of neo-isolationism in America today, a mood that nicely complements the view among many Europeans that America is meddling too much in everyone else's business and taking too little time to mind its own. The existence of the Soviet Union disciplined Americans and made them see that their enlightened self-interest lay in a relatively generous foreign policy. Today, that discipline is no longer present.

The world's crossing guard?

In other words, foreign grumbling about American hegemony would be merely amusing, were it not for the very real possibility that too many Americans will forget—even if most of the rest of the world does not—just how important continued American dominance is to the preservation of a reasonable level of international security and prosperity. World leaders may want to keep this in mind when they pop the champagne corks in celebration of the next American humbling.

WANT TO KNOW MORE?

The Spring 1993 issue of *International Security* invited a number of authors to comment on American hegemony in a forum entitled **"Primacy and its Discontents."** In his article **"The Unipolar Illusion: Why New Great Powers Will Rise,"** UCLA professor Christopher Layne cites Kenneth Waltz and employs neorealist theory to argue that multipolarity will blossom again sometime between 2000 and 2010; Columbia University professor Robert Jervis, in his article **"International Primacy: Is the Game Worth the Candle?,"** argues that primacy is no longer a worthy goal, since "with the development of nuclear weapons, the spread of liberal democracy, and the diminution of nationalism, war among the most powerful actors is unlikely"; and Harvard University's Samuel Huntington, in **"Why International Primacy Matters,"** advances an argument for American primacy that he may no longer believe in. Charles Krauthammer, in **"The Unipolar Moment"** (*Foreign Affairs: America and the World*, Vol. 70, No. 1, 1990–91), also makes a case for American hegemony, an opinion he now seems largely to have abandoned.

A good source on American policy, already cited in this article, is John Lewis Gaddis' *We Now Know: Rethinking Cold War History* (New York: Oxford University Press, 1997). Drawing on archival material from former communist countries, Gaddis argues that Western scholars have traditionally underemphasized the role of ideology during the Cold War.

The United States Information Agency (USIA) on a daily basis compiles summaries of editorial commentary from around the world. Searchable archives of the *Daily Digest* are available online at the USIA Web site.

The Perils of (and for) an Imperial America

by Charles William Maynes

In their public discourse, Americans have come to the point where it is hard to find a foreign-policy address by any prominent figure in either party that does not make constant reference to the United States as the indispensable nation, the sole superpower, the uniquely responsible state, or the lone conscience of the world. William Kristol and Robert Kagan, editors at the conservative *Weekly Standard*, have unabashedly called upon the United States to take the lead in establishing a "benevolent global hegemony"—though how benevolent it would be is unclear since they propose to attain it through a massive increase in U.S. defense spending. Likewise, former national security advisor Zbigniew Brzezinski, in his new book, *The Grand Chessboard*, speaks openly of America's allies and friends as "vassals and tributaries." He urges, only slightly tongue-in-cheek, an imperial geostrategy designed "to prevent collusion and maintain security dependence among the vassals, to keep tributaries pliant and protected, and to keep the barbarians from coming together." In the pages of this very magazine (*Foreign Policy*), David Rothkopf, a former senior member of the Clinton administration, expressed this mood of national self-satisfaction in a form that would be embarrassing to put into print, were it not so ardently felt: "Americans should not deny the fact that of all the nations in the world, theirs is the most just and the best model for the future." (See "In Praise of Cultural Imperialism?" in FOREIGN POLICY 107.)

The taproot of this growing geopolitical delirium, of course, is the extraordinary range of America's current position internationally. Probably not since classic Rome or ancient China has a single power so towered over its known rivals in the international system: Today, only the U.S. military retains the ability to reach into any region in the world within mere hours. The U.S. economy has become the envy of the world. Others continue to copy our political system, hiring our media handlers and campaign strategists to work in countries whose languages and cultures they barely understand. Finally, the "soft" power of U.S. culture reigns supreme internationally. For what it is worth, few foreign pop stars can rival America's Madonna or Michael Jackson, and American cinema smothers all foreign competitors.

Another characteristic of U.S. power deserves mention: The price America exacts from its "vassals" is more tolerable than the one previous imperial powers extracted from

---

CHARLES WILLIAM MAYNES *is president of the Eurasia Foundation.*

their subjects. The United States imposes extraordinarily light military burdens on its allies. Britain and France made their colonies fight for the motherland in World Wars I and II, and the colonies provided many of the soldiers that policed their empires. In the Korean, Vietnam, and Gulf Wars, America permitted its Japanese and European allies to watch largely as bystanders, while American troops did most of the fighting. In a post–Cold War world, the United States remains willing to pick up a totally disproportionate share of the expense of maintaining the common defense for the indefinite future. By some estimates, the costs for NATO expansion could run as high as $125 billion by 2012, prompting European commentators, such as former German defense planner Walther Stuetzle, to declare that the United States must be prepared to "pick up the tab." What other imperial power would have remained silent while its allies made it clear by statements and actions that they would not pay a single extra penny for a common alliance objective such as NATO expansion?

Former imperial powers also made sure their colonies served the economic interests of the metropole, which maintained a monopoly in key industries and enforced schemes of imperial preference to favor the home economy. In contrast, America's imperial strategy has evolved over the years into that of importer and financier of last resort. The United States has without much debate assumed the role of world economic stabilizer, often adversely affecting its own interests. America's political tradition of constitutional democracy, much more secure after the civil rights movement, also makes it difficult for Washington to follow a harsh imperial policy, even if it were so inclined. With their belief in the "white man's burden" or "*la mission civilatrice,*" the European powers—and America for that matter in the conquest of the Philippines—were able to display, when necessary, extraordinary cruelty in the pursuit of stability. Now, in its recent imperial wars, America has been concerned about press reports of a few civilian casualties.

Ironically, of all the burdens the United States now imposes on its foreign subjects and vassals, Madonna may be the heaviest. Few foreigners accept the American position that market forces alone should dictate cultural patterns—that if the citizens want to buy it, the priests and professors should retire to their monasteries and libraries and let it happen. Many foreigners secretly sympathize with the French or Russian or Israeli position that they have the duty to protect their admittedly great cultures, even if doing so occasionally violates some of the finer points of free trade or speech. Indeed, one wonders whether American officials would cling so ardently to their own position regarding international free trade in cultural goods if it turned out that market forces were in fact overwhelming the United States with, say, the culture of the Middle East or Latin America. The number of Spanish-speaking immigrants arriving in the country, and their desire to hold on to their culture and language, represent a clear market test, yet Americans become very disturbed when these new entrants insist on maintaining their use of Spanish. The "English only" movement or the race to install V-chips in home television sets to control what minors may view each suggests that many Americans harbor some of the same concerns about preserving their culture as the French and others.

The cultural issue apart, American hegemony is benign by historical standards. Therefore, it is fair to ask, as Kagan has in several earlier articles: Why not entrench that hegemony for the betterment of all humankind? After all, one can acknowledge that one's own country is not always as principled, consistent, benign, or wise as the national self-image persistently requires that its leaders regularly affirm, yet still reach the conclusion that while American hegemony may not be the best of all possible worlds, it may be the best of all likely worlds. In other words, American hegemony may be better than any alternative hegemonic arrangement, and, historically, hegemony has proved preferable to chaos.

The Case Against U.S. Hegemony

What then is the case against Kagan's call for American hegemony? It can be summed up in the following manner: domestic costs, impact on the American character, international backlash, and lost opportunities.

Domestic Costs

Many like Kagan who support a policy of world hegemony often assert that the domestic cost of such a policy is bearable. They point out that the percentage of GNP devoted to American defense, around 3 percent, is the lowest it has been since Pearl Harbor, and the country is now much richer. True, the United

States still spends more for defense than all the other major powers combined, but it is hard to argue that it would be unable to continue carrying this burden or even to increase it.

What proponents of this school of thought fail to point out is that the defense spending to which we are now committed is not terribly relevant to the policy of global hegemony that

> *Today's new hegemonists are almost a parody of the Kaiser and his court at the beginning of this century.*

they wish to pursue. In an unintended manner, this point emerged during the last presidential campaign. Senator Robert Dole, the Republican nominee, publicly complained that his old unit, the 10th Mountain Division, had carried the brunt of America's post–Cold War peacekeeping responsibilities in places such as Haiti and Bosnia, and its men and women had gone months without rest or home leave.

He was, of course, right in his complaint. But the Clinton administration could not do much to reduce the burden placed on the 10th Mountain Division, for the United States has very few other units available for peacekeeping duty. If America is to strive to be the world's hegemon, in other words, not only will the U.S. defense effort have to be radically restructured, but the costs incurred will mount exponentially unless we are willing to cut existing sections of our military, a point on which the new hegemonists are largely silent. The U.S. commitment in Bosnia provides a glimpse into the future. The burden of U.S. involvement, initially estimated at $1.5 billion, surpassed $7 billion in April 1998 and will continue to grow for years to come.

Before the manipulation of budget estimates started in connection with the effort to gain Senate ratification of NATO expansion, even the most conservative estimates suggested that American taxpayers would be compelled to contribute $25 billion to $35 billion per year over the next 10 to 12 years to pay for NATO expansion. The true costs may well be much higher. And NATO expansion is just one of the expensive building blocks required to pursue a policy of hegemony.

There is no clear geographical limit to the obligations that a quest for hegemony would impose. The American desire to remain the dominant security power in Europe drove Washington, against its will, to establish, much like the Austrians or the Turks at the beginning of this century, an imperial protectorate over the former Yugoslavia. Now, as officials spot disorder in other important parts of the globe, there is official talk of using NATO troops in northern or central Africa, if necessary. Corridor chatter has even begun among some specialists about the need to send troops to the Caspian area to secure the oil there. Where will the interventionist impulse end? How can it end for a power seeking global hegemony?

The costs of hegemony will not just be military. Modern-day advocates of hegemony have lost sight of one of the crucial characteristics of the golden age of American diplomacy: From 1945 to 1965, America's dominant image rested more on the perception of its role as the world's Good Samaritan than as the world's policeman. Nearly 60 years ago, Henry Luce, the founder of *Time* magazine, issued one of the most famous calls for American dominance internationally. He understood that a quest for world leadership requires more than a large army. In his famous essay "The American Century," Luce urged his fellow citizens to spend at least 10 percent of every defense dollar in a humanitarian effort to feed the world. He recognized that to dominate, America must be seen not only as stronger but better. The United States needs to do its share internationally in the nonmilitary field and now, as the sad state of the foreign affairs budget demonstrates, it frankly does not. But is the country willing to pick up the nonmilitary costs of a quest for global hegemony?

With their neglect of this issue, today's new hegemonists are almost a parody of the Kaiser and his court at the beginning of this century. Like their German cousins, the new hegemonists are fascinated by military might, intoxicated by the extra margin of power America enjoys, and anxious to exploit this moment to dominate others. They want to reverse almost completely the direction American foreign policy has taken for most of the period following World War II. America's goal has always been to lift others up. Now, it will be to keep them down. In Kagan's own words,

American power should be deployed to control or prevent the "rise of militant anti-American Muslim fundamentalism in North Africa and the Middle East, a rearmed Germany in a chaotic Europe, a revitalized Russia, a rearmed Japan in a scramble for power with China in a volatile East Asia."

His choice of words is instructive. America's goal would be not simply to protect this country and its citizens from actions that militant Islam might direct against American interests but to prevent the very rise of militant Islam. We would not only stand up to Russia were it to become hostile to U.S. interests but would try to prevent the very revival of the Russian people and state. And we would attempt to control the spread of "chaos" in the international system. All these tasks would require the United States to intervene in the internal affairs of other states to a degree not seen since the immediate postwar period, when the United States and the Soviet Union stationed their vast land armies on the soil of former enemy territories.

One of the most bitter lessons of the Cold War was that when American and Soviet soldiers sought to impose a political order on populations (or at least resolute parts of them) that resisted such efforts—namely in Afghanistan, Korea, and Vietnam—casualties began to mount. If the United States attempts a policy of global hegemony, Kagan and other proponents cannot claim it will incur low costs by citing the size of the current defense budget or referring only to the dollars spent. The character of that budget will have to change, and the price will be not only in dollars spent but in bloodshed. Is the country prepared for that, particularly when those asked to die will be told it is in the name of hegemony, not national defense? Will Americans be comfortable with an image of their country as the power always brandishing the clenched fist and seldom extending the helping hand?

Impact on the American Character
A quest for hegemony would have a corrosive effect on the country's internal relations. The United States could carry out such a quest only by using the volunteer army, which fills its ranks predominately with people who come from a segment of America that is less internationally minded than those who wish to use the U.S. military for geopolitical purposes. Former secretary of labor Robert Reich, among others, has pointed out that America is developing into two societies—not so much black versus white but cosmopolitan versus national, or between those who have directly, even extravagantly, reaped the benefits in recent years from the new globalized economy and those who have paid its price in terms of military service, endangered jobs, and repressed wages. The former may represent between 15 to 25 percent of the population. Its representatives travel widely, speak foreign languages (or at least can afford to hire a translator), and feel as at home in Rome or Tokyo as they do in New York. Almost none of their sons and daughters serve in the U.S. military. Facing them are the vast majority of citizens who will no doubt be asked to pay the price of their country's policy of hegemony.

Can America embark on a quest for global primacy with those responsible for pursuing this course paying almost no price for its execution? Will American democracy permit a situation like that of ancient Rome, where the rich sit in the stands to watch the valiant exertions of those less fortunate below?

In the early days of the post–Cold War period, it was not at all uncommon to hear foreign-policy practitioners refer to the American military in terms that suggested they were modern Hessians, available for deployment to any corner of the globe that policymakers wished to pacify or control. Ironically, prominent among the new interventionists were a number of humanitarian-aid officials—who are normally not enthusiastic about military deployments abroad—arguing that since the U.S. army consisted of volunteers who had accepted the king's shilling and, after all, had little to do in a post–Cold War world, they should be ready to serve in humanitarian missions, even if these were not related to core American security concerns.

The ease of victory in the Gulf War contributed to this new enthusiasm for the use of military force. If Iraq, with one of the most powerful armies in the world, could be so easily subdued, how could there be much danger or pain in deploying U.S. troops into the growing number of ethnic or religious conflicts emerging around the world? After the disaster in Somalia, one heard less of such talk. But empires need to have either Hessians or a populace anxious to march off to war. Fortunately, America has neither. Not to understand this fundamental point risks causing a major political explosion domestically at some unexpected moment in the future. Of course, the argument that the United States

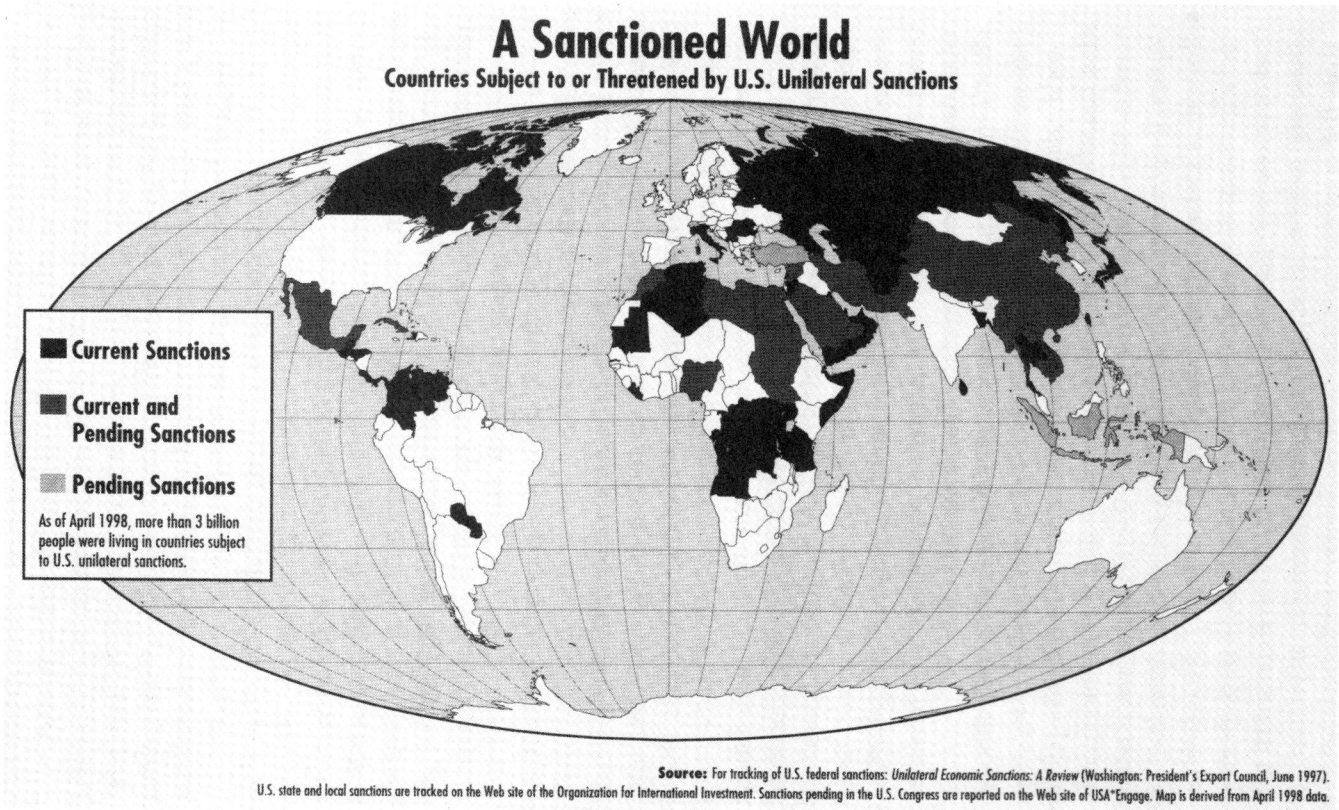

should not seek global hegemony does not mean America should not work with others to develop a shared response to some of the new challenges on the international agenda . . . but that is a different subject and article.

International Backlash
Suppose, despite all of these obstacles, a quest for world hegemony could succeed. We still should not want it. As Henry Adams warned in his autobiography, the effect of power on all men is "the aggravation of self, a sort of tumor that ends by killing the victim's sympathies." Already the surplus of power that America enjoys is beginning to metastasize into an arrogance toward others that is bound to backfire. Since 1993, the United States has imposed new unilateral economic sanctions, or threatened legislation that would allow it do so, 60 times on 35 countries that represent over 40 percent of the world's population.

Increasingly, in its relations even with friends, the United States, as a result of the interplay between administration and Congress, has begun to command more and listen less. It demands to have its way in one international forum after another. It imperiously imposes trade sanctions that violate international understandings; presumptuously demands national legal protection for its citizens, diplomats, and soldiers who are subject to criminal prosecution, while insisting other states forego that right; and unilaterally dictates its view on UN reforms or the selection of a new secretary general.

To date, the United States has been able to get away with these tactics. Nevertheless, the patience of others is shortening. The difficulty the United States had in rounding up support, even from its allies, in the recent confrontation with Iraqi president Saddam Hussein was an early sign of the growing pique of others with America's new preemptive arrogance. So was the manner in which the entire membership of the European Union immediately rallied behind the French in the controversy over a possible French, Malaysian, and Russian joint investment in the Iranian oil industry that would violate America's unilaterally announced sanctions policy against Iran. In March 1998, while reflecting on President Bill Clinton's visit to South Africa, President Nelson Mandela strongly rejected a trade agreement with the United States that would limit transactions with any third country, declaring that "we resist any attempt by any country to impose conditions on our freedom of trade."

Lost Opportunities

Perhaps the biggest price Americans would pay in pursuing world hegemony is the cost in lost opportunities. Even those who propose such a policy of hegemony acknowledge that it cannot succeed over the longer run. As Kagan himself has written, we cannot "forget the truism that all great powers must some day fall." One day, in other words, some country or group of countries will successfully challenge American primacy.

There is an alternative. We could use this unique post–Cold War moment to try to hammer out a new relationship among the great powers. Today, the most inadequately examined issue in American politics is precisely whether or not post–Cold War conditions offer us a chance to change the rules of the international game.

Certainly, there is no hope of changing the rules of the game if we ourselves pursue a policy of world hegemony. Such a policy, whether formally announced or increasingly evident, will drive others to resist our control, at first unsuccessfully but ultimately with effect. A policy of world hegemony, in other words, will guarantee that in time America will become outnumbered and overpowered. If that happens, we will once and for all have lost the present opportunity to attempt to change the rules of the game among the great powers.

Why should we believe there could be an opportunity to alter these rules? There are at least three reasons:

- War no longer pays for the great powers. For most of history, wars have paid. The victor ended up with more land and people. Over time, almost all of the latter accepted the sway of the new occupier. That is how most of the great nations of the world were built. With the rise of modern nationalism, however, it has become more and more difficult to absorb conquered territories without ethnic cleansing. Successful recent examples of seizing territory include the Russian, Polish, and Czech border changes after World War II, which involved brutal exchanges of populations. Unsuccessful examples of seizing territory include those in which the indigenous populations have remained, such as Israel's occupation of the West Bank, Indonesia's occupation of East Timor, and India's incorporation of Kashmir. Moreover, although ethnic cleansing does still take place today in a number of locations worldwide, those carrying out such practices are not the great powers but countries still in the process of nation-building along nineteenth-century lines. For most of the great states, in other words, war is not an option for power or wealth seeking. War is reserved for defense.

- Instead of seeking international power and influence through external expansion, most established powers now seek both through internal development. Postwar Germany and Japan have confirmed that these are more reliable paths to greater international prominence than the ones pursued since 1945 by Britain and France, both of which have relied on military power to hold their place in the international system only to see it decline.

- The behavior of great states in the international system that have lost traditional forms of power in recent decades has been remarkably responsible. Postwar Germany and Japan, as well as post–Cold War Russia, have all accepted being shorn of territories with notably few repercussions. A principal reason was the treatment of the first two by their rivals and the hope of the third that the rest of the world would not exploit its weaknesses so as to exclude Russia from the European system, but would instead take aggressive steps to incorporate it. In this regard, a policy of hegemony sends exactly the wrong message, particularly if one of our purposes is to prevent Russia from ever "reviving" in a way that threatens us.

Regrettably, as we approach the millennium, we are almost at the point of no return in our post–Cold War policy. We are moving along a path that will forsake the chance of a lifetime to try to craft a different kind of international system. Like France at the beginning of the nineteenth century, Britain in the middle, and Germany at the end, the United States does much to influence international behavior by the model it sets. It is still not too late to make a real effort to write a new page in history. If we pass up this opportunity, history will judge us very harshly indeed.

WANT TO KNOW MORE?

In their article "**Competing Visions for U.S. Grand Strategy**" (*International Security*, Winter

1996–97), Barry Posen of MIT and Andrew Ross of the U.S. Naval War College analyze the principal theoretical trends that have emerged in response to America's "unipolar" moment. In particular, the authors examine the practical policy implications of neo-isolationism, selective engagement, cooperative security, and U.S. hegemony.

By making use of historical case studies, Josef Joffe, editorial page editor of the *Süddeutsche Zeitung*, suggests that post–Cold War America could learn a lesson or two from imperial Germany. In his article **"Bismarck or Britain?"** (*International Security*, Spring 1995), Joffe argues that the United States should update and improve the Bismarckian model of great-power relations by pursuing alliances that inexorably link the welfare of others with America's and that discourage foreign nations from coalescing into rival power blocs.

In **"Less is More"** (*National Interest*, Spring 1996), Christopher Layne of Harvard's Kennedy School of Government relies on East Asia as a case study to argue that the United States should pursue a "minimalist grand strategy" that depends upon "global and regional power balances to contain newly emerging powers." Because of America's "relative immunity" from external threats, Layne endorses a "buck-passing" strategy that encourages regional U.S. allies to take the lead in dealing with East Asian security issues. In his book *Isolationism Reconfigured* (Princeton: Princeton University Press, 1995), the late Eric Nordlinger of Brown University argues that America's military supremacy offers a unique opportunity to cut defense spending, end security alliances, and address problems primarily through multinational institutions.

Previous articles in FOREIGN POLICY that have addressed the issue of American primacy in the international system include: Albert Coll's **"America as the Grand Facilitator"** (Summer 1992), Christopher Layne and Benjamin Schwarz's **"American Hegemony: Without an Enemy"** (Fall 1993), and Charles William Maynes' **"Bottom-Up Foreign Policy"** (Fall 1996).

For a specific case study of the spiraling costs and potential pitfalls of American hegemony, readers should consult *NATO Enlargement: Illusions and Reality*, edited by Ted Galen Carpenter and Barbara Conry (Washington: CATO Institute, 1998). Richard Haass, director of Foreign Policy Studies at the Brookings Institution, warns of the potential pitfalls of unilateral American sanctions, in his article **"Sanctioning Madness"** (*Foreign Affairs*, November/December 1997).

Several recent public-opinion surveys illustrate the widening gap in attitudes between the general public and foreign-policy practitioners, particularly with regard to America's perceived duties and obligations as a world leader: *American Public Opinion and U.S. Foreign Policy 1995*, edited by John Rielly (Chicago: Chicago Council on Foreign Relations, 1995), *America's Place in the World II* (Washington: Pew Research Center for the People & the Press, October 1997), and *The Foreign Policy Gap*, by Steven Kull, I.M. Destler, and Clay Ramsay (College Park: Center for International and Security Studies at the University of Maryland, October 1997).

A New Realism
Ronald Steel

Ronald Steel is professor of international relations at the University of Southern California and the author of Temptations of a Superpower.

The most troublesome concepts are the ones we take for granted. This is not only because they are familiar but because they are imbedded in our way of thinking. They roll off our tongues without our ever stopping to think what they really mean. We come to take them as established truths, like Biblical injunctions.

One of these concepts lies at the very heart of our thinking about the outside world: the concept of "national security." It is central to the apparatus of government and enjoys the highest priority over our resources and our lives. Yet like many other familiar terms, it is not a neutral description of an external reality. It is a social construct. It came into being at a specific time and in response to a specific set of circumstances. Those circumstances governed the way we defined the term then and continue to define it now.

It was 50 years ago this summer that President Harry S Truman signed the National Security Act. The very terminology reflected a new American approach to the world and eventually itself became the justification for that approach. The legislation provided for a limited unification of the armed forces, preserving the army and navy, and establishing the air force, as separate departments. In response to enormous pressure from the navy and its supporters—including James Forrestal, then navy secretary and later the first secretary of defense, and also Carl Vinson and other influential legislators—the navy retained its air arm (which it saw as the engine of its future growth) and successfully blocked the full merger of the services and the creation of a general staff.

In addition to partial unification of the armed forces, the act also established the National Security Council to coordinate foreign policy operations, the National Security Resources Board, and the Central Intelligence Agency. The act reflected the arguments favored by the navy and the air force, which sought the lion's share of future budgets, and of the influential Eberstadt Report, which heralded the nation's "new international commitments" and declared that these "have greatly enlarged the sphere of our international obligations, reflecting present concepts of our national security in terms of world security."

The phrasing is significant: "national security in terms of world security." No definition is given, of course, as to what "world security" might mean. It is presumably self-evident. Herein then lies an indication of how, and how early, the new concept of "national security" embraced and then went far beyond the traditional notion of "defense." Indeed, it would have been appropriate to have had, instead of a modestly titled "Defense Department" (which replaced the plain vanilla War Department), a "National Security Department."

Although the familiar phrase can be traced far back, it did not enter the common vocabulary until after the Second World War. It was first popularized by Walter Lippmann in his influential 1943 book, *U.S. Foreign Policy: Shield of the Republic*. There, he wrote that America's long insulation from European quarrels was not due to any inherent virtue on America's part but was a consequence of its protection by two great oceans and a benevolent British navy. This fortuitous combination of circumstances had, he argued, "diverted our attention from the idea of national security."

The phrase, and with it the entire concept, quickly caught on. It captured the feeling of power and exuberance that followed from the victory over Germany and Japan. It repudiated the discredited refuge of isolationism, and it suggested a far broader involvement of the United States in world affairs. In arguing for policies based on what he called a hard calculation of "national interest," Lippmann also added a caveat. A workable foreign policy, he maintained, "consists in bringing into balance, with a comfortable surplus of power in reserve, the nation's commitments and the nation's power." This later came to be honored as much in the breach as in the observance.

What Lippmann inherently recognized—and what later became abundantly clear—was how broadly the new concept of "national security" could be construed. Unlike the term "defense," which connotes repelling an invasive force, it suggests not just resistance to aggression but an outward reach to anticipate and neutralize dangers that might still be only potential. It draws a security perimeter that is determined, in practice, only by the reach of national power. A regional power will have a regional security perimeter; a global power will be satisfied with nothing less than a global one. The perimeter expands in relation to the amount of power available. And the definition of security expands with it.

For this reason security gets unhinged from its geographical moorings. It becomes a function of power and an aspect of psychology. It becomes internalized. It is not a specific reality, and it does not exist entirely in space. It is a function of definition and can be defined broadly or narrowly. Small and weak states define it narrowly, large and powerful ones define it broadly. Security, then, is a reflection of a nation's (or at least of a nation's elite's) sense of its power. It is an operating mechanism, and at the same time an abstraction.

The Paradox of Insecurity
It is striking how quickly the American sense of security, confirmed by the wartime victories and the development of the ultimate weapon, the atomic bomb, developed into a sense of insecurity. The postwar quarrels with the Soviet Union, intensified by a communist ideology that was, in its aspirations (or pretensions), global in sweep—as was, in its own way, the American counter-ideology of democratic capitalism—gave way to a pervasive sense of insecurity.

Virtually no place seemed to be really secure. Where there were not Soviet legions there were communist believers, or sympathizers, enemies without and enemies within. Everything came to seem crucial and everything was up for grabs. This new sense of global security (and as its inseparable companion, global insecurity) was enshrined in the Truman Doctrine of 1947.

Fifty years ago this March, President Truman went before Congress to ask for a relatively modest amount of money to assist the anticommunist governments of Greece and Turkey. But the request was wrapped in packaging that turned out to be far more important than the contents. The packaging was what came to be known as the Truman Doctrine. To legislators who had little inkling of what these modest words would soon justify, Truman declared that Americans must commit themselves to aiding what he described as "free peoples who are resisting attempted subjugation by armed minorities or by outside pressures."

What few asked at the time was how he defined "free peoples," or whether "armed minorities" was not another way of saying "civil war," or what he meant by "outside pressures." Just what kind of situations was he suggesting that the United States get into? "Totalitarian regimes imposed upon free peoples, by direct or indirect aggression," Truman continued, "undermine the foundations of international peace and hence the security of the United States."

Again, there was a little problem of vagueness. Which free peoples, and how free must they be to qualify? What was "indirect aggression," and how did the United States propose to counter it? Furthermore, what was "international peace"? Taken at face value, it meant a beatific state of affairs that had probably never existed. Most troublesome of all was the key word "hence"—as in "hence the security of the United States" was threatened by the absence of international peace.

Drawing the Line
What Truman was saying was that threats to free (that is, anticommunist) governments anywhere were a security threat to the United States. While presumably one was not supposed to take this literally, what his speech was intended to do was to lay out a new definition of international engagement, one global in scope and without clear political or geographical definition. It was inevitable that at some point the desire of policymakers to push the definition of national security to its outer limits would collide head-on with the anxieties of a public unpersuaded of its necessity. The excesses of globalism, and the disaster that was Vietnam, were foretold in the exuberant language of the Truman Doctrine.

If the first problem with the concept of "national security" is its vagueness, the second is its expansiveness. In its effort to simplify the issue and to win public support for a global level of engagement, the Truman Doctrine often failed to distinguish between the vital and the desirable, the critical and the peripheral. It suggested that everything was vital and security a seamless web. But then some things turned out not to be so vital after all, like South Vietnam. Where does one draw the line? If South Vietnam was not really vital, then how about South Korea, or NATO? If security is to some degree arbitrary, then are interests arbitrary as well?

An example of expansiveness carried to its ultimate extreme as a security doctrine can be found in a declaration by the Clinton administration's former national security adviser, Anthony Lake, that the enemies of the United States, now that the Cold War is over, include no less than "extreme nationalists and tribalists, terrorists, organized criminals, coup plotters, rogue states, and all those who would return newly free societies to the intolerant ways of the past." Aside from the welcome news that intolerant ways are now largely confined to the past, one wonders whether there is anyone left, by this definition, who is not an enemy of the United States.

An Attitude, Not a Policy
The major reason for the intellectual confusion evidenced by such statements lies in the unmooring of the concept of "national security" from the more explicit and narrow concept of defense. Defense is a policy, national security is an attitude; defense is precise, national security is diffuse; defense is a condition, national security is a feeling.

The doctrine of national security emphasizes the nation-state. It came to prominence at a time when states were viewed not only as the dominant but as virtually the only actors. Nothing, however, has deflated the role of the state more than the end of the Cold War. There are two reasons for this. First, the state enjoys, by definition, a monopoly on military power. The Cold War, for all its ideological overlay, was primarily a contest between powerful, militarized states. But as the end of the war has decreased the relevance of military power, so, too, has it reduced the importance of the state.

A second reason for the decline of the state is the growing importance of trade, production, and wealth as determinants of power and influence. The central arena in which advanced industrial societies compete has shifted dramatically from the instruments of war to the instruments of wealth. In this new competition a former military superpower has become a supplicant, and former puny protectorates such as Taiwan, Singapore, and South Korea, not to mention Japan, have become powerful players. In the past, the great trading states—France, Germany, Britain, Japan, Spain, and even Venice—were, for the most part, major military players as well. Today, the economic giants are, for the most part, content to remain militarily weak.

The Security Dilemma
The governing theoretical model for international relations during the Cold War—the "paradigm" in political science talk—was that of realism, or power politics. The state was deemed to be the paramount actor, its sovereignty an absolute, and its protection the ultimate purpose of its military and diplomatic forces. States, being considered independent actors, could be threatened only by other states. Since states exist in a Hobbesian world of international anarchy, they must protect themselves from envious rivals. They must accrue military power (or put themselves under the tutelage of a powerful protector). That this may provoke anxieties among other states and make *them* feel threatened is the self-fulfilling prophecy of the security dilemma. Under these rules, security is defined as the prevention of war with other states, or victory in any conflict that occurs.

This is all very well, if the nation-state is the dominant reality of public life and if it has the ability to command undiluted loyalty. But in some areas of the world, the state has collapsed (as in central Africa), or is an instrument of drug lords and local oligarchies (as in parts of Latin America), or is run by a single family or clan (as in much of the Middle East and the Third World). In these cases, it commands not loyalty, but fear, and rules by intimidation. And instead of providing security for its citizens, it actually threatens it.

In such a case, what allegiance is owed the state? The question is not an abstract one. In recent years, we have seen the disintegration of established states, such as Yugoslavia and the Soviet Union, and the hollowing-out of others that exist only at the convenience of outside forces that sustain their ruling regimes, as in the former African colonies of France. Even in parts of the industrialized world, the state is sometimes incapable of providing security for some of its citizens. One has only to look to the slums of major U.S. cities for confirmation of this sorry fact—or even to affluent areas, with their guarded gates and private police forces.

The problem is not simply that the state is often unable to provide security, which is, after all, the major justification for its existence. It has also become increasingly secondary, even superfluous, to the economic life of peoples everywhere. The export and import of capital, the shifting of hundreds of billions of dollars around the world each day, the decisions over investment and employment, wages, and production—all these are made primarily by private forces under little or no state control. Within the economic realm, we are approaching the condition described by Karl Marx (albeit under different circumstances) where the state seems to be withering away.

No longer can any single state make decisions impervious to market forces and market commands: not unless it wants to commit economic suicide. States, like Gulliver, are confined by an ever-widening web of agreements, regulations, and prohibitions that lay outside their control. The American government, for example, has learned that it cannot enforce against its own European allies and Canada its self-declared embargo against Cuba—not even when it declares the matter to be one vital to its "national security"—which it has recently done. If "national security" now means that store clerks from Toronto and homemakers from Cologne must not be allowed to sun themselves on Cuban beaches, then Karl Marx has once again been proved right in observing that events reappear in history the first time as tragedy and the second time as farce.

What is taking place on every level—in the economy, in communications, in the environment, in public health—is the decline of the state as an autonomous actor. It will continue to exist for a long time, but shorn of its former pretense and majesty: a victim of forces it cannot control. Increasingly, the greatest threats to the well-being of citizens come not from other states, not from independent actors, but from *conditions*: resource scarcity, population growth, rampant urbanization, mass migration, environmental degradation, individual and group terrorism, economic exploitation.

Traffic Cops

How does the so-called realist paradigm—which declares states to be the dominant force of international life and their unhindered pursuit of their self-defined "interests" to be the duty of their citizens—help us to deal with this reality? What indeed are we to make of the concept of "statecraft" when the state itself is only one of the actors, or forces, that influences our lives? And beyond that, what happens to the concept of the majestic state when its role is reduced to that of a facilitator of private transactions?

Consider the international trade organizations that have become so important in the past few years: the North American Free Trade Agreement (NAFTA) and the World Trade Organization (WTO). These entities are really little more than giant trade groups whose purpose is to increase the flow of commerce. They do this by eliminating government regulations and ignoring international frontiers. Their purpose is to make national governments irrelevant. What is novel about them, and a telling mark of their power, is that they have enlisted governments to do this work for them. Governments are being reduced to the role of traffic cops, ensuring that everyone follows the regulations that are, of course, written by and for the most powerful corporations.

In some places, this process has gone so far that the state can hardly be said to exist at all. By this I do not mean such narco-states as Colombia, Mexico, Burma, and Pakistan, where drug lords rule independent fiefdoms. Rather, I have in mind Russia, where the new giant corporate entities (themselves former state enterprises stolen from the people by their former managers and the new mafia entrepreneurs) control the government and refuse to pay taxes to a state that they consider, quite understandably, the servant of their ambition. In effect, the role of such a state is to keep the population in line, to deflect criticism of commercial operations by invoking appeals to patriotism, such as the war in Chechnya, and to keep out competitors.

Russia may be an extreme example, but it is not a unique one. The phenomenon can be seen, to one degree or another, throughout the industrialized world. What this means is that national security, as traditionally conceived, has lost its meaning. There is military security, which is designed to protect the nation-state against other nation-states. This will obviously remain important, just as police forces remain important within cities. But there is another realm for which it is largely irrelevant: the realm of interests that is impervious to borders. Here the tools are far more subtle and complex, and the nation with the biggest military force may well not be best equipped to preserve these interests.

Cultural Identities

In this sense, national interest is an important interest but not the only one. Other interests claim the loyalty of individuals; people do not define themselves only as citizens. In recent years, we have had reason to become aware of cultural sources of identity. Modern Islam furnishes a dramatic, but not unique, example of identities that transcend, and even seek to eradicate, frontiers. We have been told that the conflicts of the post–Cold War world will be of a different nature than those of the past: that the clash of states will give way to the clash of civilizations. Although we need not adopt the apocalyptic conclusions of that analysis, it is clear that states are not always the ultimate objects of loyalty, that societies can be riven from within by individuals whose deeply held social values make their own state itself the enemy. We may think of Algiers, but we need look no farther than Oklahoma City for demonstration of this.

Societies today are being torn apart. There is a deadly struggle between traditionalists and modernists, between those who have embraced technological and social change and those who fear and resist it. The fault lines of future, and even present, wars lie not only between civilizations or between religions, but within them. In this struggle the state, when it is not actually considered to be the enemy, is, at best, irrelevant.

Whether or not war is, as Joseph Schumpeter has written, the health of the state, it is the way by which the state demands its citizens' loyalties and affirms its own primacy. It justifies this by the claim that it is the ultimate, and most reliable, guarantor of its citizens' welfare. Yet there has been an increasing tendency to question the central premise of *raison d'état*.

The U.S. Senate came very close to rejecting President Bush's call for war against Iraq for its invasion of Kuwait. The expeditionary force in Somalia (like the one earlier in Lebanon) had to be pulled out when it encountered casualties, and the intervention in Bosnia was delayed for several years until it became clear that American troops would not likely be drawn into the fighting. Even today it is unlikely that the president would be able to keep U.S. forces there if the intercommunal war resumed.

Only in the case of Haiti was there support for military intervention, and that was because there was a clear national interest at stake: keeping unwanted refugees out of the United States. The American people will apparently not presently support direct participation in other people's civil wars: not even where considerations of "national security" are claimed.

If wars are harder to justify, it may also be that, at least for the foreseeable future, great wars are less likely to occur. There have been no wars between major powers for more than 50 years. If the United States and the Soviet Union, for a variety of good reasons, did not choose to fight each other, what major states can we now imagine doing so—and for what stakes? What possible victory is worth the cost? And what society, democratic or not, would be willing to pay it?

While I would not go so far as to argue that nuclear proliferation is a good thing because it tempers hotheads who might otherwise go to war, the fact is that the possession of nuclear weapons has probably saved Israel and dissuaded India and Pakistan from open war. They are also likely to restrain China in its pursuit of great power status, and also other states that contest its right to do so.

There are other reasons why war among major states may be less likely in the future. One is that industrial societies, under the pressures of economic competition and innovation, are perforce becoming more democratic. Democratic states, while not necessarily peace-prone, are harder to arouse to war against other democratic states than are authoritarian ones. A further, and to my mind more compelling, reason is that the great trading states—those with the capacity to fight major wars—have become far more interdependent than in the past. This is one beneficial result of the global economy. With these economic links come a whole chain of other dependencies, all of which make war more self-defeating than in the past.

Where Are the Threats?
If the danger of a major war has diminished, at least so far as the great powers are concerned, what kind of traditional security threats does the United States face? By "traditional" I mean threats from another state. The fact of the matter is that—insofar as we can envisage the future—there is no one out there capable of causing the United States serious harm.

Russia is a deeply wounded state that was always weaker than Americans believed and that will take decades to recover even a semblance of its former power. For a long time, it will remain the sick man on the fringes of Europe: a problem but not a threat.

Japan is a mercantilist, pacifist society, single-mindedly obsessed with enriching itself, and determined not to make the same mistake that it did in the 1930s. It has no higher ambition than to be America's number one creditor, number one supplier, number one investor, and number one protectorate.

And what of Europe, the potential superpower: more populous, richer, more experienced in the evil ways of the world than the United States? Will it one day be a serious rival? Not likely. Europe—if by that term we mean a political entity equipped and willing to make independent foreign policy decisions involving issues of war and peace—does not exist. Nor, despite the hopes and pretensions of Brussels bureaucrats, is it likely to come into being.

In fact, the movement is quite the other way—away from visions of a European superstate capable of challenging, or even being an equal partner with, the United States. Even the effort to create a common currency—let alone a common defense and foreign policy—has proven to be so costly and contentious that it is problematic whether it will happen at all. The Eurocrats were overly ambitious and their American well-wishers overly optimistic.

This leaves China. Traditionally, Americans have had a paternalistic attitude toward China, an exploited nation that they felt would, with proper guidance, follow U.S. leadership to the promised land of capitalism and Christianity. The Chinese rudely betrayed Americans' hopes, and the smiling Little Brother became his doppelganger, the Yellow Peril. Now America does not know how to think about China: as a limitless market or an unending problem.

With its immense population and burgeoning economy, China is, to be sure, a potential great power. But it also has immense problems of governance, national unity, and political legitimacy. The world has come to enjoy low-cost Chinese exports; but it can do without them. China, however, if it is to prosper, needs strong economic and political ties with the rest of the world. The government has tied its legitimacy to its ability to provide a rising standard of living for the Chinese people. It cannot do that through a path of aggression. For the United States this means that China must be engaged, not confronted. To treat it as a national security threat will contribute to making it one.

If the danger of major war has decreased, what do we mean when we speak of security threats? How will we recognize them when they do not entail the survival of the nation, or even its well-being? Just as the so-called "other side" has disappeared with the end of the Cold War, so has the old meaning of the word "threat." What once seemed clear is now vague, ambiguous, diffuse, and unpredictable both in its source and its impact.

Policymakers draw up a long list of potential security threats. That is one of the things they are paid to do. These range from the emergence of another evil empire at one extreme, to "coup plotters and tribalists" at another. But if we get serious, it is striking how few threats from another state the United States today faces.

America Invulnerable
For all practical purposes, the country is invulnerable. It cannot be invaded. It has no enemy interested in destroying it that has the capacity to do so. It is not dependent on foreign trade, even though parts of the economy benefit from it. It feeds itself. It enjoys allies but has no compelling need for them—and in fact never relied on them for defense during the Cold War. The United States spread its net of protection, and of foreign bases, very wide, but not in self-defense. Because of its economic and military strength, its physical resources, its loyal population, and its privileged geographical position, the United States can afford to ignore a good deal of the turbulence in much of the rest of the world.

There are other reasons why America should involve itself with other nations, but defense, or national security, is not a compelling one. That is why it may seem odd that the class of specialists we call "national security managers" has set out for itself a task of global management. This can be seen in a number of policy pronouncements, strategy scenarios, and Pentagon wish lists but perhaps nowhere more dramatically than in a 1992 Defense Department document that argued that the United States must "discourage the advanced industrial nations from challenging our leadership or even aspiring to a larger regional or global role."

When word of this ambition got around, the document was quickly toned down. But it was an accurate reflection of an attitude that is common in Washington policymaking circles today. It comes out of the quick fix of the Gulf War, but even more from the way the Cold War ended—with not only the retreat of the Soviet Union, but its collapse and disintegration. Because this left only one great power, it gave birth, not surprisingly, to the notion of a unipolar world led by the United States and dedicated to the promulgation of American values. Woodrow Wilson would be resurrected in the body of General Patton.

This ambition is sold to the American public in the name of "security" (since the public has little enthusiasm for running the world), and justified to other nations by claiming that it is good for them. It obviates the need for them to develop powerful armed forces of their own, since America pledges to defend their true interests. It is not surprising that this curious notion has been greeted with less than universal acceptance and even outright skepticism.

Those most compliant are the Europeans and Japanese, who quite rightly see this as a way of avoiding the full cost of their own defense. This does not, of course, prevent them from challenging the United States on economic issues, which are the kinds that concern them most deeply. They are content to let us defend them so long as it does not get in the way of more important things. Thus, too, the expansion of NATO, which they agree to because Washington wants it, and because it spares the west Europeans the costly alternative of admitting the east Europeans into their privileged economic club.

The Costs of Leadership
This leadership strategy is an expensive one. NATO expansion alone is scheduled to cost some $100 billion for the upgrading of east European armed forces. No wonder military contractors like it. Even without it, the United States continues to spend militarily at Cold War levels. Currently, it costs about $100 billion a year to "reassure" the Europeans (though against what is unspecified), and another $45 billion or so to "protect" the Japanese and Koreans.

Today, more than 50 percent of all discretionary federal spending is still devoted to national security, even in the absence of an enemy. While other nations invest for production, the United States borrows for consumption—and in the process becomes further indebted to the trade rivals whose interests it seeks to protect.

There is much the United States can and should do in the world, particularly in the economic and humanitarian realms. But it cannot undertake this task while it tries to maintain a pretense of global primacy that rests on a diminishing leverage in the military and diplomatic realms. It is time to balance America's foreign policy as well as its budget: to bring resources, in Lippmann's useful phrase, into line with commitments, and to take a serious look at other demands on those resources. The American people want the nation to be strong and to stick by its ideals. But they are not interested in grandiose plans of global management.

Americans are not by nature or by inclination imperialists. America is a strong and resilient society that is burdened with serious social needs that require urgent attention. Some of these problems not only prevent the United States from competing more effectively in the international arena, but also threaten the well-being and safety—that is, the security—of Americans. A national security policy that does not take that into account is inadequate, unrealistic, and unworthy. It also is doomed to fail.

A Sense of the Feasible
America's primary foreign policy interests are critical but few. They are to protect the American homeland from destruction and to preserve its institutions and form of government. Beyond this, it has a secondary interest in the expansion of the market economic core that contributes to U.S. prosperity, in access to natural resources, in the protection of the common environment, and in peaceful processes of change in areas to which it is intimately linked culturally and politically. Finally, at a tertiary level, it seeks to promote democracy not because this contributes to U.S. security in any tangible sense, but because it reflects American values.

This is a big list for a country with only 4 percent of the world's population and a steadily declining proportion of its wealth and production. If America is not to exhaust itself in pursuit of grandiose ambitions it must reestablish a sense of the feasible. This is the kind of realism of which the United States is most in need.

Specifically, it should abandon the pretense of global military control, turn over regional security tasks to the major powers of those regions, end its high-cost and high-risk dependency on Persian Gulf oil, focus on global competitiveness as the prime objective of its military posture, transform its role from that of global enforcer to that of conciliator and balancer, and address far more seriously the other kind of national security: the threats to the well-being of people that lies beyond the competition among states.

Security is, after all, not a condition, but a feeling and a process. It is also an abstraction. We may feel secure and not be so, or be secure and not feel so. We are all vulnerable in ways we cannot imagine and cannot fully protect ourselves against. That is our human condition. So therefore let us not seek absolutes but instead measure. And let us put security in its proper place, which is as a means to a greater end but not an end in itself. In a real sense it is true, in the mournful words of Macbeth, that the unbridled pursuit of "security is mortals' chiefest enemy."

Note

This essay is based on presentations given at Dickinson College, the U.S. Army War College, and the George Washington University during the spring of 1997.

Democracy at Risk
American Culture in a Global Culture

Benjamin R. Barber

Benjamin R. Barber is the director of the Walt Whitman Center for the Culture and Politics of Democracy at Rutgers University and the author of numerous books, including Strong Democracy, Jihad vs. McWorld, *and, most recently,* A Place for Us: How to Make Society Civil and Democracy Strong.

Is American culture global? Internationalists often insist that it is, but it comes closer to the truth to say that global culture is American—increasingly trapped within American culture in its technologically facilitated, free market supported, globalizing form. While it is fashionable to try to tame the idea of the Americanizing of global culture by referring to dialectical interactions and two-way interfaces that make America global even as the globe becomes American, to me this is either wishful thinking on the part of those subjected to the depredations of what I have called "McWorld,"[1] or diplomatic rationalization by the corporate beneficiaries of globalization who want to disguise their new soft hegemony in a still softer ideological cloak.

This cloak deploys the metaphors of reciprocity and mutual assimilation, which suggest that dominant cultures are themselves modified by the cultures they affect to modify. But this is a peculiar reciprocity—the reciprocity of the python who swallows the hare: "Oh look!" cry fans of the hare, "the python has not swallowed the hare, the hare has swallowed the python! For see how like a hare the python looks!" But of course after a week or two of active digestion, the hare is gone and only the python remains.

McWorld does take on the colors of the cultures it swallows up—for a while: thus the pop music accented with Reggae and Latino rhythms in the Los Angeles barrio, Big Macs served with French wine in Paris or made from Bulgarian beef in Eastern Europe, Mickey speaking French at EuroDisney. But, in the end, MTV and McDonald's and Disneyland are American cultural icons, seemingly innocent Trojan-American horses nosing their way into other nations' cultures.

McWorld represents an American push into the future animated by onrushing economic, technological, and ecological forces that demand integration and uniformity and that mesmerize people everywhere with fast music, fast computers, and fast food—MTV, Macintosh, and McDonald's—pressing nations into one homogeneous global culture, one McWorld tied together by communications, information, entertainment, and commerce.

Even where McWorld is opposed by forces of reactionary tribalism and traditional religion, it trumps its opponents. Iranian zealots may keep one ear tuned to the mullahs urging holy war, but the other is cocked to Rupert Murdoch's Star Television, which beams in *Dynasty* reruns or *The Simpsons* from hovering satellites. Underneath their chadors, Iran's women wear Western high-fashion outfits, which, the moment they leave the transparency of public space and enter the opaque safety of the private, they flaunt as if they were in Paris or Rome. The Russian Orthodox Church may remain a bastion of faith in Russia's privatizing world, but it has nonetheless managed to enter into a joint venture with California businessmen to bottle and sell natural waters from the Saint Springs. Brooding neo-Nazis in America's far-right "militias" are comfortable recruiting on the Internet, and both the far left and the far right have turned to rock music to get their traditional messages out to the new generation.

Democracy at Risk
This new globalizing culture is likely to displace not only its reactionary critics but its democratic rivals, who dream of a genuinely internationalized civil society made up of free citizens from many different cultures. For America's global culture is not so much hostile as indifferent to democracy: its goal is a global consumer society comprised neither of tribesmen (too commercially challenged to shop) nor of citizens (too civically engaged to shop), both of whom make lousy clients, but of consumers. Consumers are a new breed of women and men who are equal (potential customers all) without being just; and who are peaceful (placid and reactive rather than active) without being democratic.

In Europe, Asia, and the Americas, markets have already eroded national sovereignty and given birth to a new global culture of international banks, trade associations, transnational lobbies like OPEC, world news services like CNN and the BBC, and multinational corporations, the new sovereigns of a world where nation-states scarcely know how to regulate their own economies, let alone control runaway global markets. While mills and factories sit on sovereign territory under the eye and potential regulation of nation-states, currency markets and the Internet exist everywhere, but nowhere in particular. And although they produce neither common interests nor common law, common markets do demand, along with a common currency, a common language (English, which Japanese teenagers now prefer to use whenever possible and which is an official, if not the official, language of every international conference held today).

Moreover, common markets produce common behaviors of the kind bred by cosmopolitan city life everywhere. Commercial pilots, computer programmers, film directors, international bankers, media specialists, oil riggers, entertainment celebrities, ecology experts, movie producers, demographers, accountants, professors, lawyers, athletes—these comprise a new breed of men and women for whom religion, culture, and ethnic nationality are marginal elements in a working identity. It is shopping that has a common signature today around the world. Cynics might even suggest that some of the recent revolutions in Eastern Europe had as their true goal not liberty and the right to vote but well-paying jobs and the right to shop. It is perhaps no surprise that as the Communists and nationalists return to power in Russia and Hungary and elsewhere, it is not shopping but only democracy that is put at risk.

Shopping means consumption and consumption depends on the fabrication of needs as well as goods. As I argued in *Jihad vs. McWorld*, the new global culture is a product of American popular culture driven by expansionist commerce. Its template is American, its form is style. Its goods are as much images as material, an aesthetic as well as a product line. It is about culture as commodity, where what you think is defined by what you wear and apparel becomes a species of ideology. Think about those Harley-Davidson motorcycles and Cadillac motorcars that have been hoisted from the roadways to the marquees of global-market cafés like the Harley-Davidson and the Hard Rock. They are not about transportation anymore. You no longer drive them, their iconographic messages drive you. They conjure up synthetic behavior from old movies and new celebrities, whose personal appearances are the key to such popular international café chains as Planet Hollywood.

The new churches of this global commercial civilization are shopping malls, the privatized "public" squares and neighborless "neighborhoods" of suburbia. The new products are not so much goods as image exports that help create a common world taste around common logos, advertising slogans, celebrities, songs, brand names, jingles, and trademarks. Hard power here yields to soft, while ideology is transmuted into what I have called a kind of videology that works through sound bites and film clips. Videology is fuzzier and less dogmatic than traditional political ideology; as a consequence it may be far more successful in instilling the novel values required for global markets to succeed.

These values are not imposed by coercive governments or authoritative schools, but bleed into the culture from such pseudo-cultural products as films and advertising, which feel neither coercive nor intrusive but are often linked to a world of material goods, fast food, fashion accessories, and entertainment. *The Lion King* and *Jurassic Park* are not just films; they are global merchandising machines that sell food, music, clothes, and toys. *Titanic* is a billion-dollar movie, which makes it much more than just a movie.

America's global culture is nearly irresistible. Japan has, for example, become more culturally insistent on its own traditions in recent years, even as its people seek an ever greater purchase on McWorld. Burgers and fries now dominate noodles and sushi, and Japanese teens struggle with English phrases they hardly understand to project a sense of global cool. In France, another country that prided itself on resistance to McWorld, and where less than a decade ago cultural purists complained bitterly of a looming *Sixième République* ("*la République Americaine*") and assailed the corruptions of *franglais*, economic health is today measured in part by the success of EuroDisney just outside of Paris. And though the Socialist government of Lionel Jospin struggles to preserve some sense of France's commitment to social welfare against the tide of privatistic market thinking that is sweeping across the Western world, France becomes more and more commercial in a manner that is more and more American. The sudden appearance of "*Aloween*" as a holiday to alleviate the shopping doldrums of the pre-pre-Christmas season is only the most appealing (and appalling) example of this tendency.

Macro-Peace

Homogenization is not the whole story, of course. In light of the continuing existence of tribal bloodshed, terrorism, religious extremism, right-wing fanaticism, and civil war throughout the world, prophecies about the end of history look terminally dumb. But if microwars persist, McWorld's pacifying markets are likely to establish a macro-peace that favors the triumph of commerce and consumerism and gives to those who control information, communications, and entertainment ultimate (if inadvertent) control over global culture—and over human destiny. This suggests that the historian Paul Kennedy's worry about the decline of America,[2] predicated largely on the decline of its traditional "hard goods" economy, is misplaced and that a renewed American hegemony is far more likely—although it will be a hegemony rooted in information and technology, not in GNP or the potential of the manufacturing sector.

Unless we can offer an alternative, the triumph of globalization is increasingly likely to mean not a global multiculture or a framework for cooperation in the context of difference, but the sacrifice of both variety and democracy to a totalizing consumerism that, without coercion, will rob us of our freedom and our character. The first casualty of McWorld is citizenship. The second is democracy. For a world of the ubiquitous consumer is a world of choice without power, of democracy without citizens, and in a world without citizens—although private economic choice may be maximized—there can be little real freedom and no democracy.

The mantra of free markets is globalism's siren call. Is there any activity more intrinsically globalizing than trade, any ideology less interested in nations than capitalism, any challenge to frontiers more audacious than the market? In a number of ways, corporations are today more the central players in global affairs than either nations or tribes. We say these global corporations are multinational, but they are more appropriately termed postnational, or even antinational. They abjure the very idea of national boundaries or any other parochialism that limits them in time or space.

On "Planet Reebok," boasts the familiar athletic shoe campaign, "there are no boundaries." The ads for Ralph Lauren's designer perfume collections also reject boundaries, while a Coca-Cola campaign for the 1996 summer Olympics in Atlanta featured a blimp circumnavigating the globe trying to foment a "global" cola party among obviously distinct cultures, with each quickly succumbing to the lure of assimilationist cola consumerism.

A popular protectionist bumper sticker in the United States (one that predates the North American Free Trade Agreement) reads, "Real Americans Buy American," and many Americans believe that, in backing NAFTA, Washington sold out the country's labor interests. The trouble is that it is hard to know which car is really more American: The Chevy built in Mexico primarily from non-American imported parts and then shipped to the United States so American consumers can "buy American." The Ford built in Germany by Turkish workers for export to the Nigerian market. Or the Toyota Camry thought up at Toyota's Newport Beach (California) Design Center, built by American workers at the Georgetown, Kentucky, Toyota plant from parts that, other than the engine and drive train, are almost exclusively American, and test-driven at Toyota's 12,000-acre Arizona proving grounds.

To combat this creeping "foreignization" of American products, the government has instituted a system of automobile labels by which consumers are supposed to be informed of content percentages, foreign or American, but no one really knows how to do the calculations.

No wonder so many corporations refuse to define themselves in terms of their labor force. In the global economy, the determining factors are neither capital nor work nor material but rather how these three are manipulated by information, communications, and administration—the true levers of the new economics.

These levers are virtual rather than material, and they resist the kinds of physical and territorial regulation typical of traditional governmental monitoring (which itself has been hobbled by deregulatory ideology and the concept of the minimal state). The phrase "virtual corporation," which when Robert Kuttner, the economist and coeditor of *The American Prospect*, first used it a few years ago seemed novel, is now widely accepted.[3] In Kuttner's thinking, the corporation as a physical entity with a stable mission or location was likely to give way to a shifting set of temporary relationships connected by computer networks, telephone, and fax.

Invisible Bonds
Can globalization defined in these ways support traditional understandings of democratic national sovereignty—the authority people supposedly exercise over the shaping of their communities and their lives? On the contrary, it would seem to be a calamity not just for nations but for their citizens. We talk about democratic markets and market democracy, but in truth markets decisively constrain democracy. The new bonds of the market are, however, invisible, even comfortable, accompanied as they are by a pleasant rhetoric of private choice and personal consumer freedom. "We give you liberty" proclaims an advertisement for a Midwestern baked potato chain, "because we give you the choice of toppings!" Global liberty looks more and more like the choice of toppings in a world where chain store spuds are the only available fare.

In the 1960s, the critical theorist Herbert Marcuse prophesied a conformitarian world brought to heel by technology rather than terror, in which civilized humanity would be reduced to "One Dimensional Man." But in the sixties, the other side of Marcuse's dialectic—the power of protest— prevailed, and his prophecy seemed hyperbolic, even to him. For though he foresaw totalizing, even "totalitarian" tendencies in industrial culture, he also foresaw forces that might break the containment (he had celebrated the radical moment of resistance in Hegel's dialectic in his earlier *Reason and Revolution*).

Today, the potential of the market for assimilation of all distinctions and rebelliousness and the blurring of all ideological opposition (abetted by the fuzziness of borders between news and entertainment, information and amusement) give Marcuse's fears renewed currency. Global consumerism threatens a totalizing society in which consuming becomes the defining human essence. One-dimensionality achieves a palpable political geography in the controlled (and controlling) architecture of the shopping mall, where public squares have been supplanted by private spaces designed to maximize commerce. Malls are the privatized public squares of the new fringe city "privatopia" that secedes from the larger common society (vulgar, multiracial, and dangerous) to a gated world of placid safety.

Market Panaceas
Supporters of free market ideology continue to dismiss this line of criticism as a stale rehearsal of Marcuse's overheated prophecies. Many argue that consumer society, though it may debase taste, nevertheless enhances choice and thus entails a kind of democracy: the sovereignty of consumers. But however "sovereign" consumers may feel, voting dollars or yen or euros is not the same as voting a common political will. Market relations are not a surrogate for social relations. The problem is not with capitalism per se, but with the notion that capitalism alone can respond to every human need and provide solutions to all of our problems.

Just as statist progressives may once have thought that a paternalistic government could solve every human problem, antistatist conservatives today are convinced not only that the state can solve no human problem, but that the market can now do everything that the state has failed to do. Where statist panaceas once were sovereign, market panaceas now seem to reign—with calamitous consequences. For privatization annihilates the very idea of the public and removes from under us the ground of our commonality.

Much of my earlier analysis of McWorld turned on my analysis of market mania: the disastrous modern confusion between the moderate and mostly well-founded claim that flexibly regulated markets remain the most efficient instruments of economic productivity and wealth accumulation, and the zany, overblown claim that naked, wholly unregulated markets are the sole means by which we can produce and distribute everything we care about—from durable goods to spiritual values, from capital development to social justice, from profitability *today* to sustainable environments into the next century, from Disneyland kiddie-play to serious culture, from private wealth to the essential commonweal.

This second claim has moved people who fear government to insist that goods as diverse and obviously public as education, culture, penology, full employment, social welfare, and ecological survival be handed over to the profit sector for arbitration and disposal. Having privatized prisons (nearly one out of every six inmates in the United States is now incarcerated in a privatized for-profit facility), will we next "outsource" the electric chair, turning over to the private sector the sovereign state's defining power over capital punishment? Crime pays, after all!

The disappointment with bureaucratic interventionalism in the name of well-meaning paternalistic welfare states has led to governmental downsizing, which has probably been a good thing for individual liberty and for civil society. But the effects of democratization via devolution are quite different from the effects of privatization. Partnership between government and citizens of the kind being promoted by moderates on both sides of the political divide today is one thing; a modest devolution of power to state and municipal governments may improve the efficiency of the public sector even as it empowers civil society to take on greater responsibility. But wholesale privatization—which has become the magic potion of those who would restore the antique notion of the market's "invisible hand"—is a recipe for the destruction of our communities and our commonality, our sovereignty and our power to shape our common lives.

The End of Democracy

Privatization is not to be confused with decentralization, which involves the devolution of power to municipal and local governments and to the citizens who make them work. Privatization is not about the limitation of government; it is about the termination of democracy. For the "government" dismantled in our name is actually the only common power we possess to protect our common liberties and advance our common interest. Its destruction does less to emancipate us than to secure our servitude to global corporatism and consumer materialism.

American conservatives like William Bennett and Pat Buchanan have recognized as much, and the radical right in Europe is capitalizing on anxiety arising in the face of globalization (the export of jobs, the import of redundant labor) by engendering a new politics of fear. If the end of big government leaves big business with a monopoly over our needs and desires, the prospects for individual liberty and a robust civil society will diminish.

Markets, which permit us private rather than public modes of discourse, are simply not designed to do the things democratic communities can do. They allow us as consumers to tell producers what we want (or allow producers by means of advertising and cultural persuasion to tell us what we want), but prevent us from speaking as citizens to one another about the social consequences of our private consumer choices. As a consumer, I may want a car that goes 130 miles an hour, but as a citizen I can still vote for a reasonable speed limit that will conserve gasoline and secure safe streets. As a consumer, I prefer inexpensive goods, but that is not to say that as a citizen I will be unwilling to pay a surcharge to guarantee that what I buy is not manufactured by child labor.

There is no contradiction here: just the difference between the consumer and the citizen. The consumer in me and the citizen in me. Hence, as a private consumer, I may say, "I want a pair of expensive running shoes." But as a citizen I may say, "How about better athletic facilities in our public schools?" As a consumer I may pay to see violence-saturated Hollywood thrillers and listen to woman-hating rap lyrics, but as a citizen I may support rating systems and warning labels that help us and our children make prudent moral judgments. The point is that markets preclude "we" thinking and "we" actions, trusting in the power of aggregated individual choices (the famous invisible hand) to somehow secure the common good. Only it does not work that way. The quest by consumers for private satisfaction and of producers for private profit simply does not add up to the satisfaction for citizens of their public interests.

Markets are contractual rather than communitarian: they stroke our solitary egos, offering durable goods and fleeting dreams, but not a common identity or collective membership, thus opening the way to more savage and undemocratic forms of identity such as tribalism. One of the twentieth century's most poignant lessons, taught by the sad history of the Weimar Republic as well as by the modern story of urban gangs, is simply this: if we cannot secure *democratic* communities to express our need for belonging, *undemocratic* communities will quickly offer themselves to us. From them we will get the warm fraternity and membership we look for in community, but at the expense of liberty and equality. Gangs instead of neighborhood associations, blood tribes instead of voluntary associations, misogynist fraternities instead of communities of common interest, an "Aryan Nation" instead of a democratic nation.

Global Markets

At the global level, the failure of institutions to provide meaningful forms of democratic membership (which is precisely global consumerism's failure) is likely to spawn new forms of global tribalism. Much of the opposition to "Europe" in democratic countries like Denmark and Switzerland arose out of a conviction that Europe was insufficiently democratic: too technocratic and bureaucratic and legalistic, good for corporate entities but less obviously beneficial to citizens. Markets give us the goods but not the lives we want; they provide prosperity for some but lead to despair for many and dignity for none. The world's 26,000 or more international nongovernmental organizations (NGOs) are no match for the Fortune 500 multinational corporations of McWorld. The institutions that are our nation's most formidable expression of sovereignty may no longer be able to rival McWorld's power.

The questions I raised five years ago in writing *Jihad vs. McWorld* are more relevant than ever. What, I asked then, is the Pentagon compared to Disneyland? Today, the Pentagon is reluctant to risk a single soldier's life in pursuit of American interests abroad, while Disney has taken over a major network, bought a baseball team, founded a sovereign synthetic living community in Celebration, Florida, salvaged (but sanitized) Times Square, and made an attempt to "recreate" a battlefield of the Civil War on the "useless" turf where the war was actually contested. What then is G. I. Joe compared to the Mouse?

Can the U.S. Information Agency pretend to project America's image more cannily than Hollywood? What is the United Nations or—in the face of the Asian currency crisis—the International Monetary Fund, compared to the trillion-dollar-a-day global currency market? Such global institutions do not even have an address: you can call your broker to sell a declining stock, but who can Indonesia call when its currency goes down the drain (not George Soros, though it tried). Similarly, you can write to someone *on* the World Wide Web, but you cannot write *to* the Web itself, which is a virtual abstraction lost in the very cyberspace it defines, with neither a fax number nor a Web address.

Markets do not even know how to regulate themselves to survive, let alone to nurture democratic civic communities. They are unable to produce the kinds of regulatory antibodies they need in order to protect themselves from the self-generating viruses of monopoly and infectious greed: left to their own devices, corporations downsize until they have in effect fired not only their employees but their customers as well—since, as Henry Ford understood, their employees turn out to be one and the same as their customers.

That is the paradox of McWorld. It cannot survive the conditions it inevitably tends to create unless it is checked and regulated by civic and democratic forces it inevitably tends to destroy. It destroys the financial base of the consumers it needs on the way to selling them products at more efficient prices. It overproduces goods and underproduces employment, unable to see the connection between them. It needs democracy more than democracy needs it, yet while democracy cultivates free markets, markets often fail to cultivate democracy. It is not an accident that China, the world's last great communist political system, without abdicating its totalitarian control, has become the world's fastest-growing market economy, even in these years of the Asian slowdown.

In spring 1996, Pepsi-Cola's director of East European operations allowed, "We think we can survive and prosper, whatever regime is going to be here [in Russia]." Governments may turn the clock back on democracy, but "whatever happens" they will not "turn back the clock on consumers and deny them modern, Western brands." Inundating frustrated peoples in transitional democracies with consumer goods they have identified with life in the "democratic West" has become a favorite ploy of governments wanting to retain dictatorial control. Consumerism may turn out to be to the new converts of free-market ideology what bread and circuses were during the Roman Empire: seductive diversions that give the appearance of freedom (shopping) without granting its real substance (self-government). That is certainly one of the lessons from China.

Advocates of privatization and markets have of course insisted that markets not only reinforce democracy but are themselves inherently and deeply democratic. This is again to confuse private choices made by consumers with civic choices made by citizens. It is to be deluded to think that the liberty to choose between 27 varieties of aspirin and the liberty to choose an affordable health system to which everyone will have full and equal access are the same.

The pretended autonomy of consumers permits producers to talk like populists: If we dislike the homogeneity of McWorld, don't blame its purveyors, indict its consumers. If popular taste is plastic, popular standards meretricious, and popular consumption homogenizing, impeach the populace whose choices are determinative, not the corporations whose profits depend solely on their faithfully serving that populace. The public is two-faced, conclude populist merchandisers: people say they detest television scandal mongering, but they watch it avidly. Exhausted by the Monica Lewinsky-Clinton coverage, news anchor Peter Jennings confesses that he does "not know how to account for the fact that the public is clearly fed up but continues to watch."

As if the quarter of a trillion dollar annual advertising expenditures of these same corporations were but window dressing; as if consumer tastes are established in a vacuum; as if the desires and wants on the basis of which markets prosper are not themselves engendered and shaped by those very same markets. As if consumer tastes were established in a vacuum rather than through what a recent *New Yorker* essay calls the "science of shopping," which has become a big business among consumer industry consultant who tell retailers where to strategically place goods and how to orchestrate store atmospherics. As if, finally, human beings were not complex and divided, often loathing what they "like," often finding it hard to live up to what they believe in.

"Save us from what we want!" has become the plaintive motto of unhappy moderns inundated with products they neither approve of nor feel able to resist. Living in a world where the puerile, the ignorant, the tawdry, and the base are everywhere privileged and rewarded, how can they honor the promise of their better selves? It may be that consumers want what they are proffered, but what they are proffered has a great deal to do with what they want.

Soft Power
The manipulation of wants has been accelerated by the interactive character of buying and selling in McWorld's ever softer markets. Hard consumer goods are becoming linked to soft technologies rooted in information, entertainment, and life style, and products are emerging that blur the line between goods and services. With the saturation of traditional markets and what the socio-economic commentator William Greider has described in his recent critique of global markets as a vast surfeit of goods, capitalism can no longer afford to serve only real needs and wants.[4] In the traditional economy, products were manufactured and sold for profit to meet the demand of consumers who made their needs known through the market. In the new postmodern capitalist economy, needs are manufactured to meet the supply of producers who market products through promotion, spin, packaging, advertising, and cultural persuasion.

Whereas the old economy, mirroring hard power, dealt in hard goods aimed at the body, the new economy, mirroring soft power, depends on soft services aimed at the mind and spirit. "I don't want customers to think that they are walking into a clothing store," says designer Donna Karan (DKNY). "I want them to think that they are walking into an environment, that I am transforming them out of their lives and into an experience, that it's not about clothes, it's about who they are as people."

Where once the body more or less spoke up for its natural needs, today the mind and spirit must be manipulated into wanting and needing all kinds of things of which neither the body could have demanded nor the autonomous mind dreamed. Why should millions of music lovers replace perfectly good vinyl LP collections for a marginal, indeed a quite controversial improvement in sound or size in the forms of CDs? And now the industry has announced that we have a new "need"—for DVD-RAM digital technology that will make the recent CD and videotape innovations obsolete. This compulsory obsolescence of what appear to be perfectly adequate technologies may pay tribute to human ingenuity, but more often than not it is a recognition of market greed.

The targeting of mind and spirit by corporations seeking to transform how humans think about "need" leads material markets into strange territory. As it assimilates and transforms so many other ideologies, postmodern capitalism has not shied away from assimilating and transforming religion. If Madonna can play erotic games with a crucifix, why shouldn't Mazda and American Express work to acquire some commercial purchase on the Holy Spirit? "Trucks," intones a gravelly voiced pitchman in a 1993 Mazda television ad, "are a spiritual thing for me." The new Mazda pickup is "like a friend... with a new V-6 and a soul to match."

To create a global demand for such American products as cigarettes, soft drinks, and running shoes—for which there can be said to be no natural "need"—need must be globally manufactured. For Coca-Cola, Marlboro, Nike, Hershey, Levi's, Pepsi, Wrigley, or McDonald's, selling American products means selling America, its popular culture, its putative prosperity, its ubiquitous imagery and software—and thus its very soul. Merchandizing is as much about symbols as about goods, about selling not life's necessities but life styles. The style being marketed is uniquely American yet potentially global. It is an incoherent and contradictory yet seductive style that is less "democratic" than physical-culture youthful, rich urban, austere cowboy, Hollywood glamorous, Garden of Eden unbounded, good-willed to a fault, socially aware, politically correct, mall-pervaded, and ironically often dominated by images of black ghetto life—black, however, as in Michael Jordan hip and rapper cool, rather than as in welfare-poor miserable and prison-bound squalid.

Manipulating Habits
Because sales depend less on autonomous choices by independent buyers than on the manipulated habits and shaped behavior of media-immersed consumers, those who control markets cannot help but address behavior and attitude. Tea drinkers are improbable prospects for Coca-Cola sales, so when it entered the Asian market, the Coca-Cola company quite literally found it necessary to declare war on Indian tea culture. Long-lunch, eat-at-home traditions obstruct the development of fast food franchises. However, successful fast food franchises have inevitably undermined Mediterranean long-lunch, eat-at-home rituals, inadvertently corrupting "family values" as thoroughly as Hollywood action movies have done. For fast food is about accommodating a culture in which work is central and social relationships are secondary, in which fast trumps slow and simple beats complex. Highly developed public transportation systems attenuate automobile sales and depress steel, cement, rubber, and petroleum profits. Agricultural life styles (rise at daybreak, work all day, go to bed at dusk) may be inhospitable to television watching. People uninterested in spectator sports buy fewer athletic shoes. The moral logic of austerity that might appeal to serious Muslims or Christians or secular ascetics gets in the way of the economic logic of consumption. Tobacco companies have to target the young since use of their products tends to erode their consumer base.

Notice how so many of the new technological gadgets marketed as innovative ways of "liberating" us from the office and the workplace actually imprison us in an expanding zone of work. Do fax machines, cellular telephones, and home computer modems free us up or tie us down with electronic tentacles that make work ubiquitous? Even the Sony Walkman, that invitation to bring music to our leisure and work worlds, is in truth a device that artificially enhances the need to buy cassettes for 24-hour-a-day listening, even as it turns listening to music from a social into a solitary occupation and links it to other consumption-enhancing activities like jogging. Walkmen sell not just music but cassettes, and not only cassettes but athletic shoes as well—just as athletic shoes sell Walkmen and cassettes. You can take a walk in the woods (if you can find some woods) in a comfortable pair of old shoes and tune into nature's music for free; jogging to the music of a Whitney Houston movie sound track, on the other hand, means big profits for McWorld, as shoes, tapes, electronics, and a film are all sold at once.

Can responsible corporate managers then be anything other than irresponsible citizens in McWorld's new era of sovereign consumer markets? There is no conspiracy here, only an inadvertent triumph of the logic of private profits over the logic of public goods. To sell all that McWorld has to sell, sometime citizens must be made over into full-time consumers. That's why in place of our old town squares and multi-use urban downtowns we now have enclosed malls that offer nothing but commerce. These malls are not totalitarian in the same way that fascist and communist states once were, but they *are* in a similar fashion focused on monobehavioral activity, constructing a "new man" around activities suited to the obsessive preoccupation with profit. To this degree, we may call them "totalizing," if not totalitarian.

Malls are the capital cities and theme parks of McWorld's expanding nation: no community theater, no childcare center, no Hyde Park Speakers' Corner, no church or synagogue, no town hall, no grange, no schoolhouse—just one store after another and the demand that we shed every other identity except that of consumer, that we shed our sociability and our citizenship for the solitary pleasures of shopping. Nowadays, malls do not even pretend to sell "necessities" (no dry cleaners, no hardware store, no grocery store). Theme boutiques and gadget outlets—the Disney Store, the Sharper Image, Brookstone, and the Nature Store—predominate, and sell you nothing that you want until you get inside and realize you "need" everything they sell. To date, only in the pure suburbs like those on Long Island and in New Jersey do we find spaces with no public squares or sidewalks or multi-use centers of sociability. But imagine all the world as New Jersey.

The Illusion of Competition
The autonomy of consumers is an illusion—the market's most democratic illusion. But there is another illusion, more basic and antique, in the arguments of those who insist that markets are democratic: this is that the market in which consumers shop is any freer than the shoppers themselves. Ironically, approximately egalitarian capitalist competition only began to exist under the watchful eye of interventionist, Keynesian democratic governments that used regulation and law to assure a competitive evenhandedness that markets were incapable of on their own. In this era of deregulation and government downsizing the competitive vitality of markets has never been in greater jeopardy. Particularly in the newly sovereign market domain defined by information, entertainment, and telecommunications (the "infotainment telesector," as I have called it elsewhere), conglomeration and monopoly are becoming the rule.

Take Disney for example. Having domesticated the Lion King and the Beast, and having successfully annexed and tranquilized New York City's tenderloin district in Times Square, it also acquired Capital Cities/ABC for $19 billion, and now owns the Anaheim Angels baseball team. Likewise, Rupert Murdoch's News Corporation has bought the Los Angeles Dodgers in order to broadcast their games on its Fox television network and thus compete with Ted Turner's Atlanta Braves and Wayne Huizinga's (Blockbuster Video) winning World Series team, the Florida Marlins. "Content" is the key to the new technology, and there is no point in owning broadcast networks or cable systems if you have nothing to put on them.

The fashionable word for all this vertical corporate integration is synergy, but synergy turns out to be just another word for monopoly. Like so many of the new conglomerates of McWorld, Disney owns not just film studios, theme parks, and sports teams, but trademark tie-ins, publishing houses, television stations, newspapers, and entire new towns. One manager gushed that, in taking over ABC, Disney had become not just a world-class but a "universe class" operation. Disney has simply followed the modern corporate imperative, which is to own deep and own wide. And so Paramount acquired Simon and Schuster, which owned Madison Square Garden and the Knicks basketball and Rangers hockey teams, only to be acquired itself by Viacom, the cable company—a big fish eaten by a bigger fish. If you own hardware, the rule goes, buy software; thus Japan's Sony swallowed up Columbia Pictures and took a big (apparently indigestible) bite of Hollywood. If you own television stations, buy film libraries; thus Ted Turner bought and "colorized" the MGM film library; thus Bill Gates of Microsoft bought the rights to reproduce the works of art in museum collections on CD-ROM—after also having bought into the new production company started by ex-Disney executive Jeffrey Katzenberg, record producer mogul David Geffen, and megahit film director Steven Spielberg. DreamWorks itself is helping to corrupt the boundary between news and entertainment. Its first film, *The Peacemaker*, a disappointing action drama about stolen ex-Soviet nuclear weapons, had an earlier incarnation as a television news special.

Entrepreneurship and capitalist competition suffer at the hands of these new postcapitalist monopolists. Bill Gates has been including his Web browser free on all computers delivered with his Microsoft Windows software in order to put Netscape, a competitor, out of business. The U.S. Justice Department finally arose from its slumber to take antitrust action. Rupert Murdoch's News Corporation uses his Harper Collins publishing firm to help market the Murdoch empire in China, most recently by voiding a book contract with Christopher Patten, the former governor of Hong Kong, who is highly critical of the Chinese government. If pluralism and the enhancement of choice are rationales for McWorld's global activities, the theory is flatly contradicted by the practices.

Poised on the edge of the twenty-first century, Disney's and McWorld's other telecommunication conglomerates seem to yearn to return to the nineteenth-century world of monopoly in which there were no antitrust laws. Michael Eisner is no John D. Rockefeller, Bill Gates is no Cornelius Vanderbilt, and Steven Spielberg is no Andrew Carnegie. But that is only because Eisner, Gates, and Spielberg are far more powerful that these robber barons ever were. Are they really the harbingers of new realms of liberty, these titans who exercise an inadvertent sovereignty not over oil, steel, and railroads, the muscles of our postindustrial world's body, but over the pictures, information, and ideas that are the sinews of the postmodern soul?

Reilluminating Public Space
McWorld thus does little for consumer autonomy, less for competition, and nothing at all for the kinds of liberty and pluralism essential to political freedom. But perhaps still more dangerous to liberty, McWorld has encroached upon and helped push aside public space. Its greatest victory—and here it has been mightily assisted by the antigovernmental privatizing ideology that has dominated politics in recent years—has been its contribution to the eradication of civic space.

Yet, once upon a time, between the oppositional poles of government and market, there was a vital middle choice. Though in eclipse today, the powerful imagery of civil society held the key to America's early democratic energy and civic activism (just as it helped Eastern Europeans break away from the Soviet Empire). For it was the great virtue of civil society in days past that it shared with government a sense of things public and a regard for the general good, yet (unlike government) made no claims to exercise a monopoly over legitimate coercion. Rather, it was a voluntary "private" realm devoted to public goods.

Civil society is the domain that can potentially mediate between the state and the private sector, between the rabid identity of an exclusive tribe and the exhausting identity of the solitary consumer, between Jihad and McWorld. Civil society offers women and men a space for activity that is simultaneously voluntary and public; a space that unites the virtue of the private sector—liberty—with the virtue of the public sector—concern for the general good.

Civil society is thus a dwelling place that is neither a tribal fireside nor a shopping mall; it asks us to vote neither our political opinions nor our consumer desires but only to interact with one another around common concerns. It shares with the private sector the blessing of liberty; it is voluntary and made up of freely associated individuals and groups. But unlike the private sector, it aims at common ground and cooperative action. Civil society is thus public without being coercive, voluntary without being private.

My model for a genuinely democratic global culture would be a global civil society, hooped together by the many bands of civic associations represented by NGOs, churches, foundations, citizen organizations, and other civic groups. International organizations like Civicus and Civitas, which bring together civic associations from many nations to explore transnational agendas, represent the seedlings of a new global society. It is precisely here, where markets thrive even as subnational tribes make war on them, that civil society and a space for citizens is most needed. And it is here that Civicus does its most important work—not just as a club for like-minded NGOs but as an association that develops countervailing power in the face of a totalizing global consumerism, countervailing power that may one day carve out civic and social space for citizens and for some meaningful form of transnational democracy.

The task today in theory, no less than in practice, is to reilluminate public space for a civil society in eclipse. Unless a third way can be found between private markets and coercive government, between McWorld's anarchistic individualism and Jihad's dogmatic communitarianism, we may survive as consumers and clansmen, but we will cease to exist as democratic citizens.

Notes

This essay was adapted from a paper given at a conference, "American Culture in a Global Culture," held at Bard College, November 1997.

1. See my *Jihad vs. McWorld* (New York: Times Books, 1995).

2. Paul Kennedy, *The Rise and Fall of the Great Powers: Economic Change and Military Conflict from 1500 to 2000* (New York: Random House, 1987).

3. Robert Kuttner, "Brave New Corporate 'Workplace of the Future,'" *Berkshire Eagle*, August 1, 1993.

4. William Greider, *One World, Ready or Not: The Manic Logic of Global Capitalism* (New York: Simon & Schuster, 1996).

Unit 2

Unit Selections

Russia
5. **The United States and the New Russia: The First Five Years,** Raymond L. Garthoff
6. **Is Russia Still an Enemy?** Richard Pipes

Asia
7. **Testing the United States–Japan Security Alliance,** James Shinn
8. **South Asian Arms Race: Reviving Dormant Fears of Nuclear War,** Barbara Crossette

Europe
9. **America and Europe: Is the Break Inevitable?** Werner Weidenfeld
10. **Why Are We in Bosnia?** Richard Holbrooke

The Developing World
11. **Pivotal States and U.S. Strategy,** Robert S. Chase, Emily B. Hill, and Paul Kennedy
12. **The Middle East Peace Process: A Crisis of Partnership,** Madeleine Albright
13. **Africa, the 'Invisible Land,' Is Gaining Visibility,** Salih Booker

Key Points to Consider

❖ Construct a list of the top five regional or bilateral problems facing the United States. Justify your selections. How does this list compare to one that you might have composed 5 or 10 years ago?

❖ What are the forces that are straining the United States–Japan Security Alliance? What forces are holding the Alliance together?

❖ What developing countries should be on a list of "pivotal states"? How does your list compare to the one discussed in the reading for this unit?

❖ What direction do you expect Russian foreign policy to take, and how much influence does the United States have on this choice?

❖ What is the most underappreciated regional or bilateral foreign policy problem facing the United States? How should the United States go about addressing it?

❖ What are U.S. interests in Africa? What potential does the Clinton administration's new Africa policy have for furthering these goals and for bringing about constructive change in Africa?

DUSHKIN ONLINE Links
www.dushkin.com/online/

7. **Center for Russian, East European, and Eurasian Studies**
   http://reenic.utexas.edu/reenic.html
8. **Inter-American Dialogue (IAD)**
   http://www.iadialog.org/
9. **World Wide Web Virtual Library: International Affairs Resources**
   http://info.pitt.edu/~ian/index.htm

These sites are annotated on pages 4 and 5.

The United States and the World: Regional and Bilateral Relations

Having a clear strategic vision of world politics is only one requirement for a successful foreign policy. Another is the ability to translate that vision into coherent bilateral and regional foreign policies. What looks clear-cut and simple from the perspective of grand strategy, however, begins to take on various shades of gray as policymakers grapple with the domestic and international realities of formulating specific foreign policy.

Part of the difficulty lies with the fact that foreign policy problems do not arrive on the agenda in an orderly fashion. An example from the Clinton administration illustrates the point. President Bill Clinton entered office hoping to focus on domestic issues, only to find U.S. troops in Somalia on a humanitarian mission that was becoming embroiled in political controversy; a refugee influx from Haiti looming on the horizon; and an escalating conflict in Bosnia. Not only did these foreign policy problems detract from the administration's ability to focus on domestic issues, but its many about-faces in trying to solve these problems became a major political liability at home and abroad.

If the Clinton administration often seemed hesitant in dealing with regional and bilateral issues in its first term, it often appears eager to do so in its second term. A catalog of major initiatives would include supporting an Irish peace treaty, sponsoring NATO enlargement, a presidential trip to China, participating in the IMF-bailouts of the East Asian economies, and undertaking retaliatory bombings in response to terrorist attacks on American embassies in Africa.

These actions help bring into focus the reality that no single formula exists for constructing a successful foreign policy for dealing with these nations and organizations. Still, it is possible to identify three questions that should be asked in formulating a foreign policy. First, what are the primary problems that the United States needs to be aware of in constructing its foreign policy toward a given country or region? Second, what does the United States want from this relationship? That is, what priorities should guide the formulation of that policy? Third, what type of "architecture" should be set up to deal with these problems and realize these goals? Should the United States act unilaterally, with selected allies, or by joining a regional organization?

Each succeeding question is more difficult to answer. Problems are easily cataloged. The challenge is to distinguish between real and imagined ones. Prioritizing goals is more difficult because it forces us to examine critically what we want to achieve with our foreign policy and what price we are willing to pay. Constructing an architecture is even more difficult because of the range of choices available and the inherent uncertainty that the chosen plan will work.

The readings in this section direct our attention to some of the most pressing bilateral and regional problem areas in American foreign policy today. Which of these is most important to the American national interest is a hotly debated topic.

The first two readings in this unit examine U.S. relations with Russia. Raymond Garthoff, in "The United States and the New Russia: The First Five Years," asserts that by 1993 the "honeymoon" period in U.S.–Russian relations had ended. He outlines a number of sources of friction in this relationship and states that the greatest failure of U.S. diplomacy has been that of bringing Russia fully into a new European security architecture. Richard Pipes, in "Is Russia Still an Enemy?" reviews the internal debate within Russia over what type of foreign policy to pursue. He argues that the ambitions of Russia's elite are pulling it in two different directions. Will Russia's foreign policy be pro-Western or anti-Western?

The second two readings examine U.S. relations with Asia. In the first article, "Testing the United States–Japan Security Alliance," James Shinn observes that this long-standing relationship is at risk. His article examines what forces are pulling it apart, how the U.S.–Japanese alliance might be tested, and the potential consequences of failure. With the detonation of nuclear devices by India and Pakistan, South Asia has moved to the top of the agenda of American foreign policy. Barbara Crossette, in "South Asian Arms Race: Reviving Dormant Fears of Nuclear War," reviews events leading up to these nuclear tests and looks at their implications for the future.

U.S.–European relations are the subject of the third set of essays. Werner Weidenfeld in "America and Europe: Is the Break Inevitable?" observes that although U.S.–European relations today are generally seen in a positive light, changes are taking place on both sides of the Atlantic that suggest this may not be the case in the future. Weidenfeld calls for creating a new transatlantic community. Richard Holbrooke, in "Why Are We in Bosnia?" presents a personal perspective on the road leading to American involvement. He cautions that, if the United States does not lead, its European allies could falter and that "there will be other Bosnias in our lives."

The final set of readings examines the complex issues of dealing with the developing world. In the first essay, the authors call for a more selective U.S. foreign policy. They argue for giving priority to the "pivotal states," states who are struggling with internal problems but whose size and stature cause them to cast a shadow over their regions. The next essay focuses on the Middle East. Secretary of State Madeleine Albright in "The Middle East Peace Process," reviews the history of peace negotiations and outlines the logic of the American approach to overcoming the current impasse. The final reading examines U.S. foreign policy toward Africa. Salih Booker, in "Africa, the 'Invisible Land,' Is Gaining Visibility," outlines the emerging framework for the new American policy toward Africa.

> "In 1997 there is renewed talk of a 'partnership' [between the United States and Russia,] but it will be harder to realize in the wake of the mockery that NATO enlargement has made of the post–cold war partnership with Russia proclaimed earlier by the Bush and Clinton administrations... Managing the impact of that decision is probably the principal task for United States policy for the next five years."

The United States and the New Russia: The First Five Years

RAYMOND L. GARTHOFF

In a brief address to the nation on December 25, 1991, President George Bush declared that "the United States recognizes and welcomes the emergence of a free, independent, and democratic Russia, led by its courageous president, Boris Yeltsin," and the creation of a Commonwealth of Independent States (CIS) replacing the Soviet Union.

The former Soviet Union was also succeeded by 11 other newly independent states (because they had been recognized as independent four months earlier, the 3 Baltic states were not "successor" states). The United States, within a few weeks, extended full recognition to all 12 countries. Russia was not only the largest and most important of the successor states, it was also for political and legal reasons regarded as the sole "continuing successor." It inherited the Soviet Union's seat on the UN Security Council, and was recognized as the sole succeeding nuclear weapons state under the Non-Proliferation Treaty (NPT) and as the sole signatory of several strategic arms limitation agreements.

Relations between the United States and Russia since 1991 have reflected the impact of multiple transitions. The world has been adjusting to the aftermath of a cold war that had defined the previous half century. Russia itself has been seeking to reconfirm its identity, not only on a postcommunist, post-Soviet basis, but also on a postimperial basis, since the country is now roughly confined within borders it has not known since the seventeenth century. Europe has been trying to readjust its economic, political, and security relationships as a whole continent rather than one divided by an Iron Curtain. Finally, the United States, as the surviving superpower, has had the task of determining what role it will play and how it can help to fashion a new world order, even as change in the very elements of national power and the structure of international relations foreshadows the emergence of a new multipolar world.

FIRST TASKS

One of the highest priorities for the Bush administration was to assure maintenance of responsible control over the nuclear weapons of the former Soviet Union. The overriding objectives were to prevent the emergence of additional nuclear states, to ensure the integrity and security of the former Soviet nuclear arsenal, to prevent nuclear weapons from becoming a cause or a resort in any possible conflict among the successor states, and to deny a precedent for other potential new nuclear weapons states.

RAYMOND L. GARTHOFF *is a diplomatic historian and retired diplomat. His books include* The Great Transition: American-Soviet Relations and the End of the Cold War *(Washington: Brookings, 1994) and* Détente and Confrontation: American-Soviet Relations from Nixon to Reagan, *rev. ed. (Washington: Brookings, 1994). He is associated with the Brookings Institution.*

Although initially discouraged by the Bush administration, the Nuclear Threat Reduction Act (later termed the Cooperative Threat Reduction—CTR—program, but better known as the Nunn-Lugar program after its legislative authors, Senators Sam Nunn (R-GA) and Richard Lugar (R-IN)) was nonetheless passed by Congress in December 1991, just as the Soviet Union was dissolving. The administration soon reversed itself and welcomed the act's authorization of the transfer of $400 million from Defense Department funds to assist Russia in dismantling weapons on its territory and to aid in gathering nuclear weapons from the other former Soviet republics.

Tactical nuclear weapons had already been withdrawn to Russia from central and eastern Europe, and from the outlying Soviet republics, between 1989 and 1991. In December 1991, Ukraine, Kazakhstan, and Belarus also agreed to send their tactical nuclear weapons to Russia, and all were transferred in the first six months of 1992. More complex was the question of several thousand former Soviet strategic nuclear weapons still deployed in those three former republics. Early agreements in the framework of the nebulous CIS were either reinterpreted, ignored, or repudiated, making any understanding on command and control, as well as ownership, of these strategic nuclear forces uncertain.

The first important step was a United States–brokered agreement between Russia, Ukraine, Belarus, and Kazakhstan reached at Lisbon in May 1992. In a "Lisbon Protocol" to the United States–Soviet/Russian Strategic Arms Reduction Treaty (START I), Ukraine, Belarus, and Kazakhstan agreed to assume nonnuclear weapons status and remove all nuclear weapons to Russia. Many questions remained open, however, especially ownership of the fissionable materials in the warheads and the current nuclear status of the other three republics.

In Ukraine the question of giving up all nuclear weapons remained controversial in 1992 and 1993. The United States and other Western powers made it clear that economic assistance and the general development of relations depended on resolving this problem, which led Ukraine to realize that it could not afford to be a nuclear power (political considerations were also reinforced by growing awareness of military technical difficulties and the high cost of any attempt to do so).

The United States share of international economic assistance [to the former Soviet Union] was not in any way commensurate with American economic strength.

In January 1994, the Clinton administration, which had continued and pressed the position taken by its predecessor, succeeded in getting a tripartite agreement between the United States, Russia, and Ukraine on a number of issues that opened the way to the withdrawal of strategic nuclear warheads from Ukraine. Part of the understanding that was not made public was a Ukrainian commitment to complete the transfer of nuclear weapons to Russia within three rather than seven years. In 1994 Belarus, Kazakhstan, and Ukraine acceded to the NPT as nonnuclear weapons states, and ratified the Lisbon Protocol and START I by the end of the year. All remaining nuclear warheads in the three countries were sent to Russia before the end of 1996, and missiles and silos were being dismantled and destroyed.

American and Russian interests coincided in seeking the return of all nuclear weapons to Russia, but United States diplomacy played an important role in gaining Russian concessions (in particular on reimbursement to the other three countries for the fissionable materials in the weapons) as well as in inducing the others to agree. All in all, it was a substantial success for United States policy and for international stability.

Concern also arose over the security of nuclear weapons, fissionable materials, and nuclear scientific know-how in Russia itself. The Nunn-Lugar program was expanded to assist in creating new scientific research opportunities for former Soviet nuclear weapons specialists. It also provided technical assistance and funding to assist in transporting, storing, and dismantling nuclear weapons, and in storing fissionable materials, especially plutonium. These tasks were addressed at the first Bush-Yeltsin summit, in February 1992, and efforts were greatly expanded under the Clinton administration. One of the most notable agreements, in February 1993, provided for the United States purchase of some 500 metric tons of highly enriched uranium (for use as reactor fuel) over a 20-year period for about $12 billion.

HONEYMOON'S END

Although in the short term the question of the nuclear arsenal of the former Soviet Union was most important for United States security, for the long run the future political and economic evolution of Russia was of the greatest importance. American diplomacy (together with that of the other principal Western powers) played an important part in facilitating Russia's adjustment to the new world order, especially in 1992 and 1993. President Bush had three summit meetings with President Yeltsin in 13 months. In February 1992 at Camp David, the two presidents agreed that their countries would not regard one another as "potential" enemies, a step forward from the 1989 Malta accord that the United States and the Soviet Union would not regard each other as "enemies." In June in Washington they signed a "charter" on Russian-American relations. Finally, in January 1993 in Moscow another major strategic arms reduction treaty (START II) was signed.

President Bill Clinton, soon to become, for Yeltsin, "my friend Bill," held the first of his many summit meetings with Yeltsin at Vancouver in April 1993, where they envisioned not merely a Europe stretching from the Atlantic to the Urals but a community of friendship encircling the northern hemisphere, from Vancouver to Vladivostok. By mid-1997 it was becoming difficult even to keep count of all their meetings (my count is 12 in the four and a half years Clinton has been in office, including 7 full-fledged bilateral summit meetings). This in itself tells us a great deal and is a sign of growing normalcy in the relationship. Moreover, from mid-1993 on there have been regular semiannual meetings of a joint commission chaired by Russian Prime Minister Viktor Chernomyrdin and United States Vice President Al Gore, which has developed into a particularly useful and successful collaboration at an authoritative level not requiring the constant direct engagement of the presidents (and with less demanding media pressures for dramatic "news"). Some 97 formal agreements between the United States and Russia were signed in the five years between 1992 and 1996 (almost as many as the 101 signed with the Soviet Union in the half century from 1933 through 1985, and up from the 78 signed in the preceding five years, 1986 through 1991).

In retrospect, it has become clear that the United States–Russian relationship in 1992 and 1993 was, as it sometimes has been called in Russia, the "honeymoon" period. But by the end of 1993 there were increasing strains in the relationship. It is important to note that while these frictions grew out of various actions by the United States and Russia, including internal Russian developments, they also stemmed in part from an American failure to recognize the tentativeness and fragility of Russia's idealistic globalist "new thinking" and reliance on "common interests," and of Russia's almost embarrassingly pro-Western stance from January 1992 to mid-1993. Perhaps this was due in part to the fact that American leaders, especially Bush, had become accustomed to taking Russia for granted after overcoming earlier reservations as to Gorbachev's new thinking, and in part to the early efforts by Yeltsin and his foreign minister, Andrei Kozyrev, to outdo Gorbachev in displaying pro-Western new thinking. In any case, the failure of this Russian stance to prevent a worsening economic situation, and a growing United States tendency to assume that it would lead and Russia would follow in international relations, led most Russians to become disenchanted with the "honeymoon" and to conclude that Russia would have to act to defend its own national interests rather than assume that the other powers would honor them.

The Bush and Clinton administrations, while seeking to establish good relations with Russia, failed to understand the need to validate Russia's self-effacing "new thinking" instead of taking actions that would, even if inadvertently, undermine it. Another reason for the failure of United States policy to meet Russian expectations was that some Russian actions were interpreted in the United States as reflecting a neo-imperialist desire to reestablish hegemony in the former Soviet republics. Finally, unreasonably high Russian expectations also contributed to the failure.

THE ILLUSION OF LARGESSE

The dominant, and arguably most important, component of United States (and other Western) relations with Russia at least over the first three years was economic. For most Russians it was also the primary issue.

The Bush administration acted swiftly to convene and chair a "Coordinating Conference on Assistance to the Newly Independent States." The convening of the meeting, in Washington in mid-January 1992, was announced on December 12, even before the dissolution of the Soviet Union was complete. It had in fact originally been planned as a meeting to coordinate assistance to the Soviet Union, and to build on Western economic aid to the Soviet Union that had begun a year before. The United States sought to take a leadership role but also to submerge its own modest aid in a broader package that it hoped would emerge from the meeting of 47 countries. The meeting proved a stopgap before the more important commitment of a package of $24 billion in aid drawn up by the Group of Seven (G7) and announced by President Bush on April 1. The United States share of the package was approximately $6.6 billion. But the "support package" as a whole was an amalgam of various kinds of economic assistance, nearly half of it previously pledged to the Soviet Union, and over half in new repayable short-term loans, deferral of debt interest payments, and credit guarantees to Western enterprises. (This obfuscation exaggerating the extent of aid even led some to refer to the package as an April Fools' Day gift.)

Following the January coordinating conference, the United States announced a short-term emergency aid program supplying surplus food stocks and medicines to the successor states of the Soviet Union called Operation Provide Hope. With later extensions, this program in 1992 and 1993 provided some $73 million in quick assistance, mostly flown in by the United States Air Force.

Subsequent meetings of the coordinating conference were held in Lisbon in May 1992 and Tokyo in October, and in April 1993 the G7 came up with another catchall package of $28.4 billion, of which the United States share was a pledge of $2.5 billion.

The appearance of massive Western economic assistance in 1992 and 1993, although well intentioned, was counterproductive in several respects. Although intended to facilitate Western contributions to a common effort, it sometimes had the effect of suggesting the task could be left to the international community—despite the fact that the multilateral "packages" were made up of individual national aid commitments and larger commitments by multilateral organizations such as the IMF and World Bank (to which Russia and other successor states were admitted in June 1992) that also depended on national funding. Similarly, while the aid was intended to bolster Russian confidence as well as the reform program, even President Yeltsin and most of his advisers did not understand that direct economic assistance would be limited and incremental, and that much of it would not be grants of money placed at the disposition of the Russian government. The most direct economic aid, from the IMF and World Bank, was also subject to fairly stringent conditions that tied disbursement to continued onerous if necessary economic and financial reform measures. Although sound, and helpful to Russian economic reform, such conditionality has been interpreted by many Russians as interference in their internal affairs, and by some even as designed to prevent Russian resurgence as an independent world power.

In June 1992, the United States granted normal nondiscriminatory most favored nation trade status to Russia for the first time since MFN was withdrawn from the Soviet Union in 1974. It has subsequently been renewed annually under a waiver of the Jackson-Vanik amendment to the 1974 Trade Act, but that discriminatory legislation still has not been repealed. In March 1994, the multilateral Coordinating Committee (COCOM) that established Western export controls was abolished as a remnant of the cold war, and the United States relaxed substantially its own more stringent export controls.

The United States share of international economic assistance in the first years after the Soviet Union's dissolution was not in any way commensurate with American economic strength. Of all Western economic aid in 1991 and 1992, the United States share was only about 10 percent (roughly $2 billion), in contrast to Germany's 60 percent (about $12 billion). From January to April 1992, the Bush administration was slow to act. From April to October the Congress in turn was slow, not unmindful that it was an election year, despite an unusual bipartisan letter of support signed by all living former presidents (Richard Nixon, Gerald Ford, Jimmy Carter, and Ronald Reagan). In October 1992 the Freedom Support Act was finally enacted, providing a long-planned $12 billion contribution to the IMF and $1.2 billion in new bilateral assistance to Russia, mainly through credit and loan guarantees by the Overseas Private Investment Corporation, the Export-Import Bank, and the United States Department of Agriculture.

In 1993, the Clinton administration carried forward the bilateral and multilateral economic assistance programs begun by the Bush administration (including the Nunn-Lugar aid in securing and dismantling nuclear weapons and materials). As noted, this included a composite aid package for Russia and the other successors totaling about $2.5 billion. The same sum was appropriated in 1994, but that proved to be the high point. In 1995 United States assistance appropriations dropped to $850 million, and in 1996 to $640 million. (In 1996 the IMF came up with a third package of $10 billion, just in time to give a boost to President Yeltsin's reelection bid;

> *What some Americans view with apprehension Russians see as no more than their equivalent of the Monroe Doctrine.*

the United States appropriation was not passed until after his election).

In sum, from 1991 through 1995 the United States obligated about $8.7 billion in assistance to the former Soviet successor states (of which about $4 billion went to Russia), and about $11 billion in credits (again, about $4 billion to Russia). Over these years, there was a deliberate shift in assistance from Russia to the other successor states, in particular Ukraine and Armenia. During the "honeymoon" years of 1992 and 1993, the United States gave about two-thirds of its economic assistance to Russia, and one-third to Ukraine and the other states, more or less in line with the relative size of the countries' populations. By 1995 and 1996 this ratio was reversed, with about one-third going to Russia and two-thirds to the others. By this time Ukraine had agreed to give up its nuclear weapons and had belatedly embarked on economic reform, whereas Russian-American frictions had risen and Russia was thought (in 1994 and 1995) to be less dedicated to reform and to a postimperial nationhood than it had seemed earlier. By early 1997 Ukraine was not only receiving more United States assistance than Russia, but had become the third largest United States aid recipient. In 1997 the administration has requested an increase to a total of $900 million for all the successor states, of which $240 million is earmarked for Russia.

It remains a nagging question whether the United States and the West seized the challenge of aiding the newly independent Russia with sufficient vigor and resources. To be sure, Russia's economic recovery and reform must ultimately rest on its own efforts. It is also clear that simply to have poured money into the "wild capitalism" of Russia since 1992 would not have yielded a sufficient trickledown effect to justify open-ended assistance. Moreover, there are domestic political constraints in the United States and other countries on the amount of economic assistance that can be authorized. And a major constraining factor has been the uneven internal institutional development of the Russian political economy (and that of Ukraine and the other successor states). It remains an important and as yet unanswered question whether a bolder effort might have yielded greater results. The Bush and Clinton administrations seem to have merited at least a grade of "C" or perhaps "B"; not "A," but not "F."

ARMS AND ARMS CONTROL

Presidents Bush, Clinton, and Yeltsin shared an interest in establishing a close and highly visible personal relationship. They also shared an interest in preventing nuclear proliferation and in maintaining arms control efforts, in particular strategic arms control and reduction. As earlier noted, President Bush succeeded in concluding a second strategic arms reduction treaty (START II) just before leaving office in January 1993. In January 1994 at a Moscow summit, Clinton and Yeltsin agreed to a largely symbolic "detargeting" of missiles on alert aimed at their two countries (although they could be retargeted in seconds). By the Helsinki summit of March 1997, after the United States Senate had consented to ratification of START II, new guidelines were agreed on for still deeper nuclear weapons cuts (from levels of 3,000–3,500 in START II to 2,000–2,500, and including warheads as well as missiles), but these were dependent not only on further negotiation but on ratification of START II by the Russian Duma, which remained an uncertain prospect.

Long negotiations on permissible Theater Missile Defenses below a threshold of capability that would contravene the Anti-Ballistic Missile (ABM) treaty limits on strategic ballistic missile defenses also produced an agreement (largely on American terms) at that same summit, but again ratification in both countries was questionable under prevailing circumstances. Moreover, interest in deploying strategic ballistic missile defenses for the United States remained strong in the Republican Congress, casting further doubt on the longevity of the ABM treaty and the future of the entire strategic arms control regime.

The United States and Russia set aside minor differences and agreed on a common position in support of the Chemical Weapons Convention (CWC) in 1993, the indefinite extension of the nuclear Non-Proliferation Treaty (NPT) in 1995, and a Comprehensive Nuclear Test Ban (CTB) in 1996 (although Russia has lagged in ratifying the CWC because of a lack of funding to meet its deadlines on destruction of existing chemical weapons stocks).

The 1990 multilateral treaty on Conventional Forces in Europe (CFE) presented two problems. First, while it had been concluded by the Soviet Union, its provisions directly concerned several of the other successor states in addition to Russia. A division of arms quotas was negotiated among these states in 1992, and all adhered to the treaty. The second problem concerned some collateral subceilings of arms holdings in the so-called flank areas (as seen from a central European focus). Russia and Ukraine were unduly constrained by these subceilings. Russia, while well within the severely reduced overall arms levels of the treaty, had not reduced to the required level in the North Caucasus flank area. When the treaty came into full effect in November 1995, Russia was thus not in compliance with that limitation. The United States assisted in obtaining a consensus of CFE parties to accept revised interim flank constraints that dealt with this problem pending a full review and revision of the CFE treaty, now under negotiation.

In direct United States–Russian military relations, contacts between the military establishments begun in the late 1980s with the Soviet Union were continued and expanded. Joint field exercises on a modest scale were held in 1994 and 1995 (and naval exercises even earlier), and the first joint high-level war game was held in 1994. In May and October 1994, United States Defense Department delegations in Moscow for consultations presented unprecedented detailed briefings on the new American defense review and nuclear posture review. By late 1995 Russia had agreed not only to participate in the NATO-led peacekeeping operation in Bosnia, but to place its troops under United States command (which they preferred to "NATO" command). With misgivings and hesitation, Russia also joined the NATO Partnership for Peace program launched in 1994.

Collaboration in the exploration of outer space, building on earlier United States–Soviet cooperation, was also carried forward, beginning in 1992. The main problem has not been political or technological, but Russia's difficulty in funding its share of the joint program.

Many other examples of the normalization of United States–Russian relations could be cited. Perhaps the most prosaic but telling is the lifting in May 1995 of a nearly 50-year-old ban by the United States embassy in Moscow on embassy personnel fraternization with Russian citizens.

FRICTION IN THE RELATIONSHIP

A number of sources of friction have also arisen in the United States–Russian relationship. As earlier noted, some of these stemmed from the initial self-effacing posture of the Russian government in 1992 and 1993, to which the United States became accustomed. Many prominent Americans in Congress and the public seem to have had difficulty in distinguishing the defeat and collapse of the Soviet Union from the emergence of Russia as its principal successor; there has been a tendency to treat Russia as a defeated adversary rather than a liberated successor. Many political figures in Russia, in turn, have been disposed to see the West, and above all the United States, as determined to maintain or expand its global hegemony and to keep Russia down and weak.

Thus there has been some concern in the United States with what is sometimes seen as Russian "neo-imperialism," or an attempt to restore hegemony in the "near abroad," as many Russians refer to the other former republics of the Soviet Union. There also was a backlash of negative reaction to the protracted internal war in the breakaway Russian republic of Chechnya in 1994–1996.

Russia has sought to strengthen the CIS (with only limited success), and does see the other new independent republics of the former Soviet Union as an area of vital interest to Russia. There is a small Russian military presence in a number of these countries, by agreement (except in the Transdniestr of Moldova). On the other hand, the Russian government has consistently reaffirmed the territorial integrity of all these states, rejecting opportunities to accept incorporation of actual or would-be separatists in Ukraine (Crimea), Moldova, and Georgia. What some Americans view with apprehension Russians see as no more than their equivalent of the Monroe Doctrine.

If some Americans are concerned by Russian activities in the "near abroad" and at home, Russians have been concerned by the failure of the United States to consult Russia over the use of force in other regional disputes, mostly against former Soviet clients (and current debtors to Russia). Thus United States air strikes against Libya in 1993, Serbs in Bosnia in 1994, and Iraq in 1995 and 1996 brought Russian protests. And in peacemaking, Russia resented being left out when the United States met with China and the two Koreas over the North Korean nuclear proliferation problem in 1995.

Although the United States and Russia agree on the principle of controlling exports of weapons and military high technology, in a number of specific cases they have differed. The United States, for example, strongly objected in 1993 to a Russian sale of rocket boosters and associated technology to India for its civilian space program. (Russia agreed to renegotiate the provisions on providing technology in exchange for a United States purchase of some Russian space components.) The United States also objected strongly to Russian assistance in construction of nuclear reactors in Iran, even though it was being done in conformity with International Atomic Energy Agency safeguards. And the United States has objected to Russian sales of diesel submarines to Iran and naval cruise missiles to China. Russia, in turn, sees the United States as attempting to deny it opportunities to take its share of international trade in the arms and space field. For example, the nuclear reactors Russia is building for Iran are the same type that the United States and South Korea have agreed to supply to North Korea as part of a deal to close down another reactor that produces weapons-grade fissionable material. Moreover, American companies are aggressively selling weapons to former Warsaw Pact countries to replace their Soviet weapons (which Russia can service) with NATO arms.

In an echo from the cold war, concerns over compliance with arms control agreements have been revived. Russia, evidently because of a lack of funds, failed to meet its promised schedule for destroying old chemical weapons stocks and surplus armaments earlier withdrawn from Europe beyond the Urals. Much more serious was evidence that Russia had been slow to end research on biological weapons and had not dismantled standby infrastructure for production of such weapons, continuing a violation inherited from the Soviet Union. The Russians for their part have been concerned about the extensive United States research and development of advanced ballistic missile defense systems and tentative plans to deploy a national defense despite the ABM treaty, which they see as a threat not only to the treaty but to the entire strategic arms control process.

One of the most persistent irritants in United States–Russian relations stems from the American political process, rather than United States government policy. Congress has continually sought to influence Russian policy and behavior, or at least to gain domestic support for attempts to do so, on a wide range of issues. Legislative riders are frequently introduced and even enacted that would require Russia to accede to one or another demand or lose economic assistance or benefits of agreements negotiated on a basis of reciprocal advantage. For example, riders enacted would have cut off economic assistance if Russia had not withdrawn its troops from Latvia and Estonia by a prescribed date. Other riders have sought to do the same for withdrawal of Russian forces from Moldova, and even to demilitarize the Kaliningrad (formerly Koenigsberg) district of Russia itself. Riders have demanded that Russia not supply space technology to India, nuclear reactors to Iran, and anti-ship missiles to China, and that it not complete a power reactor in Cuba. Still others would require Russian acceptance of United States positions in ongoing arms control negotiations or compliance with United States interpretations of various arms agreements. Most of these, it will be noted, are issues that the United States government has taken up with Russia and in many cases resolved. Sometimes the congressional punitive threats may have some effect. But they are always resented, since they imply an American right to dictate Russian policies.

THE GREATEST FAILURE

Relations between the United States and Russia during the first five years consolidated a shift already begun in the final post–cold war years of the Soviet Union, a shift to a normal mix of cooperation and competition, collaboration on areas of congruent national interests, and reconciliation or acceptance of divergent interests. Relations are no longer seen as a zero-sum interaction, as in the cold war.

The area of greatest failure has been in bringing Russia fully into a new security architecture for Europe. The responsibility for that failure rests primarily with the United States. This is particularly regrettable because it was largely owing to a United States policy initiative that had not been intended to have the negative impact it has had. The enlargement of NATO to the east, giving membership to former Warsaw Pact allies of the Soviet Union and diminishing the nonaligned belt of states between NATO and Russia, has engendered wide concern in Russia. To many Russians, the renewal of the cold war Western military alliance by absorbing former members of the defunct Warsaw Pact when there is no threat from Russia can only been seen as creating a new threat to Russia. Why else should NATO, now enjoying enormous conventional as well as nuclear superiority, feel it necessary to advance to the very borders of Russia itself? The United States, as the acknowledged leader of NATO and the principal progenitor of NATO expansion, is held responsible.

Most Russians do not place this issue at the forefront of their concerns. Moreover, the signing in May 1997 of the Founding Act on Relations between Russia and NATO defused any immediate crisis in relations as NATO embarks on its enlargement. Nonetheless, it remains a palliative to an undesirable initiative. And it does not dispel all concerns or answer questions about why the United States and NATO should wish to expand to the East.

NATO enlargement has come to be seen, especially by its prospective new members, at least in part as a hedge against a resurgent threat from Russia. But hedging should be a contingent response if negative changes occur; it should not be a preemptive initiative that may contribute precisely to such undesired changes. While most Russians do not see an expanding NATO as a direct military threat, many are disquieted. The essence of the problem is not that NATO expansion stirs exaggerated Russian fears, but that it tends to impinge on legitimate Russian security interests. It represents an effort to create a new security architecture for Europe based on NATO. Expansion of NATO—but not including Russia—means to marginalize, if not to exclude, Russia from meaningful participation in European security arrangements. The Russian-NATO Founding Act is a belated effort to redress that error inherent in the original idea, even if not in its purpose.

The drive for NATO expansion was launched in early 1994 when President Clinton declared that the question was not whether, but when, NATO would enlarge. Later he extended this commitment to future rounds of enlargement after the initial round in 1997–1999, which is to bring Poland, Hungary, and the Czech Republic into the alliance. Clinton's first serious discussion of the issue with President Yeltsin did not come until two acrimonious encounters in September and December 1994. While bilateral relations developed productively in 1995 and 1996, the issue of NATO expansion continued to corrode the overall relationship until the two sides succeeded in March 1997, through strenuous efforts, in devising the Founding Act.

NATO enlargement had several sources, but President Clinton's advocacy has been the driving force. He sees the enlargement of NATO as a way for the United States, under his administration, to assume sponsorship of a project that would serve a number of purposes: it would reinvigorate NATO, reconfirm American leadership in Europe, gain the gratitude of the central European aspirants most eager for incorporation in "the West" (and, not incidentally, the gratitude of the millions of their progeny in the American electorate), and it would be an initiative coming to fruition in 1999 and capping the achievements of his administration in foreign affairs.

Paradoxically, NATO expansion seemed so easy precisely because Russia was no longer a threat. Because there was no real military threat, it could be done with no real risk or security cost. It was not directed against Russia, and Clinton was confident he could reassure "his friend Boris." Although it was recognized that Russia would feel left out, it was clear that Russia would have no recourse and it was assumed that rhetorical reaffirmations of friendship would suffice. The Founding Act was an afterthought that was to act as damage control when Russian objections were belatedly recognized to be broader and deeper than originally envisaged.

NATO expansion and its impact on Russian–United States (and Western) relations is far from settled. A great deal will depend on the future course of a continuing process of NATO expansion, the evolution of NATO, and not least the application and implementation of the Founding Act. It has considerable potential, but that potential must be realized. One unresolved issue is the effect of possible later expansion of NATO membership to the Baltic states and even to Ukraine on Russian relations with the West. A particularly important question is the future course of Russian politics, especially after Yeltsin.

In 1997 there is renewed talk of a "partnership," but it will be harder to realize in the wake of the mockery that NATO enlargement has made of the post–cold war partnership with Russia proclaimed earlier by the Bush and Clinton administrations. That initiative is not easy to square with the conception of an undivided, reunified Europe extending from the Atlantic to the Urals, as celebrated at the Paris summit of 1990 marking the end of the cold war, and even reaching across the continents from Vancouver to Vladivostok, as Clinton and Yeltsin proclaimed at their first summit in April 1993.

United States relations with Yeltsin's Russia have developed sufficient resilience to withstand the negative impact of the expansion of NATO. It is less certain that a successor government in Moscow will be as complaisant. In any case, an initiative not designed or undertaken as United States policy toward Russia has become probably the single most important decision about, and the most important negative influence on, that relationship in the first five years of the new Russia. Managing the impact of that decision is probably the principal task for United States policy for the next five years.

Is Russia Still an Enemy?

Richard Pipes

Treat your friend as if he will one day be your enemy, and your enemy as if he will one day be your friend.

DECIMUS LABERIUS, FIRST CENTURY B.C.

IT IS OFFICIAL: Russia no longer considers the Western democracies antagonists. The military doctrine that the government of the Russian Federation adopted in 1993 declares that Russia "does not regard any state to be its adversary." The May 1997 NATO-Russia agreement reaffirmed the premise. Although not admitted to NATO, Russia has been given a seat on the alliance's Permanent Joint Council, which assures it, if not of a veto, then of a voice, in NATO deliberations. Given that in last year's presidential election Russian voters rejected the communist candidate for one committed to democracy and capitalism, it is not unreasonable to assume that in time Russia will become a full-fledged member of the international community.

RICHARD PIPES is Professor of History, Emeritus, at Harvard University. He was Director of Eastern European and Soviet Affairs at the National Security Council in 1981–82. His recent books include *A Concise History of the Russian Revolution* and *The Unknown Lenin*.

6. Is Russia Still an Enemy?

Yet doubts linger because so much about post-communist Russia is unfinished and unsettled. Fledgling democracy contends with ancient authoritarian traditions; private enterprise struggles against a collectivist culture; frustrated nationalist and imperialist ambitions impede the enormous task of internal reconstruction. Russians, bewildered by the suddenness and the scope of the changes they have experienced, do not know in which direction to proceed. A veritable battle for Russia's soul is in progress.

Its outcome is of considerable concern to the rest of the world, if only because Russia's geopolitical situation in the heartland of Eurasia enables it, weakened as it is, to influence global stability. Whether it indeed joins the world community or once again withdraws into its shell and assumes an adversarial posture will be decided by an unpredictable interplay of domestic and external factors.

FROM WELL-WISHER TO COLD WARRIOR

OVER THE past three centuries, Russia has had its share of conflicts with what are now NATO countries—notably Turkey, Britain, and Germany—but Russian relations with the United States before the Bolsheviks' seizure of power were exceptionally friendly. In the early decades of the nineteenth century, the two countries had some differences over the northwestern territories of the North American continent, but these they peacefully resolved by treaty in 1824. The czarist government permanently eliminated that source of friction in 1867 when, unwilling to bear the costs of administering and defending Alaska, it persuaded a reluctant U.S. Congress to take the territory off Russia's hands for a nominal payment. During the American Civil War, Russia boosted the morale of the Northern states by dispatching naval units to New York and San Francisco. Secretary of State William Henry Seward declared at the time that Americans preferred Russia over any other European country because "she always wishes us well."

Relations deteriorated to some extent toward the end of the nineteenth century because of the wave of pogroms against Jews that broke out after the assassination of Czar Alexander II and persistent discrimination against American Jews visiting Russia. Another irritant was Russia's expansion in the Far East: in the 1904–05 Russo-Japanese War, U.S. opinion openly favored the Japanese. But all was forgotten when Russia joined the Allied cause on the outbreak of World War I. The United States was the first country to recognize the Provisional Government that took over after the czar's abdication in March 1917.

The seven decades of U.S.-Russian hostility that followed the Bolshevik coup d'état were the result not of a conflict of interests but of the peculiar needs of Russia's conquerors, the Soviet ruling elite. The Bolsheviks seized power in Russia not to reform their country but to secure a base from which to launch a worldwide revolution. They never thought it possible to establish a socialist society in a single country, least of all their own, where four-fifths of the inhabitants were peasants rather than Marx's industrial workers. To remain in power, they needed revolutions to break out in the industrialized countries of the West, by which they meant in the interwar years principally Germany and Britain, and after World War II, the United States. The Cold War was an artificial conflict initiated and aggressively pursued by a dictatorship that invoked to its people phantom threats to justify its illegitimately acquired and lawlessly enforced authority. No concessions to the communist regime could attenuate its hostility because its very survival depended on it: as in the case of Nazi Germany, belligerency and expansionism were built into the system.

Indeed, as soon as the Communist Party fell from power, the government that succeeded it abandoned all pretense that the country faced threats from without. If the Soviet regime required international tension, its democratic successor needs peaceful relations with other countries so that it can cut military spending and attract foreign capital. It is clearly in Russia's interests to be on the best of terms with the rest of the world, especially the United States.

FIGHTING THE CULTURE

YET SELF-INTEREST has to contend with a political culture based in traditions of empire-building and reliance on military power for stature rather than security. For, unfortunately, Russia has not made a clean break with its Soviet past.

The bloodless revolution of 1991 that outlawed the Communist Party, oversaw the peaceful dissolution of the Soviet Union, and installed democracy is in many respects incomplete. The new coexists with the old in an uneasy symbiosis. No fresh elites have emerged: the country's political, economic, military, and cultural institutions are run by ex-communists who cannot shed old mental habits. The Duma, the lower house of parliament, is dominated by communists and nationalists equally suspicious of the West and equally determined to reclaim for Russia superpower status.[1] Unlike the Bolsheviks, who on coming to power promptly obliterated all the symbols of the overthrown czarist regime, Russia's democrats have left in place the myriad memorials glorifying their predecessors without substituting pervasive symbols of their own.

Russia is torn by contradictory pulls, one oriented inward, hence isolationist, the other imperialist. The population at large, preoccupied with physical survival, displays little interest in foreign policy, taking in stride the loss of empire and the world influence that went with it. People pine for normality, which they associate with life in the West as depicted in foreign films and television programs. Depoliticized, they are unresponsive to ideological appeals, although not averse to blaming all their troubles on foreigners. But for the ruling elite and much of the intelligentsia, accustomed to being regarded as citizens of a great power, the country's decline to Third World status has been traumatic. They are less concerned with low living standards than the loss of power and influence, perhaps because inwardly they doubt whether Russia can ever equal the West in anything else. Power and influence for them take the form of imperial splendor and military might second to none.

In contrast to the Western states, which acquired empires after forming nation-states, in Russia nation-building and empire-building proceeded concurrently. Since the seventeenth century, when Russia was already the world's largest state, the immensity of their domain has served Russians as psychological compensation for their relative backwardness and poverty. Thus the loss of empire has been for the politically engaged among them a much more bewildering experience than for the British, French, or Dutch. Unable to reconcile themselves to the loss, they connive in various ways to reassert control over the separated borderlands and regain superpower status for the motherland.

The situation in today's Russia is highly volatile. There are really two Russias. One is led by the younger, better-educated, mostly urban population that is eager to break with the past and take the Western route; the new deputy prime minister, Boris Zemtsov, is a representative spokesman for this constituency. The other Russia is made up of older, often unskilled, preponderantly rural or small-town citizens, suspicious of the West and Western ways and nostalgic for the more secure Soviet past; their principal mouthpiece is the head of the Communist Party of the Russian Federation, Gennadi Zyuganov.

At present the pro-Western contingent runs the country, but it is by no means firmly in the saddle. In the first round of the June 1996 presidential election, incumbent Boris Yeltsin received the most votes (35 percent), but had the anti-liberal opposition combined

---

1. The preponderance of communists in parliament grossly overstates their popularity. It came about because in regional elections they present a single slate, while the disunited democratic parties are prone to field a dozen or more candidates.

forces it would have decisively defeated him: Zyuganov won 32 percent of the vote, the extreme nationalist Vladimir Zhirinovsky nearly 6 percent, and the authoritarian Aleksandr Lebed over 14 percent, to produce a theoretically absolute majority of 52 percent. Three years ago, when asked what they thought of communism, 51 percent of Russians polled said they had a positive image of it and 36 percent a negative one. (It is, however, indicative of the prevailing confused mood that fewer than half those who expressed a positive attitude toward communism wanted to see it restored.) The popular base of democracy in the country is thus thin and brittle; the political climate can change overnight. Countries like Russia, lacking in strong party organizations and loyalties, are capable of swinging wildly from one extreme to another, often in response to a demagogue who promises quick and easy solutions.

For Russians, the road to a civil society is long and arduous because they have to overcome not only the communist legacy but also that of the czars and their partner, the Orthodox Church, which for centuries collaborated in instilling in their subjects disrespect for law, submission to strong and willful authority, and hostility to the West. Russia bears a heavy burden of history which has taught its people better how to survive than how to succeed.

> There are two Russias, one eager to take the Western route, one highly suspicious of it.

Their present striving for what they conceive of as normality is further hampered by a mindset formed in a harsh rural environment that bred suspicion of anyone who did not belong to the community and demanded social leveling within it. (Although the majority of the Russian population lives in cities, the bulk of city dwellers are first- or second-generation peasants who have never been truly urbanized.) As anthropologists have noted, peasants, dependent on a fluctuating but unchanging Nature, tend to believe that the good things in life, such as hunting grounds or farmland, are available only in finite quantities. Having had no opportunity to learn that an economic milieu that enables some to profit more than others can, in the end, benefit all, numerous Russians, like others of the same background, resent anyone more affluent or distinguished than themselves because they believe that such affluence and distinction are purchased at their expense. This attitude impedes both the evolution of market institutions and friendly relations with foreigners. It will come as a surprise to Americans that many Russians, possibly the majority, believe that U.S. aid and investments are a ploy to acquire their country's resources at liquidation prices.

AN EMPIRE RECLAIMED

MOSCOW ACKNOWLEDGED the sovereign status of the former Soviet republics, but it is a recognition that comes from the head, not the heart. The patrimonial mentality embedded in the Russian psyche, which holds that everything inherited from one's forefathers is inalienable property, works against accepting the separation of the borderlands as a fait accompli. It prompts Moscow to strive for their gradual economic, political, and military "reintegration" with Russia—which, given the disparity in their respective size and population, can only mean reducing the former republics once again to the status of clients. In this endeavor the government is abetted by the Orthodox Church, which claims authority over all Orthodox Christians of what was once the Soviet Union.

In December 1991, immediately after the dissolution of the U.S.S.R., Moscow created the Commonwealth of Independent States, ostensibly to enable the former Soviet republics to resolve common problems by common consent. In time, ten of the 15 republics joined the CIS, some enrolling of their own free will, others under duress. In 1992, at Moscow's insistence, CIS members signed a mutual security treaty, which in effect entrusted the defense of their territories to the only military force on hand, the Russian army.

Despite the declared objectives of the CIS covenant and its security treaty, Moscow has used the documents, especially the latter, as excuses to meddle in the affairs of the borderlands. At first the preferred technique was economic pressure, which Russia had at its disposal because it owns the bulk of the industries of the defunct Soviet Union as well as the principal developed energy resources. Such pressure became less effective when foreigners began to pour capital investment into the other former republics. The fledgling states have further enhanced their economic independence by signing commercial treaties with each other and friendly neighbors like Poland and Turkey.

The main instrument of "reintegration" today is the Russian army, and this is worrisome because its formidable officer corps is society's most embittered and vindictive group. Anyone who spends an hour with Russian generals cannot but feel the intensity of their resentment against the West as well as against their own democratic government for reducing to the status of a negligible force the army that defeated Nazi Germany and was acknowledged by the U.S. military as a peer. The dethroned Communist Party nomenklatura has adapted to the new era by appropriating some of the state's wealth and continuing to manage much of the rest. But the generals, dependent on government allocations, have had no such opportunity, and they seethe with humiliation both personal and professional. Most analogies between contemporary Russia and Weimar Germany fall wide of the mark, but parallels between the general officers of the two are striking: one sees the same sense of degradation and thirst for revenge. As in Weimar Germany, civilian authorities in Russia exert only nominal control over the military; the Ministry of Defense has a single civilian executive.

Although Russia's armed forces are demoralized and starved for money, their command structure remains largely intact and extends over most of what was once the Soviet Union. With the exception of the three Baltic states and Azerbaijan, Russian troops are deployed in every one of the ex-Soviet republics: 24,000 in Tajikistan, 15,000 in Turkmenistan, 5,000 in Uzbekistan, and so on. In Armenia, which has traditionally relied on Russia for protection from Turkey and other Muslim neighbors, Moscow has secured a 25-year basing right for its troops, in return for which it sent Armenia $1 billion worth of military equipment. The ostensible mission of these Russian expeditionary forces is to defend the former republics' borders and protect their ethnic Russian residents. In reality, they also serve as the vanguard of Russia's imperial drive. Moscow interprets the terms of the mutual security treaty as giving it license to intervene militarily in any CIS country where, in its judgment, the commonwealth's security is threatened. Russian troops guarding the border between Tajikistan and Afghanistan have engaged in desultory clashes with Muslim fundamentalist forces. A Russian general stationed in Central Asia declared recently that if hard-line Islamist Taliban units from Afghanistan menaced Tajikistan, his troops would intervene. Thus a modified Brezhnev Doctrine is still in force: Moscow regards any country that was once part of the Soviet Union as falling within the sphere of its security interests. Decolonization has been quite halfhearted.

Georgia is a classic case of Moscow's use of military power for imperial objectives. Moscow overcame Georgia's reluctance to join the CIS by inciting a 1992 rebellion of the Abkhaz minority inhabiting the northwestern region of the country. With Russian political and military backing, the Abkhazians expelled 200,000 ethnic Georgians and declared independence. Unable to quell the rebellion, Tbilisi was forced to request aid

6. Is Russia Still an Enemy?

> A modified Brezhnev Doctrine is still in force. Decolonization has been halfhearted.

from Moscow, which consented to provide it so long as Georgia joined the CIS and acquiesced to 15,000 Russian troops on its territory, along with a Russian "peacekeeping" force in Abkhazia. As soon as Tbilisi met these conditions, the Abkhaz rebellion abated. President Eduard Shevardnadze's efforts to rid his country of the putative Russian peacekeepers have so far proved unavailing. Russian forces guard Georgia's land and sea borders with Turkey; since other troops are stationed on Armenia's western border, Russia has direct access to Turkey along the old Soviet frontier.

Moscow's encroachments on the sovereignty of its onetime dependencies present a serious potential threat to East-West relations. The situation is not entirely clear-cut, since the West tacitly recognizes all lands that were once part of the Soviet Union as Russia's legitimate sphere of influence while insisting that Russia respect the sovereignty of the separated republics. If the past is any guide, in the event of an overt conflict between Russia and another of the former republics, the European allies are unlikely to go beyond expressions of regret. The United States, however, is almost certain to react more harshly, especially if the victim of Russian intimidation is Ukraine or one of the countries adjoining the Caspian Sea—the former because of its geopolitical importance, the latter because of those oil-rich states' potential contribution to the world economy.

The existence of petroleum in the Caspian region has been known since antiquity; in late czarist Russia Baku was the center of the empire's oil production. Since 1991 Western companies have engaged in intensive exploration around the Caspian, which has led to the discovery in Turkmenistan, Azerbaijan, and Kazakhstan of oil reserves estimated to be at least as large as those of Iraq and perhaps equal to those of Saudi Arabia. International consortia are pouring hundreds of millions of dollars into the three former republics to extract the oil and natural gas and ship them to world markets. Direct foreign investment in the three countries nearly equals that in Russia.

Having lost these assets, Russia for the time being contents itself with pressing its claim to their transport, demanding that all oil from the Caspian region be sent by pipeline across Russian territory to the Black Sea port of Novorossiysk. This damaged pipeline runs through Chechnya, which for years has been torn by ethnic strife. For security reasons, as well as to prevent Moscow from using the pipeline for political or economic blackmail, the oil-producing republics and their foreign backers prefer an alternate route running across Azerbaijan and Georgia to the Black Sea and from there to the Mediterranean coast of eastern Turkey. The issue is a matter of keen competition between Russia and foreign oil firms, in which the other republics concerned, for both economic and political reasons, lean toward the latter.

DREAMS OF THE GENERALS

MANY INFLUENTIAL persons in Russia want to regain not only the empire but the status of superpower. Russia cannot attain the latter objective by economic means, which in the modern world confer such rank; its partial inclusion in the Group of Seven is little more than a public relations ploy to compensate it for its forced acquiescence to the expansion of NATO into Eastern Europe. Russia's claim to be a world power has traditionally rested on military prowess, and the temptation is to resort to this expedient once again.

It is common knowledge that Russia's armed forces are destitute and demoralized. Officers drive taxis; soldiers engage in crime for the money. There is so much draft-dodging that officers are believed to constitute half of military personnel. While some generals find the situation intolerable and virtually threaten mutiny, the more far-sighted view it as a temporary setback that they can exploit to revamp the armed forces. Their ambition is to lay the groundwork for a military establishment so effective that its mere presence will guarantee Russia what they deem its rightful place among nations.

That projected force differs greatly from Russia's traditional army, which relied on masses of foot soliders storming enemy positions without regard to casualties. For one thing, Russia no longer commands unlimited manpower. The death rate exceeds the birthrate; the percentage of babies with genetic defects is well above normal. Nor is there money to rebuild and maintain a large standing force, let alone switch to an all-volunteer army, which President Yeltsin mentions from time to time. Apart from these constraints, Russia's strategists have absorbed the lessons of the Persian Gulf War, which conclusively demonstrated the superiority of modern weapons technology over conventional forces. They were awed by the Americans' ability, before the battle was even joined, to disable Iraq's large and well-equipped army through the electronic suppression of its military communications network, cutting off forces in the field from the command. They were no less impressed by precision missiles' ability to strike and destroy key enemy installations. Those lessons have persuaded them to abandon Russian canon and adopt what American military theorists have designated the revolution in military affairs.

Russia's new military doctrine, approved by the Yeltsin government in 1993, following U.S. practice calls for a shift in defense allocations from procurement to research and development. Hoover Institution Fellow Richard F. Staar estimates that 1997 expenditures on high-technology R&D will account for 40 percent of the defense budget. Drawing on Russia's excellent scientific talent in the field of military technology, the new doctrine projects designing, with the help of supercomputers imported from the United States, prototypes of directed-energy weapons, electronic warfare equipment, and stealth aviation. Naval weaponry is to be emphasized as well. Russia recently established an Academy of Military Sciences to study "military futurology" so as to anticipate developments among potential enemy nations and thus insure itself against shocks like Operation Desert Storm. Such a program can be carried out with the limited funds currently allocated the armed forces. First Deputy Defense Minister Andrei Kokoshkin boasts that it will enable Russia to produce weapons "that have no equivalent in the world."

Until they have designed the new military hardware and secured sufficient funds to procure it—a period of between ten and 20 years, in their estimation—Russian generals intend to rely on the nuclear deterrent. They have revoked Brezhnev's 1982 "no-first-use" pledge and, in view of the superiority of NATO's conventional forces, adopted NATO's own flexible response strategy, formulated when Soviet conventional forces enjoyed the upper hand.

Of what use will such a modernized force be to Russia? The new military doctrine speaks of protecting Russia's "vital interests," but these are nowhere defined, an omission that reflects widespread confusion in the country about its place in the world. Certainly, apart from restoring to Russia the prestige of a great power, the new force will enable it to insist on a sphere of influence in adjacent regions, thereby again becoming a leading player on the global stage.

Even in its present reduced state, Russia still has the world's longest frontier, bordering Europe and East Asia, neighboring on the Middle East, and even touching North America. Its capacity for exploiting instabilities along its borders is therefore undiminished. Historically, whenever it has suffered setbacks in one sector of its frontier, Russia has shifted attention to the others. The pattern seems to be repeating itself: feeling rebuffed by Europe, Moscow is turning to the Middle East and East Asia. Yeltsin declared in May that to counter the "Western alliance's expansion plans" his administration has designated the integration of the CIS and the strengthening of ties with China its principal foreign policy goals. Moscow is also cultivating Iran and the other fundamentalist Muslim states. Given the interest of Western powers in Caspian oil and the desire of former Soviet republics in that region to escape Russian pressures for dissolution in the CIS by drawing closer to Turkey, a new political alignment appears to be emerging along Russia's southern frontier. With it, a new East-West geopolitical fault line, running somewhere across Central Asia and the Caucasus, seems to be opening up.

THE CHOICE

IT IS IMPOSSIBLE at this time to foresee which path Russia will choose, pro-Western or anti-Western. The country's political structures are too fragile and the mood of its people too volatile for predictions. Russia's true national interests demand a pro-Western alignment and integration into the world economy. The ambitions and emotional needs of Russia's elite, however, pull in the opposite direction: away from the global economic order dominated by the industrial democracies and toward reliance on military power as well as rapprochement with countries that for one reason or another are hostile to the West. The latter course is alluring because catching up with the West militarily would be much easier for Russia than catching up economically.

Yet it would be an error of historic proportions if Russia threw away the chance of becoming a genuine world power to pursue the illusion of power based on the capacity to threaten and coerce. Russia was acknowledged as a superpower during the Cold War not by virtue of economic might, technological leadership, or cultural achievement, but solely because it possessed weapons capable of wreaking universal destruction—in other words, because of its ability to blackmail the world. The hollowness of Russian claims to superpower status became apparent immediately after the collapse of the Soviet Union: having abandoned its adversarial posture in order to carry out long overdue internal reforms, Russia stood revealed as a second-class power, dependent on foreign loans and exports of raw materials.

The next few years will confront Russia with a supreme test. Can the nation realize its aspirations through internal reconstruction and international cooperation, or will it once again seek to make its mark by resorting to military force and exploitation of international tensions?

> Generals believe that revamping the military can reestablish Russia as a great power.

Each year that Russia continues as a partner of the West strengthens the forces that favor development over expansionism. A younger generation aspiring to be Western gradually replaces the older one mired in nostalgia for the Soviet past. A business class emerges that has little use for militarism, along with a new breed of politicians who cater to an electorate more concerned with living standards than imperial grandeur.

The choice will be made by the Russians themselves; the West can influence the decision only marginally. The situation calls for a subtle policy that mixes toughness with understanding of Russian sensitivities. No special favors should be granted. They only whet the appetites of nationalists who interpret undeserved concessions to mean that the world is so anxious to bring Russia into the international community that it is prepared to show boundless tolerance for its behavior. Moscow should not be allowed to increase its forces in the country's southern regions in violation of the 1990 Conventional Forces in Europe Treaty, or to bully its erstwhile republics and ex-satellites. The world must not acquiesce to a new Brezhnev Doctrine.

At the same time, Western leaders should consider ways of avoiding actions that, without any real bearing on their countries' security, humiliate Russians by making them keenly aware how impotent they have become under democracy. These leaders should consider whether extending NATO to Eastern Europe to forestall a putative military threat to the region is worth alienating the majority of politically active Russians, who see the move as permanently excluding their country from Europe and giving it no alternative but to seek allies in the east. The ambiguity of a "gray zone" between Russia and the present members of NATO would actually help assure Russia that even if it is not politically and militarily part of Europe, it is also not categorically excluded. Projected joint military exercises of forces from the United States and the Central Asian nations scheduled for September in Kazakhstan and Uzbekistan are certain to be perceived in Moscow as a deliberate provocation: what purpose do they serve? Assistance of any kind, no matter how well-meaning, must take into account Russian people's suspicions of the motives behind it, irrational as these may be. Immense patience and empathy are required in dealing with Russia's halting progress toward democracy; failure to display them only helps anti-Western forces.

Is Russia then still an enemy? It is not and it ought not to be. But it might become one if those who guide its destiny, exploiting the political inexperience and deep-seated prejudices of its people, once again aspire to a glory to which they are not yet entitled save by the immensity of their territory, meaningless in itself, vast mineral resources that they cannot exploit on their own, and a huge nuclear arsenal that they cannot use. Russia could again become an adversary if, instead of building their country from the ground up after seven decades of destruction such as no nation in history has ever inflicted on itself, its leaders once again were to seek to escape the difficulties facing them through self-isolation and grandstanding. I fear that if it fails to confront reality and tries to make up for internal shortcomings by posturing on the global stage, Russia may not be given another chance.

> "If, as some Japanese critics have charged, this is not really an alliance at all but rather a patron-client relationship, then it is a peculiar relationship, one in which the patron commits to the defense of the client and the client commits to little in return. To paper over this asymmetry, the benefits of the alliance have been undersold to the Japanese public and oversold to the American public." But this is about to change.

Testing the United States–Japan Security Alliance

JAMES SHINN

The United States–Japan security alliance is at risk. In the words of Japanese diplomat Okamoto Yukio, "We have a security alliance that works fine in peace but which will fail the most likely tests of war."

If the United States becomes embroiled in a military clash in Asia—other than repelling an attack on Japan—Tokyo may well do nothing, or do too little, too late. The public backlash in the United States would destroy the alliance. And Japan would be forced to chart an independent course through the murky security waters of North Asia.

The alliance weathered the tests of the cold war for 40 years. Now the cold war is over, yet the alliance has not adapted to changed circumstances. Japan's self-imposed limits on the use of force other than in the defense of the Japanese homeland have kept its Self-Defense Forces (SDF) and the United States military at arm's length. Cautious bureaucrats and risk-averse politicians in Tokyo have imposed a host of limitations on Japan's ability to support the American military beyond a narrow range of peacetime supply missions. As a result, the SDF remains "planned out" of the United States Defense Department's preparations for dealing with a wide range of Asian security problems.

If, as some Japanese critics have charged, this is not really an alliance at all but rather a patron-client relationship, then it is a peculiar relationship, one in which the patron commits to the defense of the client and the client commits to little in return. To paper over this asymmetry, the benefits of the alliance have been undersold to the Japanese public and oversold to the American public. But the current review of the United States–Japan alliance by Tokyo and Washington will cast that asymmetry in stark relief, reopen the debate over the purposes of the alliance, and resurrect the prospect of Japan as a "normal country," with an independent security strategy in an uncertain world.

DON'T ROCK THE BOAT

Thoughtful officials on both sides of the Pacific are acutely aware of the risk that this perception gap poses for the alliance, and have been modifying its terms to make it less of a patron-client relationship and more of a traditional alliance among equals. The bureaucratic shorthand for this process is the "Nye Initiative," named after Joseph Nye, who provided the impetus for the process when he served as assistant secretary for international security affairs during the first Clinton administration. A milestone in this process is "The U.S.-Japan Guidelines for Defense Cooperation of 1997," which was negotiated by diplomats and officials on both sides throughout 1996 and 1997 and whose recommendations are being submitted to politicians in Tokyo and Washington for approval in 1998.

Tinkering with the wording of the alliance in diplomatic obscurity is one thing—the guidelines review has been covered only sporadically by the press, and has barely registered in the public consciousness—but altering the terms of the alliance in the glare of media attention is another matter. Even the modest recommendations of the guidelines review could ignite considerable controversy in Japan, prompt recrimination in the United

---

JAMES SHINN *is a senior fellow at the Council on Foreign Relations.*

States, and raise hackles among Japan's Asian neighbors.

This glare of publicity presents the officials engaged in the extended Nye Initiative with a serious dilemma. If the change is too fast, it could trigger a backlash among Japanese citizens, among whom the alliance has never been terribly popular. Attempts to modify the alliance to deal with post–cold war realities also collide with three of the most salient aspects of politics as usual in Japan: distributive budgeting, bureaucratic delegation, and consensus coalitions in the Diet.

On the other hand, if change in the alliance is too slow, frustration with Japan will grow in the United States and Japan will remain planned out of United States security strategy for Asia. In the meantime, the alliance faces a window of vulnerability during which, if tested, it may fail.

The magnitude of this risk is rarely mentioned in official discourse between Tokyo and Washington. Nor are the consequences of a test of the alliance—especially a failed test—dealt with explicitly. Instead, politics as usual in Japan has confined bilateral discussions to the edges of the issue, making only minor concessions in terms of Japanese willingness to be planned in, and getting bogged down in the minutiae of logistical cooperation rather than tackling the underlying problem of adjusting the alliance to fit the needs of the post–cold war world order.

No political leader in Japan is willing to grasp the nettle of collective self-defense, and no bureaucrat in Tokyo is in a position to force the issue. And no one in official Washington is eager to press the case on Tokyo too strongly: the pessimists discount the ability of the Japanese government to make strategic choices, the caretakers do not want to attract more attention to the underlying asymmetry of the alliance, and the strategists are simply overwhelmed by the prospect of a "normal" Japan.

This article seeks to make these uncomfortable questions explicit. What kind of a test of the alliance is likely? As officials tinker and politicians dawdle, what underlying forces are pulling the alliance together, and what forces are pulling it apart? What will happen to the alliance if it is not tested—if Tokyo and Washington deal with the alliance through "politics as usual"? If the alliance is tested, what will be the impact on United States–Japanese relations, and on Japanese "politics as usual"? Most ominously, what will happen if the alliance fails a test?

Basic disagreement over the scope and underlying purpose of the alliance. . .is the strongest force pulling [it] apart.

FROM SPECULATION TO PREPARATION

The alliance was at the top of the agenda at the April 1996 summit meeting of Prime Minister Ryutaro Hashimoto and President Bill Clinton. The meeting took place against a backdrop of lingering friction over Okinawa, uncertainty about North Korea, and alarm over Chinese intentions—the People's Liberation Army (PLA) had launched a series of missile "tests" in Taipei's direction following Lee Teng-hui's election as president of Taiwan a few weeks earlier.

This cluster of events made the prospect of a test of the alliance more real in the minds of decision makers in Washington and Tokyo alike. Several scenarios were dissected. One was a meltdown in Pyongyang, followed by a military clash on the Korean Peninsula and the accompanying need to evacuate noncombatants, assist a flood of refugees, and deter North Korean commando attacks on United States bases in Japan. The second scenario was a contingency farther afield, such as a second Persian Gulf War or a complete government collapse in Cambodia. A third scenario—the least likely but the most dangerous—was a conflict involving China across the Taiwan Strait.

China has emerged as a potential threat to Japan only recently; for decades the alliance's prime reason for existence was the menace posed by the Soviet Union. Every time the Soviet threat began to fade in the mind of the average Japanese citizen, it would be refreshed by headlines about incidents at sea around the disputed northern islands, or by heavy-handed Soviet military maneuvers in the Sea of Japan.

The collapse of the Red Army not only knocked out a foundation of the alliance, it also underscored one of its basic asymmetries. If the cold war turned hot, Japan's role was to bottle up the Soviet Pacific Fleet as it dashed for the open Pacific. By merely defending its nearby waters Japan was performing an important role and thereby defending the United States. But now that the once-formidable Soviet Pacific Fleet is rusting at anchor or being sold for scrap, the SDF's purely defensive role is much less valuable to the United States.

From the standpoint of the United States, the value of the alliance depends on Japan's willingness to provide support in regional contingencies, including a possible clash with Chinese forces. Japan, however, has little enthusiasm for letting the

SDF take part in any regional contingency—a lack of enthusiasm shared by Japan's neighbors. This basic disagreement over the scope and underlying purpose of the alliance—reflected in the current inability of Japan and the United States to plan together for Asian military contingencies—is the strongest force pulling the alliance apart.

THE COSTS OF THE "SOUND OF FREEDOM"

The daily friction of hosting foreign troops on Japanese soil is also straining the alliance. The 25,000 young, racially diverse American soldiers are difficult to integrate with Japan's tightly knit, racially homogenous, largely middle-class communities.

In the early days of the American occupation, when Americans seized airfields from the imperial Japanese army, the landing strips were in the countryside, surrounded by rice paddies. Since then, the "miracle years" of Japan's economic growth have pushed urban sprawl up to the barbed wire fences. Now F-15s scream over apartment buildings and attack helicopters bank in over schools. When Japanese civic groups complain about the deafening noise, offended American officers retort, "That's the sound of freedom." Both sides are aware that simmering friction could explode into heated opposition to the United States military in Japan should a jet plow into a school or a chopper crash on a shopping center.

The American soldiers are reminded of their cool welcome, and of their own relative poverty, whenever they venture off their bases into the world's priciest consumer society. This leads to a kind of wear and tear on the American side, aggravated by years of widely publicized trade friction. Why should young American soldiers put their lives on the line to defend Japanese who resent their presence? Why should struggling American taxpayers defend rich Japanese?

It is old news that both Tokyo and Washington are laboring under fiscal deficits, as swelling entitlement spending, especially health costs, edges out discretionary spending such as defense. The United States defense budget is likely to flatten out at $250 billion per year, and Japan's defense budget will settle at around 4.7 trillion yen, or about $40 billion at current exchange rates. Most defense analysts agree that this is not enough money for Japan or the United States to maintain current force levels, train them adequately, and continue the present pace of buying new equipment. Hard choices will have to be made soon among these three areas. These choices are unlikely to favor the alliance.

Overseas deployment of United States forces is a likely target. It is expensive, has no hometown congressperson rooting for it, and is not popular with many Americans. So far both official and unofficial reviews of the Defense Department's long-term plans, including the Quadrennial Defense Review, have endorsed the principle of continuing to deploy troops at forward bases in Japan. Japanese burden-sharing payments of $25 billion over five years have been used to make the case that it is cheaper to keep these American forces abroad than at home. But missing from the calculation is the true marginal cost of defending Japan. When push comes to shove and the United States military must choose between these forward deployments and other programs, this enthusiasm may fade.

Japan is also not immune from similar budget pressures. As the Japanese defense budget gets squeezed, burden-sharing is a probable target for cuts when the current defense agreement runs out in 2002. This will become a hot topic for debate, even though both the press and the Diet now support a tighter alliance.

THE END OF A TABOO

During the cold war there was little realistic debate in Tokyo over Japan's national security, which was the result of lingering guilt over World War II, a knee-jerk leftist bias among many Japanese reporters, and the hothouse effect of the alliance itself—the world is a simple, safe place if somebody else makes all the tough choices and protects you if things go wrong.

The taboo on defense discussions lifted abruptly in the 1990s. A spirited debate on Japan's national security future is being conducted in Tokyo's influential daily newspapers, the exuberant weekly *shukanshi* magazines that are a cross between *Time* and the New York *Daily News*, and on television talk shows. War guilt is an alien notion to young Japanese. News reporters are more objective and better informed about security affairs. And ominous noises from both Beijing and Pyongyang periodically remind Japanese citizens that they live in a rough neighborhood. America's strong reaction to Japan's do-nothing stance during the 1991 Persian Gulf War was a wake-up call to many thoughtful observers in Tokyo, a reminder that America's indulgence in a one-sided alliance cannot be counted on indefinitely.

There has also been a profound shift in the Diet. A centrist clustering of politicians has forged a new consensus on the importance of the alliance to

Japan. The 1996 election devastated the Socialists and marginalized the Communists; both parties objected to the alliance on principle. A solid majority of the Diet, including members of the governing Liberal Democratic Party (LDP) coalition as well as the opposition New Frontier Party (NFP), now favors the alliance with the United States.

The devil, as usual, is in the details. These centrist parties disagree on how close the alliance should be, and they especially disagree on the proper interpretation of the bounds of "collective self-defense." A restrictive interpretation would keep Japan planned out and on the sidelines of a regional contingency; a looser interpretation has enough slack to plan Japan in.

The fault line on collective self-defense runs right through the center of the LDP. One wing, represented by Kato Koichi, with party elders such as Miyazawa Kiichi behind him, holds the dovish view. The other wing, represented by figures such as Kajiyama Seiroku, with party elders such as Nakasone Yasuhiro behind him, holds the more hawkish view. A decision on collective self-defense would fracture the LDP in two. Such a split would produce a radical realignment, with the hawkish wing merging with the NFP (referred to in Japanese political shorthand as a *ho-ho-rengo*, or conservative-conservative coalition), and the dovish wing making common cause with the socialists.

Prime Minister Hashimoto presides uneasily over this potential split. This fault line accounts for the extreme care with which he has dealt with the security alliance, and for the extreme interest that Japanese politicians of all stripes have taken in the finer points of the collective self-defense debate.

Some observers in Japan believe that Ozawa Ichiro, the architect of the NFP, intends to use the debate over the United States alliance not only to force a fundamental change in Japan's national security strategy, but also to do away with the very aspects of "politics as usual" in Japan that hinder a stronger alliance. Ozawa took aim at all three aspects in his 1993 book *Blueprint for a New Japan*, in which he explicitly linked "politics as usual" with Japan's inability to devise a realistic national security strategy based on a strong alliance with the United States.

Politics as usual in Tokyo has, as was noted, three features: distributive budgeting (using fiscal largesse rather than hard decisions to defuse policy differences); bureaucratic delegation (elected politicians defer to officials on the formulation of policy, including security policy); and least-common-denominator consensus (hard choices are avoided or papered over in the interfactional maneuvering to form a governing coalition).

Japanese budgets are notoriously incremental, with most departments across the board getting the same level of funding increase each year. Despite ritual calls for fiscal reform and belt-tightening, the Japanese central government budget is still swollen with public works expenditures and a host of quasi-automatic entitlements (such as farm subsidies and health care programs) that have created a river of red ink: the deficit-to-GDP ratio is around 7 percent, versus 1 percent for the United States. As for bureaucratic delegation, Diet "debates" on defense issues are broadly scripted by diplomatic and defense officials, to the point of writing the questions posed by lawmakers and the answers given by cabinet ministers. Finally, the Hashimoto government is a perfect example of risk-averse consensus coalitions; the prime minister would rather expose the alliance to a window of vulnerability than face splitting his fragile governing coalition with a decision on the question of collective self-defense.

China is the preoccupation of strategic thinkers in Japan.

On the United States side, the alliance is less acutely politicized, at least for the moment, and none of the measures required to make it more resilient necessarily conflict with business as usual, Washington-style. But, ironically, even as the centrist consensus favoring the alliance is strengthening in Tokyo, its traditional constituency in Washington is weakening.

The Clinton administration has a relatively free hand in its security dealings with Japan, and mainstream voices in Congress and the defense community still believe that the alliance is the bedrock of United States security in Asia. Yet the alliance is coming under fire from several different quarters in Washington. First, isolationists are deeply suspicious of any military entanglements in Asia; that Japan may be "free riding" on the alliance is incidental to their opposition. A second group of critics, the trade hawks and the so-called revisionists, make the free-rider issue central to their criticism of the alliance. Yet a third vocal group is composed of influential sinocentric Asia strategists in academia and officialdom who argue for a looser alliance with Japan, pointing out that the United States has far more at stake in its dealings with

China, and that this critical relationship with Beijing—already tense for other reasons—is only complicated by the alliance with Japan.

MUDDLING THROUGH

China is the preoccupation of strategic thinkers in Japan as well, since they want to avoid a contest of wills with Beijing. No test of the alliance—indefinitely prolonging the status quo—would enable Tokyo to pursue a low-profile, UN–centered foreign policy; the alliance could be downplayed in all discussions with Beijing, while Tokyo focused on confidence building and military transparency under the auspices of the Association for Southeast Asian Nations (ASEAN) Regional Forum.

Under an indefinite "no test" scenario, there is one major bump in the road: should Japan succeed in gaining a permanent seat on the UN Security Council, the price for that seat would be full support of peacekeeping operations, shoulder-to-shoulder with the other great powers, which would mean sending combat troops abroad. The UN enjoys such high prestige among Japanese citizens that this undertaking may be politically acceptable at home. In fact, some hawkish Japanese politicians are counting on the UN question to force a decision on collective self-defense, breaking through the restrictive definition in exchange for a Security Council seat.

Under a no test scenario the alliance would slowly erode, and the chief danger would be an accident or a lurid crime by United States forces in Japan. Okinawa would remain a source of low-level friction.

Internally, if the alliance were not tested, Japan could continue to practice politics as usual. Distributive budgeting choices in order to curry favor with powerful domestic constituencies would continue, albeit on a reduced scale. Japan's budget squeeze would steer money away from burden-sharing troops and training in favor of wealthy commercial interests—construction firms and defense contractors—who can express their gratitude through political contributions.

Japan's no test military budget would create a smaller, well-equipped, high-tech military, although of questionable readiness and efficacy. The budget would likely include larger allocations for research and development and expensive projects such as indigenous aircraft and satellites. Conversely, projects that would rely largely on United States suppliers, such as theater missile defense, would be far less attractive.

Bureaucratic delegation is unlikely to change much under the no test scenario, which also means no large change in the relative power of the ministries involved in national security, principally the Foreign Ministry and the National Defense Agency. The policy focus of the so-called *boei-zoku* or "defense tribe" of Diet members would remain budget allocation, not security strategy per se, which means that they would spend more time lobbying Defense Agency bureaucrats on spending priorities and less time holding the bureaucrats accountable for national security policy.

The no test scenario would also perpetuate consensus politics in Japan. In the absence of an external test of the alliance, it is difficult to imagine that the NFP would succeed in splitting the governing LDP coalition with a vote on collective self-defense.

TESTING THE ALLIANCE

Whether passed or failed, a test of the alliance would fundamentally alter Japan's national security strategy. The most likely test, that of a conflict in Korea, would be the easiest for the alliance to weather, since the demands placed on Japan would focus on support rather than combat. In any case, Washington would be more likely to justify a continued military presence on the peninsula if Korea were unified by force of arms rather than by peaceful political means. Similarly, the expectations for Japanese performance in a second Gulf War, or in a large-scale UN peacekeeping operation, would be relatively modest. Indeed, a peacekeeping operation would give Japan an opportunity to play to its strengths in terms of nation-building and financial leverage.

A test involving China would be radically different. Even modest Japanese support for the United States in a military face-off with China would trigger hostility and suspicion in Beijing. This would lead to a cycle of confrontation and threat, with a belligerent PLA on one side and a hardened alliance on the other.

Passing a test is the quickest route to an ironclad alliance in which the United States military and the SDF have similar war-fighting-doctrines, equipment, and training, and the basis for joint command and control. An ironclad alliance would lead to a division of labor between the two militaries, and to the partial withdrawal of United States forces from Japan. For example, if the American military could count on decisive Japanese support in a pinch, it could remove redundant facilities and equipment from Japan.

But decisiveness in passing a test is not without other risks. If the Japanese government were to suddenly commit forces to a military contingency, after years of pious statements of pacifism and invocations of the no-war constitution, suspicions would be raised throughout Asia. Japan's military capability may be perfectly transparent, note the skeptical Chinese, but Japan's strategic intent is opaque.

Passing a test would require Japanese politicians to suspend both bureaucratic delegation and consensus politics and to override some domestic resistance. If the test came before Japan were effectively planned in, even for support activities, then the ruling party would have to ignore the nuances of the collective self-defense question and possibly resort to supralegal authority to get things done quickly. A test would also trigger Ozawa's desired political reshuffle in Tokyo and strengthen the hand of the right-center political forces in the Diet.

It would also require a permanent departure from distributive budgeting. A real test of the alliance would remind politicians and bureaucrats alike that SDF budgets should be driven by realistic war-fighting roles and missions, not by parochial commercial interests.

THE DOWNSIDE TO FAILING

What constitutes a Japanese failure to fulfill United States expectations for the alliance is not clear-cut, although the direction the alliance takes after the test is likely to be strengthened in one case, abrogated in the other.

Failure in the case of Korea would destroy the alliance; Japan's support role is essential, the theater is geographically close to Japan, and conflict would be bloody. Moreover, the United States would reduce its military presence after unification, weakening the rationale for keeping troops in Japan—especially if Japan had failed to support the United States operation on the peninsula.

Failure in the case of a second Gulf War has the most room for slack, for no one knows what level of support the United States might receive from its European allies, even for a UN-sanctioned operation. United States policy in the Middle East is sufficiently at odds with the strategy of both the Europeans and Japan, not to mention China, that the test of the alliance would be muddied.

Failure in the case of a China conflict would destroy the alliance. Taiwan is the most likely flashpoint. Both Japan and the United States have long taken refuge in strategic ambiguity about their response to a Chinese threat to Taiwan. This ambiguity has the virtue of obscuring a basic point of disagreement with Beijing, but makes it hard to coordinate United States and Japanese response to Chinese belligerence across the Taiwan Strait. Moreover, China is a nuclear power; Beijing would certainly brandish the thermonuclear sword in a military conflict over Taiwan in order to crack the alliance. Without theater missile defense or a retaliatory capability, Japan is vulnerable to such a threat.

The net effect on Japan's national security of a failed test would be destruction of the alliance. Japan would be on its own, providing its own defense with its own armed forces and forced either to become a normal country, to become neutral, or to strike a new alliance, such as "bandwagoning" with the emerging Chinese superpower in Asia. All three options require a radical rethinking of Japan's military power, including the obvious question of nuclear weapons.

Internally, any of these three options would mark the end of distributive budgeting. The cost of national security would increase dramatically. Japan's defense budget would be driven by cold military realities rather than by incremental negotiations with the Ministry of Finance. As the price tag of national security soared, bureaucratic delegation would wane, since the ruling party would be forced to make hard choices between guns and butter—never a popular choice in any country. Forging a consensus policy in Tokyo regarding any of these options and building on the rubble of a collapsed alliance with the United States would be a hazardous proposition for any Japanese leader.

COLD WINDS

The end of politics as usual in Japan may be the price of becoming a normal country again. Indeed, the renewed debate over the goals and structure of the alliance may reveal that Tokyo's distinctive "politics as usual" was an unusual phenomenon that flourished only within the protective hothouse of a patron-client alliance with the United States, a phenomenon that will disappear in the harsh climate of Asian insecurity once the alliance itself is normalized. Historians may look back on the last 40 years of Japanese politics as a curious by-product of the cold war, and merely one stage in Japan's reemergence as a normal country in the twenty-first century.

THE RIVALRY

South Asian Arms Race: Reviving Dormant Fears of Nuclear War

By BARBARA CROSSETTE

UNITED NATIONS, May 28—In a matter of weeks, covert nuclear programs in India and Pakistan, rivals who have three times gone to war, have turned into an open nuclear arms race, raising alarms about what comes next—and where.

Diplomats and arms control experts see this arms race as particularly dangerous because Pakistan and India, unlike the United States and Russia during the cold war, have not held serious negotiations over outstanding problems for decades or concluded agreements that reduced the number of weapons aimed at each other.

These experts now fear that Pakistan and India could be drawn into a nuclear war over Kashmir, a territory that has been in dispute since the two countries gained independence in 1947. They also worry that nuclear testing by India and Pakistan could encourage other nations that have long sought nuclear arms to acquire these weapons.

"We are at perhaps the most dangerous period since the beginning of the nuclear age—with the exception of the Cuban missile crisis," said Thomas Graham, a former negotiator for the United States Arms Control and Disarmament Agency who is now president of the independent Lawyers' Alliance for World Security.

The United Nations, and the nuclear powers who hold Security Council seats, are left standing by helplessly. Since the end of the Cold War, few nations have much leverage with either India or Pakistan.

"They don't want outside help, at least the Indians don't," said Mr. Graham. "They think it's too much like colonialism. The Indians have probably not been very interested in confidence-building measures because in their heart of hearts they probably thought they would one day eliminate Pakistan."

Michael Krepon, president of the Henry L. Stimson Center, in Washington, an independent military research organization, said that years of watching the two nations sign agreements and then ignore or circumvent them led him to conclude that these pacts were used for little more than scoring points off one another.

Furthermore, neither India nor Pakistan has signed the treaty against the spread of nuclear weapons or the nuclear test-ban treaty.

Pakistani officials and several former American diplomats said today that public outrage at threats by Lal Krishna Advani, India's Home Minister and policy maker on Kashmir, that India might attack Pakistan along the Kashmir border, overwhelmed cautious civilian politicians in Islamabad and made the tests inevitable.

The United States, which had been surprised by India's nuclear explosions, did not offer Pakistan, a country that feels friendless and surrounded by dangers in a tumultuous region, any real incentives not to test, said Stephen P. Cohen, an expert on India-Pakistan military affairs who is joining the Brookings Institution in Washington as its first South Asian policy scholar in the fall.

"Two things didn't happen," Mr. Cohen said today. "The price we offered was not close to what we offered North Korea." Pyongyang got $4 billion in American assistance to cap its nuclear program; Pakistan was given vague promises that it might finally be given the 28 F-16 aircraft it bought and paid for almost a decade ago.

"And we and the Chinese were unwilling to offer the Pakistanis security guarantees that would have made them feel comfortable," Mr. Cohen said.

Furthermore, said Robert Oakley, Ambassador to Pakistan in 1990, Pakistan thought its national security was compromised by Washington, because a legal provision known as the Pressler Amendment cut off economic and military assistance to Pakistan because of its nuclear program, but did not similarly punish India, which had already set off a nuclear explosion in 1974.

"For eight years Pakistan has been deprived of everything, and therefore we severely weakened their conventional military capability, which was predicated on the use of American equipment," Mr. Oakley said today. "We certainly weakened their confidence in the United States."

"At the same time, India was getting stronger," he said. "So what could the Pakistanis rely upon? Missiles and nuclear capability."

The decision to test not only brings down crippling economic sanctions on the country, but has also prompted India's Prime Minister, Atal Bihari Vajpayee, to assert that Indian explosions were now fully justified, since Pakistan had proved how dangerous it is. Furthermore, the Pakistani military, which has only recently been pushed back from the center of political power, now has the bomb.

From Pakistan's perspective, pleas from around the world—and several long telephone appeals from President Clinton—were not enough to overcome visceral fears of India, a country of nearly a billion people that looms large over the border.

"Pakistan is a profoundly insecure state," Mr. Cohen said. "It is a state that feels itself surrounded by enemies, beginning with Iran, a security problem. Afghanistan has turned out to be a terrible disaster for them. The Indians are as troublesome as ever. Their friends are not really friends. The U.S. has moved out of the region, and the Chinese are cool. Add to that the domestic troubles."

India, better armed by virtually every measure, has kept Pakistan off balance since they were created from the partition of British India in 1947.

It was the Indian Army that seized a large part of Kashmir in 1947, when raiders from Pakistan entered the territory, then still under a Hindu Maharaja, who called for help. In 1971, the Indian Army came to the rescue of a nationalist Bengali movement and severed East Pakistan—now Bangladesh—from the rest of the country.

"Pakistan refuses to accept Indian primacy and India refuses to accept anything else," Richard H. Haass, a former member of the National Security Council in the Bush Administration, wrote in 1990. That core problem was often at the heart of the two nations' disputes.

Richard Murphy, senior fellow for the Mideast at the Council on Foreign Relations and a former Assistant Secretary of State for the region, said today that policy makers cannot now rule out the possibility that Iran will react to the Pakistani tests.

"The Pakistan-Iranian relationship is edgy—totally hostile no, but really quite edgy—and there have been a number of incidents of terrorism, assassination in Pakistan that they have blamed on Iranian instigation," Mr. Murphy said. "Don't rule out the chain reaction—that this will add to the motivation of Iranians to go for a nuclear weapons program, although they have said in various U.N. forums that they stand for a nuclear-free zone in the Persian Gulf."

In India as in Pakistan, the decision to test was also explained by fears of neighbors' weapons and intentions. India singled out China, but many diplomats and experts on the South Asian region and [i]n China rule this out as a serious consideration.

"There hasn't been any increased threat to India's security at all from China or Pakistan," said Mr. Oakley, the former Ambassador who is now at the National Defense University in Washington.

Several experts said that they believe that the Indians, now under a new Hindu nationalist leadership also seeking to broaden its political support, were determined to acquire a world-power image they believe has been unfairly denied them.

That point was made clear in a statement on nuclear policy presented to India's Parliament on Wednesday by Prime Minister Vajpayee. The bomb, he said, "is India's due, the right of one-sixth of mankind."

America and Europe: Is the Break Inevitable?

Werner Weidenfeld

APART FROM A few contentious trade issues, a cursory look at U.S.–European relations today reveals a general picture of harmony. In particular, an almost perfect symbiosis has prevailed in U.S.–German relations ever since the United States lent unparalleled support for German reunification. President Bill Clinton spoke of a "unique partnership" during his visit to Berlin in 1994. The often wearisome discussions during the 1980s on the deployment of medium- and short-range missiles, the heated dispute between the United States and Europe on the Soviet gas pipeline deal, and the anti-American demonstrations of the 1970s and '80s in front of U.S. embassies and consulates in Europe, so hurtful to the United States, are now forgotten.

Yet, despite U.S.—European congeniality, the way each side views its partner and the expectations placed on cooperation are currently undergoing radical change. Europe's significance in U.S. politics has diminished drastically since the end of the Soviet threat. Western Europe is no longer considered to be threatened militarily from the outside. As a result, less and less attention is being paid to internal developments on the old continent. The United States used to be keen to promote a positive image of itself to the European public to preserve the cohesion of the Western defense community. This required Americans to devote a great deal of effort to assessing the mood in Europe. Today, interest in Europe has been reduced to certain spheres: as an ally in resolving international crises and perhaps as a trading partner—that is, as a market for U.S. goods.

The America Houses in Munich and Hamburg are now under threat of closure. The U.S. cultural institutes in Hanover and Stuttgart were closed in 1995. U.S. exchange programs with Europe are being cut drastically at all levels, a prime example being the renowned Fulbright scholarships. U.S. consulates are closing their doors. In the last few years, 200,000 U.S. troops left European bases, and now the official U.S. political and cultural presence in Europe is noticeably diminishing, too.

Washington points to financial difficulties, claiming that, because of the desire to balance the U.S. budget, public funds are no longer available in abundance and that, in any case, relations with Europe today are far more relaxed than they were during the Cold War. Reducing the U.S. commitment to Europe was thus something less than dramatic.

The results of the 1996 U.S. elections gave further momentum to this change in Americans' view of Europe. It is of secondary importance to Europeans which party the U.S. president belongs to or whether Republicans or Democrats have the majority in Congress. What does matter is that the emergence of a new generation of politicians further accelerated the dramatic decrease in knowledge about Europe. Fourteen senators with proven experience in issues related to the Atlantic Alliance—among them, Sam Nunn, Bill Bradley, and Claiborne Pell—did not stand for reelection last year and were replaced by younger and less-experienced colleagues. Although the younger generation of politicians generally has a large measure of goodwill toward Europe, it seems reluctant to follow European affairs closely. In 1995, not one member of Congress visited Bonn. In 1996, only five visited Germany. Europe is in danger of disappearing from the radar screen of U.S. politics.

In Europe as well, a radical change is taking place in self-perception and in expectations of the United States as a partner. The forthcoming deepening and enlargement of the European Union (EU) is increasingly the all-pervasive domestic and foreign policy issue. Reshaping Europe following the end of the Cold War requires that all European countries undertake painful reform, in particular the reform of their social welfare systems and the abolition of government subsidies.

At the same time as Europe is becoming more introspective, however, the call is getting louder from the outside, especially from the United States, for the Union to assume global politi-

---

Werner Weidenfeld is the coordinator for German–American Cooperation in the Foreign Ministry of the Federal Republic of Germany and member of the Executive Board of the Bertelsmann Foundation.

cal responsibility. Demands on Europeans to carry an ever larger share of the joint international burden are mounting as the United States's own resources are increasingly needed to master domestic challenges.

Flagging interest coupled with heightened expectations about Europe's capability to act decisively and cohesively in the field of foreign policy will inevitably lead in the medium term—5–10 years—to a dangerous alienation within the transatlantic relationship. The already perceptible weakening of U.S.–European networks are thus only harbingers of a much more radical development: The United States and Europe are at risk of experiencing a political and cultural continental drift. Even a complete break is possible.

The transatlantic community as it was during the days of the East–West conflict no longer exists. Certainly, the alliance remains, but without the mentality of a defense organization designed to protect against a major attack. Certainly, the political links are still in place, but without the challenge of an antagonistic system of values. The partnership still exists but it lacks a definition of what specific contribution it has to make in responding to issues arising in international politics. The old loyalties will not be enough to provide the necessary political and analytical parameters for the next phase in U.S.–European cooperation. Sooner or later, Europe and the United States will find themselves redefining their interests.

It would be desirable if this were a process that resulted in positive gains for both sides. But it is entirely possible that the opposite will happen—in terms of foreign policy, a drifting apart of the partners under the influence of the centrifugal forces of international crisis; in terms of economic policy, an escalation of transatlantic trade rivalries; and in social and cultural terms, a refocusing of interests away from the transatlantic partner.

This negative scenario would mean more than just a difficult restructuring of foreign policy priorities for Europe and the United States. In fact, it would shake the very foundations of the European and U.S. self-image. Historically speaking, each partner has always formed part of the other's identity. The commitment of the United States to the reconstruction of Europe after World War II is a central element in their collective consciousness. For the United States too, the contribution made by Europeans toward the development of politics and society has become a basic element of the U.S. psyche—beyond demographical and ethnic shifts. Thus, for both sides, the loss of their transatlantic partner would do more than just inflict damage in foreign policy terms—it would lead to a cultural split with disastrous consequences. So, if the redefinition of the transatlantic relationship is to succeed, is has to offer both partners not only a common agenda in practical terms, but also a redefinition of their own identity that incorporates the partner on the other side of the Atlantic.

For a new era of transatlantic cooperation to emerge, the political elites of Europe and the United States will have to display the sort of vision shown by the founders of the postwar order. A reorientation of the relationship is inevitable, but it remains to be seen whether it will be possible to develop further this valuable transatlantic friendship and enable it to operate effectively under new conditions.

The United States in a New Era

The end of the Cold War allowed both Europe and the United States to turn to internal problems that had been neglected or concealed for decades. In Europe, the fall of the Iron Curtain made dramatically clear the wretched state of the economies of the formerly socialist half of the continent, with all the consequences that the economic demise of Eastern Europe poses for the nations of Western Europe. In the United States, the full attention of politicians and the public turned for the first time in decades to the country's domestic economic and social difficulties. Paradoxically, the election of President Clinton in 1992 and the Republican landslide victory at the 1994 congressional elections sent the same message: U.S. society is less interested in the "new world order" proclaimed by former president George Bush than in solving domestic problems that have grown dramatically.

The United States is now engaged in a debate unprecedented in its sheer breadth—a dialogue that, albeit superficially, contrasts strangely with the carefully celebrated restoration of U.S. self-confidence vis-à-vis the outside world, a restoration that had taken place only a few years earlier under presidents Ronald Reagan and George Bush. At the center of the debate lies concern about the serious structural problems of the U.S. economy that, in the view of many Americans, will be an increasing burden on current and future generations. For instance, the total federal debt has grown from $3 trillion in 1991 to a current figure of more than $5 trillion. Each year, approximately $300 billion—or approximately 20 percent of the federal budget—goes toward paying interest on this debt.

The problem of the budget deficit is made worse by the extremely low level of savings in the United States. On average only 5 percent of disposable income is saved, whereas the figures for Germany and Japan are 12 percent and 15 percent respectively. Thus, the deficit in the United States has to be financed from foreign sources to a much greater degree than in Europe. This has led to a situation whereby, in the space of a few years, the United States has moved from being the world's biggest creditor country to being the biggest debtor country. Internationally, it is some $650 billion in the red. At the same time, the effects of economic globalization are now making their full impact felt on the United States. Cheap suppliers from East Asia have surpassed many U.S. producers in their own market: Color televisions, for example, are no longer manufactured in the United States. This and similar developments are reflected in the already chronic U.S. trade deficit, which has reached record levels the last two years. The United States's technological lead, which in the eyes of Americans is the crucial factor underlying the country's leading role in the world, has disappeared completely in many areas and has been noticeably reduced in others. Growth in productivity and investment are currently not high enough in the United States to turn the situation around in the short term—that is, in 2–3 years. Americans have, quite simply, been consuming too much for too many decades and neglecting the modernization of the country's infrastructure and production sites in the process.

The concrete results of this for most Americans are stagnant or sinking real wages. For example, the income of employees without a college degree has dropped by 18 percent during the last 15 years. Although greater wage flexibility means that the United States does not have the European problem of mass unemployment, the fact is that, in the United States, a job does not guarantee a secure income: More than 3 million Americans living below the poverty line have full-time jobs. The phenomenon of the "working poor" has become a stock-in-trade of the U.S. social debate.

Furthermore, the increasingly visible shortcomings in social integration are closely connected to the state of the economy. An ever greater number of Americans is missing out on the American dream. Today, nearly 15 percent of the population—37 million U.S. citizens—is officially classified as poor. Likewise, about 37 million Americans have no health insurance whatsoever. The increasingly evident shortcomings in the education system pose a particularly severe problem, in that they contribute to the growing marginalization of large sections of the population. At its best, the U.S. education system leads the world. But a concentration on excellence at the top end has led to an increasing neglect of education and training for the masses.

In view of these facts it is not surprising that many Americans demanded a fundamental change in policy and saw the dissolution of the Cold War system as an opportunity to question aspects of domestic and foreign policy that until then had been taken for granted. President Clinton tried to react to the new mood with a fundamental reform of health and social policy during his first years in office. The attempt failed because the majority of Americans viewed the expansion of "big government," rather than the administration's lack of action, as the root cause of economic decay. The main target of all reform attempts during the last two years—both those of the Republican majority in Congress and those of the Clinton administration—has therefore been the federal deficit, which both sides hope to master through an endless succession of budget cuts in the areas of domestic, social, and foreign policy.

The new approach is far more radical than all previous attempts to consolidate the budget. The current focus of U.S. politics almost solely on the national agenda could be seen as a relapse into provincialism. Against the background of the ambitious domestic agenda, for example, voters generally find a [number] of Congress's overseas contacts highly suspect because they distract attention from what are perceived as the real tasks at hand.

Yet, the effects of budget cuts on the actual content of U.S. foreign policy have been even more dramatic than this shifting of priorities. Since 1994, influential elements—the leadership in Congress in particular—have devoted themselves to a far-reaching reinterpretation of U.S. foreign policy, using domestic challenges as a guideline for foreign policy initiatives. As with home affairs, they view U.S. foreign policy as being unnecessarily constrained by excessive bureaucracy and inefficiency and generally take the view that it has drifted too far from the ideas and interests of the American public. Thus, various members of Congress have called for the abolition of institutions such as the United States Information Agency that have long been part of the U.S. foreign policy "establishment." Furthermore, they demand budget cuts for development aid, personnel and the number of U.S. diplomatic missions abroad, and exchange programs such as Fulbright scholarships.

The proponents of this new U.S. foreign policy strategy vehemently reject the suggestion, already made by some Europeans, that budget cuts constitute a prelude to a new period of U.S. isolationism. On the contrary, they say, they are concerned about reasserting the United States's claim to lead the world and wish to rid the foreign policy establishment of unnecessary ballast in the form of both government bureaucracy and multilateral commitments. The proponents of the strategy can thus be best described as "unilateralists." Their criticism that the United States has failed to assert its claim to world leadership in recent years may well be justified. Yet, it would be a mistake to conclude that the continued need for U.S. involvement and leadership in the world can be served by a reduction in the country's foreign policy resources.

U.S. policies to reduce "big government" in domestic affairs cannot automatically be applied to the field of U.S. foreign policy. It is precisely because the United States must concentrate increasingly on its own economic and social problems that it must also renew its foreign policy efforts: to ensure that the burden of U.S. international involvement, which is as necessary as ever, can be shared more efficiently with its allies and partners.

Europe in Transition

Like the United States, Europe is undergoing far-reaching changes in its self-perception and experiencing internal upheavals of an unpredictable nature. Processes of integration are occurring concurrently with processes of disintegration, and both are affecting the European Union. Supranational political interweaving is running parallel to new splits along social and ethnic lines. The old borders between Catholic and Orthodox Europe, between the Ottoman and Habsburg empires, have reemerged. It is less clear than ever before where Europe begins and ends. The acceleration in the process of developing the EU is being met with a growing degree of skepticism at the national level. The importance of national and regional concerns is increasing.

At the same time, the internationalization of economics and politics is intensifying, and creating several problems. But the development of appropriate decision-making structures at the European level continues to lag and cannot yet offer an adequate response to pressures that are already too great for individual nation-states. Europe is trapped: On the one hand, the magnet of integration is attracting more and more politicians and states—specifically, Eastern European ones—keen to accede to the EU; on the other, the structures that would enable the Union to take political action at the supranational level are not being developed quickly enough. The continent is in danger of becoming a victim of its own success.

In a transitional era like the present one, the foreign policy of many states has reverted to a familiar pattern in the European context—the maintenance of a "balance of power." Behind the multilateralist rhetoric of the Conference on Security and Cooperation in Europe (CSCE), behind the wrangling about the heritage of the Soviet Union and the question of the timetable for accepting new members into the EU, there lie national calculations as to the best way to counterbalance the potential power wielded by neighboring states.

In Western Europe, integration has become an instrument for such an approach. The shift in the internal balance caused by German unification has prompted France to offer to deepen the European Union. Britain has countered the prospect of greater integration with the prospect of widening, in the expectation that this will lead to a looser type of integration.

Yet, under present conditions, this process should not be seen as a return to the European tradition of grand diplomacy by nation-states. One of the peculiarities of the present-day policy of maintaining a balance of power is that it combines classic diplomacy with modern levels of integration. Even within the European Union, it is possible to pursue a policy of national interest. European politicians now face the task of giving form to this complex, transitional constellation. National ambitions need to be brought into harmony with the challenges resulting from the situation.

This simultaneity of contrasting developments is what makes Europe such a special case. And it is from this complex Europe that the United States will demand a clear definition of interests. It will expect Europe to have at its disposal the instruments necessary to pursue clearly defined policies. Thus, any realignment of the transatlantic partnership is going to require that Europeans do some very basic homework.

No action based on maintaining equilibrium can be considered an adequate solution or an appropriate way of solving far-reaching challenges. In particular, balance of power policies do not do justice to U.S. expectations concerning a more mature partnership. Rather, current political problems demand that European politicians devise strategic policies to meet four specific goals: to change the institutions responsible for integration, including their capacity to act; to develop the EU further along the path toward a true political, economic, and monetary union; to stabilize and integrate Central and Eastern Europe; and to preserve peace and security on the continent. The European Union's Intergovernmental Conference (IGC) for 1996–97 will determine the way forward; it is intended to give the process of integration new impetus and pave the way for amendments to the Treaty on the European Union. The whole idea of taking integration further will thus be subjected to careful consideration.

At first glance it appears paradoxical: Of all the times to start raising the issue of the continent's leading role, the United States has to do so in a period of deep-seated insecurity in Europe about the Union's future shape. Yet, given its increasing problems at home and its lonely position as the sole global superpower following the collapse of the Soviet Union, the United States is understandably applying increasing pressure on Europeans to play a greater role in solving global problems. It is thus in the U.S. interest that Europe learn, as soon as possible, to speak with one voice politically, militarily, and economically—or at least to channel the chorus of voices more effectively. The United States, as Europe's main partner, has the important role of constantly reminding the Europeans not to get tied up in seemingly trivial internal quarrels relating to European integration and not to lose sight of wider global challenges.

Europe has to bear responsibility worldwide simply because of its economic might; together with the United States, Europe is one of the main sources of hope in the developing world in terms of support for democracy and economic liberalization. In the future, the United States will increasingly remind Europe of its duty to take on political responsibilities commensurate with its position as a world economic power.

Today, Europe has the full potential to take on this new role of equal partner to the United States. One condition for the full exploitation of this potential is that Europe be politically aware of the new international challenges that have emerged in the wake of the end of the Cold War. If it fails to react to these challenges, or if it reacts inadequately, it risks permanent erosion of the transatlantic community: The United States, in searching for partners prepared to share its burdens, will increasingly begin looking outside Europe if it does not believe the Union is up to the task.

The Rise and Fall of the Transatlantic Community

Internal social and political changes taking place on both sides of the Atlantic will have several consequences on the transatlantic relationship. Both parties find themselves in a relatively serious identity crisis and lack a firm sense of direction. It is becoming increasingly difficult for Europe and the United States to calculate one another's actions—especially given the shifting political importance of economy, security, and culture. Under circumstances such as these, conflicts could be triggered very easily.

Crises beyond the domain of the North Atlantic Treaty Organization (NATO), trade conflicts both within and outside the Western community, and global challenges such as environmental pollution or nuclear terrorism have moved to the fore as topics demanding high-level political decision-making, yet the transatlantic partners have no commonly accepted guidelines for dealing with them. Differences on individual issues that have always existed are now becoming clearly visible and are being allowed to develop unchecked.

Yet, for the foreseeable future, no alternative exists to the transatlantic relations that have developed over the last 50 years. Europe and the United States have created a network of relations unprecedented throughout the world; they have succeeded in building more common understanding concerning democracy, pluralism, human rights, and the market economy than has ever before existed. Moreover, this common understanding is accepted by, and serves as a model for, more and more nations all over the world. This fact is increasingly ignored or forgotten because the West lacks a common orientation and a new agenda to take into account altered external conditions.

To establish transatlantic consensus, the West continues to use the old structures left over from the era of East–West conflict. But these structures cannot meet new challenges. New guiding principles for common action are needed to change the old backdrops and to form a consensus on how to tackle the tasks of the future. The ability of the Western partners to develop a new outline for a common direction in transatlantic relations will ultimately decide their fate.

If the West does not step up to this challenge, U.S.–European relations seem headed for a cultural split, one whose effects would radically question the structure of 50 years of transatlantic links. This split in the culture of political and social contact would not come about in the form of abrupt cuts or spectacular arguments. Rather, it would lead decisionmakers on both sides of the Atlantic in the medium term to drift apart in terms of their attitudes and subjective political and social designs.

Signs of a possible start of this process have already become manifest in the creeping erosion of bilateral links. Thus, the parliamentary contacts between Europe and the United States have recently been thinning visibly. According to U.S. insiders in the policy planning staff of the U.S. executive, the transatlantic relationship is also moving to the fringe of the operative radar screen. If this trend continues and extends to other fields, in the medium term the ability to conduct transatlantic policy will disappear.

As this erosion is below the surface, the whole extent of the current split would become visible only when the damage could no longer be repaired by using the reliable pattern of direct contacts and pulling the relevant strings. Strings can be pulled only when they exist—that is, when political and social contacts are constantly cultivated and a high level of agreement exists concerning the expectations each party has toward the other. As the attitudes of leading opinion makers in Europe and the United States drift apart, the basis for short-term successful crisis management will also vanish.

This process would not only lead to a far-reaching drift of political and social orientations, but also, in the worst case, to a direct political division between Europe and the United States—in other words, to a complete abandonment of the concept of the fundamental community of interests. The danger of such a split can be surmounted only if a future-oriented concept for deepening the transatlantic relationship can be developed that takes both partners' topical interests into consideration. Without a renewal of the U.S.–European community along such strategic lines, the very existence and success of the transatlantic relationship will be in jeopardy.

Creating a New Transatlantic Community

Players on both sides of the Atlantic have felt the increasingly painful unraveling of the network of transatlantic relations, the lack of a common new direction, and the ensuing dangers of substantial erosion of the U.S.–European partnership. Thus, politicians are, with increasing intensity, creating new models for the future prospects of U.S.–European cohesion. Leading European and U.S. politicians, in particular the German minister for foreign affairs, Klaus Kinkel, and his previous U.S. counterpart, former secretary of state Warren Christopher, declared their support for new treaty arrangements between Europe and the United States, as well as for the drawing-up of a binding transatlantic agenda or the establishment of new forums for cooperation at all conceivable levels.

All these approaches have one thing in common: namely, the worry about the creeping erosion of the transatlantic partnership following the disappearance of a common foe. To reshape cooperation to bring it in line with the times—a move that is absolutely imperative—the partners must develop a structure that is binding for all involved.

The task of finding a new direction can certainly be compared to that facing the transatlantic partners after World War II, one that demanded a radical paradigmatic shift on both sides of the Atlantic. The founders of the postwar order were aware that this change of direction and the quality of the U.S.–European ties they hoped to achieve would not be possible if relations within the Western community were governed only by loose arrangements. The degree of organization within the Western community had to be improved and this improvement found expression in the form of NATO, complemented by its economic counterpart, the Marshall Plan.

Today's new challenges, too, call upon the U.S.–European partnership to take a great step forward in terms of commitment. The first step must be the renaissance of the transatlantic community uniting the United States and the European Union. This task involves defining a clear vision of a continued transatlantic success story, in the face of different external conditions, that is obvious to both domestic and external observers and that will give all partners involved a highly exigent, common goal toward which to work. Furthermore, the new community has to create an organizational framework that enables the diverse and far-reaching common traits of the transatlantic partners to be developed into a coordinated and well-defined strategy for political action.

New Structures for Political Cooperation

Unlike during the period of East–West confrontation, when all partners could rely on a common security policy, no all-encompassing *raison d'être* exists today as a basis for reestablishing the transatlantic community. The creation of new binding structures must therefore revolve around issues in which the partners have an obvious interest in joint action as a matter of paramount importance.

If one considers the focus of European or U.S. political action, the need for binding structures is evident particularly in the coordination of strategy in response to global challenges and/or international crises. Today, Europe and the United States remain the only reliable makers or guarantors of stability in the world. The variety of burning issues in international politics calls for action by the transatlantic partners almost daily, often in regions where the existing institutions of the Atlantic Alliance have no jurisdiction. Thus far, no permanent mechanism exists to coordinate European and U.S. policy to deal with these issues. Moreover, both the United States and members of the European Union have fallen prone to navel-gazing because of problems and challenges at home. Yet, now that the traditional security partnership has been somewhat watered down, there is an increasing danger that the fallout from these conflicts may affect the transatlantic community, too.

Therefore, it is vital to establish a binding structure for transatlantic political consultation and cooperation that would give the transatlantic partners a reliable mandate to coordinate all issues relevant to the transatlantic agenda. The structure of this consultation and cooperation could be similar to that of the European Political Cooperation (EPC) forum, introduced in 1970 as the first permanent forum for coordinating the common policy of the members of the European Economic Community, as the EU was then known. It is now time for the transatlantic partners to institute a similar mechanism, to set up some form of Euro-American Political Cooperation (EAPC), which could deal with all the issues that the international community directs at the transatlantic partners but for which no organizational form has yet been found.

Creating a Transatlantic Common Market

Nowhere is the level of existing transatlantic interdependency more visible than in economic relations. This policy area constitutes one of the central vehicles of previous—and future—progress in transatlantic integration. Great care must therefore be taken to shape the political framework for this tightly woven network of relations so it can become the catalyst driving integration forward rather than—as has often been the case—the brakes holding it back. The high degree of transatlantic economic interdependency somehow seems to evade the collective consciousness of the European and U.S. populations. What they never fail to notice, however, are the recurring clashes over trivial matters such as bananas, feta cheese, or spaghetti, although the respective trade volumes in these goods account for a mere fraction of their governments' economic interests.

Similarly unheeded by the public at large, countless negotiating teams of European and U.S. officials in various different forums endeavor to thrash out progress concerning individual aspects of transatlantic trade, such as liberalizing public procurement, standardizing product norms, and dismantling export subsidies.

If one measures the results of this dialogue on regulatory policy against both the extent and the dynamic potential of real economic trade between Europe and the United States, however, a serious policy deficit emerges. Transatlantic settlement mechanisms lag far behind the supranational vitality of trade between Europe and the United States and seriously hamper the further development of trade relations.

Removing existing barriers to trade can succeed only if Europe and the United States manage to make their removal part of a strategic vision and manage to win over their populations by means of proactive arguments. Europe and the United States must categorically declare their faith in a revival of their trade relations; the founding of a Transatlantic Common Market, anchored in an agreement between the European Union and the United States, would be an optimal way of achieving this aim. This agreement should provide for specific objectives aimed at dismantling existing tariffs that hamper trade and, furthermore, it should formulate the timetable for a standardized U.S.–European economic area. In other words, it should dismantle any barriers to trade caused by regulatory policy.

Founding a Transatlantic Learning Community

The internal challenges facing the members of the transatlantic partnership increasingly require consultation between Europe and the United States, too. Concerning problems such as international crime, drug trafficking, and immigration, a need for joint action is clear. But other issues, such as reform of social security systems, appear merely to have a national character. Yet, strategies aimed at solving domestic problems can draw on models from other countries within the transatlantic community.

By way of example, President Clinton's health care reforms were clearly inspired by European models. By the same token, U.S. limits on automobile emission levels were crucial for European policymakers in this field. Countless other examples illustrate how the transatlantic partners can learn from each other's experiences. This has created the ideal conditions for founding a transatlantic learning community that would give some structure to the contacts and cross-referencing that have, until now, been somewhat ad hoc.

For the strategic planning of such a learning community, one must realize that the future of international relations will no longer be governed by the *raison d'être* of the security partnership—that is, by a so-called superior motive. In the future, such exchanges will have to serve a specific aim or make a practical contribution to the future lives of citizens on both sides of the Atlantic. It is the job of politicians to tap this potential appropriately, to create the optimum space for it to unfold as creatively as possible, and in so doing, to increase the acceptance of transatlantic relations among both Americans and Europeans.

Using the Opportunities of a New Beginning

The tenacity of the institutions of the postwar order has, until now, stalled the tendency for Europe and the United States to drift further apart. For example, no one seriously calls into question the existence of NATO, although the reason for its inception—the threat from Eastern Europe—has been reduced considerably. The after-effects of Western cohesion during the

East–West confrontation will be available to the transatlantic partners as spiritual armor for some time yet. The imminent celebrations commemorating the fiftieth anniversary of the Marshall Plan, the Berlin airlift, and the founding of NATO will certainly contribute to this.

Furthermore, the potential for differences of opinion between the Western partners has decreased considerably since the end of the Cold War. Constant points of friction over the appropriate reaction to the Soviet threat have disappeared. Compared to the controversies of the 1980s, the present state of transatlantic relations exudes considerable harmony. Yet, the current risk is that of increasing transatlantic indifference on a scale to match the disputes of old. Potential sources of friction concerning security policy coordination have ceased to exist, dealing with one's partners seems less and less necessary, and, given the more promising topics of everyday politics, cooperation is now frequently seen as a tiresome obligation.

Any analysis of transatlantic circumstances and options brings us to this central dilemma. On the one hand, as indicated above, no two other regions in the world enjoy such close ties, characterized by friendship and shared common values as well as by political and economic efficiency, as do Europe and the United States. On the other hand, the historical development of this alliance over the last 50 years makes it clear that, without a revitalization of these ties that is both forward-looking and geared toward the changing geopolitical situation, the two partners will inevitably grow apart.

The closeness of the transatlantic community in recent decades has been possible only because the security partnership founded in the postwar era provided the necessary framework. In the future, this framework will no longer be available. Thus far, only the initiated have been able to discern the first tiny cracks in the superstructure, demonstrated by the sharp decline in the number of visits to Europe by members of Congress and the cutbacks in U.S. funding for transatlantic cultural exchanges.

On both sides of the Atlantic, the everyday routine of politics is creating ever-greater distance between what were once the closest of partners. If this tendency is not halted, this slight indifference will eventually develop into more sharply defined differences of perception concerning international politics and strategies. This will become visible as a serious problem for Europe and the United States only when this perceptual difference turns into conflict, most likely when the partners face a concrete international challenge, such as peacekeeping in a crisis region of the world. The expectation that tried-and-tested methods of long-standing transatlantic cooperation will be able to solve this conflict of ideas may be deceptive.

Successful U.S.–European conflict management rests on the permanent agreement between policymakers and their public on a common direction. If this agreement is lacking on the minor issues, or if politicians begin to prefer solving domestic problems at the cost of dealing with their foreign partners (for example, in trade policy), then, when a serious issue arises, neither the politicians nor the general public will see the value of maintaining a transatlantic consensus. The ultimate consequences of such a split could be a permanent break in the transatlantic culture of close political and social interaction.

Eventually, all parties involved will have to ask how transatlantic relations can be placed on a new footing for the future. The longer it takes to answer this question, the more difficult a new beginning will be. For now, however, the opportunity to refound the transatlantic community is still ripe. The latest discussions on a Transatlantic Treaty, a Charter, or a "New Agenda" have made major political, industrial, and social policymakers aware of the need for a new initiative. The generation of committed supporters of the transatlantic partnership from the days of the East–West conflict are still involved in policymaking and opinion-shaping. Both Europe and the United States must therefore make decisive use of these conditions for a new beginning.

No one should make the mistake of thinking that such a new foundation will be easy to build. It will require a lot of effort on both sides and, more specifically, new and unconventional strategies. At the moment, because of the dominance of domestic issues, it is more difficult to gauge how much foreign policy strain Europe and the United States can take. Founding the transatlantic community anew would require both partners to open up unreservedly toward each other in areas such as trade, economic relations, and the transfer of experiences in social affairs.

In the coming decades, these new forms of cooperation will give both sides entirely new chances for development. In the short term, however, they could lead to painful adjustments, especially for the guardians of certain individual interests desirous of protection, such as agriculture or textiles. Transatlantic renewal requires Europeans and Americans to change their attitudes to a degree, not unlike reestablishing relations after World War II. Citizens on both sides of the Atlantic have to be won over if this new beginning is to succeed.

It is only by opening up the transatlantic community to the challenges of the future that we can ensure its continued existence and success. Merely preserving the status quo based on a transfigured romantic view of the past would be the surest way to guarantee the erosion of this partnership. Europe and the United States must seize this historic opportunity to found the transatlantic community anew before the emerging tendency to ignore solidarity means it slips through our fingers for good.

WHY ARE WE IN BOSNIA?

The road to American involvement was sometimes unmarked.

BY RICHARD HOLBROOKE

By 1995, as the crisis in Bosnia approached its climax, America's armed forces could look back proudly on the skill and courage with which they had handled a decade of challenges in Kuwait, Panama, Haiti, and elsewhere. But the memory of Vietnam still shadowed the Pentagon, which was now led by men who had served as company or field-grade officers in Southeast Asia. The lesson they drew from that experience was eloquently summarized by General Colin Powell, who wrote in his 1995 memoir, "Many of my generation, the career captains, majors, and lieutenant colonels seasoned in that war, vowed that when our turn came to call the shots, we would not quietly acquiesce in halfhearted warfare for half-baked reasons that the American people could not understand or support."

In addition, three post-Vietnam tragedies haunted the military: the failed attempt to rescue the American hostages in Teheran in 1980, which left eight Americans dead; the loss of two hundred and forty-one marines whose barracks in Beirut were bombed in

---

RICHARD HOLBROOKE is the former Assistant Secretary of State for European and Canadian Affairs and the author of *To End a War*, which was published in June 1998 by Random House.

The author and the President in April, 1997, on a day that led to unexpected policy consequences.

1983; and the firefight of October 3, 1993, when eighteen Americans, serving as part of a United Nations force in Somalia, were killed while trying to capture a clan leader. The wound from that most recent disaster was still fresh, and, together with the ghost of the much greater disaster a generation earlier, had saddled Washington's deliberations on Bosnia with what might be called a "Vietmalia syndrome."

To be sure, there were fundamental differences between Bosnia and "Vietmalia." The Bosnian Serbs were neither the disciplined, ruthless revolutionaries of North Vietnam nor the drunken, ragtag thugs who raced their "technicals" around Mogadishu, guns blazing. But discussion of such distinctions was unwelcome.

American military leaders were generally opposed to involvement in Bosnia. They feared that the mission would be "fuzzy"—imprecise, like the one in Somalia. Of course, General John Shalikashvili, the chairman of the Joint Chiefs of Staff, had made sure that the American military, if it should be ordered into action, would respond quickly and effectively. But the military regarded almost anything beyond self-protection and the carrying out of the military provisions of any peace agreement as constituting "mission creep"—that is, an undesirable broadening of their mission.

The United States, under both Presidents Bush and Clinton, had decided not to commit American soldiers to Bosnia. But there was a critical and little-noticed exception: President Clinton had pledged that American troops would support any massive withdrawal of the United Nations peacekeeping troops already stationed there. As the situation in Bosnia deteriorated dramatically in the spring of 1995, and many countries began talking openly of withdrawing from the peacekeeping force, NATO completed and formally approved a highly classified planning document that covered every aspect—from bridge-building to body bags—of the alliance's projected role in supporting a U.N. pullout. This plan, known as Operations Plan (or OPLAN) 40104, projected the participation of twenty thousand American soldiers.

In June of 1995, in my role as Assistant Secretary of State for European and Canadian Affairs, I asked for a briefing on the plan. After some initial Pentagon resistance, Air Force Lieutenant General Howell Estes III, the Pentagon operations director, came to my office and showed my deputies and me plans that left us stunned. As General Estes told us, it was bold and dangerous. American casualties, he warned, were virtually certain. To take such risks for a withdrawal, when we had not taken them to prevent "ethnic cleansing," seemed inconceivable to me.

As soon as General Estes finished, I rushed to the office of Secretary of State Warren Christopher and urged him to get the same briefing. He did so the next day, and what he heard about OPLAN 40104 left him as worried as I was. But the status of the plan remained less than clear. According to complicated Cold War-era procedures that had never been tested, OPLAN 40104 would become an operational order, adjusted for specific circumstances, if a U.N. withdrawal started. Once that order was given, American troops would be deployed in the Balkans as part of a NATO force under an American commander. But, under our Constitution, only the President of the United States—not the NATO Council or any other international body—can decide to deploy American troops. And, despite the NATO Council's approval of the plan, the President had not approved it, or even been given a formal briefing on it.

U.N. withdrawal would open the way for the greatest disaster yet for the Bosnians. Sending American ground troops to fight the war was out of the question, but something had to be done, or else a Serb victory—and more "ethnic cleansing"—was inevitable. I had long favored NATO air strikes against the Bosnian Serbs, but that proposal had run into fierce opposition a withdrawal from Bosnia? That, as the British and French told us bluntly, would be a transatlantic catastrophe. It was not an overstatement to say that America's post-Cold War role in Europe was at stake. It was a terrible set of choices, but it was clear that Washington could not avoid direct involvement much longer.

As we faced these dark prospects, Jacques Chirac arrived in Washington, on June 14, 1995, for his first visit as President of France. It was not for nothing that Chirac had acquired the nickname Le Bulldozer: he was as direct and blunt as his predecessor, François Mitterrand, had been opaque and elegant. He lost no time in threatening to withdraw French troops from Bosnia unless the United States got more deeply involved.

What happened that day has been described, in slightly different form, by Bob Woodward in "The Choice." Late in the morning, we held the "pre-brief," normally a routine session to prepare the President for an important visitor. It quickly degenerated into an angry, contentious discussion of Bosnia. The initial presentation seemed, in my view, misleading about the desperate nature of the situation, and especially about the likely consequences and complications of America's promise to assist a U.N. withdrawal. When I began to set forth the implications of OPLAN 40104, the President, obviously disturbed that he was receiving contradictory information so soon before his meeting with Chirac, cut me off. Vice-President Al Gore intervened with a pithy summation of the situation—the most accurate, in my view, at the meeting. Then, as people offered differing views, Christopher and I had to excuse ourselves, in order to go to the French Embassy, where Chirac was expecting us for lunch. In the car, Christopher and I, astonished at what had just happened, agreed that we had to talk to the President again as soon as possible about the true status of the NATO planning process.

The rest of the day was hectic. The President met alone with Chirac for well over an hour, instead of the scheduled twenty minutes, while Gore, Christopher, and half the American Cabinet waited in the Cabinet Room. The President asked Chirac to visit the Senate Majority Leader, Bob Dole, and the Speaker of the House, Newt Gingrich, hoping that the French President would be able to persuade the Republican leaders to give the Administration greater support on Bosnia. Chirac's meetings on the Hill, while cordial, changed nothing. He then returned to the White House for a small "family" dinner, which was spent, for the most part, in conversation about subjects other than Bosnia.

After Chirac left, I stood in the main entrance hall of the White House, in front of the North Portico, with Christopher, Samuel (Sandy) Berger, who was then the deputy national-security adviser, and Madeleine Albright, who was then the American Ambassador to the U.N. The President and the First Lady danced briefly to the music of a Marine Band ensemble that had played during dinner, and then they walked over to us. It was a beautiful June evening, and the White House glowed with its special magic. I looked at Christopher, concerned that we would lose the moment. He nodded. The President broke the ice. "What about Bosnia?" he asked suddenly, looking at me.

"I hate to ruin a wonderful dinner, Mr. President," I began, "but we should clarify something that came up during the day. I'm afraid that we may not have that much flexibility left. Under existing NATO plans, the United States is already committed to sending troops to Bosnia if the U.N. decides to withdraw."

"What do you mean?" the President asked me. "I'll decide the troop issue if and when the time comes."

There was silence for a moment. "Mr. President," I said, "NATO has already approved the withdrawal plan. While you can always stop it, it has a high degree of automaticity built into it, especially since we have committed ourselves publicly to assisting the NATO troops if they decide to withdraw."

The President looked at Christopher. "Is this true?" he asked.

"Yes, it appears to be," Christopher said tersely.

"I suggest that we talk about it again tomorrow," the President said, and he walked off without another word, holding Mrs. Clinton's hand.

THE next day, as he flew to Halifax for a G-7 summit, the President began to press for better options; he understood that sending troops to Bosnia to implement a failure was unacceptable. But events in Bosnia were moving faster than the policy-review process in Washington. While the Administration deliberated, the Bosnian Serbs went on the attack again. This time, their actions would horrify the world.

General Ratko Mladic, the commander of the Bosnian Serb Army, now focussed pressure on three isolated Muslim enclaves in eastern Bosnia—Srebrenica, Zepa, and Gorazde—that had been completely surrounded by Serb forces since early in the war. A small number of U.N. peacekeepers had been sent to each enclave, but they had been bottled up, unable to relieve the siege conditions of the three towns. Mladic decided to eliminate the enclaves from the map.

On July 6, 1995, his forces began shelling Srebrenica. What took place over the next ten days was the biggest single mass murder in Europe since the Second World War. The outside world did nothing effective to stop the tragedy. Precise details of the atrocities were not known at the time, but there was no doubt that something truly horrible was going on. By coincidence, I soon had an additional source of information about Srebrenica beyond the official reporting: my younger son, Anthony, who was twenty-five, had gone to Tuzla that week to help interview refugees. Anthony had been working in a refugee camp in Thailand when the president of Refugees International, Lionel Rosenblatt, summoned him to Bosnia. Anthony and Rosenblatt arrived in central Bosnia just as the first, desperate survivors from Srebrenica and Zepa reached the safety of the Muslim-controlled airfield outside Tuzla. They were joined by two key State Department officials: John Shattuck, the Assistant Secretary for Human Rights, and Phyllis Oakley, the Assistant Secretary for Population, Refugees, and Migration.

Together, the four of them interviewed shell-shocked survivors of Srebrenica, and heard the stories that would soon horrify the world: how the Serbs, directed by General Mladic, had rounded up all the Muslims in the town and piled them into buses; how most of the men were never seen again; how people were herded onto soccer fields and school grounds and killed in large numbers; how men in the thousands were still trying to escape through the woods toward Tuzla.

On July 13th, as the Serbs were systematically killing Muslims, President Chirac called President Clinton. He said that something had to be done, and proposed that American helicopters carry French troops into Srebrenica to relieve the town. This proposal had already been discussed through official French channels, and had run into fierce opposition from the British and the Pentagon and also from Chirac's own generals. It had no chance of being accepted.

No more energy was left in the international system. Everywhere one turned, there was numb confusion in the face of the Bosnian Serbs' brutality. The first line of opposition to any air strike against the Serbs—which I recommended—was the Dutch government, which refused to consider air strikes until all its soldiers were out of Bosnia. Through every channel available, in London, Paris, and NATO headquarters, we pressed for some response, but the Europeans had reached their limits: with their own soldiers at risk, they were not going to agree to any action that endangered the Dutch. The Serbs knew this, and held the bulk of the Dutch forces captive in the U.N. compound at the nearby village of Potocari until their own forces had finished their dirty work at Srebrenica. According to the International Committee of the Red Cross, the toll of Muslims dead or missing and presumed dead in Srebrenica was seven thousand three hundred. Most of the victims had been unarmed, and almost all had died in ambushes and mass executions. Nothing else in the war had matched, or ever would match, Srebrenica. The name would become part of the language of the horrors of modern war, alongside Lidice, Oradour, Babi Yar, and the Katyn Forest.

THE destruction of Srebrenica was an enormous shock to the Western alliance, and to the conscience of the West. President Clinton pressed his national-security team once again to make an all-out effort to bring peace to Bosnia. As a result, in early August of 1995, after more bureaucratic twists, a last-ditch diplomatic effort was launched, which I was asked to lead. Less than a week into that effort, three of the four members of our negotiating team—Robert Frasure, Joseph Kruzel, and Nelson Drew—were killed when their vehicle, travelling some fifty yards behind mine, slipped off the narrow and dangerous Mt. Igman road as we tried to reach Sarajevo, the besieged capital of Bosnia.

The deaths of these three highly respected and treasured colleagues wrenched the Washington policy discussions into focus. And then—on August 28, 1995, the day our newly reconstituted team resumed the diplomatic shuttle—the Bosnian Serbs killed some thirty-eight people in the Sarajevo marketplace with a single mortar shell. It was, at last, an outrage too far. Within forty-eight hours, under urging from President Clinton and with strong support from our negotiating team, NATO finally did what it should have done years earlier: it launched massive air strikes against Bosnian Serb positions.

Events now accelerated dramatically. We negotiated a lifting of the siege of Sarajevo in mid-September and a general ceasefire in early October. On November 1, 1995, at Wright-Patterson Air Force Base, outside Dayton, Ohio, we convened a risky, all-or-nothing peace conference involving all three Balkan Presidents and senior diplo-

10. Why Are We in Bosnia?

matic representatives from Russia, Great Britain, France, Germany, and the European Union. For twenty-one days, we cajoled, harassed, and pressured the participants, coming to the very brink of failure on the morning of the last day. Finally, on November 21st, after a last-minute intervention by President Clinton, the three Balkan Presidents initialled the Dayton Peace Agreement.

Dayton marked a turning point in America's post-Cold War role in Europe. It put an end not only to the war in Bosnia but also to several years of widespread concern that the United States was in the process of turning its back on Europe. Even America's harshest critics acknowledged that without the Administration's leadership the war would have ended disastrously—and only after much more carnage.

But Dayton was not the end of the story. On paper, it was a good agreement: it called for a single, multiethnic country and a central government. Countless diplomatic agreements, however, survive only as case studies in failed expectations. Dayton's true place in history would be determined by its implementation.

Dayton's first military deadlines were met easily, and without incident. The first major civilian deadline of the Dayton agreement—and in many ways the most important—was the unification of Sarajevo, which took place on schedule, on March 19, 1996. But on the eve of that achievement the Bosnian Serbs exploited the passivity of the NATO-led Implementation Force, or IFOR, to reassert themselves. Two weeks before Sarajevo's scheduled unification, in a cynically brutal act designed to reinforce ethnic partition, the Bosnian Serb leadership began to order all Serbs in the Sarajevo area—some forty thousand or more—to burn down their own apartments and leave the city. Detailed instructions were broadcast on how to set the fires: pile all the furniture in the middle of the room, douse it with kerosene, turn the gas on, and throw a match into the room as you leave. Often, those Sarajevo Serbs who resisted were beaten by Serb thugs who roamed the streets, while NATO troops stood by. The result was a severe blow to the multi-ethnic country called for at Dayton, and it would take more than sixteen months to undo the damage.

Even when a President is reëlected, his Administration goes through a transition period, although it may be mostly invisible to the public. At the beginning of 1997, the Clinton Administration effected a smooth transition in most areas, and especially at State, where the new Secretary, Madeleine Albright, was familiar with the major issues from her U.N. tour, and on the National Security Council, where Sandy Berger simply moved up to replace Tony Lake as national-security adviser. (Although I had left the government in February of 1996 to return to private life in New York, I would continue to work closely with the Administration on Bosnia, returning three times to assist my former colleagues.)

At State, Albright's well-known tough line on Bosnia made her the ideal person to reinvigorate the policy. Nonetheless, by April of 1997 there was a general impression that "Clinton II" was downgrading Bosnia; the emphasis in Europe was almost entirely on a critical summit meeting with Boris Yeltsin, planned for Helsinki, that would determine the future of the Administration's plan to enlarge NATO. Sensing that high-level American interest had declined, Radovan Karadzic, the indicted war criminal who had founded the Bosnian Serb Republic, ventured once more into public view, flagrantly violating a July 18, 1996, agreement he had negotiated with me, in which he had pledged to withdraw "permanently" from public life. His reëmergence went unchallenged by NATO, and suggested, as many journalists noted, that NATO was simply counting the days until its forces left. But as soon as the Helsinki summit ended successfully, with Yeltsin's acceptance of a larger NATO, President Clinton focussed again on Bosnia, ordering a full-scale review of American policy.

At about that time, Liz Stevens gave a combined birthday party in honor of her husband, the filmmaker George Stevens, Jr., and my wife, the writer Kati Marton—a party that would have unexpected policy consequences. On arriving early, we found Secret Service agents all over the house. Without telling us, Liz had invited the Clintons, and a few minutes later, ahead of the other guests, they walked in.

To be precise, Hillary walked; the President limped in, on crutches. A month earlier, he had taken a nasty fall outside the home of the golfer Greg Norman. As it happened, I had injured myself at about the same time, tearing ligaments in my ankle, and I, too, was on crutches. We spent a few minutes comparing our rehabilitation programs. As he left, the President pulled me aside for a moment and said, "Come by tomorrow and we can do some therapy and talk."

The next day, I presented myself at the White House and was ushered upstairs to the family quarters, where I found the President pedalling away on a stationary bicycle. We worked out together in silence for a while. Then we adjourned to another room to cool down. Members of the family, including Hillary and her mother, Dorothy Rodham, stopped to chat. Just as I was starting to wonder if we would ever get around to talking about Bosnia, the President said, "Let's go downstairs." With that, we hobbled down to his office in the family quarters.

"What's going on out there?" the President began. It is in the nature of the hierarchical structure of the executive branch that a conversation like the one we then proceeded to have—informal, candid, and alone—would have been next to impossible while I was still in the government; there are simply too many layers between an assistant secretary and the Chief Executive. I had decided, at the enthusiastic urging of Strobe Talbott, to be as frank as I could. I listed the series of reverses and lost opportunities since December.

"While NATO enlargement and your achievement with Yeltsin have been historic, Bosnia has gone nowhere," I said. "These issues are interrelated. People out there are not even sure we still support Dayton, or still care what happens in Bosnia."

I urged the President to give his full backing to Albright and Robert Gelbard, a career diplomat whom Albright had chosen to be the "czar" for implementation of Dayton. I had first asked Gelbard, a tough, no-nonsense official, to visit Bosnia at the end of 1995. His assumption, in April of 1997, of full-time responsibility for implementing the Dayton agreement would soon produce results, and he and I would make a productive trip to the region together in August of 1997 to accelerate the process.

When the President visited Sarajevo, last December, he said that implementation was running about a year behind schedule—a judgment that coincided with my own. But the situation in Bosnia has greatly improved. There has been no fighting for two years; the three communities have begun rebuilding ties at the local level; Sarajevo, reunified, is rebuilding; large quantities of weapons have been destroyed; four airports have opened for civilian traffic; numerous refugee "open cities" have been created; the odious Bosnian Serb television transmitters, once Karadzic's greatest asset, have finally been seized by NATO and turned over to broadcasters who are not preaching race hate; Banja Luka, the center of a new, more moderate Serb leadership, has grown in strength. And all this has been done without a single NATO soldier's being killed or wounded by hostile action since Dayton.

In January, a new moderate Bosnian Serb, Milorad Dodik, was named Prime Minister of the Serb portion of Bosnia, and pledged full compliance with the Dayton agreement. When the Karadzic forces threatened a coup against him, NATO moved rapidly, in a manner not previously seen, to head off the threat. If such actions continue, the anti-Dayton forces will be progressively weakened, and the chances of creating a viable multi-ethnic state will improve dramatically.

Still, while the blood lust of 1991-95 has subsided, it is not gone; people on all sides carry deep scars, and many continue to seek revenge instead of reconciliation. Most troubling, the same leaders who started the war are still trying to silence those who call for multi-ethnic coöperation. The two most dangerous men in the region, the indicted war criminals Karadzic and Mladic, remain at large more than two years after Dayton.

If the United States does not lead, its European allies could falter as they did in the early part of this decade. Indeed, since earlier this year, the old pattern has threatened to repeat itself; in Kosovo, an Albanian Muslim region in Serbia, Serbian police have cracked down on ethnic Albanians. This time, though, the United States immediately condemned the aggressors, and Secretary of State Albright called for fresh sanctions against Belgrade. "We will keep all options open to do what is necessary to prevent another wave of violence from overtaking the Balkans," she said in March. As Kosovo reminded us, there will be other Bosnias in our lives.

Pivotal States and U.S. Strategy

Robert S. Chase, Emily B. Hill, and Paul Kennedy

Robert S. Chase is a Ph.D. candidate in economics at Yale University. Emily B. Hill is a Ph.D. candidate in history at Yale University. Paul Kennedy is Professor of History at Yale University.

THE NEW DOMINOES

HALF A DECADE after the collapse of the Soviet Union, American policymakers and intellectuals are still seeking new principles on which to base national strategy. The current debate over the future of the international order—including predictions of the "end of history," a "clash of civilizations," a "coming anarchy," or a "borderless world"—has failed to generate agreement on what shape U.S. policy should take. However, a single overarching framework may be inappropriate for understanding today's disorderly and decentralized world. America's security no longer hangs on the success or failure of containing communism. The challenges are more diffuse and numerous. As a priority, the United States must manage its delicate relationships with Europe, Japan, Russia, and China, the other major players in world affairs. However, America's national interest also requires stability in important parts of the developing world. Despite congressional pressure to reduce or eliminate overseas assistance, it is vital that America focus its efforts on a small number of countries whose fate is uncertain and whose future will profoundly affect their surrounding regions. These are the pivotal states.

The idea of a pivotal state—a hot spot that could not only determine the fate of its region but also affect international stability—has a distinguished pedigree reaching back to the British geographer Sir Halford Mackinder in the 1900s and earlier. The classic example of a pivotal state throughout the nineteenth century was Turkey, the epicenter of the so-called Eastern Question; because of Turkey's strategic position, the disintegration of the Ottoman Empire posed a perennial problem for British and Russian policymakers.

Twentieth-century American policymakers employed their own version of a pivotal states theory. Statesmen from Eisenhower and Acheson to Nixon and Kissinger continually referred to a country succumbing to communism as a potential "rotten apple in a barrel" or a "falling domino." Although the domino theory was never sufficiently discriminative—it worsened America's strategic overextension—its core was about supporting pivotal states to prevent their fall to communism and the consequent fall of neighboring states.

Because the U.S. obsession with faltering dominoes led to questionable policies from Vietnam to El Salvador, the theory now has a bad reputation. But the idea itself—that of identifying specific countries as more important than others, for both regional stability and American interests—is sensible. The United States should adopt a discriminative policy toward the developing world, concentrating its energies on pivotal states rather than spreading its attention and resources over the globe.

Indeed, the domino theory may now fit U.S. strategic

needs better than it did during the Cold War. The new dominoes, or pivotal states, no longer need assistance against an external threat from a hostile political system; rather, the danger is that they will fall prey to internal disorder. A decade ago, when the main threat to American interests in the developing world was the possibility that nations would align with the Soviets, the United States faced a clear-cut enemy. This enemy captured the American imagination in a way that impending disorder does not. Yet chaos and instability may prove a greater and more insidious threat to American interests than communism ever was. With its migratory outflows, increasing conflict due to the breakdown of political structures, and disruptions in trade patterns, chaos undoubtedly affects bordering states. Reacting with interventionist measures only after a crisis in one state threatens an important region is simply too late. Further, Congress and the American public would likely not accept such actions, grave though the consequences might be to U.S. interests. Preventive assistance to pivotal states to reduce the chance of collapse would better serve American interests.

A strategy of rigorously discriminate assistance to the developing world would benefit American foreign policy in a number of ways. First, as the world's richest nation, with vast overseas holdings and the most to lose from global instability, the United States needs a conservative strategy. Like the British Empire in the nineteenth and early twentieth centuries, the interests of the United States lie in the status quo. Such a strategy places the highest importance on relations with the other great powers: decisions about the expansion of NATO or preserving amicable relations with Russia, China, Japan, and the major European powers must remain primary. The United States must also safeguard several special allies, such as Saudi Arabia, Kuwait, South Korea, and Israel, for strategic and domestic political reasons.

The United States has the most to lose; thus, its interests lie in the status quo.

Second, a pivotal states policy would help U.S. policymakers deal with what Sir Michael Howard, in another context, nicely described as "the heavy and ominous breathing of a parsimonious and pacific electorate." American policymakers, themselves less and less willing to contemplate foreign obligations, are acutely aware that the public is extremely cautious about and even hostile toward overseas engagements. While the American public may not reject all such commitments, it does resist intervention in areas that appear peripheral to U.S. interests. A majority also believes, without knowing the relatively small percentages involved, that foreign aid is a major drain on the federal budget and often wasted through fraud, duplication, and high operating costs. Few U.S. politicians are willing to risk unpopularity by contesting such opinions, and many Republican critics have played to this mood by attacking government policies that imply commitments abroad. Statesmen responsible for outlining U.S. foreign policy might have a better chance of persuading a majority of Congress and the American public that a policy of selective engagement is both necessary and feasible.

Finally, a pivotal states strategy might help bridge the conceptual and political divide in the national debate between "old" and "new" security issues. The mainstream in policy circles still considers new security issues peripheral; conversely, those who focus on migration, overpopulation, or environmental degradation resist the realist emphasis on power and military and political security.

In truth, neither the old nor the new approach will suffice. The traditional realist stress on military and political security is simply inadequate—it does not pay sufficient attention to the new threats to American national interests. The threats to the pivotal states are not communism or aggression but rather overpopulation, migration, environmental degradation, ethnic conflict, and economic instability, all phenomena that traditional security forces find hard to address. The "dirty" industrialization of the developing world, unchecked population growth and attendant migratory pressures, the rise of powerful drug cartels, the flow of illegal arms, the eruption of ethnic conflict, the flourishing of terrorist groups, the spread of deadly new viruses, and turbulence in emerging markets—a laundry list of newer problems—must also concern Americans, if only because their spillover effects can hurt U.S. interests.

Yet the new interpretation of security, with its emphasis on holistic and global issues, is also inadequate. Those who point to such new threats to international stability often place secondary importance (if that) on U.S. interests; indeed, they are usually opposed to invoking the national interest to further their cause. For example, those who criticized the Clinton administration in the summer of 1994 for not becoming more engaged in the Rwandan crisis paid little attention to the relative insignificance of Rwanda's stability for American interests. The universal approach common to many advocates of global environmental protection or human rights, commendable in principle, does not discriminate between human rights abuses in Haiti, where proximity and internal instability made intervention possible and even necessary, and similar abuses in Somalia, where the United States had few concrete interests.

Furthermore, the new security approach cannot make a compelling case to the American public for an internationalist foreign policy. The public does not sense the danger in environmental and demographic pressures that erode stability over an extended period, even if current policies, or lack thereof, make this erosion inexorable and at some point irreversible. Finally, the global nature of the new security threats makes it tempting to downplay national governments as a means to achieving solutions.

A pivotal states strategy, in contrast, would encourage integration of new security issues into a traditional, state-centered framework and lend greater clarity to the making of foreign policy. This integration may make some long-term consequences of the new security threats more tangible and manageable. And it would confirm the importance of working chiefly through state governments to ensure stability while addressing the new security issues that make these states pivotal.

HOW TO IDENTIFY A PIVOT

ACCORDING TO which criteria should the pivotal states be selected? A large population and an important geographical location are two requirements. Economic potential is also critical, as recognized by the U.S. Commerce Department's recent identification of the "big emerging markets" that offer the most promise to American business. Physical size is a necessary but not sufficient condition: Zaire comprises an extensive tract, but its fate is not vital to the United States.

What really defines a pivotal states is its capacity to affect regional and international stability. A pivotal state is so important regionally that its collapse would spell transboundary mayhem: migration, communal violence, pollution, disease, and so on. A pivotal state's steady economic progress and stability, on the other hand, would bolster its region's economic vitality and political soundness and benefit American trade and investment.

For the present, the following should be considered pivotal states: Mexico and Brazil; Algeria, Egypt, and South Africa; Turkey; India and Pakistan; and Indonesia. These states' prospects vary widely. India's potential for success, for example, is considerably greater than Algeria's; Egypt's potential for chaos is greater than Brazil's. But all face a precarious future, and their success or failure will powerfully influence the future of the surrounding areas and affect American interests. This theory of pivotal states must not become a mantra, as the domino theory did, and the list of states could change. But the concept itself can provide a necessary and useful framework for devising American strategy toward the developing world.

A WORLD TURNING ON PIVOTS

TO UNDERSTAND this idea in concrete terms, consider the Mexican crisis a year ago. Mexico's modernization has created strains between the central and local governments and difficulties with the unions and the poorest groups in the countryside, and it has damaged the environment. Like the other pivotal states, Mexico is delicately balanced between progress and turmoil.

Given the publicity and political debate surrounding the Clinton administration's rescue plan for Mexico, most Americans probably understood that their southern neighbor is special, even if they were disturbed by the means employed to rescue it. A collapse of the peso and the consequent ruin of the Mexican economy would have weakened the U.S. dollar, hurt exports, and caused convulsions throughout Latin America's Southern Cone Common Market and other emerging markets. Dramatically illustrating the potency of new security threats to the United States, economic devastation in Mexico would have increased the northward flow of illegal immigrants and further strained the United States' overstretched educational and social services. Violent social chaos in Mexico could spill over into this country. As many bankers remarked during the peso crisis, Mexico's troubles demonstrated the impossibility of separating "there" from "here."

Because of Mexico's proximity and its increasing links with the United States, American policymakers clearly needed to give it special attention. As evidenced by the North American Free Trade Agreement, they have. But other select states also require close American attention.

EGYPT

EGYPT'S LOCATION has historically made its stability and political alignment critical to both regional development and relationships between the great powers. In recent decades, its proximity to important oil regions and its involvement in the Arab-Israeli peace process, which is important for the prosperity of many industrialized countries, has enhanced its contribution to stability in the Middle East and North Africa. Furthermore, the government of President Muhammad Hosni Mubarak has provided a bulwark against perhaps the most significant long-term threat in the region—radical Islamic fundamentalism.

The collapse of the current Egyptian regime might damage American interests more than the Iranian revolution did. The Arab-Israeli peace process, the key plank of U.S. foreign policy in this region for the past 20 years, would suffer serious, perhaps irreparable, harm. An unstable Egypt would undermine the American diplomatic plan of isolating fundamentalist "rogue" states in the region and encourage extremist opposition to governments everywhere from Algeria to Turkey. The fall of the Mubarak government could well lead Saudi Arabia to reevaluate its pro-Western stance. Under such conditions, any replay of Operation Desert Storm or similar military intervention in the Middle East on behalf of friendly countries such as Kuwait or Jordan would be extremely difficult, if not impossible. Finally, the effect on oil and financial markets worldwide could be enormous.

Egypt's future is not only vital, but very uncertain. While some signs point to increasing prosperity and stability—birth rates have declined, the United States recently forgave $7 billion of debt, and Egypt's international reserves reached $16 billion in 1995—the preponderance of evidence paints a dimmer picture. Jealously guarding its power base and wary that further privatization would produce large numbers of resentful former state employees, the government fears losing control over the economy. Growth rates lurch fitfully upward, and although reform has improved most basic economic indicators, it has also widened the gap between rich and poor. Roughly one-third of the population now lives in poverty, up from 20–25 percent in 1990.

A harsh crackdown on fundamentalism has reduced the most serious short-term threat to the Mubarak regime, but a long-term solution may prove more elusive. The government's brutal attack on the fundamentalist movement may ultimately fuel Islam's cause by alienating the professional middle class; such a policy has already greatly strengthened the more moderate Muslim Brotherhood and radicalized the extremist fringe.

Environmental and population problems are growing. Despite the gradually decreasing birthrate, the population is increasing by about one million every nine months, straining the country's natural resources, and is forecast to reach about 94 million by 2025.

Recognizing Egypt's significance and fragility, successive U.S. administrations have made special provisions to maintain its stability. In 1995 Egypt received $2.4 billion from the U.S. government, making it the second-largest recipient of American assistance, after Israel. That allocation is primarily the result of the Camp David accords and confirms Egypt's continuing importance in U.S. Middle East policy. Current attempts by American isolationists to cut these funds should be strongly resisted. On the other hand, the U.S. government and Congress should seriously consider redirecting American aid. F-16 fighters can do little to help Egypt handle its internal difficulties, but assistance to improve infrastructure, education, and the social fabric would ease the country's troubles.

INDONESIA

WHILE EGYPT'S prospects for stability are tenuous, Indonesia's future appears brighter. By exercising considerable control over the population and the economy for the last several decades, Indonesia's authoritarian regime has engineered dramatic economic growth, now expected to be about 7 percent annually for the rest of the decade. Poverty rates have dropped drastically, and a solid middle class has emerged. At first glance, Indonesia's development has been a startling success. However, the government now confronts strains generated by its own efforts.

Along with incomes, education levels, and health status, Indonesia's population is increasing dramatically. With the fourth-largest population in the world and an extra three million people added each year, the country is projected to reach 260 million inhabitants by 2025. The main island of Java, one of the most densely populated places on earth, can scarcely accommodate the new bodies. In response, the government is forcing many citizens to migrate to other islands. This resettlement program is the focal point for a host of other tensions concerning human rights and the treatment of minorities. The government's brutal handling of the separatist movement in East Timor continues to hinder its efforts to gain international respect. President Suharto's regime has made a point of cooperating with Chinese entrepreneurs to boost economic expansion, but ethnic differences remain entrenched. Finally, the government's favoring of specific businesses has produced deep-rooted corruption.

Because of the government's tight control, it can maintain stability even while pursuing these questionable approaches to handling its people. However, as a more sophisticated middle class emerges, Indonesians are less willing to accept the existing concentration of economic and political power. These opposing forces, one for continued central control and one for more dispersed political power, will clash when Suharto leaves office, probably after the 1998 elections.

If Indonesia falls into chaos, it is hard to see its region prospering.

A reasonable scenario for Indonesia would be the election of a government that shares power more broadly, with greater respect for human rights and press freedoms. The new regime would maintain Indonesia's openness to foreign trade and investment, and it would end favoritism toward certain companies. Better educated, better paid, and urbanized for a generation, Indonesians would have fewer children per family. Indonesia would continue its leadership role in the Association of Southeast Asian Nations (ASEAN) and the Asia-Pacific Economic Cooperation forum (APEC), helping foster regional growth and stability.

The possibility remains, however, that the transfer of power in Jakarta could trigger political and economic instability, as it did in 1965 at the end of President Sukarno's rule. A new regime might find it more difficult to overawe the people while privately profiting from the economy. Elements of the electorate could lash out in frustration. Riots would then jeopardize Indonesia's growth and regional leadership, and by that stage the United States could do nothing more than attempt to rescue its citizens from the chaos.

Instability in Indonesia would affect peace and prosperity across Southeast Asia. Its archipelago stretches across key shipping lanes, its oil and other businesses attract Japanese and U.S. investment, and its stable economic condictions and open trade policies set an example for ASEAN, APEC, and the region as a whole. If Indonesia, as Southeast Asia's fulcrum, falls into chaos, it is hard to envisage the region prospering. It is equally hard to imagine general distress if Indonesia booms economically and maintains political stability.

Despite the difficulty, the United States must have a strategy for encouraging Indonesia's stability. Part of this will involve close cooperation with Japan, which is by far the largest donor to Indonesian development. A more sensitive aspect of the strategy will be encouraging the regime to respect human rights and ethnic differences. The strategy also calls for calibrated pressure on Indonesia to decrease its widespread corruption, which in any case is required to achieve the country's full integration into the international business world.

BRAZIL

BRAZIL BORDERS every country in South America except Ecuador and Chile, and its physical size, complex society, and huge population of 155 million people are more than enough to qualify it as a pivotal state.

Brazil's economy appears to be recovering from its 1980s crisis, although the indicators for the future are inconsistent. President Fernando Henrique Cardoso's proposals for economic reform, which include deregulation and increased openness to foreign investment in key industries, have advanced in Brazil's congress. Many basic social and economic indexes point to a generally improving quality of life, including the highest industrial growth since the 1970s (6.4 percent in 1994), declining birth and death rates, increasing life expectancy, and an expanding urban infrastructure. In the longer term, however, Brazil must address extreme economic inequality, poor educational standards, and extensive malnutrition. These realities, together with a burgeoning current account deficit and post-peso crisis skittishness, help diminish investor confidence.

Were Brazil to founder, the consequences from both an environmental and an economic point of view would be grave. The Amazon basin contains the largest tropical rain forest in the world, boasting unequaled biodiversity. Apart from aesthetic regrets about its destruction, the practical consequences are serious. The array of plants and trees in the Amazon is an important source of natural pharmaceuticals; deforestation may also spread diseases as the natural hosts of viruses and bacteria are displaced to other regions.

A social and political collapse would directly affect significant U.S. economic interests and American investors. Brazil's fate is inextricably linked to that of the entire South American region, a region that before its debt and inflation crises in the 1970s bought large amounts of U.S. goods and is now potentially the fastest-growing market for American business over the decades to come. In sum, were Brazil to succeed in stabilizing over the long term, reducing the massive gap between its rich and poor, further opening its markets, and privatizing often inefficient state-run industries, it could be a powerful engine for the regional economy and a stimulus to U.S. prosperity. Were it to fail, Americans would feel the consequences.

SOUTH AFRICA

APARTHEID'S END makes South Africa's transition particularly dramatic. So far, President Nelson Mandela's reconciliation government has set an inspiring example of respect for ethnic differences, good governance, and prudent nurturing of the country's economic potential. In contrast to other conflicts, in which different groups have treated each other with so much acrimony that they could not negotiate, the administration has successfully overcome some of its political divisions: it includes both former apartheid president Frederik Willem de Klerk and Zulu Chief Mangosuthu Buthelezi. Moreover, South Africa is blessed with a strong infrastructure, a sound currency, and vast natural resources. These assets make its economy larger and more vital than any other on the continent, accounting for a colossal 75 percent of the southern African region's economic output. No longer an international pariah, it is working to develop robust trade and financial links around the region and the globe. A hub for these connections, South Africa could stimulate growth throughout the southern cone of Africa.

There are indications, however, that South Africa could succumb to political instability, ethnic strife, and economic stagnation. Power-sharing at the cabinet level belies deep ethnic divisions. Any one of several fissures could collapse this collaboration, plunging the country into civil war. Afrikaner militias may grow increasingly intransigent, traditional tribal leaders could raise arms against their diminished influence, and when Mandela no longer leads the African National Congress, the party may abandon its commitment to ethnic reconciliation.

As Mandela's government struggles to improve black living standards and soothe ethnic tensions, the legacy of apartheid creates a peculiar dilemma. It will be hard to meet understandable black expectations of equity in wages, education, and health, given the country's budget deficits and unstable tax base. As racial inequalities persist, blacks are likely to grow impatient. Yet if whites feel they are paying a disproportionate share for improved services for blacks, they might flee the country, taking with them the prospects for increased foreign direct investment.

South Africa can show other ethnically tortured nations the way to democracy.

While the primary threats to South Africa's stability are internal, its effectiveness in containing them will have repercussions beyond its borders. Even before apartheid ended, South Africa had enormous influence over the region's political and economic development, from supporting insurgencies throughout the "front-line states" to providing mining jobs for migrant workers from those same countries. If South Africa achieves the economic and political potential within its grasp, it will be a wellspring of regional political stability and economic growth. If it prospers, it can demonstrate to other ethnically tortured regions a path to stability through democratization, reconciliation, and steadily increasing living standards. Alternatively, if it fails to handle its many challenges, it will suck its neighbors into a whirlpool of self-defeating conflict.

Although controlling the sea-lanes around the Cape of Good Hope would be important, especially if widespread trouble were to erupt in the Middle East, American strategic interests are not otherwise endangered in southern Africa. Yet because South Africa is the United States' largest trading partner in Africa and possesses vast economic potential, its fate would affect American trading and financial interests that have invested there. It would also destabilize key commodity prices, especially in the gold, diamond, and ore markets. More generally, instability in South Africa, as in Brazil and Indonesia, would cast a large shadow over confidence in emerging markets.

American policy toward South Africa should reflect its importance as a pivotal state. While recognizing South Africa's desire to solve its problems without external interference, the United States should promote South Africa's economic and political stability. Of $10.5 billion in American economic aid given in 1995, a mere one percent ($135 million) was for South Africa. A strategy that acknowledges this nation's importance to American interests would surely be less parsimonious.

ALGERIA AND TURKEY

ALGERIA'S geographical position makes its political future of great concern to American allies in Europe, especially France and Spain. A civil war and the replacement of the present regime by extremists would affect the security of the Mediterranean sea-lanes, international oil and gas markets, and, as in the case of Egypt, the struggle between moderate and radical elements in the Islamic world. All the familiar pressures of rapid population growth and drift to the coastal cities, environmental damage, increasing dependence on food imports, and extremely high youth unemployment are evident. Levels of violence remain high as Algerian government forces struggle to crush the Islamist guerrilla movement.

While a moderate Islamist government might prove less disturbing than the West fears, a bloody civil war or the accession of a radical, anti-Western regime would be very serious. Spain, Italy, and France depend heavily on Algerian oil and gas and would sorely miss their investments, and the resulting turbulence in the energy markets would certainly affect American consumers. The flood of middle-class, secular Algerians attempting to escape the bloodshed and enter France or other parts of southern Europe would further test immigration policies of the European Union (EU). The effects on Algeria's neighbors, Morocco and Tunisia, would be even more severe and encourage radical Islamic elements everywhere. Could Egypt survive if Algeria, Morocco, Tunisia, and Muammar al-Qaddafi's Libya collaborated to achieve fundamentalist goals? Rumors of an Algerian atomic bomb are probably premature, but the collapse of the existing regime would undoubtedly reduce security in the entire western Mediterranean. All the more reason for the United States to buttress the efforts of the International Monetary Fund and for the Europeans to improve Algeria's well-being and encourage a political settlement.

Although Turkey is not as politically or economically fragile as Algeria, its strategic importance may be even greater. At a multifold crossroads between East and West, North and South, Christendom and Islam, Turkey has the potential to influence countries thousands of miles from the Bosporus. The southeast keystone of NATO during the Cold War and an early (if repeatedly postponed) applicant to enlarged EU membership, Turkey enjoys solid economic growth and middle-class prosperity. However, it also shows many of the difficulties that worry other pivotal states: population and environmental pressures, severe ethnic minority challenges, and the revival of radical Islamic fundamentalism, all of which test the country's young democratic institutions and assumptions. There are also a slew of external problems, ranging from bitter rivalries with Greece over Cyprus, various nearby islands' territorial boundaries, and Macedonia, to the developing quarrel with Syria and Iraq over control of the Euphrates water supply, to delicate relationships with the Muslim-dominated states of Central Asia. A prosperous, democratic, tolerant Turkey is a beacon for the entire region; a Turkey engulfed by civil wars and racial and religious hatreds, or nursing ambitions to interfere abroad, would hurt American interests in innumerable ways and concern everyone from pro-NATO strategists to friends of Israel.

INDIA AND PAKISTAN

CONSIDERED separately; the challenges facing the two great states of South Asia are daunting enough. Each confronts a population surge that is forecast to take Pakistan's total (123 million in 1990) to 276 million by 2025, and India's (853 million in 1990) to a staggering 1.45 billion, thus equaling China's projected population. While such growth taxes rural environments by causing the farming of marginal lands, deforestation, and depletion of water resources, the urban population explosion is even more worrisome. With 46 percent of Pakistan's and 35 percent of India's population under 15 years old, according to 1990 census figures, tens of millions of young people enter the job market each year; the inadequate opportunities for them further strain the social fabric. All this forms an ominous backdrop to rising tensions, as militant Hindus and Muslims, together a full fifth of the population, challenge India's democratic traditions, and Islamic forces stoke nationalist passions across Pakistan.

The shared borders and deep-rooted rivalry of India and Pakistan place these pivotal states in a more precarious position than, for example, Brazil or South Africa. With three wars between them since each gained independence, each continues to arm against the other and quarrel fiercely over Kashmir, Pakistan's potential nuclear capabilities and missile programs, and other issues. This jostling fuels their mutual ethnic-cum-religious fears and could produce another bloody conflict that neither government could control. What effect a full-scale war would have on the Pakistan-China entente is hard to predict, but the impact of such a contest would likely spread from Kashmir into Afghanistan and farther afield, and Pakistan could find support in the Muslim world. For many reasons, and perhaps especially the nuclear weapons stakes, the United States has a vital interest in encouraging South Asia's internal stability and external peace.

Could this short list of important states in the developing and emerging-markets regions of the globe include others? Possibly. This selection of pivotal states is not carved in stone, and new candidates could emerge over the next decades. Having an exact list is less important than initiating a debate over why, from the standpoint of U.S. national interests, some states in the developing world are more important than others.

BETTER WISE THAN WIDE

THE UNITED STATES needs a policy toward the developing world that does not spread American energies, attention, and resources too thinly across the globe, but rejects isolationist calls to write it off. This is a realistic policy, both strategically and politically. Strategically, it would permit the United States, as the country that can make the greatest contribution to world security, to focus on supporting pivotal states. Politically, given the jaundiced view of Americans and their representatives toward overseas engagements, a strategy of discrimination is the strongest argument against an even greater withdrawal from the developing world than is now threatened.

As the above case studies suggest, each pivotal state grapples with an intricate set of interrelated problems. In such an environment, the United States has few clear-cut ways to help pivotal states succeed. Therefore, it must develop a subtle, comprehensive strategy, encompassing all aspects of American interaction with each one. Those strategies should include appropriate focusing of U.S. Agency for International Development assistance, promoting trade and investment, strengthening relationships with the country's leaders, bolstering country-specific intelligence capabilities and foreign service expertise, and coordinating the actions of government agencies that can influence foreign policy. In short, the United States must use all the resources at its disposal to buttress the stability of key states around the globe, working to prevent calamity rather than react to it. Apart from avoiding a great-power war, nothing in foreign policy could be more important.

This focus on the pivotal states inevitably means that developing states not deemed pivotal would receive diminished attention, energy, and resources. This will seem unfair to many, since each of the pivotal states examined above enjoys a higher per capita GDP than extremely poor nations like Mali and Ethiopia. Ideally, U.S. assistance to the entire developing world would significantly increase, but that will not happen soon. A pragmatic refocusing of American aid is better than nothing at all being given to the developing world, which may happen if the isolationist mood intensifies.

Such a refocusing could improve the American public's confidence that its money can be used effectively abroad. Relative to what other states give for development, the American contribution is declining. By continuing to spread those resources across a broad swath of developing countries, the United States might further diminish the impact of its assistance in many countries. In contrast, concentrating on a few pivotal states would increase American influence in them and improve the chances of convincing the public to spend resources overseas.

Current patterns of assistance to developing and emerging countries do not reflect American global security interests and in many cases seem glaringly inconsistent with U.S. strategic priorities. While conceding that by far the largest amounts of American aid will go to Israel and Egypt, is it not curious that India, like South

Africa, receives less than one percent of total U.S. assistance? Pakistan receives virtually nothing. Algeria receives nothing. Brazil is given one-fifth of the aid awarded to Bolivia. Turkey gets less than Ethiopia (although, like Egypt, Ankara is given a large amount of military assistance that is hard to explain in the post-Cold War environment). Surely this requires serious examination?

A pragmatic refocusing of aid is better than no aid at all.

In changing these patterns, diplomatic and political objections will be inevitable. Questions will arise about countries not on the list, particularly when one of them faces a crisis. Some will plead that exceptions be made for states that have been encouraged to undertake internal political changes, like Haiti, El Salvador, and the Philippines. Foreign service professionals will caution against making this strategy part of the declared policy of the United States, for that could indicate likely American reactions in a crisis. The more critics raise theme problems, the more controversial this idea will become.

However, the pivotal states strategy merits such a debate, and it is high time for such a policy discussion to begin. As Mackinder pointed out, democracies find it difficult to think strategically in times of peace. All the above-mentioned problems and reservations, far from weakening the case for helping pivotal states, point to the importance of identifying how better to order U.S. policies in different parts of the world. A debate over pivotal states would also provide a way of checking the extent to which American agencies already carry out a discriminative strategy and the degree to which they recognize that the traditional types of external threats are not the only sources of danger to countries important to U.S. interests.

Would this formula solve all of America's foreign policy challenges? By no means. Priority should always be given to managing relations with the other great powers. In view of the international convulsions of the past 10 years, who would be rash enough to predict American relations with Russia, Japan, and China a decade or more hence and the dire implications if they go badly? Yet even if those countries remain our primary concern, the developing world still needs a place in U.S. global strategy. By identifying pivotal states to Congress and the public and providing the greatest possible support to those countries, this strategy has a greater chance of coherence and predictability than vague and indiscriminate assurances of good will to all developing countries, large and small. America's concern about traditional security threats would then be joined by a heightened awareness of the newer, nonmilitary dangers to important countries in the developing world and the serious repercussions of their collapse. Whichever administration steers the United States into the next century, American priorities would be ordered, and its foreign policy toward the developing world would have a focus—that of supporting those pivotal states whose future affects the fate of much of the planet.

The Middle East Peace Process

A CRISIS OF PARTNERSHIP

Address by MADELEINE ALBRIGHT, *United States Secretary of State*
Delivered to the National Press Club, Washington, D.C., May 12, 1998

Thank you very much. I am very pleased to be here. Good afternoon. Two weeks ago, before departing for Asia and talks in London on the Middle East, I attended a dinner sponsored by Seeds of Peace. This is a group that brings young people together from all around the Middle East to learn about and from each other, to go beyond the stereotypes and to understand how much they have in common.

At that dinner, I was given a letter signed by Arab and Israeli youngsters, which I hand-delivered, in London, to Prime Minister Netanyahu and Chairman Arafat. I want to begin my remarks today by quoting from that letter: "In our history books, the Middle East has always appeared as a magnificent crossroads. Yet we have not tasted its grandness, for we are blinded by its destructive wars. We at Seeds of Peace had a taste of what it is like to co-exist peacefully. We learned to accept the fact that both sides, Arabs and Israelis, have a right to a home in this disputed holy land. We are writing this letter as people who have experienced peace temporarily and we enjoyed the taste, but we want the whole pie. However, this is up to you. It is up to you to shape or build our future."

That is a part of the letter that I delivered.

I would have liked very, very much to have been able to return to the United States this past weekend with the news that the prayers of those young people had been answered and that a new milestone in the Middle East peace process had been reached. It was our hope that this week would have marked the start of permanent status negotiations between Prime Minister Netanyahu and Chairman Arafat, hosted by President Clinton.

Unfortunately, despite exhaustive and exhausting efforts to remove them, there remain obstacles to an agreement that would allow those permanent status talks to begin. However, I look forward to meeting with Prime Minister Netanyahu here in Washington tomorrow to see if it is possible to clear the way.

Today, I want to do two things. First, on behalf of President Clinton, I want to reaffirm America's commitment to the pursuit of Arab-Israeli peace and our determination to continue exploring every possible avenue for helping the parties to achieve it. We do this because it is in our interest and because it is right. The peoples of the Middle East deserve a future free from terror and violence, a future in which they can prosper in security and peace.

Second, I want to explain the logic of our approach and provide some perspective about what we have been doing in recent months to overcome the impasse that has developed in Israeli-Palestinian negotiations.

The past year has been the most disappointing since the Oslo Accords were signed in 1993. It was 16 months ago that active U.S. mediation helped to produce an agreement on Hebron. Since then, a crisis of confidence has arisen between Israelis and Palestinians that has stalled progress at the bargaining table and put at risk both historic accomplishments and future hopes.

In only two years, we have gone from a situation where Israel had some form of peace negotiation, relationship, or promising contact with every Arab state except Iraq and Libya to a stalemate which has eroded regional cooperation on issues such as water, economic integration, the environment and refugees, stalled Arab-Israeli contacts, and caused optimism to be replaced by a sense of fatalism and helplessness about the future.

At the root of the stalemate is a crisis of partnership between Israelis and Palestinians wherein short term tactical considerations have too often trumped broader understandings of common interest and cooperation. Indeed, we have gone from a situation where no problem was too big to solve to a situation where every issue is argued about. We have seen tragic incidents of terror, unilateral actions and provocative rhetoric undermine the historic accomplishments of the Israeli-Palestinian negotiations.

For more than a year now, the United States has been working hard to revive the missing spirit of partnership. We have been trying literally to restore the ability of the parties to talk constructively with each other, to overcome mistrust, to solve problems, to arrive at agreements and to implement obligations.

Early last year, we were approached by Prime Minister Netanyahu with an idea for reorienting the process. He argued that the confidence building period provided for under the Oslo Accords had begun, instead, to destroy confidence; and he was right. The Prime Minister argued that it therefore made sense to move directly into final status negotiations, and to do so on an accelerated timetable. He asked President Clinton to help achieve this purpose; and as Israel's ally and friend, the President decided to try to do so.

Beginning last spring and throughout the summer of 1997, we sought an agreement that would put the process back on track by focusing the parties on the importance of getting to permanent status talks. In August, I proposed in a speech here in Washington that the parties "marry the incremental approach of the interim agreement ... to an accelerated approach to permanent status."

Then, last September the Israelis and Palestinians agreed on a four-part agenda that included accelerated permanent status talks and three other issues: security with the emphasis on pre-empting and fighting terror; the further redeployment of Israeli troops; and a time-out on unhelpful unilateral steps. There followed several months of intensive discussions on that agenda, along with resumed negotiations on key interim issues.

During this period there was some narrowing in the differences between the parties, but very substantial gaps remained. Despite our efforts, we could not get the Israelis and Palestinians to agree to an accord. Both urged us, nevertheless, to persist and to help them find a way to bridge their differences. By early this year we had come to the conclusion that even if the parties could not be responsive to each other's ideas, they might respond to ours. Working closely and quietly with both sides, we began to share our views on how the parties might resolve their differences over the four-part agenda.

In January, here in Washington, President Clinton met with Prime Minister Netanyahu and Chairman Arafat. And I met with them when I traveled to the region in February, and then again in Europe in March. Ambassador Ross and Israeli and Palestinian negotiators have been in almost constant contact. Throughout, we continued to urge the parties to sort out the issues directly with each other.

Unfortunately, none of these discussions produced sufficient results. It was clear that tough decisions were required if Israelis and Palestinians were to reach an agreement that neither side was prepared to make.

Having worked since January to share our thoughts informally with the parties at the highest level, it was logical that we should at some point share a more fully integrated set of ideas in an effort to facilitate decisions. We took this step not because we wanted to, but because there seemed no other way to break the dangerous logjam that had developed.

Our ideas stemmed from intensive consultations with both sides and take into account both the obligations each side has accepted and the vital interests each must protect. They are balanced, flexible, practical and reasonable. They are based on the principle of reciprocity — another concept stressed by Prime Minister Netanyahu and embraced by us because of our belief that parallel implementation of each side's obligations is the only way to restore the partnership between Israelis and Palestinians.

In presenting our ideas, we made it clear that we were offering them as suggestions, not as an ultimatum or an effort to impose a settlement. Both parties have their own decision-making processes and interests, which we respect. Our purpose was only, in response to the parties' request, to help them find the way forward.

The role of the mediator is never an easy one. The challenge is how to meet the needs of both sides in a way that is acceptable to the other. Logically, that presents both sides with the need to be flexible and to make decisions that reflect the concerns not just of one party, but of two. In this regard, our ideas were designed to find that balance and to persuade each side that the balance could be struck in a way that addressed their particular requirements.

Now, let me try to explain our approach as it relates to addressing Israel's requirements, foremost of which is security. Let me say at the outset that there should be no doubt about the commitment of the Clinton Administration or of America to Israel's security. That commitment is unshakable and has been demonstrated over and over again, not only in words but in actions; in our joint struggle against terrorism; in the assistance to Israel that the American people have so long and so generously provided; and in the steps we have taken to ensure Israel's qualitative military edge.

These include providing Israel with the F-15-I, the most advanced fighter aircraft in the American arsenal; the pre-positioning of American military stocks and material in Israel for possible joint use; and jointly-funded research and development projects designed to enhance Israel's ability to protect itself against long range missiles and Katyusha rockets. And let me add that our commitment to Israel's security does not come with a time limit. There is no expiration date. It will continue today, tomorrow and for as long as the sun shall rise. I said that in Israel last year and I meant it. And that's true whether there is progress in the Middle East peace process or not — or whether we have differences with Israel at a particular moment or not.

At the same time, we have agreed with Israeli leaders from Prime Minister Ben Gurion to Begin and from Rabin to Netanyahu that the key to long term security for the Israeli people lies in lasting peace. That is why we have been working so hard to resolve the present impasse. In so doing, we would not for a minute assert for ourselves the right to determine Israel's security needs. That is — and must remain — an Israeli prerogative.

Moreover, both in our ideas and in the way we presented them, we took fully into account Israeli concerns both about process and substance. For example, we have given the parties many weeks to consider our ideas in private. We did not launch a public campaign on their behalf. And in response primarily to Israeli requests, we allowed more time and then more time and then more time for our suggestions to be studied, considered and discussed.

Moreover, the ideas we presented posed some very difficult choices for the Palestinians. They were required to make substantial changes in their negotiating position. Nevertheless, Chairman Arafat agreed to our ideas in principle.

The real centerpiece of our efforts to address Israeli requirements focused on dealing with Israel's fundamental and legitimate security concerns. It was no coincidence that security was the first point on our four-point agenda. Creating the right environment for negotiations had as its focus the issue of ensuring that Israeli-Palestinian security cooperation was functioning at 100 percent, and that Palestinians were exerting 100 percent effort to take effective unilateral steps against terror. That's why our ideas on security create a structure to ensure that the fight against terror will not be episodic, but that it endures.

From the beginning, we have made the security issue the center of our dialogue with the Palestinians. We have pressed them to understand that the fight against terror is a basic Palestinian interest. And what we have seen, especially over the past several months, is a concerted Palestinian effort — even in the absence of an agreement with Israel on the four-part agenda — against those who would threaten peace with terror and violence. The Palestinian Authority deserves credit for taking on such groups, but it is essential as they do that others in the region who tell us they support peace refrain from greeting with cordial hospitality and financial backing the enemies of peace.

Our suggestions for Israeli redeployments were also formulated with Israel's prerogatives and concerns in mind. We recognize, as reflected in the Christopher letter, that further redeployment is an Israeli responsibility under Oslo, rather than an issue to be negotiated. But it is in the nature of partnership that Israel should take Palestinian concerns into account, while following the terms of its agreement. Otherwise, the peace process cannot move forward.

In presenting our ideas, we did not define the areas from which Israel should redeploy. Our ideas placed a premium on Israel retaining overall security responsibility in the areas affected by the proposed redeployment. And our suggestion about the size of the next redeployment came down far closer to Israel's position than to that of the Palestinians.

Why did we suggest a size? Because that is the only way to reach the agreement on launching permanent status talks that Prime Minister Netanyahu asked us to achieve. In presenting

12. Middle East Peace Process

and discussing our ideas, we have acted with discretion and patience. Because we realize the difficulty of the decisions the parties were being asked to make, we have gone the extra mile — in fact, the extra 20,000 miles, back and forth across the Atlantic many times. And we have done so without complaint, because America will always go the extra mile for peace.

I want to mention at this point also that America's commitment to peace and security in the Middle East has historically been a bipartisan commitment, stretching from the administrations of Truman and Eisenhower to Bush and Clinton. Because that commitment involves the security of a cherished ally and the vital strategic interests of the United States, our leaders have historically stood together in support of Israel, and shoulder to shoulder with our Arab friends in pursuit of peace. If America is to play its proper role in promoting stability in the Middle East, it is imperative that our leaders now — in the Executive Branch, in Congress, and within the Jewish-American and Arab-American communities — continue to work together on behalf of shared goals.

Tomorrow, I will meet with Prime Minister Netanyahu again, and I very much look forward to the meeting. We are working hard to overcome differences and I hope we will be able to make progress.

But the key point that I have been emphasizing to both Israeli and Palestinian leaders is that although America remains committed to the pursuit of peace, it is up to them — not to us— whether peace is achieved.

Over the past months, we have played the role of mediator, counselor, friend, shuttler, cajoler and idea-maker. We have responded whenever called at literally any time of the day or night. We have done this because we care about Israel and its people; and we care about the Palestinians and Arabs; and we care about the future peace and stability of the region.

We are not giving any ultimatums, and we're not threatening any country's security. We are not trying to make any party suffer at the expense of another. All we are trying to do is find the path to peace, as the parties have repeatedly urged us to do. And what we have especially been trying to do in recent weeks is to issue a wake-up call. The leaders of the region have reached a crossroads. Act before it is too late. Decide before the peace process collapses. And understand that in a neighborhood as tough as the Middle East, there is no security from hard choices, and no lasting security without hard choices.

The parties must understand, as well, that there is urgency to this task. For time is no longer an ally of this process; it has become an adversary. The historic accomplishments that flowed from the Oslo process represented a strategic opportunity for peace that is now being put at risk. Consider that just two years ago, at Sharm al-Sheikh, representatives from Israel and a host of Arab states gathered at the Summit of the Peacemakers to say no to terror and yes to peace. They saw Israel as a partner. Unfortunately, that exhilarating sense of partnership has been lost.

Second, the very idea that negotiations can peacefully resolve the Arab-Israeli conflict is now under threat. Unless the leaders are willing to make hard choices, the field will be left to extremists who have no interest in peace.

Third, the clock continues to tick. The interim period under Oslo concludes on May 4, 1999 — less than a year from now. Those who believe that drifting is acceptable, or who believe they can declare unilateral positions or take unilateral acts when the interim period ends, are courting disaster. Both sides must understand that the issues reserved for permanent status discussions —including the status of the West Bank and Gaza and of settlements — can only be settled by negotiation. That was the spirit and logic of Oslo.

America's interest and goal is a comprehensive Arab-Israeli peace based on U.N. Security Council Resolutions 242 and 338, including the principle of land for peace. That will require decisive progress on all tracks, including the Israel-Lebanon track and the Israel-Syria track.

We are not a party to the negotiations. As President Clinton has repeatedly emphasized, it is not our right, nor our intention, nor is it within our capacity, to dictate terms or impose a settlement. At the same time, our credibility and interests are indeed affected by what the Israelis, Palestinians and Arabs do or fail to do. We are prepared to support their efforts as long as we judge they are serious about wanting to reach an agreement — and serious enough to make the decisions necessary to achieve it.

For too long, too many children in too many parts of the Middle East have grown up amidst violence, deprivation and fear. Too many lives have been cut short by the terrorist's bomb, the enemy's shell and the assassin's bullet. Too many opportunities have been lost to heal old wounds, narrow differences and transform destructive conflict into constructive cooperation.

Everyone with a stake in the Middle East has an obligation to do what can be done to seize the strategic opportunity for peace that now exists, and thereby to make possible a future of stability and prosperity for all the people of the region.

The United States believes this kind of future is within our grasp. But the peoples of the region will not realize that future if their leaders do not reach out with a vision as great as the goal to overcome past grievances, treat neighbors as partners and undertake in good faith the hard work of cooperation and peace. All that is required is for each to accord dignity and accept responsibility, and to act not out of passion and fear, but out of reason and hope.

For the peoples of the region who have suffered too long, the path out of the wilderness is uphill, but clearly marked. The time has come now, before the dusk obscures the guideposts, to move up that road; and by so doing, to answer the too-long denied prayers of the children — all the children — of the Middle East.

Thank you very much.

Africa, the 'Invisible Land,' Is Gaining Visibility

Clinton's visit may signal a new relationship based on mutual national interests

By Salih Booker

The ancestors of at least one-tenth of the American population came to America in slave ships from Africa. The continent is three times the size of the United States, represents one-quarter of the earth's land mass and is home to 53 sovereign nations and some 800 million people. Yet, in the 222 years of U.S. history, no American president had ever made an extensive visit to Africa until President Clinton did.

The continent, like Ralph Ellison's "Invisible Man," has been the invisible land. Indeed, American perceptions of Africa often have had little to do with African realities and everything to do with the projection of our fears, fantasies, racism and ignorance onto the enormous canvas that is Africa.

As President Clinton pointed out in his speech in Uganda, the cardinal sin in American relations with Africa has been that of neglect. Thus his 11-day, six-nation tour of sub-Saharan Africa—with stops in Ghana, Uganda, Rwanda, South Africa, Botswana and Senegal—is truly historic. It may also mark the beginning of a new era of cooperation with Africa based on mutual respect and mutual interests.

The president's visit to Africa certainly was based firmly on America's national interests. The increase of stability and the spread of democracy there are creating new opportunities for trade and greater participation by Africa in global affairs.

At the same time, the administration has at last assembled the ingredients of the United States' first real Africa policy, intended to move Africa from the back of the bus of the foreign policy agenda.

The new Africa policy will promote greater private business involvement in Africa, trade incentives conditional on democratic political change and military cooperation to produce a collective African peacekeeping force. Unfortunately, absent are additional funds for development and for the relief of the debts of African nations, a willingness to commit U.S. troops for peacekeeping on the continent and specific efforts to support democratic movements in crucial countries such as Nigeria and Sudan.

It may surprise some Americans—who have noticed only the tragedies in Rwanda and Burundi—but this is the most promising period for Africa since the heyday of African independence 40 years ago. Although the continent's continuing problems should not be understated, in just the past eight years Africa has celebrated the independence of Namibia and Eritrea; an end to war in Ethiopia, Mozambique and Liberia; a peace agreement in Angola; and of course, an inspiring transition to democratic majority rule in South Africa.

Several despots hang on, but their days are probably numbered. Elections have swept away one-party systems or long-standing dictatorships in Zambia, Malawi and Ivory Coast, with 26 African states conducting presidential elections in the past two years. The emergence of a strengthened civil society and the incorporation of women in positions of power are also helping to create the conditions in which governments can be held accountable by the people.

On the economic front, more than two-thirds of African countries are implementing reform policies that emphasize growth, private-sector development and greater openness to the global economy. Aggregate growth rates for these 35 reforming countries have averaged around 5 percent over the past three years.

America has just begun to recognize the opportunity for doing business with Africa. U.S. trade with the 12 nations of southern Africa alone is greater than U.S. trade with the 15 independent states of the former Soviet Union combined, while trade with South Africa is greater than U.S. trade with all of Eastern Europe.

The Clinton administration has benefited from a sharper focus on Africa over the past three years by Congress, which has been working with indefatigable nongovernmental human-rights, development and relief organizations to produce a trade liberalization bill called the African Growth and Opportunity Act. It passed the House on March 11, just in time for Clinton's travels. The legislation promotes freer trade with sub-Saharan Africa, based on eligibility criteria that include market reforms and respect for human rights.

Last year, the Clinton administration, needing something to take to the G-8 summit of industrialized nations in Denver where Africa was to figure prominently on the agenda, embraced the Africa trade bill and announced the President's Partnership for Growth and Opportunity in Africa. This effort is aimed at opening up U.S. markets to more African goods, creating a high-level annual forum for discussing economic issues with African partners and instituting federally insured investment funds for Africa.

The legislation gave rise to an important debate regarding the right mix of assistance, debt reduction and trade needed to promote investments for economic development in Africa, and to a consensus that Africa's recovery will require all of these types of economic engagement. The president has made passage one of his top legislative foreign policy priorities.

In 1996, the administration, without African consultation, hastily unveiled a plan for training peacekeepers in a handful of African armies under an "Africa Crisis Response Initiative." This has now been recast as a program offering communications equipment and military training to help several countries develop rapidly deployable peacekeeping units that could respond to crises as a combined force. The motivation for a crisis-response initiative came from a desire to avoid new U.S. military commitments in Africa following the 1992 debacle in Somalia, and a simultaneous concern that the conflict in Burundi might produce a crisis on the scale of the genocide in Rwanda. The White House feared a scenario in Africa where the only options would be U.S. intervention or no intervention.

Though many political questions have been left unanswered, the initiative represents a new framework for cooperation on security and conflict resolution that even its critics welcome.

THE FINAL ELEMENT OF THE NEW POLICY FRAMEwork is the development of a coherent approach to democratization and human rights in Africa. The appointment last year of the Rev. Jesse Jackson to the post of special envoy for the promotion of democracy in Africa is part of this effort, though it seemed to result more from domestic political considerations than a thorough review of the requirements for promoting democracy in Africa.

Indeed, Jackson's first trip in December to Kenya and Zambia was widely criticized for its perceived embrace of the heads of both states at a moment when they were resisting pressure to reform from democratic forces in their countries. His second trip in February to Kenya, Congo and Liberia, demonstrated a far more visible commitment to supporting pro-democracy groups. Initially considered a potential liability by Africa policymakers and human-rights groups, the special envoy is now viewed as an asset.

That the White House failed to integrate these efforts into a creative new Africa policy before Clinton's trip is partly the result of the happenstance manner in which they emerged. It was also a reminder that Africa's sheer size and diversity require an approach tailored to specific countries and regions rather than one that lumps them together.

The new initiatives for Africa as a whole provide a framework for the administration. But it will need to pursue it differently in each of Africa's five subregions—Southern, West, Central, Eastern and Northern—with a special eye on the key countries of South Africa, Nigeria, Congo, Kenya, Sudan and Algeria.

In the context of this new debate on where the United States should concentrate in Africa, suggestions have tended to emphasize partnerships with "successfully reforming states" and/or with states whose leaders are considered to represent the new generation of African leaders, such as Ethiopia or Uganda.

These approaches are more opportunistic than strategic. The administration needs to consider the subregional context within which states are seeking to make economic and political progress. There is significant agreement among those closest to events on the ground that subregional cooperation will be crucial to the success of any new chapter in African affairs.

South Africa's new roles as an engine for economic growth in southern Africa, an anchor for security cooperation and a leader on issues of democracy and human rights demonstrate the importance of one key nation's influence in supporting positive change regionally.

Without this refinement, various new U.S. initiatives may miss opportunities now emerging, or fail to solve problems in key countries that threaten to undermine the progress being achieved by their neighbors.

The real work must now begin. Acknowledging the critical need for greater development cooperation and debt reduction to help African nations create an attractive environment for trade and investment, Clinton will need to secure more money from Congress and get the trade bill enacted if he is to "walk the talk" that he offered in Africa.

There are already constituencies in the United States that care about Africa and can help provide the political support needed for these new initiatives. Among them, and not mutually exclusive, are newly interested businesses, non-government development and human-rights organizations, environmentalists, churches and labor. And central to the effort will be the mobilization of the African American community.

By changing the generally uninformed mind-set of Americans about Africa, Clinton's trip could broaden the base further by engaging the public at large in the African renaissance.

Salih Booker is a senior fellow and director of the Africa Studies Program at the Council on Foreign Relations.

Unit 3

Unit Selections

The Public, Public Opinion, and the Media
The Role of American Values

14. **The Common Sense,** John Mueller
15. **Netanyahu and American Jews,** Jonathan Broder
16. **On American Principles,** George F. Kennan
17. **Globalization: The Great American Non-Debate,** Alan Tonelson

Key Points to Consider

❖ Should policymakers listen to the U.S. public in making foreign policy decisions? Defend your answer.

❖ What types of issues are the American public most informed about?

❖ In what ways is U.S. foreign policy true to traditional American values? How did these values apply during the cold war? What role should American values play in making foreign policy?

❖ What is the most effective way for Americans to express their views to policymakers on foreign policy?

❖ Does global involvement threaten to destroy American national unity? If so, what steps might be taken to prevent this from happening?

DUSHKIN ONLINE Links

www.dushkin.com/online/

10. **Carnegie Endowment for International Peace**
    http://www.ceip.org/
11. **RAND**
    http://www.rand.org/

These sites are annotated on pages 4 and 5.

The Domestic Side of American Foreign Policy

Conventional political wisdom holds that foreign policy and domestic policy are two very different policy arenas. Not only are the origins of and gravity of the problems different, but the political rules for seeking solutions are dissimilar. Where partisan politics, lobbying, and the weight of public opinion are held to play legitimate roles in the formulation of health, education, or welfare policy, they are seen as corrupting influences in the making of foreign policy. An effective foreign policy demands a quiescent public, one that gives knowledgeable professionals the needed leeway to bring their expertise to bear on the problem. It demands a Congress that unites behind presidential foreign policy doctrines rather than one that investigates failures or pursues its own agenda. In brief, if American foreign policy is to succeed, politics must stop "at the water's edge."

This conventional wisdom has never been shared by all who write on American foreign policy. Two very different groups of scholars have dissented from this inclination to neglect the importance of domestic influences on American foreign policy. One group holds that the essence of democracy lies in the ability of the public to hold policymakers accountable for their decisions, and therefore that elections, interest group lobbying, and other forms of political expression are just as central to the study of foreign policy as they are to the study of domestic policy. A second group of scholars sees domestic forces as important because it is the fundamental nature of a society that determines a country's foreign policy. These scholars direct their attention to studying the influence of such forces as capitalism, American national style, and the structure of elite values.

The debate over how much emphasis to accord domestic influences in the study of American foreign policy went largely unresolved during the cold war, with all sides able to maintain the essential correctness of their position. One of the most visible signs that American foreign policy is undergoing important changes in the post–cold war era is the amount of attention now being given to domestic forces. The altered agenda of the post–cold war era breathed new life into this debate and refocused attention on the domestic side of American foreign policy. Today it seems quite natural to include a discussion of interest groups, public opinion, elections, the nature of American values, and the media in any accounting of American foreign policy.

This certainly has been the case in the Clinton administration. Such diverse first-term policy initiatives as support for the North American Free Trade Agreement (NAFTA), proposing to end the ban on gays in the military, the reluctance to act in Bosnia, and the perceived need to act in Haiti were all influenced by considerations of domestic politics. Many contend that a similar pattern is emerging in the second Clinton administration. NATO expansion and involvement in the Irish peace talks are linked to a desire to court ethnic votes in this country, and the retaliatory bombing for terrorist attacks on U.S. embassies in Africa came just days after Clinton admitted having a relationship with Monica Lewinsky.

What is not yet clear is which of these public voices will be the loudest or what they will say. Some fear that rather than serving as a check on policymakers or ensuring that their decisions are in accordance with the will of the American people, domestic forces may stampede policymakers into undertaking rash actions, bring about abrupt shifts in the direction of American foreign policy, or forestall any type of change. Because of these uncertainties, debate continues over whether the increased prominence of domestic factors in formulating American foreign policy is to be applauded or condemned.

The readings in this section provide us with an overview of the ways in which U.S. domestic politics and American foreign policy interact. The first set of articles highlights the growing influence of the public voice in making foreign policy. In "The Common Sense," John Mueller presents 10 propositions regarding public attitudes toward foreign policy. Then, Jonathan Broder, in "Netanyahu and American Jews," provides us with insight into the activities of one of America's most powerful ethnic lobbying groups. His article examines the divisive effect that Netanyahu's leadership has had on the American Jewish community and what that means for American foreign policy.

The second set of readings focuses on the enduring influence that American values have on U.S. foreign policy. George F. Kennan, one of the leading architects of containment, asserts that the best way for the United States to help small states is to lead by the power of example. Finally, Alan Tonelson, in "Globalization: The Great American Non-Debate," examines the extent to which globalization could threaten America's future as a cohesive and successful society. He asserts that the trend toward globalization of production could represent the greatest challenge to American unity since the Civil War.

The Common Sense

John Mueller

A FEW YEARS ago international politics experienced the functional equivalent of World War III, only without the bloodshed. In a remarkably short time, virtually all the major problems that haunted international affairs for a half century were solved. The Cold War evaporated, the attendant arms race was reversed, intense disagreement over Eastern Europe and the division of Germany was resolved, and the threat of expansionist international communism simply withered away. In the wake of this quiet cataclysm, we have entered an extraordinary new era: If we apply conventional standards, the leading countries are today presented at the international level with minor, immediate problems and major long-range ones—but no major immediate problems or threats.

Some international relations scholars and writers have been trying, at times a trifle desperately, to refashion constructs and theories originally designed for an era with compelling threats to fit one that lacks them. Despite their efforts, however, a policy consensus seems to be emerging among those who actually carry out international affairs in the leading countries. It stresses as a primary goal economic enrichment through open markets and freer trade (rather than through empire or triumph in war as in days of old); it allows for the inclusion into the club of those less developed countries that are able to get their acts together; and it seeks cooperatively to alleviate troubles in other parts of the world if this can be done at low cost (particularly in lives), and to isolate and contain those troubles that cannot be so alleviated.

In this new world dominated by unthreatened wealth seekers, public opinion will play its role in U.S. foreign policy, and as always it will be an important one. Many have rued this condition, George Kennan famously among them, but looked at over time, the general sense of the American public on core issues of foreign policy has often been rather coherent and reasonable—sometimes more so than that shown by the country's elites.

There is a considerable cache of good data about public opinion on foreign policy, some of it sufficiently consistent in design over time to show reliable patterns.[1] Such data do not, of course, announce their own interpretations, but their meaning can be teased out. Based on extensive analysis of this data—but without drowning the narrative in a half ton of documentary footnotes—I offer here ten proposi-

---

John Mueller is professor of political science at the University of Rochester. Among his books are *Retreat From Doomsday: The Obsolescence of Major War* (Basic Books, 1989), and *Policy and Opinion in the Gulf War* (University of Chicago Press, 1994).

[1] Huge quantities of public opinion survey results—hundreds of thousands of questions going back to the 1930s—are stored, and readily available for research, at such organizations as the Roper Public Opinion Research Center at the University of Connecticut.

tions about American public opinion that bear important implications for the practice of foreign policy in our new era. Some of these propositions will strike many readers as obvious, others may seem counterintuitive—but not necessarily to the same readers.

1 Two facts are central: The public pays little attention to international affairs, and nothing much can be done about it; this, however, does not mean that Americans have become, or are becoming, isolationist.

Even in an age in which international interdependence is supposedly increasing by the minute, Americans principally focus on domestic matters. From time to time their attention can be diverted by major threats, or by explicit, specific, and dramatic dangers to American lives. But once these troubles vanish from the scene, the public returns to domestic concerns with considerable alacrity. So strong is the evidence on this score that it must be accepted as a fact of life that no amount of elite cajoling or uses of the bully pulpit will ever change.

According to the data, over the last sixty years the few events that have notably caused the public to divert its attention from domestic matters include the Second World War, the Korean War, the Vietnam War, and certain Cold War crises before 1963. Also included in this list, fleetingly at least, were the Iran hostage crisis of 1979-80, perhaps embellished by concern over the Soviet invasion of Afghanistan; the apparent prospect in the early to mid-1980s of nuclear war; and the Gulf War. That's about it; at no time since the 1968 Tet Offensive have foreign policy concerns outweighed domestic ones in the public eye—even in the midst of the Gulf War.

Nevertheless, the data suggest that the public has not become newly isolationist—it is about as accepting of involvement in foreign affairs as ever. That the American public has been able to contain its enthusiasm for sending American troops to police such trouble spots as Bosnia and Haiti does not mean that it has turned isolationist. Americans were willing, at least at the outset, to send troops to die in Korea and Vietnam because they subscribed to the view that communism was a genuine and serious threat to the United States that needed to be stopped wherever it was advancing. But polls from the time make clear that they had little interest in risking American lives simply to help out beleaguered South Koreans or South Vietnamese. Moreover, poll questions designed directly to measure isolationism find little change in the wake of the Cold War. In other words, the public does not pay much attention to foreign affairs most of the time, but it seems ready to care about foreign affairs if there is a clear, obvious reason to do so. This trait has been fairly consistent over many years.

2 The public undertakes a fairly sensible cost-benefit accounting when evaluating foreign affairs and, not unreasonably, the key to its definition of cost is the high value it places on American lives.

Public opinion analysis generally supports the proposition that the American people will tolerate a substantial loss of American lives if the enemy is seen to be powerful and set on jeopardizing vital American interests. But the notion that Americans should die to police a small, distant, perennially troubled, and unthreatening place has always proved difficult to sell. Nor has it been possible to generate much support for the notion that American lives should be put at risk in order to encourage democracy abroad.

After Pearl Harbor the American public had no difficulty accepting the necessity, and the human costs, of confronting the threats posed by Germany and Japan. And after the war, it came to accept international communism as a similar source of threat and was willing to support military action to combat it. However, as the Cold War's hot wars progressed in Korea and Vietnam, the data show clearly that the public undertook a continuing reevaluation of these premises, and, as it did, misgivings mounted. The data also suggest that these misgivings were primarily a function of cumulating American casualties, not of television coverage and, in the case of Vietnam, definitely not of antiwar protest.

Policy in the Gulf War was subject to a similar calculus. Many Americans bought George Bush's notion that it was worth some American lives—perhaps one or two thousand, far lower than in Korea or Vietnam—to turn back Saddam Hussein's aggression in Kuwait. But it is clear from poll data that support for the effort would have eroded quickly if significant casualties had been suffered.

While the public's concern about American lives often seems nuanced, there are times when it becomes so obsessive, so unreasonable by some standards, that policy may suffer in consequence. In the case of Vietnam, public opinion essentially supported the war until American prisoners-of-war held by Hanoi were returned; after that burden was eased, the weight of growing misgivings overtook any inclination to press on. Although some might question the wisdom of continuing a war costing thousands of lives to gain the return of a few hundred prisoners, it would be difficult to exaggerate the political potency of this issue. In a May 1971 poll, 68 percent agreed that U.S. troops should be withdrawn from Vietnam by the end of the year. However, when asked if they approved of withdrawal "even if it threatened [not *cost*] the lives or safety of United States POWs held by North Vietnam", support for withdrawal plummeted to 11 percent.

The emotional attachment to prisoners-of-war has been a recurring theme in the politics of U.S. military interventions. It was central to the lengthy and acrimonious peace talks in Korea, and outrage at the fate of American POWs on Bataan probably generated as much hatred for the Japanese during the Second World War as the attack on Pearl Harbor. Saddam Hussein's decision to parade captured American pilots on television early in the Gulf War ranks among his many major blunders. The preoccupation with hostages held by Iran during the crisis of 1979-81, and after that the fate of a few abducted Americans in Lebanon—a concern that helped to generate the Iran-Contra scandal—are also cases in point.

On the other hand, Americans seem quite insensitive to casualties suffered by foreigners, including foreign civilians. During the Gulf War Americans displayed little animosity toward the Iraqi people. However, the available data show that this view did not translate into sympathy for Iraqi casualties. Extensive coverage of civilian deaths in an attack on a Baghdad bomb shelter had no effect on attitudes toward U.S. bombing policy. Similarly, images of the "highway of death", and early postwar reports that 100,000 Iraqi soldiers had died in the war (a figure too high probably by a factor of more than ten), scarcely dampened the enthusiasm of the various "victory" parades and celebrations.[2]

These basic characteristics of American opinion are also illustrated by the public response to the international mission to Somalia in 1992-93. American policy there has been labeled a "failure" because, although tens and probably hundreds of thousands of foreign lives were saved, a few Americans were killed in the process. In essence, when Americans asked themselves how many American lives peace in Somalia was worth, the answer was rather close to zero.

3 The public's attitudes on foreign affairs are set much more by the objective content of the issue and by the position of major policymakers (including the political opposition) than by the media.

The media are not so much agenda setters as purveyors and entrepreneurs of tantalizing information and, like any other entrepreneur, they are susceptible to market forces. If they give an issue big play, it may arrest attention for a while, but this is no guarantee the issue will "take." As with any business enterprise, media moguls follow up on those proffered items that stimulate their customers' interest. In that very important sense, the media does not set the agenda, the public does.

Concern about the Ethiopian famine of the mid-1980s, for example, is often taken to have been media-generated since it was only after the problem received prominent play that it entered the public's agenda. However, the media were at first reluctant to cover the issue because they saw African famine as a dog-bites-man story. Then NBC television decided to buck the consensus and do a three-day sequence on it, and this in turn inspired a huge public response, whereupon NBC gave the crisis extensive follow-up coverage while its television and print competitors scrambled to get on the bandwagon. There is a sense, of course, in which it could be said that NBC put the issue on the public's agenda. But the network is constantly doing three-day stories, and this one just happened to catch on, to strike a responsive chord. It seems more accurate, then, to say that NBC put the item on display—alongside a great many others—and

---

[2] On Iraqi casualties, see my essay, "The Perfect Enemy", *Security Studies* (Autumn 1995).

that it was the public that found it there, picked it out, and took it home.

4 The "CNN effect" is vastly exaggerated. It follows from the above that the argument that television pictures set the public's agenda and policy mood—the so-called CNN effect—is hard to credit. This effect is usually taken to mean that televised images can cause intense interest where there might otherwise be none, and that such interest can have important effects on policy. Sometimes this might be the case, but, on balance, the CNN effect is exaggerated, and some interpretations of it seem well off the mark.

Essentially, believers in the CNN effect contend that people are so unimaginative that they react only when they see something visualized. However, Americans were outraged and quickly mobilized over the Pearl Harbor attack months before they saw any pictures of the event. Less obvious but more important, the Vietnam War was not noticeably more unpopular than the Korean War for the period in which the wars produced comparable American casualties, despite the fact that the later war was a "television war", while the earlier one was fought during that medium's infancy.

The conventional wisdom about the CNN effect amounts to a triumph of myth over matter. After all, for years we were deluged by pictures of horrors in Bosnia and, while these pictures may have influenced the opinion of some editorial writers and columnists, there was remarkably little public demand to send American troops over to fix the problem. Nor did poignant and memorable pictures inspire a surging public demand to do much of anything about Rwanda or Haiti. The reason, it would seem from the data, is disarmingly simple: Whatever the pictures showed, the public saw no serious threat to American security in either of these cases that could justify risking American lives.

On those rare occasions when pictures have—or seem to have—an impact, as over Ethiopia in the mid-1980s, observers eagerly note the fact. But when pictures fail to have an impact, the same observers fail to notice *that* fact—or come up with tortured accountings to explain the media's lack of impact. This slippery process is nicely illustrated by the case of the journalist Jack Germond.

As the Haitian crisis was heating up in 1994, Germond pointedly noted that "We're seeing the coverage of children starving and ill and so forth." When it was pointed out to him that the polls were suggesting that most Americans did not want troops in Haiti because it was not in the country's vital national interest, Germond responded, "The numbers might change if we keep getting all this film about the starving kids there." However, when the numbers didn't change, he later mused, "It's interesting that three or four years ago in Somalia, for example, television film of starving children was enough to make the country act. Now, television film of starving children in Haiti and atrocities is not enough." Groping for an explanation, Germond philosophized, "No one wants to say so, but there's a race factor here. There's no question about that."[3] That the starving children in Haiti happened to be of the same race as those in Somalia did not dampen his punditry in the slightest.

Another example: One explanation offered for the unwillingness of the American public to send troops to Bosnia is that the constant suffering shown on television happened not to "sensitize" the public but rather "inured" it.[4] We are supposed to believe that whether the public, in its collective wisdom, concludes that troops should or should not be sent, television is always somehow the cause. It isn't.

5 Foreign policy has become less important in judging the performance of the president and of presidential contenders.

During the Cold War, foreign policy was often important in presidential elections, but in its wake the general tendency of the American public to ignore foreign policy in national elections has been given free reign. Banking on his Gulf War success and on his opponent's lack of experience in foreign policy, George Bush tried hard to make foreign

---

[3] Quotations taken from transcripts of "The McLaughlin Group", Public Broadcasting Service, July 1 and September 16, 1994.
[4] See Clifford Orwin, "Distant Compassion: CNN and Borrioboola-Gha", *The National Interest* (Spring 1996).

affairs a central issue in the 1992 campaign, but failed. His ratings for handling the economy plummeted within days of the end of the war as the public quickly refocussed its attention on domestic matters. And when candidate Bill Clinton went out of his way to deliver a few serious foreign policy speeches, he found them generating little public or press attention. As suggested by the 1996 campaign, this phenomenon is likely to continue.

6 The advantage to a president of a success in a minor foreign policy venture is marginal; the disadvantage to a president of a failure in such a venture is more than marginal, but still far from devastating unless the failure becomes massively expensive.

If George Bush found little lasting electoral advantage in a large dramatic victory like the Gulf War, smaller accomplishments are likely to be even less rewarding in an era of great foreign policy inattention. America's recent venture into Haiti has been a success by most reasonable standards. Yet, while surely a feather in his cap, this venture has garnered Bill Clinton little credit—though it probably helped to diffuse his reputation for foreign policy ineptitude as a potential Republican campaign issue. Something similar could be said for his successes—possibly of historical importance—on the North American Free Trade Agreement and on the General Agreement on Tariffs and Trade.

Although messing up marginal ventures can be politically damaging by contrast, particularly if seen to fall within a pattern of poor performance, the costs need not be high. This stems from the fact that the public has shown a willingness to abandon an overextended or untenable position after American lives have been lost: The deaths of eighteen U.S. soldiers in Somalia in 1993, for example, led to outraged demands for withdrawal, not for calls to revenge the humiliation.

This episode, as well as the withdrawal from Lebanon after a truck bomb killed 241 U.S. Marines in 1983, suggests that when peacekeeping leads to unacceptable deaths, peacekeepers can be readily removed with little concern for saving face. If a venture is seen to be of little importance in terms of serious American interests, a president can, precisely because of that, cut and run without fear of inordinate electoral costs—though it will hardly be something to brag about. U.S. military interventions, then, need not become "quagmires."

7 If they are not being killed, American troops can remain in peacekeeping ventures virtually indefinitely with little public criticism; it is not important to have an "exit strategy", a "closed-end commitment", or "a time-certain for withdrawal" except for the purpose of selling an intervention in the first place.

Although there is an overwhelming political demand that casualties be extremely low in ventures deemed of minor importance, there seems to be little problem with keeping occupying forces in place as long as they are not being killed. After the deadly Somalia firefight, the Americans stayed on for several months and, since there were no further casualties, little attention was paid or concern voiced. Similarly, although there was scant public or political support for sending U.S. troops to Haiti, there has been almost no protest about keeping them there since none have been killed. And Americans have tolerated—indeed, hardly noticed—the stationing of hundreds of thousands of U.S. troops in Europe, Japan, and South Korea for decades on end. If they are not being killed, it scarcely matters whether the troops are in Macedonia or in Kansas.

On the other hand, if American troops start to take casualties while on peacekeeping missions, there will be demands to get them out quickly, whatever "date-certain" for withdrawal had been previously arranged. Thus, despite calls for knowing in advance what the endgame will look like, the only real "exit strategy" required is the tactical flexibility to yank the troops abruptly from the scene if things go awry.

8 A venture deemed of small importance is best sold not with cosmic internationalist hype, but rather as international social work that can be shrugged off if it goes wrong.

Most of the knotty and dramatic international problems that occupy the headlines are of remarkably little concern to the United States if one applies commonly accepted standards of what constitutes the national interest—and the public seems to be applying exactly those standards. Many problems are, in fact, mainly humanitarian in nature, exercises in what Michael Mandelbaum has called international "social work."[5]

But the notion of the United States doing international social work is not necessarily a non-starter. There is, after all, adequate support for domestic social work. International social work might best be sold in the same way as the domestic variety—as a good faith effort that can be abandoned if the client proves untreatable, rather than wrapped in the false guise of strategic interest. By contrast, in 1995 President Clinton argued that, "If war reignites in Bosnia, it could spark a much wider conflagration. In 1914, a gunshot in Sarajevo launched the first of two world wars"—a historical parallel that was wildly overdrawn, as numerous commentators promptly pointed out. Despite Clinton's claim that a new war in Bosnia "could spread like a cancer throughout the region", the "conflagration" in Bosnia seems, if anything, to have been successfully contained.

In principle, grandiloquent rhetoric can restrict later policy flexibility: If the fate of Europe really does hinge on tiny Bosnia (Clinton: "Europe will not come together with a brutal conflict raging at its heart"), failure there would be disaster. Fortunately, however, the public often seems more sensible on such matters than its leaders. When he sent the Marines to help police Lebanon, Ronald Reagan declared that "in an age of nuclear challenge and economic interdependence, such conflicts are a threat to all the people of the world, not just to the Middle East itself." Despite such an overblown sales pitch, however, the public had no difficulty accepting Reagan's later decision to have the Marines "re-deployed to the sea" after 241 of them were killed by a truck bomb.

The American people clearly do not spend a lot of time musing over public policy issues, particularly international ones. But they *are* grown-ups and, generally, they react as such. Policymakers might do well occasionally to notice this elemental and important fact.

---

[5]Michael Mandelbaum, "Foreign Policy as Social Work", *Foreign Affairs* (January/February 1996).

9 A danger in peacekeeping missions is that Americans might be taken hostage, something that can suddenly and disproportionately magnify the perceived stakes.

Because of the overriding importance Americans place on American lives, policy in low-valued ventures remains vulnerable to hostage-taking. As noted, peacekeeping missions need not become quagmires because the president can still abruptly withdraw troops from an overextended position with little long-lasting political cost. However, this flexibility can be dramatically compromised if American troops are taken hostage.

This is illustrated by some evidence from the Somalia episode. In the debacle of October 1993, a Somali group captured one American soldier. Polls clearly demonstrated that the public was determined that U.S. forces remain until the prisoner was recovered and only then to withdraw. Some opposition to placing U.S. soldiers on the Golan Heights between Israel and Syria has rested in part upon fear that U.S. personnel might be taken hostage by Syrian-supported Shi'a fundamentalists—and perhaps killed as well, as was the fate of Lt. Col. William Higgins in 1989. While such fears may be exaggerated, and sometimes pressed into political service for ulterior reasons, the concern is by no means baseless.

10 Nuclear weapons in the hands of rogue states and international terrorism remain potentially attention-arresting concerns.

In an era free of compelling threats, few concerns can turn the public's attention to foreign affairs. However, polls show that from time to time nuclear weapons do seem to retain some of their legendary attention-arresting aura, and the same may hold for biological and chemical weapons.

While it is not entirely clear what a country like North Korea, Iran, Iraq would actually do with a nuclear weapon or two—confronted as they are by countries that have thousands of them—alarm over such a possibility can rise to notable levels. In 1994, 82 percent of the public (up from 58 percent four years earlier) identified "preventing the spread of nuclear weapons" as a very important foreign policy goal—putting it in third place in the poll's sixteen-item list. (The top two goals were really more of domestic than of foreign policy concern: "stopping the flow of illegal drugs into the U.S." and "protecting the jobs of American workers.") The public also selected "the possibility of unfriendly countries becoming nuclear powers" as the top "critical threat" to the United States.

The public's fear of international terrorism is also quite robust. On average, international terrorism kills fewer Americans each year than lightning, or colliding with a deer. But though terrorism is rather unimportant in that literal sense, it generates fear and concern far out of proportion to its objective significance; it was almost as oft-cited a "critical threat" as nuclear proliferation in the 1994 poll.

IN THE END, it seems, misanthropes and curmudgeons are the only truly happy people: no matter how much things improve, there will always be something to complain about and to worry over. When one problem is solved, another is quickly promoted to take its place. Thus, now that life expectancy has increased to a level that would have tested the credulity of our ancestors a century ago, we, their progeny, worry about the huge budget deficit substantially caused by the fact that people now live so long. Most Americans believe that there has been an increase over the last twenty years in air pollution and in the number of elderly living in poverty, when the reverse is decidedly the case. "Status quo", as Ronald Reagan reportedly liked to put it, "is Latin for 'the mess we're in'", and there is, reliably, always some mess somewhere to be in.

This general phenomenon carries over to international affairs as well. When a peace mission helps peoples in the former Yugoslavia to stop killing each other, pundits are quick to find fault because it is unable to entice them to love each other as well. Thus there is a school of thought that contends that the post-Cold War era is just as dangerous as the one we have left behind, and it counsels keeping commitments and defense spending high, and tolerance for the mischief of others low. So, even in a state of considerable peace the catastrophe quota will always remain comfortably full. Although the chances of a global thermonuclear war—or indeed of any war among major developed countries—have diminished to the point where remarkably few even remember the terror it once inspired, one can concentrate on more vaporous enemies like insecurity, uncertainty, instability, and what one European foreign minister, the late Johan Jørgen Holst of Norway, darkly labeled "unspecified risks and dangers."[6] Or one can declare our new era to be profoundly, even dangerously, "complex" by conveniently forgetting the difficult and painful choices of the Cold War: The United States once had to treat Mobutu Sese Seko of Zaire as a dictator who brought his country to ruin, but who had been on the right side in the Cold War; today it can treat him merely as a dictator who has brought his country to ruin.

In any event, it is clear that alarums about uncertainty and complexity from academics and pensive foreign diplomats will not cure the attention deficit disorder that, as usual, characterizes the American public's approach to international affairs. In an era free of compelling threats, the public is likely to continue happily to focus its ennui and its *Weltschmerz* on parochial matters, not foreign ones—at least until there is good reason for them to do otherwise. Given the record of its generally good sense, that is perhaps not such a tragedy.

---

[6]Johan Jørgen Holst, "European and Atlantic Security in a Period of Ambiguity", *The World Today* (December 1992), p. 218.

Netanyahu and American Jews

Jonathan Broder

On the evening of October 6 last year, ten senior American Jewish leaders arrived at the White House and took their seats at a formally set dinner table across from President Clinton, Vice President Al Gore, Secretary of State Madeleine Albright, and National Security Adviser Sandy Berger. Though the occasion was a state dinner for Israel's ceremonial president, Ezer Weizman, the gathering was anything but ceremonial. Earlier that day, the Israeli Policy Forum, a New York–based think tank, had released a poll indicating that an overwhelming majority of American Jews—84 percent of those questioned—favored U.S. "pressure" on both Israel and the Palestinians to save the faltering Middle East peace process.[1] When it comes to Israel, "pressure" is one of those terms that is so politically sensitive that State Department officials refer to it as "the P-word." Anticipating resistance from Israeli Prime Minister Benjamin Netanyahu, Clinton wanted to know whether the Jewish leaders would affirm the poll or disavow it.

Clinton did not have to wait long for an answer. In an opening statement, Melvin Salberg, head of the Conference of Presidents of Major American Jewish Organizations, lavishly praised Clinton as "the most pro-Israel president in Israel's history" and pledged the community's undiluted support for his efforts to advance the peace process. According to those present, Clinton then went around the room, soliciting the individual opinions of each Jewish leader. One after another, they endorsed the president's efforts to bring together Netanyahu and Yasir Arafat, chairman of the Palestinian Authority, some citing the poll to underscore they spoke not only for their organizations but for the broader Jewish community.

Undergirding the Jewish leaders' responses was their acute disappointment with Netanyahu's leadership, an endless series of blunders, provocations, and self-inflicted wounds that had brought the once-promising Oslo peace process to its knees. First there was the three-day gunbattle with Palestinians in September 1996, provoked by Netanyahu's opening of an entrance to an archeological tunnel in Jerusalem's Old City. Then there was Netanyahu's decision last March to construct a new Jewish neighborhood in disputed East Jerusalem, a move widely blamed for bringing the peace talks to a halt. And who could forget Netanyahu's attempt to assassinate a Hamas leader in Jordan—a bungled adventure that alienated Israel's last friend in the Arab world, King Hussein, and further undermined Arafat, Netanyahu's only negotiating partner among the Palestinians?

Indeed, there had been a quiet acknowledgment among most American Jewish leaders that no Israeli prime minister, not even the rigid Yitzhak Shamir, had ever inspired such distrust and derision, not only among opponents in Israel but also among U.S. officials and broad swathes of American Jewry. Yet, even this closely guarded sentiment burst into the open at the White House dinner when Daniel Abraham, a major Democratic donor, asked, "Does anyone in this room believe that Prime Minister

Netanyahu really wants peace?" Tellingly, not one American Jewish leader spoke up in Netanyahu's defense. It fell to the patrician Weizman, and ultimately to Clinton himself, to defend Netanyahu's intentions. Even then, Clinton noted: "I'm not sure he can do it with the cabinet he's put together."

In American Jewry's long history of relations with Israel and successive American administrations, the October gathering represented a watershed. Never before had the community's top leadership effectively given the administration a green light to apply pressure on Israel to be more forthcoming in peace talks. "Any other time, they would have walked into the White House prepared to explain why such a poll was wrong or misleading," says J. J. Goldberg, a longtime commentator on American Jewish affairs and author of *Jewish Power: Inside the American Jewish Establishment*. "Instead, they walked in, and everybody's message was, 'Do what you must do, Mr. President. We love you.' Period."[2]

The Fracturing Factor

Cracks in American Jewry's deep emotional bond with Israel are nothing new. When Menachem Begin came to power in 1977 at the head of Israel's first right-wing Likud-led government, many American Jews, accustomed to familiar Labor Party figures like Golda Meir and Moshe Dayan, reacted with dismay to Begin's hard-line policies. Many prominent American Jews also expressed their opposition to Israel's 1982 invasion of Lebanon, its expansion of Jewish settlements in the occupied West Bank, and its bone-breaking response to Palestinian protesters during the uprising that erupted in 1987. But ultimately these were disagreements over style, not substance. Back then, the American Jewish leadership could always line up comfortably behind Israel's elected governments because of one simple reason: neither Israel nor the United States had recognized the Palestinian Liberation Organization (PLO) yet. At the end of the day, no matter how much American Jews may have disliked Israel's excesses, they could always claim there was no one with whom Israel could talk peace.

Today, the situation is dramatically different. Ever since the 1993 Oslo Accords, Israel and the PLO have recognized one another and agreed on the fundamental principle of trading land for peace. An internationally recognized Palestinian Authority now rules Gaza and the principal cities and towns of the West Bank. There is a PLO office in Washington, with a representative who enjoys the rank and status of an ambassador. Meanwhile, the Arab boycott of Israel has ended, and Israeli officials and businessmen now regularly attend Middle East economic summits alongside their Arab counterparts. In Israel and the Palestinian-controlled territories, foreign investment has reached unprecedented levels. The Israeli Policy Forum poll showed that 94 percent of American Jews agree that these new realities, though tested too often by Palestinian suicide bombings, still offer the last best hope for Middle East peace. And by margins as sweeping as 79 percent, the poll also confirmed that American Jews interpret Netanyahu's policies of continued settlement construction, land confiscations, and house demolitions as an attempt to turn the clock backward.

As a result, the cracks in the Jewish-Israeli relationship have turned into deep fractures. Deepening those fissures are the wounded sensibilities of key American Jewish leaders, who complain of Netanyahu's arrogance, his failure to consult them, and his turn to Christian fundamentalists and shrill right-wing Jewish groups for support against the Clinton administration.

Then there are the other irritants that have nothing to do with Netanyahu's anachronistic peace policies. For American Jews, 85 percent of whom belong to the Reform and Conservative denominations, the most damaging has been Netanyahu's declared intention to support his Orthodox coalition partners in passing a law that would delegitimize Reform and Conservative Jews in Israel. It is hard to underestimate how corrosive this issue has become. American Jews, enraged by the thought that their brand of Judaism might be outlawed by the Netanyahu government, have begun to cut back on their donations to Israel. For many Jews, their anger over the religious issue has combined with their doubts about Netanyahu's peace policies, producing a potent brew of hurt and hostility. And increasingly, more and more American Jews are simply tuning out. Offended by Netanyahu's policies, many are simply turning inward, toward their own local communities and their personal identities as Jews.

Whatever the causes, the result is the same: Israel's most powerful political constituency in the United States is now deeply alienated from the Netanyahu government and solidly behind President Clinton. For Clinton, that means more political leeway to press ahead with the Middle East peace process than any American president has ever enjoyed. The burning question now is, will he use it?

Distrustful Leaders
In the movie *Patton*, there is a scene toward the end of film in which the legendary Second World War general, played by George C. Scott, deliberately refuses to join his Soviet counterpart in a toast to their joint victory over the Germans. "Tell the general I do not wish to drink with any Russian son of a bitch," Patton instructs an interpreter to say. Stung, the Soviet commander counters that he has no wish to drink with any American son of a bitch. Hearing this, Patton laughs, raises his glass to the Russian and says, "From one son of a bitch to another." Warily locking arms Russian-style, the two men then down their drinks, never taking their suspicious eyes off one another.

That, essentially is where U.S.-Israeli relations stand right now. When Netanyahu arrived in Washington in January for talks with President Clinton, his first meeting, to the astonishment of the White House and American Jewish leaders, was with the Reverend Jerry Falwell, a fierce critic of the president who has produced and peddled a widely discredited video that accuses Clinton of murder, drug smuggling, and cocaine addiction. At the end of the meeting, Falwell publicly pledged to mobilize America's 70 million–strong evangelical community to Netanyahu's side. In another breach of protocol, Netanyahu then met with House Speaker Newt Gingrich, receiving reassurances that the Republican majority in Congress would side with Israel in any confrontation with the administration. With his divisions arrayed on the battlefield, only then did Netanyahu go to the White House.

Clinton was able to make light of Netanyahu's provocations. According to one of his aides, Clinton jokingly told the Israeli leader that in view of the administration's open backing for Netanyahu's opponent in Israel's 1996 elections, Labor Party leader Shimon Peres, he, the president, probably had it coming. "I guess we're even," Clinton was said by the aide to have told Netanyahu. But beneath the diplomatic veneer, the two leaders, like Patton and the Russian, remain deeply distrustful of one another. One White House aide likened the personal chemistry between Clinton and Netanyahu to that between Socks and Buddy, Clinton's cat and his new dog.

Moreover, the stage is now set for a major U.S.-Israel confrontation. During his Washington talks with Netanyahu and later with Arafat, Clinton presented his own plan for renewed negotiations, becoming directly and personally involved in the peace process for the first time. The Clinton plan calls for a rapid Israeli withdrawal from 12 to 15 percent of the West Bank, broken into three phases, as called for under the Oslo agreement. Under the Clinton plan, these Israeli pullbacks are to be implemented in parallel with specific Palestinian commitments to bolster Israeli security. After the withdrawals are completed, final status talks on the most difficult issues—refugees, final borders, Jewish settlements, and the future status of Jerusalem—can begin.

For his part, Netanyahu is willing to give up only 9 percent of the West Bank in one combined phase, eliminating the third stage entirely. Even then, Netanyahu insists, the Palestinians first must meet more than 50 Israeli demands, including politically sensitive conditions like the extradition of Palestinian prisoners to Israel, a commitment to cease all political activity in East Jerusalem, and the elimination of old clauses from the Palestinian Covenant calling for Israel's destruction. Only then will Israel move on to the final status talks. Standing behind Netanyahu is his fractious and narrow coalition of right-wing and religious parties, whose threats to bring down the government over any further withdrawals have allowed Netanyahu to claim he is unable to offer more.

The difficulties facing American peacemakers became evident when Secretary of State Albright returned to the Middle East at the end of January, several weeks after the Washington talks, and came away empty-handed. More talks, at a lower level, are expected to continue in Washington over the coming months, but there is now widespread skepticism that junior diplomats will succeed where Albright and Clinton himself have failed. Indeed, among a majority of Israelis, there is now a conviction that the peace process, gasping for breath since last March, is finally dead. The only thing that remains to be seen is who gets the blame.

More Blame or More Demands

Whether it comes in the form of blame or more demands for concessions, Netanyahu is bracing for more American pressure. Netanyahu is said to have believed that Clinton's need to focus on the Monica Lewinsky scandal would provide Israel with some extra breathing space, during which time Netanyahu could stabilize his razor-thin coalition. At this writing, in mid-February, there is talk that the former foreign minister, David Levy, who resigned from the government in January, may return after all, bringing his five-member Gesher faction with him. Were that to happen, Netanyahu's coalition would be back at 66 seats in the 120-member Knesset, a comfortable majority by any measure.

Netanyahu is also counting on Congress to act as a counterweight to any pressure that Clinton might apply. To help in this campaign, he has turned to the principal pro-Israel lobby, the American Israeli Public Affairs Committee, or AIPAC, as well as several small right-wing American Jewish groups. The most prominent is the Zionist Organization of America (ZOA), which tries to portray Clinton as another version of his distrusted predecessor, George Bush. "I find it extraordinary that the president who is described as the greatest supporter of Israel ever is the same president who resists moving the American embassy to Jerusalem and the same president who demands that Jews stop building settlements in Judea and Samaria [the West Bank]," said ZOA President Morton Klein in an interview with the author in early February. "Clinton has shown himself to be not only not even-handed, but pro-Arab."

Klein has won over a few dozen lawmakers, but people who are knowledgeable about the organized Jewish community say his influence, along with that of other right-wing Jewish groups, has been overblown. Within the community, their shrill voices have become an embarrassment. It is not surprising that mainstream Jewish leaders left Klein out of the delegation to the White House last October. If Klein has achieved anything, it has been to highlight the split in the Jewish community—a development that has not gone unnoticed on Capitol Hill.

As Netanyahu looks to Congress for support, two incidents last fall ought to give him pause. The first occurred last September when a teenaged murder suspect from Washington's Maryland suburbs fled to Tel Aviv and claimed Israeli citizenship because his father had been born there. Israel initially refused to return the youth, citing a law that forbids the extradition of Israeli citizens. The technicality so infuriated Rep. Bob Livingston, chairman of the House Appropriations Committee, that he suspended aid to Israel, declaring that his "sensibilities as a citizen of the United States [had] been violated." Livingston relented only after the Israeli government reversed itself and ruled that the youth should be extradited—although Republicans still grouse that the legal process in Israel could take years.

Only a month later, as the Appropriations Committee put the final touches on the 1997–98 foreign aid bill, Livingston angrily suspended aid to Israel again. This time, he lashed out because Israel had failed to keep a months-old promise to allow Congress to transfer $50 million in U.S. aid from Israel's $3 billion account to financially strapped Jordan. Chastened, Israel quickly came up with the necessary documents, and the aid was restored. Afterward, according to congressional aides, Livingston boasted: "I stood up to Israel, and they backed down."

Though on one level both incidents

were relatively minor, Congress's response was unprecedented, suggesting a new fragility in the U.S.-Israeli relationship. U.S. foreign aid to Israel is one of the most sacred cows in the U.S.-Israeli relationship, an annual tribute whose political symbolism far outweighs its economic significance. In earlier days, any congressman who even suggested a cut in aid to Israel would have faced a ferocious response from angry Jews around the country, mobilized by AIPAC's extensive phone trees. But this time, Congress acted with impunity, not once, but twice within the space of six weeks. Why?

AIPAC dismisses both incidents as "minor misunderstandings" that did not require a call to arms by the lobby's members and donors. And they add that Israel has been restored to Congress's good graces with its recent discussions on Capitol Hill over gradually phasing out the $1.2 billion that the United States provides Israel annually in economic assistance. But commentator J. J. Goldberg believes those explanations obscure the depths of the malaise now infecting the Jewish community when it comes to Israel. "The truth is that this time, the phone trees simply weren't working," he said. "It shows just how angry people are, not just at the level of the donors who are supposed to make the calls, but even at the level of the AIPAC staffers who are supposed to be mobilizing them. People are feeling this lassitude. They're asking themselves, how far are we supposed to go for this Bibi [Netanyahu's nickname] guy?"

Wounded Sensibilities
For the vast majority of American Jews, that anger can be traced directly to Netanyahu's handling of the controversial religious law now pending before the Knesset. Last year, in response to an Israeli Supreme Court decision that paved the way for greater recognition of Reform and Conservative religious rights in Israel, Netanyahu's Orthodox coalition partners, outraged that these "Hellenized" forms of Judaism might gain a foothold in Israel, tabled a bill that would codify the Orthodox's traditional monopoly over all religious affairs in Israel. The religious parties also warned Netanyahu that if he did not support the bill, they would bolt the coalition and bring down the government. Netanyahu pledged his support, drawing howls of outrage from Reform and Conservative leaders in the United States. Delegations of American Jewish leaders flew to Israel, where Netanyahu told them to stop overreacting. After all, he argued, the only American Jews who would be affected by passage of the law would be the half-dozen or so non-Orthodox converts who immigrate to Israel every year. Yes, he said, their conversions would not be recognized by Israel's Orthodox Rabbinate. So what? Is the religious status of a handful of people any reason to split the Jewish people?

The answer was a thunderous yes. What Netanyahu does not understand, says Rabbi Eric Yofe, head of the Reform movement in the United States, is that most American Jews do not pay attention to the complexities of the proposed law. Netanyahu's attempts to find a compromise to soothe the wounded sensibilities of American Jews are "too little, too late," he said. "All they know [is] they're not hearing from Israel that sense of inclusion, that embrace that they're looking for." Compounding their sense of rejection are the harsh language and the occasional acts of violence that Netanyahu's Orthodox allies have employed to attack the tiny Reform and Conservative communities in Israel. Their synagogues have been branded "whorehouses" because, unlike the strict Orthodox, Reform and Conservative Jews allow women and men to pray together. During an attempt last year by liberal American Jewish men and women to pray together at Jerusalem's Western Wall, Orthodox protesters pelted them with human excrement.

The bitter confrontation only intensified in February, when Israel's Orthodox Chief Rabbinate ruled out any cooperation with Reform and Conservative rabbis on conversions and other religious rites, accusing them of having "brought about disastrous results of assimilation among Diaspora Jewry." The Rabbinate was rejecting a government compromise that would have established a joint institute where all three branches of Judaism would be represented in preparing candidates for conversion, but which would have given the Orthodox control over the actual conversions themselves. "The sages of Israel have forbidden any cooperation with them and their method," the Rabbinate declared, referring to the non-Orthodox movements. "One cannot consider establishing a joint institute with them."

Amazingly, officials in the Netanyahu government saw in this declaration a window of Orthodox flexibility. Because the Orthodox had not been invited to "establish" the proposed institute but only to take part in it, the rabbis had not really rejected the compromise, officials said. Netanyahu hailed the Rabbinate's decision, saying, "It promotes the national consensus among the Jewish people and the State of Israel, which all of us are striving for."

But such Talmudic hairsplitting has not impressed Reform and Conservative rabbis, who now say they will resume the legal and political struggle for recognition that they shelved while a compromise was being sought. As for Netanyahu, American Jewish leaders are calling "outrageous" his attempts to portray the Orthodox as flexible.

"American Jews are profoundly offended by what's happening on the Jewish issues," Yofe said. "The Judaism that's being articulated by the Israeli leadership is so foreign to us and so vituperative when it comes to my form of Judaism. If people in Israel are saying Reform and Conservative synagogues are whorehouses and throwing handfuls of shit at us, then is it any wonder that we're turning away?"

Reluctant American Jews
Trying to quantify the extent of American Jewry's disillusionment with Netanyahu has always been difficult. Despite reservations over Israel's peace policies, American Jews have tended to keep their doubts to themselves, largely out of a sense of protective Jewish solidarity. But as the Israel Policy Forum poll suggests—as well as numerous pro-peace newspaper ads signed by prominent mainstream Jewish figures—American Jews appear to have overcome their reluctance to speak out critically. Moreover, many Jewish leaders say Netanyahu himself pried the door off that closet with his mishandling of the religious issue.

One reliable gauge of Jewish sentiment is the community's charitable donations, and here Jewish leaders detect the beginnings of a trend away from the Israel of Benjamin Netanyahu. Last year, the United Jewish Appeal (UJA), whose collections fund not only the organized Jewish community in the United States but also numerous projects in Israel, reported total donations of $758 million for 1997, 2 percent lower than anticipated. Moreover, for the first time, UJA officials say, a number of large donors earmarked their checks, directing their donations either to specific nongovernmental institutions in Israel or to Jewish institutions in the United States. Meanwhile, the New Israel Fund, a small philanthropic organization that encourages religious pluralism in Israel and reconciliation between Jews and Arabs, reported a 30 percent increase in its donations over 1996, collecting $17 million.

Some local Jewish federations have taken unprecedented steps in their fundraising efforts to distance themselves from Netanyahu and his government. Late last year, Alan Rothenberg, president of San Francisco's Jewish Community Federation, one of the largest and most active Jewish organizations in the country, felt compelled to send a letter to major donors, explicitly stating that the federation "does *not* fund the Israeli government." Rothenberg was quoted in the federation-funded *Jewish Bulletin of Northern California* of December 19, 1997, as having said that his letter came in response to contributors' deep concerns about threats to religious pluralism in Israel and to the peace process.

"I have received numerous calls from JCF donors with mixed emotions about events in Israel," he wrote in his letter. "Every day we seem to be inundated with news stories about Israel that make us shake our heads and wonder if this is the same land of milk and honey that we looked to with such pride as our spiritual and moral compass." He went on to explain the federation's collections are turned over to the UJA, which then sends a portion to the Jewish Agency, a quasi-governmental Israeli institution that helps with the absorption of immigrants.

Among those who received the letter was Fred Blum, a prominent San Francisco attorney, a past president of the American Jewish Congress, and a major donor to his local federation for the past decade. Blum told the *Bulletin* that he would reduce his annual donation by 35 percent—the proportion of each federation dollar that goes to Israel—and earmark the remainder of his donation for domestic use only.

"I don't know any other way to express what I'm feeling about the way the government of Israel is moving," the *Bulletin* quoted Blum as saying. "The issue of pluralism is the tree that broke the camel's back. It's not a straw. It's a tree. As a Jew, I have more rights in Turkey than I do in Israel. You add to this what's going on in the peace process and basically, enough is enough."

Bernard Moscovitz, the UJA's executive vice president, notes Rothenberg's letter of clarification was mild compared to the concerns raised by some other Jewish federations around the country. "Some communities are now questioning whether they should mention Israel at all in their fundraising," he says. "They have donors who don't want to hear the word anymore." In Israel, the impact of American Jewish anger is already being felt: officials of the Jewish Agency say that because of the drop-off in American donations, the 75-year-old organization is now facing bankruptcy.

A New Generation
Even without the current crises over religious pluralism and peace, long-term ethnic, religious, and political trends in Israel would be driving American Jewry and Israel apart, many observers say. Netanyahu represents a new generation of young, tough, and confident leaders whose defining experience was not the Holocaust or the creation of the state of Israel, but the Israeli army's conquest of the Arab territories during the 1967 Six-Day War. For these Israelis, the territories are not "occupied" at all, but Jewish land, to be kept or traded as they deem necessary. Moreover, this generation of leaders does not include the familiar European Ashkenazi Jews that Jewish Americans have grown accustomed to. Rather, they have risen from the ranks of Israel's dark-skinned Sephardic Jews, its recent Russian immigrants, and its black-coated ultra-Orthodox—all previously outsiders to Israel's elite establishment but now the political groups holding the balance of power. Many Israeli analysts—including some of Netanyahu's sharpest critics—have concluded that even if his government were to fall, these new Israeli power brokers would determine national policy well into the next century.

American Jewry's focus has shifted as well. As the century comes to a close, all the great struggles for Jewish survival have been won. Soviet Jewry, Ethiopian Jewry, Syrian Jewry, all have been saved, thanks in large part to the dedication of American Jews. Elderly Holocaust survivors soon will be receiving checks from the Swiss. And despite the threat of more Arab terrorism, Israel's survival is no longer in question. "All these emergencies have receded," Yofe says. "American Jews look at Israel and ask what exactly does Israel have to do with them. They want to know what's the connection, but all they get is an Israel that seems to despise them and their religion. So they're turning inward. Now they're asking, 'What about me? How does Judaism address my needs in America?' We're losing the troops in terms of Israel. Each is going its own way."

The collapse of the peace process has only accelerated these divisions. But there is one other factor: one of the most fundamental truths about the Jewish community is that no matter how secure it has come to feel in the United States, it still feels uncomfortable and vaguely threatened when Washington is at odds with Israel over Middle East peace policy. And that's especially true when the community suspects that Washington is right, as it does now.

Thus, for the first time in the history of the Middle East conflict, the strongest political constituency in the United States in favor of increased pressure on Israel is the American Jewish community itself. Publicly, Salberg and other leaders have warned that the community could turn against Clinton if he crosses the so-called red lines of the U.S.-Israel relationship—exerting pressure by withholding aid, military assistance, and intelligence cooperation. But such threats seem more political than probable, reflecting the leadership's need to placate the small but vocal right-wing groups within the community. There has been no hint that Clinton would take such measures, and virtually no one, not even anti-Clinton Arabists, believes he ever will.

The Danger of Netanyahu
For the Jewish community's mainstream leadership, the issue boils down to this: Netanyahu has become not only an embarrassment and danger to Middle East peace but, more important, a threat to their own peace of mind as a non-Christian minority in the United States. Though many Jews have channeled their anger into the religious issue, the leadership knows that the community's ultimate comfort in the United States depends on not being associated with an Israeli leader who is complicating American policy toward Iraq and Iran, interfering in Washington's efforts to stop the proliferation of Russian weapons technology, and who could provoke another war in the Middle East. So the message remains, as it was that evening in the White House last fall: Do what you must do, Mr. President. We love you.

To be sure, not everything Clinton has said or done in the Middle East so far has won Jewish accolades. The community bristled last year when administration officials suggested that Netanyahu's hard-line policies were eroding the Gulf War coalition of moderate Arab states against Iraq. It would have been far more accurate to say that Clinton's reluctance to confront Netanyahu over his hard-line policies has eroded the unity of the coalition. Last summer, when Secretary of State Albright and her deputies tried to convince moderate Arab leaders to attend, along with the Israelis, the Middle East Economic summit in Doha, the capital of Qatar, the message they heard, from Morocco to the Persian Gulf, never varied: if the United States can justify its tough stand against Iraq because of Saddam Hussein's failure to keep his agreements, then why is Netanyahu not being held to the same standard? The Arab price for remaining in the coalition was decisive U.S. action on both issues. In the case of Saddam, the Arabs wanted the Clinton administration to kill him, pure and simple. Pinprick American attacks, even a sustained air war, were not worth the Arabs' support if Saddam was to be left to exact revenge on his neighbors another day. The same goes for Netanyahu. If you are serious about Middle East peace, they are telling Clinton, you will use the power of the presidency to make Netanyahu honor Israel's commitment under the Oslo Accords. The administration's failure to reenergize the anti-Iraq coalition is a direct result of confidence it has lost among Arabs over its handling of Netanyahu.

Snubbing Bibi
How the Clinton administration will respond remains to be seen. There is no question that the tone of the relationship with Netanyahu grows colder and more distant with every passing day. Last summer, when Netanyahu requested a meeting with Clinton during a planned visit to the United States, the president made it clear he had no time for pleasantries without some substantial progress in the peace process. The same scenario repeated itself in November, prompting Netanyahu to accuse Clinton of snubbing him. During Clinton's talks with Netanyahu in January, the White House quietly scrubbed from the schedule any of the diplomatic niceties that normally attend an Israeli prime minister's visit—no lunch with the president, no joint news conference, no overnight stay at Blair House. Presidential aides let it be known that so long as Netanyahu dithers, he will be treated the same as that other ditherer, Yasir Arafat. Secretary of State Albright, with her ferociously sharp tongue, is now the administration's bad cop in the confrontation, showing no hesitancy to skewer Netanyahu and Arafat publicly for their intransigence. "Madeleine is definitely one of the arrows in our quiver," says one State Department aide.

But will that be enough to save the peace process? Some observers doubt it, saying heavier pressure is needed. But they question whether Clinton will take that step, pointing to his reluctance to alienate the American Jewish community, which gave him 80 percent of its votes in each of his campaigns for the White House. Should Vice President Al Gore run for the presidency in the year 2000, as expected, he will also need Jewish votes and campaign money, they say.

Significantly, the most forceful argument against this view comes not from the Arabists but from American Jewish leaders. "The American administration has been very cowardly on these issues," said Yofe. "There is much more they can do without crossing the red lines." Some members of the Jewish leadership have quietly begun stressing this point in meetings with State Department officials.

Short of increased pressure, some Jewish leaders are hoping that the administration's continued criticism of Netanyahu will gradually erode Israelis' confidence in him. Israelis judge their leaders on, among other things, their stewardship of the Israel-U.S. relationship, which is still considered Israel's most powerful defense against a hostile world. If Israelis conclude that their prime minister is jeopardizing that relationship, they will eventually turn him out of office. That is what happened to Yitzhak Shamir in 1992, and with a helping hand from the Clinton administration that will be Netanyahu's fate as well, the Jewish leaders say.

A Fool's Game

But predicting events in the Middle East has always been a fool's game. The American Jewish community may be prepared for the first time to support greater pressure on Israel, but there are many more ducks that need to be brought into a row or neutralized, including Congress, the Evangelical Christians, the Democratic Party, Netanyahu's coalition partners, the Israeli electorate, and the Palestinians, to mention just a few. There are events on the ground, like the possibility of another Hamas suicide bombing and American airstrikes against Iraq for its refusal to permit United Nations weapons inspections. One Iraqi missile directed at Tel Aviv and an Israeli military response, and the administration can probably kiss the Middle East peace process goodbye for the foreseeable future. American Jews will unquestionably rally to Israel's side, and it will be months, perhaps years before diplomatic efforts can reopen the window that exists today. By that time, there may be new governments in both Israel and the United States.

And finally, there is the lingering question of Monica Lewinsky, whose alleged affair with Clinton and suspected perjury on his instructions could yet bring down his presidency. The possible impact that the scandal could have on the Middle East peace process has not been lost on the American Jewish community, with some of Clinton's right-wing Jewish opponents portraying Lewinsky as a modern-day, if unwitting, Esther, the biblical Jewish woman whose love affair with a Persian king saved the Jews from destruction. Clinton's Jewish supporters dismiss such comparisons, but as the scandal grows, his detractors are taking comfort in what they see as its biblical echoes.

—*February 12, 1998*

Notes

1. The Israeli Policy Forum poll was conducted by Penn, Schoen & Berland by telephone on September 16, 17, 18, and 21, 1997. Interviews were conducted with 1,198 subjects.

2. Unless noted otherwise, all quotations in this article are taken from interviews conducted by the author during the first week of February 1998.

Jonathan Broder is the Washington correspondent for The Jerusalem Report.

On American Principles

George F. Kennan

George F. Kennan is Professor Emeritus in the School of Historical Studies at the Institute for Advanced Study in Princeton, N.J. This is his nineteenth article for Foreign Affairs. *His first, "The Sources of Soviet Conduct," appeared in July 1947 under the pseudonym X.*

THE HISTORICAL EXPERIENCE

AT A LARGE dinner given in New York in recognition of his ninetieth birthday, the author of these lines ventured to say that what our country needed at this point was not primarily policies, "much less a single policy." What we needed, he argued, were principles—sound principles—"principles that accorded with the nature, the needs, the interests, and the limitations of our country." This rather cryptic statement could surely benefit from a few words of elucidation.

The place that principle has taken in the conduct of American foreign policy in past years and decades can perhaps best be explained by a single example from American history. In the aftermath of the Napoleonic wars, and particularly in the period beginning about 1815-25, there set in a weakening of the ties that had previously held the Spanish empire together, and demands were raised by certain of the American colonies for complete independence. Pressure was brought on Washington to take the lead not only in recognizing their independence at an early stage, but also in giving them political and presumably military aid in their efforts to consolidate their independence in the face of whatever resistance might be put up by the Spanish government.

These questions presented themselves with particular intensity when James Monroe was president (1817-25). At that time the office of secretary of state was occupied by John Quincy Adams. In view of his exceptional qualities and experience, and the high respect with which he was held in Washington and throughout the country, much of the burden of designing the U.S. response to those pressures rested on him.

Adams realized that the U.S. historical experience left no choice but to welcome and give moral support to these South American peoples in their struggle for the recognition and consolidation of their independence. But he had little confidence in the ability of the new revolutionary leaders to shape these communities at any early date into mature, orderly, and firmly established states.

For this reason, he was determined that America not be drawn too deeply into their armed conflicts with Spain, domestic political squabbles, or sometimes complicated relationships with their neighbors. Adams took this position, incidentally, not just with regard to the emerging South American countries, but also in relation to similar conflicts in Europe, particularly the efforts of Greek patriots to break away from the Turkish empire and establish an independent state.

These attitudes on Adams' part did not fail to meet with opposition in portions of the American political establishment. Some people, including the influential speaker of the House, Henry Clay, remembering America's own recent struggle for independence, felt strongly that the United States should take an active part in the similar struggles of other peoples. This, of course, was directly opposed to Adams' views. For this reason, Adams felt the need to take the problem to a wider audience and enlist public support for his views. In 1823, when he was invited by a committee of citizens to deliver a Fourth of July address in the nation's capital, he promptly agreed. The address was delivered in the premises of the House of Representatives, although not before a formal session of that body. The talk was presented as a personal statement, not an official one; and Adams took care to see that the text was printed and made widely available to the public.

A considerable part of the address was devoted to the questions I have just mentioned. On this subject Adams had some firm views. America, he said, had always extended to these new candidates for statehood "the hand of honest friendship, of equal freedom, and of generous reciprocity." It had spoken to them in "the language of equal liberty, of equal justice, and of equal rights." It had respected their independence. It had abstained from interference with their undertakings even when these were being conducted "for principles to which she [America] clings, as to the last vital drop that visits the heart." Why? Because, he explained, "America goes not abroad in search of monsters to destroy. She is the well-wisher to the freedom and independence of all. She is the champion and vindicator only of her own. She will recommend the general cause by the countenance of her voice, and the benignant sympathy of her example. She well knows that by once enlisting under other banners than her own, were they even the banners of foreign independence, she would involve herself beyond the power

16. On American Principles

of extrication, in all the wars of interest and intrigue, of individual avarice, envy, and ambition, which assumed the colors and usurped the standards of freedom. . . . She might become the dictatress of the world. She would be no longer the ruler of her own spirit."

The relevance of this statement to many current problems—in such places as Iraq, Lebanon, Somalia, Bosnia, Rwanda, and even Haiti—is obvious. But that is not the reason why attention is being drawn to the statement at this point. What Adams was doing in those passages of his address was enunciating a principle of American foreign policy: namely, that, while it was "the well-wisher to the freedom and independence of all," America was also "the champion and vindicator only of her own." Those words seem to provide as clear an example as any of what the term "principle" might mean in relation to the diplomacy of this country or any other.

THE IDEAL VS. REALITY

How, THEN, using Adams' statement as a model, would the term "principle" be defined? One might say that a principle is a general rule of conduct by which a given country chooses to abide in the conduct of its relations with other countries. There are several aspects of the term, one or two of them touched on in this definition, others not, that require elucidation.

A principle was just defined as a general rule of conduct. That means that whoever adopts a principle does not specify any particular situation, problem, or bilateral relationship to which this rule should apply. It is designed to cover the entirety of possible or presumptive situations. It merely defines certain limits, positive and negative, within which policy, when those situations present themselves, ought to operate.

A government cannot play fast and loose with the interests of its people.

A principle, then, is a rule of conduct. But it is not an absolute one. The possibility is not precluded that situations might arise—unforeseeable situations, in particular—to which the adopted principle might not seem applicable or to the meeting of which the resources of the government in question were clearly inadequate. In such cases, exceptions might have to be made. This is not, after all, a perfect world. People make mistakes in judgment. And there is always the unforeseeable and unexpected.

But as new situations and challenges present themselves, and as government is confronted with the necessity of devising actions or policies with which to meet them, established principle is something that should have the first and the most authoritative claim on the attention and respect of the policymaker. Barring special circumstances, principle should be automatically applied, and whoever proposes to set it aside or violate it should explain why such violation seems unavoidable.

Second, a principle is, by definition, self-engendered. It is not something that requires, or would even admit of, any sort of communication, negotiation, or formal agreement with another government. In the case of the individual person (because individuals have principles, just as governments do), the principles that guide his life are a matter of conscience and self-respect. They flow from the individual's view of himself; the nature of his inner commitments, and his concept of the way he ought to behave if he is to be at peace with himself.

Now, the principles of a government are not entirely the same as those of an individual. The individual, in choosing his principles, engages only himself. He is at liberty to sacrifice his own practical interests in the service of some higher and more unselfish ideal. But this sort of sacrifice is one that a responsible government, and a democratic government in particular, is unable to take upon itself. It is an agent, not a principal. It is only a representative of others.

When a government speaks, it speaks not only for itself but for the people of the country. It cannot play fast and loose with their interests. Yet a country, too, can have a predominant collective sense of itself—what sort of a country it conceives itself or would like itself to be—and what sort of behavior would fit that concept. The place where this self-image finds its most natural reflection is in the principles that a country chooses to adopt and, to the extent possible, to follow. Principle represents, in other words, the ideal, if not always, alas, the reality, of the rules and restraints a country adopts. Once established, those rules and restraints require no explanation or defense to others. They are one's own business.

A drawing that appeared in *The New Yorker* magazine many years ago showed a cringing subordinate standing before the desk of an irate officer, presumably a colonel, who was banging the desk with his fist and saying: "There is no reason, damn it; it's just our policy."

Well, as a statement about policy, this was ridiculous. But had the colonel been referring to a principle instead of a policy, the statement might not have been so out of place. It would not be unusual, for example, for someone in authority in Washington today to say to the representative of a foreign government, when the situation warranted it, "I am sorry, but for us, this is a matter of principle, and I am afraid we will have to go on from there."

Let me also point out that principles can have negative as well as positive aspects. There can be certain things that a country can make it a matter of principle not to do. In many instances these negative aspects of principle may be more important than the positive ones. The positive ones normally suggest or involve action; actions have a way of carrying over almost imperceptibly from the realm of principle into that of policy, where they develop a momentum of their own in which the original considerations of principle either are forgotten or are compelled to yield to what appear to be necessities of the moment. In other words, it is sometimes clearer and simpler to define on principle the kinds of things a country will not go in for—the things that would fit with neither its standards nor its pretensions—than it is to define ways in which it will act positively, whatever the circumstances. The basic function of principles is, after all, to establish the parameters within which the policies of a country may be normally conducted. This is essentially a negative, rather than a positive, determination.

Another quality of a principle that deserves notice is that it is not, and cannot be, the product of the normal workings of the political process in any democratic country. It could not be decided by a plebiscite or even by legislative action. You would never get agreement on it if it came under that sort of debate, and whatever results might be achieved would deprive the concept of the degree of flexibility it requires to serve its purpose.

A principle is something that can only be declared, and then only by a political leader. It represents, of necessity, his own view of what sort of a country his is, and how it should conduct itself in the international arena. But the principle finds its reality, if it finds it at all, in the degree of acceptance, tacit or otherwise, that its proclamation ultimately receives from the remainder of the political establishment and from the populace at large. If that acceptance and support are not forthcoming in sufficient degree, a principle ceases to have reality. The statesman who proclaims it, therefore, has to be reasonably confident that, in putting it forward, he is interpreting, appealing to, and expressing the sentiment of a large proportion of the people for whom he speaks. This task of defining a principle must be seen as not just a privilege, but also a duty of political leadership.

Adams' statement certainly had this quality. The concept was indeed his own. But his formulation of it met wide and enthusiastic support among the people of his time, as he probably thought it would. The same could be said of similar declarations of principle from a number of other American statesmen, then and later. One has only to think, for example, of George Washington's statements in his farewell address, Thomas Jefferson's language in the Declaration of Independence, or Abraham Lincoln's in his Gettysburg speech. In each of those instances, the leaders, in putting forward their idea of principle, were speaking from their own estimate—a well-informed estimate—of what would find a sufficient response on the part of a large body, and not just a partisan body, of American opinion.

In no way other than by advocacy or proclamation from high office could such professions of principle be usefully formulated and brought forward. The rest of us may have our thoughts from time to time about the principles America ought to follow in its relations with the world, but none of us could state these principles in a manner that would give them significance for the behavior of the country at large.

THE POWER OF EXAMPLE

SO MUCH, then, for the essential characteristics of a principle and the manner in which it can be established. But there are those who will not be content with this abstract description of what a principle is, and who will want an example of what a principle valid for adoption by the United States of our day might look like.

The principle cited from Secretary Adams' Fourth of July speech was one that was applicable, in his view, to the situation then. The world now is, of course, different from his in many respects. There are those who will hold the gloomy view that such is the variety of our population and such are the differences among its various components, racial, social, and political, that it is idle to suppose that there could be any consensus among them on matters of principle. They have too little in common. There is much to be said for that view. This writer has at times been inclined to it himself. But further reflection suggests that there are certain feelings that we Americans or the great majority of us share, living as we do under the same political system and enjoying the same national consciousness, even though we are not always aware of having them. One may further suspect that if the translation of these feelings into principles of American behavior on the world scene were to be put forward from the highest governmental levels and adequately explained to the people at large, it might evoke a surprisingly strong response.

But this understanding and support cannot be expected to come spontaneously from below. It will not be likely to emerge from a public media dominated by advertisers and the entertainment industry. It will not be likely to emerge from legislative bodies extensively beholden to special interests, precisely because what would be at stake here would be the feelings and interests of the nation as a whole and not those of any particular and limited bodies of the citizenry. An adequate consensus on principles, in other words, could come from below only by way of response to suggestions from above, brought forward by a leadership that would take responsibility for educating and forming popular opinion, rather than merely trying to assess its existing moods and prejudices and play up to them.

Now, coming back to the model of Adams' Fourth of July speech, the problems now facing this country show a strong resemblance to ones Adams had in mind when he gave that address in 1823. At that time the dissolution of the great empires was only just beginning, and few—

at the most half a dozen—of the newly emerging states were looking to us for assistance. In the period between Adams' time and our own, and particularly in the wake of the Second World War, the process of decolonization has preceded at a dizzying pace, casting onto the surface of international life dozens of new states, many of them poorly prepared, as were those of Adams' time, for the responsibilities of independent statehood. This has led to many situations of instability, including civil wars and armed conflicts with neighbors, and there have been, accordingly, a great many appeals to us for political, economic, or military support.

To what extent, then, could Adams' principle of nonintervention, as set forth in 1823, be relevant to our situation today?

One cannot ignore the many respects in which our present situation differs from that which Adams was obliged to face. This writer is well aware of the increasingly global nature of our problems and the myriad involvements connecting our people and government with foreign countries. I do not mean to suggest a great reduction in those minor involvements. But what is at stake here are major political-military interventions by our government in the affairs of smaller countries. These are very different things.

First of all, we do not approach these questions with entirely free hands. We have conducted a number of such interventions in recent years, and at least three of these—Korea, Iraq, and Haiti—have led to new commitments that are still weighty and active.

There are several things to note about these interventions and commitments. First, while some may well have helped preserve peace or promote stability in local military relationships, this has not always been their stated purpose; in a number of instances, in particular, where we have portrayed them as efforts to promote democracy or human rights, they seem to have had little enduring success.

Second, lest there be any misunderstanding about this, the interventions in which we are now engaged or committed represent serious responsibilities. Any abrupt withdrawal from them would be a violation of these responsibilities; and there is no intention here to recommend anything of that sort. On the contrary, it should be a matter of principle for this government to meet to the best of its ability any responsibilities it has already incurred. Only when we have succeeded in extracting ourselves from the existing ones with dignity and honor will the question of further interventions present itself to us in the way that it did to Mr. Adams.

Third, instances where we have undertaken or committed ourselves to intervene represent only a small proportion of the demands and expectations that have come to rest on us. This is a great and confused world, and there are many other peoples and countries clamoring for our assistance. Yet it is clear that even these involvements stretch to the limit our economic and military resources, not to mention the goodwill of our people. And even if this were not a compelling limitation, there would still be the question of consistency. Are there any considerations being presented as justifications for our present involvements that would not, if consistently applied, be found to be relevant to many other situations as well? And if not, the question arises: If we cannot meet all the demands of this sort coming to rest upon us, should we attempt to meet any at all? The answer many would give to this question would be: yes, but only when our vital national interests are clearly threatened.

And last, beyond all these considerations, we have the general proposition that clearly underlay John Quincy Adams' response to similar problems so many years ago—his recognition that it is very difficult for one country to help another by intervening directly in its domestic affairs or in its conflicts with its neighbors. It is particularly difficult to do this without creating new and unwelcome embarrassments and burdens for the country endeavoring to help. The best way for a larger country to help smaller ones is surely by the power of example. Adams made this clear in the address cited above. One will recall his urging that the best response we could give to those appealing to us for support would be to give them what he called "the benign sympathy of our example." To go further, he warned, and try to give direct assistance would be to involve ourselves beyond the power of extrication "in all the wars of interest and intrigue, of individual avarice, envy, and ambition, which assumed the colors and usurped the standards of freedom." Who, today, looking at our involvements of recent years, could maintain that the fears these words expressed were any less applicable in our time than in his?

The best way for a larger country to help smaller ones is by the power of example.

These, then, are some of the considerations bearing on the relevance of Adams' principle to the present problems of our country. This writer, for one, finds Adams' principle, albeit with certain adjustments to meet our present circumstances and commitments, entirely suitable and indeed greatly needed as a guide for American policy in the coming period. This examination of what Adams said, and its relevance to the problems of our own age, will in any case have served to illustrate what the word "principle" meant in his time and what it could, in this case or others, mean in our own.

One last word: the example offered above of what a principle might be revolved primarily around our relations with smaller countries that felt, or professed to feel, the need for our help in furthering their places in the modern world. These demands have indeed taken a leading place in our diplomacy of this post-Cold War era. But one should not be left with the impression that these relationships were all that counted in our present problems with diplomacy. Also at stake are our relations with the other great powers, and these place even more important demands on our attention, policies, and resources.

The present moment is marked, most happily, by the fact that there are no great conflicts among the great powers. This situation is without precedent in recent centuries, and it is essential that it be cherished, nurtured, and preserved. Such is the destructive potential of advanced modern weapons that another great conflict between any of the leading powers could well do irreparable damage to the entire structure of modern civilization.

Intimately connected with those problems, of course, is the necessity of restraining, and eventually halting, the proliferation of weapons of mass destruction and of achieving their eventual total removal from national arsenals. And finally, also connected with these problems but going beyond them in many respects, there is the great environmental crisis our world is entering. To this crisis, too, adequate answers must be found if modern civilization is to have a future.

All of these challenges stand before us. Until they are met, even the many smaller and weaker countries can have no happy future. Our priorities must be shaped accordingly. Only when these wider problems have found their answers will any efforts we make to solve the problems of humane and civil government in the rest of the world have hopes of success.

> "Precisely because its effects are distributed in such a wildly uneven, frequently shifting manner, globalization raises serious questions about America's future as a cohesive, successful society—about American nationhood itself. [Indeed,] globalization could represent the greatest challenge to national unity since the Civil War."

Globalization: The Great American Non-Debate

ALAN TONELSON

Early in the nuclear age, Albert Einstein lamented that the atomic bomb had changed everything but the way humanity thinks. Today, the same can be said of the impact on American politics of economic globalization—the increasing integration of international markets being brought about by rapidly expanding worldwide flows of goods, services, capital, information, and sometimes people.

Prominent Americans in and out of government proclaim the new global economy to be the defining reality of our age, powerful enough (along with technological change) to transform such age-old institutions as the job, the nation-state, and the family itself. Yet aside from discrete trade policy controversies, globalization has not been meaningfully incorporated into American politics or policymaking. In fact, most social and even economic policy issues are debated in America today as if globalization did not exist, or were happening somewhere else.

Take the ongoing controversy this year about domestic monetary policy and the relationship between economic growth, employment levels, and wage pressures. Eyeing a steadily falling national unemployment rate and understandably determined to stop inflation before it starts, Federal Reserve Board chairman Alan Greenspan has been holding real interest rates high enough to keep economic growth modest and therefore labor markets loose enough to inhibit workers from seeking significant raises. Most Wall Street observers and economists have praised Greenspan, expressed amazement that inflationary pressures have not reappeared at today's unemployment levels, and continued to warn that rising labor costs must be just around the corner.

If these observers recognized the United States economy's steady internationalization, they would understand that the employment rate of American workers is no longer the only significant determinant of American wage levels. With more and more American companies hiring foreign workers for their overseas facilities, it is equally important to look at global unemployment rates. According to the International Labor Organization, roughly one-third of the world's workforce is jobless or underemployed. Moreover, given the explosive growth in the number of workers entering the world economy in huge, low-wage countries like China, India, and Indonesia, it is easy to see how American workers could continue to be afraid to press for higher pay even if United States unemployment rates sank even lower.

Welfare reform is another issue with a critical but neglected international dimension. Both supporters and most opponents of today's welfare reform schemes apparently believe that the United States economy is full of opportunities for minimally educated and generally unskilled workers to earn a liv-

---

ALAN TONELSON *is a research fellow at the United States Business and Industrial Council Educational Foundation, a Washington, D.C.-based organization studying United States national security, trade, and technology policy. His articles and reviews have appeared in* Foreign Affairs, The Atlantic, Foreign Policy, *and* The Harvard Business Review, *among other publications.*

ing wage—either through the magic of the marketplace or with a little help from retraining and reeducation programs. What both overlook is that most of the industries that paid decent wages to American workers without world-class skills and education—such as apparel, textiles, and steel—have been decimated by foreign competition and the inadequate response of United States trade policy. Moreover, wages in those jobs that remain have fallen precipitously in the past quarter century.

THE NEW RECEIVED WISDOM

The failure to fully incorporate globalization into American foreign and domestic policies has had serious consequences. As suggested earlier, it has obscured the global dimensions of—and therefore, key elements of the solutions to—many major national economic and social problems. It has also crippled American trade policy, saddling the country with narrowly conceived globalization approaches that have benefited relatively small numbers of Americans. Not coincidentally, the poll ratings for America's globalization policies keep sinking lower and lower.

American politics and policy are not taking globalization seriously enough for several reasons. One is perceptual. To most Americans in and out of government, globalization means "trade." This is especially true in discussions of globalization's impact on American living standards, which are usually brought to a premature halt with the observation that, despite 20 years of steady growth, two-way trade in goods and services still represents less than 30 percent of the United States economy. Thus it is said to be mathematically impossible for such flows to be responsible for most wage stagnation.

Leave aside for the moment the conveniently forgotten fact that mainstream economic theory emphasizes the decisive influence that even marginal changes in supply, demand, and prices (including labor prices) tend to have on each other. What about the impact of immigration on wage levels? What about investment? Technology flows? For some reason they are invariably left out of the debate—an especially ironic tendency, given that immigration is now widely blamed for about one-third of the wage decline experienced since the early 1970s by low-income Americans (a point made by Harvard professor George Borjas in the November 1996 *Atlantic*).

Other reasons for the globalization non-debate combine the emotional, the intellectual, and the ideological. Today, at the end of the twentieth century, many Americans are inhibited from thinking critically and rigorously about globalization for the kinds of reasons that inhibited their forebears at the end of the nineteenth century from thinking critically and rigorously about laissez-faire capitalism in the domestic sphere. Unfettered economic activity and the absolute sanctity of private property were that era's unassailable orthodoxy. Their moral and practical superiority were firmly established by Adam Smith's *The Wealth of Nations* and subsequent works of neoclassical economics. As Eric F. Goldman explained in his brilliant 1952 history of American reform, *Rendezvous with Destiny*, these certitudes formed the main links of a "steel chain of ideas" that created an overwhelming bias against government intervention in domestic economic and social affairs.

Today, although welfare capitalism has sunk deep roots in the industrialized world, free trade, unrestricted capital mobility, and economic integration are the watchwords of international economic policy. Their moral and practical superiority has been firmly established by two epochal events—the Great Depression and the fall of communism. Today's noninterventionist trade ethos has become so strong that even many liberals who have pushed hard to expand the welfare and regulatory state at home recoil at the thought of any regulation of international trade or investment. Indeed, no modern American political cliché has been more predictably invoked than when Vice President Al Gore confronted former presidential contender Ross Perot at their 1993 televised NAFTA debate with a photo of Senators Smoot and Hawley. Their 1929 tariff bill, after all, is almost universally—but inaccurately—blamed for deepening and even starting the Depression.

The power and persuasiveness of laissez-faire orthodoxy have another, equally important dampening effect on debating globalization—portraying globalization issues as a series of black-and-white, either-or choices. Free trade versus protectionism is how the debate is typically framed—as if anyone were advocating either removing all controls over international commerce or permitting no such commerce whatsoever. The situation is analogous to the debate over American foreign policy, with most commentators endlessly and fruitlessly debating "engagement versus isolationism," and neglecting what form engagement should take.

WHOSE GLOBALIZATION?

This dichotomous portrayal of globalization choices is convincing in large part because of the way globalization itself is depicted. Critics of current globalization policy are right to complain that its champions simply assume that the global economy will unfold along Anglo-American-style free trade lines, even though most of the world practices forms of capitalism significantly different from this approach.

But the problem runs even deeper. It entails the view of globalization as a monolithic, undifferentiated phenomenon, with a structure as interesting as a lump of coal. In fact, like any sweeping trend with widespread, profound effects, globalization is highly complex. The term describes a bewildering number of relationships and arrangements that are inevitably subject to strategic, political, social, and cultural—as well as "purely economic"—influences.

Elsewhere around the world, where mixed economic systems and the difficult trade-offs they require are more openly acknowledged, the complexity of globalization seems more apparent. Policymakers and analysts alike seem to recognize that their challenge entails not simply promoting or stopping globalization, but ensuring that its terms serve specific local, national, and regional interests. Efforts are under way to strike the right balance between benefiting from globalization's efficiency-enhancing effects and promoting the equally valid noneconomic goals set by all human communities. Eisuke Sakakibara, a vice minister in Japan's powerful Ministry of Finance, provided an unusually comprehensive statement of this position in his 1993 study, *Beyond Capitalism: The Japanese Model of Market Economics:* "Taking [the] pluralistic position that capitalism can differ across national borders and according to various historical and cultural backgrounds, our views on the world economy and world trade should be transformed as well. Indeed, in this increasingly interdependent world, many aspects of different national economies need to be harmonized. Yet to the extent that different regimes continue to be different, they will have to accommodate each other in certain ways. In some instances, these accommodations may take the form of modification of the principle of laissez-faire."

In the United States, the failure to perceive the real, highly nuanced choices presented by globalization, plus the ideological bias against intervention in the economy, severely undermines the very legitimacy of thinking critically about these matters. The clearest evidence of this is the labels that have been successfully hung on the parties in globalization disputes: supporters and opponents of prevailing policies are simply and misleadingly labeled "pro" and "anti-trade," respectively.

Proponents of current globalization policies have also been able to portray their preferences in terms connoting objectivity and inevitability. They have explicitly described themselves as the "party of the future" or, more specifically, of the "New Economy." Their depiction of their policies as "bridges to the twenty-first century" fails to provoke much protest, even from opponents.

Critics, meanwhile, are widely dismissed as voices of the past, clinging stubbornly but naively to outmoded industries and ways of life. (At least one—columnist and erstwhile Republican presidential hopeful Pat Buchanan—actually does talk openly about returning to the "Old Republic.") Paul Gigot of *The Wall Street Journal* used all of the major stereotypes in a September 12, 1997, column: "[F]ree trade has its political compensations even in a Democratic primary. It lets [Vice President Gore] seem future-oriented and presidential, instead of hostage to special interests and the old blast-furnace economy."

President Clinton, perhaps characteristically, tried to have it both ways in his September 22, 1997, speech to the United Nations General Assembly. "The forces of global integration are a great tide, inexorably wearing away the established order of things," he intoned, hastening to add, "but we must decide what will be left in its wake."

Superficially, these labels and stereotypes seem at least partly justified. After all, some of the leading champions of current globalization policies are high-tech companies like Microsoft, IBM, and AT&T, while some of the leading opponents include industrial unions, like the United Steel Workers and the United Auto Workers, which provide the workforce for the so-called blast-furnace industries.

The problem is that the high-tech companies still employ surprisingly small numbers of high-wage, highly skilled workers. Many more of these workers are employed by the blast-furnace industries, which have also undertaken a large and growing incorporation of high-tech components into their products and manufacturing processes. Still, the CEOs of the blast-furnace economy are sending production abroad just as fast—and fighting just as hard to keep United States markets open to their output—as their counterparts in high-tech industries.

American politics and policy are not taking globalization seriously enough.

Although the globalization debate often burns white hot when it erupts, the contending factions are anything but perfectly cohesive or coherent. The confusion is understandable; after all, any phenomenon with effects as powerful and wide-ranging as those of globalization is bound to stimulate myriad responses from many different interests and individuals. Still, the blurring of disagreements even over fundamental issues makes productive discussion of globalization all the more difficult.

THE DEBATE'S HISTORICAL ROOTS

For most of America's history, globalization policy has mainly meant trade policy, and its politics was mainly sectional. The manufacturing-heavy north favored high tariffs to protect and nurture its industries; the largely agrarian south, which not only imported manufactured goods but relied heavily on commodities exports, favored much more open trade. These powerful sectional influences in turn produced a clear partisan divide. Republicans were so devoted to tariffs that their presidents and especially members of Congress championed protectionist policies well into the Nixon era. Democrats generally favored more trade liberalization even after they transcended their base in the "Solid South." At the same time, it is crucial to note that the early nineteenth century triumph of federalists and nationalists in American politics and economic policy placed the nation on a predominantly mercantilist course until the mid-1930s.

During that decade, powerful domestic and international developments began to rival sectionalism as a determinant of trade politics and policy. Domestically, nationalizing forces, such as the continuing spread of manufacturing to the south and the creation of national cultural tastes and economic markets by movies and radio, started to flatten sectional differences. Internationally, protectionism was blamed for the Great Depression (and ultimately World War II). By the end of the war, a strong bipartisan consensus in favor of multilateral trade liberalization had been produced by the determination not to repeat the mistakes of the 1930s, the overwhelming supremacy of American industry and technology, and the emerging perceived need to win or aid cold war allies by unilaterally opening United States markets. In the years to follow, many politicians and analysts credited these free trade policies with sparking unprecedented peace and prosperity in the noncommunist world—further reinforcing free trade's legitimacy and popularity.

Starting in the 1970s, the fading of United States global economic predominance, the slowing of worldwide and domestic growth, and the steady decline in Americans' real wages significantly weakened the free trade consensus. Additional blows were delivered in the late 1980s by the end of the cold war and by the steady transformation of many large American companies into truly global firms. The former development undermined the strategic arguments for tolerating continued protectionism by allies even as their own economic strength burgeoned. The latter development began to open an unprecedented gap between the fortunes of American workers and those of American businesses, as companies responded to competitive pressures, new market opportunities, and investment incentives by building more factories and even laboratories abroad, exporting possibly millions of high-wage jobs in the process.

The American globalization debate has been hampered by the diversity of the nation...as well as by ideological blinders.

At the same time, one powerful countertrend enabled free traders to prevail in most of the increasingly contentious policy disputes of the 1980s. President Ronald Reagan's ringing rhetorical support for trade liberalization convinced many conservative and moderate Americans that traditional free trade policies were integral parts of the campaign against big government—even as the president approved skillfully targeted trade barriers to help hard-hit United States industries like semiconductors and autos regain competitiveness.

In the late 1980s, globalization's increasingly differentiated impact on Americans and the collapse of the cold war rationale for free trade, coupled with the end of the Reagan economic boom, greatly complicated the politics of globalization. The effect on Republicans and conservatives was especially profound, as their long-standing postwar consensus on free trade was shattered. At the end of World War II, the Grand Old Party was comprised of often vigorously clashing clusters of Eastern seaboard internationalist financiers, pro-tariff New England and Midwestern industrialists, Western and Midwestern isolationists, opportunistic McCarthyite red-baiters, and a small but influential band of paleo-conservative intellectuals battling against the modernizing, secularizing spirit of the twentieth century. The onset of the cold war persuaded them to set aside their differences and unite on an emergency basis behind interventionism, peacetime military alliances, and free trade.

Over the next three decades, these Republican factions broke up, evolved, and recombined into their contemporary forms—including laissez-faire-oriented supply-siders and libertarians, moral majoritarians, neoconservatives, nativist communitarians, deficit hawks, blue-collar ethnic "Reagan Democrats," and a dwindling band of moderates and liberals who retain influence in Congress and in Washington media circles. Yet with the cold war emergency over and the unifying presence of Reagan gone, America's conservative coalition has been pulling apart at the seams. And one of the main polarizing issues—even more at the rank and file than at the leadership level—has been globalization.

A February 1997 survey by prominent Republican pollsters Fabrizio McLaughlin and Associates showed how deep and wide the split runs. All five factions into which they divided the party—including the normally ardently pro–free trade supply-siders—showed plurality support for the proposition that recent trade agreements had sent more jobs abroad than they had created at home. Just as surprisingly, a late-July NBC–*Wall Street Journal* poll reported that Republican respondents were more strongly opposed to NAFTA than Democrats.

THE BIRTH OF THE NEW DEMOCRATS

The end of the cold war had a less dramatic impact on Democrats. Instead, their internal splits over globalization stem from the gap opened up by the Vietnam War between the party's moderate and left wings. The fault lines have remained more or less intact, but the dispute has been transformed into a battle between contrasting visions—if not realities—of the new and old economies. Moderates—most of whom eventually turned against the Vietnam War—continued to insist that cold war internationalism was a viable framework for United States foreign (and by extension, trade) policy. The left-wingers pushed a more fundamental critique of the war and the society that spawned it.

At the same time, cross-cutting issues and clashing institutional imperatives have repeatedly confused the picture. Among congressional Democrats, the hardening of organized labor's opposition to conventional free trade policies—led by unions whose leaders tended to support the Vietnam War until the bitter end—has helped shift the balance of power against current globalization initiatives.

At the presidential level, many Democratic leaders persuasively argued that electoral success depended on candidates distancing themselves from the party's best-known constituencies (including not only big labor but civil rights groups and feminists) and from the unpopular federal bureaucracies they had allegedly captured. Instead, the moderates counseled, Democrats should embrace the technological progress and entrepreneurial spirit that was fueling the booming information-based New Economy.

Greatly enhancing the New Democrats' power has been the skyrocketing costs of political campaigns. Since business—which is traditionally pro-Republican—is the greatest potential source of funds for the media advertising that can make or break candidates, Democrats have had to "follow the money" and step up their efforts to win corporate support. Under the leadership of former Connecticut Congressman Tony Coelho, the Democratic Congressional Campaign Committee turned into a big-time money machine and full-time Wall Street presence, starting in the late 1980s. In fact, one of Bill Clinton's most effective fund-raisers in 1992 was Treasury Secretary Robert Rubin, then head of the Wall Street investment giant Goldman Sachs. Because the large companies pursued by the Democrats have been the strongest proponents of current globalization policies, the New Democrats who preach that America should "compete, not retreat" in the world economy (to quote Clinton) have seen their influence grow. (The Democrats have made no special efforts to target small businesses—the vast majority of which do not export or are found in domestic-oriented service industries.)

The fly in this ointment has been the environmental issue. Although many environmentally minded voters are high-income Americans who consider themselves to be globalization's winners, many fear that uncontrolled globalization will greatly increase industrial pollution—and enhance corporations' ability and authority to pollute. Thus, major environmental organizations like the Sierra Club have been leading opponents of NAFTA and the General Agreement on Tariffs and Trade (GATT) Uruguay Round agreement that gave birth to the World Trade Organization.

GLOBALIZATION'S DRAMATIS PERSONAE

One critical result of these intraparty changes has been the emergence of nonpartisan "strange bedfellows" coalitions on globalization issues. Numerous commentators and analysts have noted that the anti-NAFTA and anti-GATT campaigns united Pat Buchanan and Jesse Jackson, Ralph Nader and Ross

Perot, paleo-conservatives and big labor. Less remarked on have been the mirror images of these pairings among globalization enthusiasts—Bill Clinton and Newt Gingrich, Henry Kissinger and Jimmy Carter, the Brookings Institution and the Heritage Foundation. At the same time, below the surface of these coalitions lurk major globalization-related disagreements that make coherent debates difficult to hold—and difficult for most voters to follow.

Today's globalization enthusiasts are divided between self-styled competitiveness advocates and free-market conservatives. The former—many of whom serve in the Clinton administration—speak of current globalization policies as integral parts of a broader "proactive" government strategy to restore America's relative economic position on the world stage. Indeed, many also favor a significant government role in developing and commercializing new technologies, as well as public sector efforts to restructure labor-management relations along more cooperative lines and improve America's primary and secondary schools. Although often insisting that trade in particular is not a zero-sum game, they repeatedly emphasize the importance of American exporters not only getting their appropriate share of foreign markets, but also beating the competition in the race for business opportunities whenever possible. Early in the Clinton administration, many of these competitiveness advocates vowed to reduce America's global trade deficits and its major bilateral trade deficits, which they blamed largely on foreign protectionism. The continued growth of these deficits, however, led them to abandon these goals in favor of simply boosting exports.

Nowhere was this approach more apparent than in the campaign to pass the original NAFTA in 1993. The agreement was sold as a way to create millions of high-wage jobs and improve the relative competitiveness of United States companies by securing for them significant advantages in Mexican consumer markets as well as important investment preferences. NAFTA supporters even warned that without these preferences valuable business opportunities would be lost to European and Asian companies allegedly poised to dominate the Mexican economy. Revealingly, the same arguments are being made today in the debate over expanding NAFTA to the rest of the Western Hemisphere.

The free-market conservative allies of these competitiveness advocates are distinctly uncomfortable with most of these arguments. They tend to see any trade expansion as a good in itself that enhances global efficiency and maximizes global welfare—thus benefiting America indirectly. Convinced (somewhat inconsistently) that international markets can, do, and should operate completely independent of international power politics, they oppose as counterproductive government efforts to shape worldwide economic flows for national advantage. The only exception entails maintaining sound macroeconomic policies.

Significantly, these conservatives' laissez-faire instincts are so strong that they vigorously oppose government trade policy activism even when market forces are fettered. In other words, true to David Ricardo's teachings (although not to Adam Smith's), they regard government as inherently so incompetent that they believe in tolerating foreign protectionism rather than retaliating. To be sure, they attribute America's trade deficits primarily to its relatively low rate of savings and high rate of consumption, not to foreign barriers. More important, however, most attach no significance to these international trade balances. Consistent with their free-market beliefs, they also oppose dedicated United States government efforts to promote exports, not to mention anything smacking of "industrial policy." Indeed, they—like Ronald Reagan's rhetoric—see opposition to protectionism as central to their plans to shrink government.

CRITICS LEFT AND RIGHT

Critics of current globalization policies face significant disagreements of their own, which tend to divide along left-right, nationalist-internationalist lines. Right-wing critics generally take a strongly nationalist view of international economics. They see the main challenge of United States globalization policy as defending and promoting purely American interests against the predations of foreign actors. Consequently, they scorn international organizations like the World Trade Organization as mechanisms largely designed by weak countries to handcuff great powers like the United States, and as unacceptable threats to America's sovereignty and the principles of representative, accountable government. In addition, they are fully confident that the unilateral use of United States power—especially regulating access to the American market—can achieve America's essential globalization policy goals, including removing foreign trade barriers and ensuring that exports to the United States are "fairly" traded. Yet like the competitiveness advocates, the right-wing globalization critics leave unclear whether they simply want a perfectly level playing field in world trade and investment and equal opportunity for American producers, or whether they want guarantees of successful outcomes.

These critics understand that promoting economic development and sound environmental policies in low-income countries can help buoy wages and environmental standards at home. But they fear that significantly closing the North-South gap will take too many years—if it can be done at all. Therefore, they tend to see the interests of American workers and their foreign counterparts as being in unfortunate but unmistakable conflict.

Most left-wing globalization critics see entirely different fault lines in the world economy. Generally unconcerned with the globalization-related tensions among countries, their main interest is the struggle they see between the world's workers and international capital. Unlike the conservative nationalists, they believe that developing world living standards can be raised relatively quickly with few sacrifices from workers in the industrialized world, and they are confident that international institutions can and should play constructive roles. The main problem they have with these institutions is not that they are anti-American, but that they are controlled by worldwide corporate interests. If only unions and consumer groups were adequately represented, these left-wing critics suggest, they would have no objections to significant reductions in American sovereignty.

At the same time, one faction on the left, convinced that multinational businesses have all the advantages in a truly global economy, seems to oppose the idea of increasing worldwide economic integration itself, and argues for greater self-reliance at the national and especially subnational levels.

ONE NATION, DIVISIBLE?

Unquestionably, the American globalization debate has been hampered by the diversity of the nation and by globalization's uncanny ability to subdivide even the factions described above, as well as by ideological blinders. The globalization of production does indeed create obstacles to identifying which firms are truly serving the entire nation's interests and therefore where and how to target globalization policy initiatives. Powerful links are forming between the prosperity of American workers and foreign countries—whether the former work in exporting industries or hold stock in foreign enterprises or major United States exporting companies. And globalization issues can pit not only different industries against each other, but different companies within industries against each other—witness the current feud among American airlines over access to Japan. At the same time, although organized labor and United States multinationals are battling tooth and nail over the trade and investment dimensions of globalization, they are cooperating to defeat a UN environmental initiative that both believe will damage American competitiveness.

Precisely because its effects are distributed in such a wildly uneven, frequently shifting manner, globalization raises serious questions about America's future as a cohesive, successful society—about American nationhood itself. Globalization's ability to set worker against manager, industry against industry, and companies within industries against each other is clear even during today's ongoing economic expansion and relative prosperity. These developments will only become more frequent and pronounced when the economy slows.

Observing the growing tendency of wealthier Americans to literally wall themselves off from the problems of their fellow countrymen with private schools, gated communities, and private security forces, writers as different as Robert Reich, the former labor secretary, and conservative military strategist Edward Luttwak warn that parts of America are starting to resemble chronically divided, class-ridden third world societies. Should these trends continue, globalization could represent the greatest challenge to national unity since the Civil War. It is, of course, certainly possible that Americans ultimately will be better off as members of transnational labor or corporate communities, or even as citizens of tightly contained subnational groups; no political form lasts forever, and the nation-state cannot automatically be assumed an exception. But questions so monumental should be confronted openly and decided deliberately, not backed into unwittingly, heedless of the full consequences.

Unit 4

Unit Selections

Law and the Courts
18. **Against an International Criminal Court,** Lee A. Casey and David B. Rivkin Jr.

State and Local Governments
19. **Paying Something for Nothing,** Kimberly Ann Elliott

Congress
20. **The Senate's Strange Bedfellows,** John Isaacs

The Bureaucracy
21. **Racing toward the Future: The Revolution in Military Affairs,** Steven Metz
22. **Why Spy? The Uses and Misuses of Intelligence,** Stanley Kober
23. **Tin Cup Diplomacy,** Hans Binnendijk

Key Points to Consider

❖ How relevant is the Constitution to the conduct of American foreign policy? Do courts have a legitimate role to play in determining the content of U.S. foreign policy? What role should international law play in making policy?

❖ Should states and local governments be restricted in their ability to conduct their own foreign policy? In what areas should they be allowed to make foreign policy? What should states do when they feel injured by American foreign policy?

❖ Is Congress best seen as an obstacle course that presidents must navigate successfully in making foreign policy? What is the proper role of Congress in making foreign policy? Is it the same for military and economic policy?

❖ Which of the foreign affairs bureaucracies discussed in this unit is most important? Which is in the most need of reform? Which is most incapable of being reformed?

❖ Prioritize which parts of the U.S. government are most in need of reform, in terms of making foreign policy. In your view, are the institutions that make American foreign policy capable of being reformed? Are institutional reforms really necessary for the content of American foreign policy to change?

DUSHKIN ONLINE Links www.dushkin.com/online/

12. **Central Intelligence Agency (CIA)**
    http://www.odci.gov/cia/ciahome.html
13. **NAFTA Border Home Page**
    http://www.iep.doc.gov/border/nafta.htm
14. **The NATO Integrated Data Service (NIDS)**
    http://www.nato.int/structur/nids/nids.htm
15. **The North American Institute (NAMI)**
    http://www.santafe.edu/~naminet/index.html
16. **United States Department of State**
    http://www.state.gov/

These sites are annotated on pages 4 and 5.

The Institutional Context of American Foreign Policy

Central to any study of American foreign policy are the institutions responsible for its content and conduct. In fact, institutions and policy are so tightly intertwined that it often becomes impossible to talk about one without the other. Vietnam quickly brings to mind images of the "imperial presidency"; Pearl Harbor is associated forever with the need for more coordination among the national security bureaucracies; the isolationist and protectionist trade policies of the 1930s can only be discussed within the context of congressional politics; and references to the Central Intelligence Agency (CIA) abound in any study of U.S. foreign policy toward Cuba, Angola, Chile, Iran, and Guatemala.

This close linkage between institutions and policies suggests that if American foreign policy is to successfully adapt to the challenges of the post–cold war era, American policy-making institutions must also change their ways. Many find it unreasonable to expect that institutions that built a political or budgetary power base around policies designed to contain communism can provide a hospitable environment for policies designed to further human rights, engage in multilateral peacemaking operations, protect the environment, or open markets to American products.

The process of bringing about institutional reform thus promises to be a long and difficult one, and one that proceeds on many levels. It may be little more than renaming congressional committees (for instance, from the House Armed Services Committee to the National Security Committee). In other places it may involve potentially significant organizational changes such as those involving the State Department's absorption of the Arms Control and Disarmament Agency, the Agency for International Development, and the U.S. Information Agency. In still other places, it may involve the formation of new organizational units such as the creation of economic development and foreign trade offices in the 50 states.

The historical record regarding institutional change in the United States also suggests a point of caution to those seeking reform. Once put into place, institutional reforms often have unintended consequences that thwart the purposes of the reform initiative or create new, unimagined problems.

It will not be enough to reform any one institution if change in American foreign policy is to be realized, because no one institution is capable of bringing about substantive changes by itself. Rather, as has long been noted, when it comes to foreign policy, the Constitution of the United States amounts to little more than an "invitation to struggle." Thinking about the institutions of American foreign policy making in terms of the need to change and their ability to do so thus requires us to think about change in a wide range of institutions.

In prioritizing institutions for change, Congress and the presidency must come first because these two bodies are the lead protagonists in the struggle to control the content and conduct of American foreign policy. The relationship between them has varied over time with such phrases as the "imperial presidency," "bipartisanship," and "divided government" being used to describe it. The Republican victory in the 1994 congressional elections brought a new intensity to the battle of wills between Congress and the presidency.

One essay examines the role that Congress plays in making foreign policy. Written before NATO expansion sailed through the Senate with little opposition, John Isaacs, in "The Senate's Strange Bedfellows," examines the political alignment of forces in the Senate as the vote neared.

A second set of institutions thought to be in need of change are the bureaucracies that play influential roles in making foreign policy by supplying policymakers with information, defining problems, and implementing the selected policies. The end of the cold war presents these bureaucracies with a special challenge. Old threats and enemies have declined in importance or disappeared entirely. To remain effective players in post–cold war foreign policy making, these institutions must adjust their organizational structures and ways of thinking or risk being seen by policymakers as irrelevant anachronisms. The three leading foreign policy bureaucracies of the cold war are the State Department, the Defense Department, and the Central Intelligence Agency (CIA).

What the future holds for each of these institutions is the subject of three articles in this section. Stanley Kober, in "Why Spy?" examines the uses and misuses of intelligence. He argues for concentrating intelligence resources on political and military challenges such as international terrorism and not on economic espionage as the Clinton administration has done. Hans Binnendijk, in "Tin Cup Diplomacy," is highly critical of the reductions that have occurred in the foreign affairs budget and the negative consequences this has had on the State Department's ability to represent effectively American interests abroad. Steven Metz, in "Racing toward the Future: The Revolution in Military Affairs," looks at the prospects for meaningful reform in the military.

A final set of institutions demands our attention not because they need reform, but because the altered agenda of world politics raises the possibility that they might become more important players in making policy. The first of these are the state and local governments. Their increased importance is tied to the greater attention being paid to international economic issues in American foreign policy. Kimberly Ann Elliott, in "Paying Something for Nothing," presents a critical evaluation of state and local government sanctions against foreign countries. She argues they are unproductive and may be unconstitutional. The courts may also play a greater role in American foreign policy due to the increased involvement of the United States in multilateral efforts. Particularly controversial is the relationship between the American legal system and international law. Lee A. Casey and David B. Rivkin Jr., in "Against an International Criminal Court," argue that the International Criminal Court Treaty is flawed and that it cannot work as advertised. They argue against U.S. participation.

Against an International Criminal Court
Lee A. Casey & David B. Rivkin, Jr.

ALTHOUGH ONE would not necessarily know it from the newspapers, a half-century of debate over the question of how to bring perpetrators of genocide and other grave crimes to justice is now coming to a head. In June, a gathering of diplomats in Rome will put the finishing touches on a United Nations-sponsored treaty to establish an International Criminal Court (ICC). This document will then be put forward for signature and ratification by the 185 member states of the world body.

Not a moment too soon, many might say. After all, the prosecution of Nazi war criminals at Nuremberg after World War II was undertaken in part to keep the horrors of mass slaughter and aggressive war from recurring. Yet, in places as disparate as Cambodia, Rwanda, and Iraq, such horrors *have* recurred, and recurred again, and the guilty parties have gone unpunished. The need for a standing International Criminal Court would thus appear self-evident, its absence itself a kind of crime.

In the United States, a variety of influential organizations—ranging from the American Bar Association (ABA) to monitoring groups like Human Rights Watch—is backing the UN initiative. With Secretary of State Madeleine Albright leading the charge, the Clinton administration, too, though quibbling about some aspects of the draft now under discussion, has expressed its approval of the treaty's basic outline, and is expected in due course to submit a version to the U.S. Senate for its advice and consent.

If the ICC were to work as advertised—its professed purpose is to indict warring despots and mass murderers, extradite them, try them, and award them their just deserts—it would be no bad thing. There is, however, a problem, and one with especially severe implications for the United States: it will not, and cannot, work as advertised.

As IT is currently conceived, the ICC will be an independent international body that will combine in one institution the functions of fact-finding, prosecution, judgment, sentencing, appeal, and pardon. The ICC's judges and prosecutors will be nominated by the signatory states, and elected by their majority vote. A complaint brought by any signatory state, or by the UN Security Council, will empower the ICC prosecutors to investigate, indict, and try individuals for such offenses as crimes against humanity and violations of the laws of war. Trials will not be by jury. Punishment, up to a maximum sentence of life imprisonment, will be decided by the court, as will requests for clemency and parole. The sole venue for appeal will be the appellate division of the ICC itself. There will be no recourse from its decisions, and no ability to overturn the law it sets.

To begin at the beginning, it is highly questionable whether the Constitution allows the U.S. government to delegate its judicial authority—to delegate, in other

---

LEE A. CASEY *and* DAVID B. RIVKIN, JR. *have both served in the U.S. Justice Department and now practice law in Washington, D.C. Their article, "Federalism (Cont'd.)," appeared in our December 1996 issue.*

words, the right to put Americans on trial for offenses (like planning an allegedly illegal military action) that they have committed on American soil—to an institution that is not a court of the United States. The defining case here is *Ex parte Milligan*, decided shortly after the Civil War, in which the Supreme Court struck down the conviction of a civilian by a military tribunal. Because the military tribunal had not been established under Article III of the Constitution, ruled the Court, it was not "part of the judicial power of the country." The same reasoning would clearly apply to the ICC and render its judgments against Americans unenforceable in the United States.

Even if a way around this could be found—and it would require, at a minimum, that ICC judges be appointed by the U.S. President, be approved by the U.S. Senate, and serve for life—the ICC would still be unconstitutional. In particular, though the ICC will be empowered to indict and try American citizens, its procedures will fail to provide American defendants who come before it the basic guarantees they enjoy under the Constitution's Bill of Rights.

Thus, the Constitution's Fourth Amendment protects Americans against unreasonable searches and seizures; the Fifth Amendment requires grand-jury indictments, forbids double jeopardy, and gives an assurance of "due process of law"; the Sixth Amendment ensures that in all criminal prosecutions the accused shall have the right to be tried "by an impartial jury of the state and district wherein the crime shall have been committed"; the Eighth Amendment forbids excessive bail and fines, as well as cruel and unusual punishment. None of these rights is adequately preserved in the ICC agreement, and most are not preserved at all.

The absence of these safeguards is all the more disturbing because the Supreme Court stated plainly in an 1890 case, *De Geofroy v. Riggs*, that the constitutional rights of Americans cannot be abridged by the federal government's power to conclude treaties. That power, stated the Court, does not enable the government to "authorize what the Constitution forbids." The Court reiterated this view in a particularly pertinent case, *In re Yamashita*, heard shortly after the end of World War II and dealing with the same subject matter that will come before the ICC. In any conflict between U.S. law and the laws of war, noted the Supreme Court, U.S. law must prevail: "[W]e do not make the laws of war but we respect them so far as they *do not* conflict with the commands of Congress or the Constitution" (emphasis added).

The fact that the constitutional case against the ICC seems straightforward has not prevented the ICC's supporters, including the American Bar Association, from blithely dismissing it. An organization ostensibly devoted to the rule of law, the ABA describes constitutional objections to the ICC as a "red herring," asserting that since the ICC will not be a "court of the United States," the Bill of Rights will not apply to its proceedings. This analysis is as simple as it is wrong. The protections offered by the Bill of Rights, as we have seen, extend to every act of the entire federal government, including its agreements with other nations.

B UT NOW suppose that the ICC treaty were somehow altered to pass constitutional muster—that is, by scrapping the current draft and starting again. Even so, compelling reasons remain for not setting up a supranational criminal court that will be empowered to stand in judgment not only of the usual despots and mass murderers but also, by definition, of the U.S. and its allies.

The danger of politicization and anti-Americanism, inherent in all international institutions, has been driven home time and again by the behavior of such bodies as the International Labor Organization, UNESCO, and the UN itself. While it is true that the level of anti-Americanism may have waned somewhat now that the cold war has drawn to an end and the Soviet Union has disappeared, the United States and its allies still have enemies, and those enemies, if they accede to the ICC treaty, will have a say in the composition of the court's personnel. Add to the mix the many countries that are not overtly hostile to the U.S. but that wish to check an assertive American foreign policy, and inevitably a tremendous potential for mischief will arise.

Here is an example of how things can go awry. The Clinton administration has asserted that if Saddam Hussein further impedes the work of UN inspectors searching for weapons of mass destruction in Iraq, the U.S. has the legal right to strike Baghdad without further action by the UN Security Council. Yet three of the five permanent members of the Council—Russia, China, and France—disagree. They maintain that a U.S. attack would be a violation of the UN mandate and consequently of international law.

If a court like the ICC were in place, a decision to hit Saddam Hussein would leave the President, and each and every American who participated in the formulation and execution of the military operation, vulnerable to investigation and prosecution. How might the court's proceedings unfold? The prosecution might root its case in the civilian casualties that Iraq would inevitably incur in the course of the U.S. strike. If the ICC determined that sufficient evidence existed to hand up an indictment for violation of the laws of war, the United States would be legally bound to surrender the individuals charged, be they military or civilian, Secretary of State or GS-7 file clerk, President or private. While there would be no enforcement mechanism on U.S. soil to compel acquiescence, the ICC could issue international warrants; those under indictment would then be unable to travel overseas for fear of arrest. The ICC could also opt to begin proceedings against U.S. officials *in absentia*.

Naturally, the President and other responsible officials would have a number of defenses at their disposal. They could claim, for example, that the attacks on Iraq had been authorized by previous Security Council resolutions and that civilians were not deliberately targeted. Ultimately, however, the merits of the case would be for the ICC to determine, and the court's findings, as noted above, could not be appealed except to the ICC itself.

A SCENARIO like this one may seem unlikely. But whether or not it ever comes to pass, the very existence of a court that can at any time initiate investigations of U.S. actions around the globe will almost certainly impose inhibitions on the conduct of American foreign policy. In fact, even the Clinton administration is troubled by the prospect of the ICC's becoming an uncontrollable rogue institution. "We do have concerns about a prosecutor who would act on his or her own authority," admits David Scheffer, the head of the U.S. delegation to the negotiations.

To keep the ICC within acceptable bounds, the administration has sought to revise the mechanism that will trigger its initiation of a case; these proposed revisions, however, fall far short of the mark. For example, the U.S. wants to require "complementarity," which means that the ICC would become involved in prosecuting individuals only if their own government had failed to bring them to justice. But this particular proposal comes with a qualification: the power to determine whether a good-faith effort at prosecution had been made would be retained by the ICC itself. It is a generous loophole, and potentially a lethal one.

The U.S. also wants to require a referral by the UN Security Council before the ICC can investigate any particular conflict or atrocity. This would allow the United States to exercise its veto when American interests are threatened. But one can easily imagine what would happen in practice: on every occasion in which the U.S. considered casting its veto to prevent the ICC from taking action, it would be accused of hypocrisy and lawlessness, and find itself under intense pressure to acquiesce. And such occasions are likely to abound, given the investigatory latitude the ICC is to enjoy.

To understand what is at stake here, let us return to the example of Iraq, and let us suppose that Kuwait, say, were to attempt to bring Saddam Hussein before the ICC for committing war crimes. An ICC investigation into this matter could easily expand to encompass an inquiry of another sort entirely—namely, into the war crimes that Saddam Hussein himself has alleged were committed by the U.S. *against Iraq*. To avert this possibility, the U.S. might then be forced to exercise its veto—and thus block even friendly states like Kuwait from initiating a referral.

Indeed, to avoid having its current or former leadership brought before an international tribunal to answer for American foreign policy, Washington might find itself compelled to veto *any* referral of *any* conflict where American arms were involved. In the end, all the ICC would then have accomplished would be to tie our foreign policy in knots. In the eyes of some around the world, to be sure, this might well seem a desirable goal; but how it would serve our own interests—or, for that matter, the interests of peace and the rule of law—is a mystery.

DO THE palpable flaws of the ICC treaty mean that the world community is helpless to bring outlaws to justice? Hardly. The UN Security Council already possesses the authority to establish tribunals to investigate and punish war crimes. It has, in fact, recently established two: the international criminal tribunal for the former Yugoslavia, and the international criminal tribunal for Rwanda. Unlike the ICC, however, their territorial jurisdiction and temporal duration are limited. Thus far, the Yugoslav tribunal has issued eighteen indictments against 74 individuals, of whom twenty are in custody. It concluded its first trial, of a Serbian concentration-camp guard, last July, sentencing him to prison for twenty years. A number of other cases are to be heard in the next few months. Some may consider this too little, too late; but with sufficient international backing, such courts can accomplish a great deal.

The ICC also promises to accomplish a great deal—but precisely what those accomplishments will be is another matter. In the name of international law, the treaty will undermine our own system of justice. In the name of bringing aggressors to account, it will diminish our own ability to do exactly that, while augmenting the possibility that we or one of our close allies will sooner or later find ourselves in the dock.

The Clinton administration's penchant for multilateralism is by now an old story. Even so, it is astonishing that it has so fervently embraced a document with such obvious faults. Is this really the straitjacket in which the world's greatest power, and its best hope for peace, wishes to place itself?

Paying something for nothing

A researcher says state and local economic sanctions against countries are counterproductive and may be unconstitutional.

BY KIMBERLY ANN ELLIOTT

The General Assembly in my home state of Maryland is debating a bill this year to impose economic sanctions against Nigeria, as well as against companies doing business there. As a constituent, I am sympathetic with the objective of bringing democracy to Nigeria. As an analyst, I am concerned that these sanctions impose a variety of under-appreciated costs at home while achieving little or no improvement in conditions in Nigeria.

Economic sanctions do not just hurt the targeted country. They also prevent the country imposing sanctions from reaping the gains from trade. In this case sanctions mean higher costs for Maryland taxpayers. When imposed at the state and local level, sanctions often undermine national policy, exacerbate relations with important allies and trading partners, and, most troubling, violate the U.S. Constitution.

The Maryland initiative, with some exceptions, would bar state agencies from purchasing goods produced in Nigeria or procuring goods or services from companies that do business

Kimberly Ann Elliott is a research fellow at the Institute for International Economics. The views expressed here are the author's and do not necessarily reflect the views of the institute's other staff, board of directors or advisory committee.

Nigeria's ruling regime is not committed to encouraging reform and democratic principles, according to the U.S. Department of State.

there. As of early March, Massachusetts and city or county governments in eight states had imposed economic sanctions against companies doing business in Burma, Nigeria, Cuba or Tibet. Like the Maryland proposal, these sanctions typically involve selective procurement rules, while some also prohibit investment of state funds in firms or banks doing business in the target country. More than a dozen similar sanctions proposals are pending at the state and local level as of mid-March (see table 1).

Economic and political costs

Taxpayers will pay more if affected firms forgo local procurement opportunities to remain in important foreign markets. That's because with fewer firms to buy from, selective procurement laws reduce competition and raise the cost of providing government goods and services. Firms in a community also could withdraw from a city or state that denies them procurement opportunities. However they respond, affected firms, which often are U.S.-based, will have to sacrifice profitable opportunities in one market or another. Replicated many times, such costs could spread beyond local procurement markets.

Evidence suggests that public officials are aware of these potential costs to taxpayers and often tailor their sanctions accordingly. A large majority (20 of 26) of subfederal sanctions target Burma, renamed Myanmar in 1989. Freedom House, a nonprofit group that tracks freedom around the world, gives its lowest ranking for political and civil liberties to Burma, which is by no means alone in that category. But the costs of imposing sanctions against the small Burmese market are not large. Many companies faced with a choice between the Burmese market or Massachusetts will choose Massachusetts. Faced with a choice between Massachusetts or Maryland and Indonesia or Nigeria, the choice is not so clear and the costs to taxpayers and the economy could be much higher.

The proposed Maryland law contains loopholes allowing the state or local government to waive sanctions if the cost of alternative suppliers is too high. But those loopholes do not mitigate other costs. Though the tangible economic losses for multinational firms would likely be small, the Massachusetts law imposing selective procurement sanctions against firms doing business in Burma triggered an international dispute with the European Union and Japan that has yet to be resolved.

During the Uruguay round of multilateral trade negotiations, completed in 1994, U.S. Trade Representative Michael Kantor elicited pledges from Massachusetts, Maryland, 35 other states (13 states chose not to participate) and seven of the 24 largest municipalities (Chicago, Detroit, Boston, Dallas, Indianapolis, San Antonio and Nashville) to abide by the rules of the Government Procurement Agreement. These commitments were then exchanged for commitments from Europe, Japan and others to increase access for U.S. firms in subfederal procurement markets in their countries. The agreement disciplines discrimination against foreign firms in procurement and bars the use of political or other arbitrary criteria in the procurement process. The EU and Japan have filed a complaint against the Massachusetts law in the World Trade Organization charging that the law violates U.S. obligations under the GPA. If the Maryland law passes, it could trigger a similar complaint. Thus, in addition to the direct taxpayer costs, state and local sanctions generate international political conflict and undermine the chances for adopting a common front against rogue states such as Burma and Nigeria.

The U.S. State Department is concerned over a lack of democracy and human rights in Burma.

While it is troubling that these disputes endanger U.S. relations with the EU and Japan, an even more fundamental issue is whether these actions are justifiable under the U.S. Constitution. Local and state government officials argue that taxpayers have the right to determine how their tax dollars are spent. The framers of the Constitution, while recognizing the legitimacy of states' rights in many areas, felt that in relations with foreign countries the nation should speak with one voice. Thus, the Constitution vests authority to conduct foreign affairs and to regulate foreign commerce in the federal government. The Constitution also provides that the laws and treaties of the United States are the "supreme law of the land" and may not be preempted by state or local actions. On this basis, the business coalition USA Engage is proposing to challenge the Massachusetts sanctions and other similar measures in a U.S. court.

Elusive benefits

Backers of these sanctions justify the costs by invoking the end of apartheid in South Africa as a model they hope to replicate in bringing democracy to Nigeria, Burma and elsewhere. In that case, the United States, European Union, Australia and other members of the British Commonwealth, Japan and a number of other countries imposed financial and trade sanctions against South Africa. A number of state and local governments in the United States also imposed procurement and investment restrictions, not on South Africa, but on companies doing business there.

But the impact of sanctions in South Africa often is exaggerated and the situation in current target countries quite different. Analysis of this case suggests that broadly supported, multilateral economic sanctions may be helpful, but rarely decisive, in changing behavior in foreign countries where domestic political conditions are propitious. The inherent unsustainability of the apartheid economic model and

---

State and local sanctions satisfy the urge to do something to punish repressive regimes, but even when imposed at the national level, they have little impact on the behavior of those regimes.

Table 1. State and local government sanctions

Jurisdiction	Sanctions target	Sanctions type*	Date enacted
Massachusetts	Burma	SP	July 1996
Dade County, FL	Cuba	SP&I	July 1992
Berkeley, CA	Burma	SP	March 1995
San Francisco, CA	Burma	SP	April 1995
Santa Monica, CA	Burma	SP	November 1995
Ann Arbor, MI	Burma	SP	April 1996
Oakland, CA	Burma	SP&I	May 1996
Madison, WI	Burma	SP	August 1996
Carrboro, NC	Burma	SP	October 1996
Takoma Park, MD	Burma	SP	October 1996
Alameda County, CA	Burma	SP&I	December 1996
Boulder, CO	Burma	SP	December 1996
Chapel Hill, NC	Burma	SP	January 1997
Cambridge, MA	Burma	SP	May 1997
New York, NY	Burma	SP&I	May 1997
Oakland, CA	Nigeria	SP&I	May 1997
Berkeley, CA	Tibet	SP	June 1997
Berkeley, CA	Nigeria	SP	July 1997
Santa Cruz, CA	Burma	SP&I	July 1997
Amherst, MA	Nigeria	SP&I	September 1997
Alameda County, CA	Nigeria	SP&I	October 1997
Palo Alto, CA	Burma	SP&I	October 1997
West Hollywood, CA	Burma	SP	October 1997
Brookline, MA	Burma	SP	November 1997
Newton, MA	Burma	SP	November 1997

* SP=Selective purchasing, SP&I=Selective purchasing and investment

Source: USA Engage, "State and Local Sanctions Watch List," updated as of March 9, 1998; online at www.usaengage.org.

Table 2. Effectiveness of economic sanctions as a foreign policy tool

	Number of successes	Number of failures	Success ratio as percentage of total
All cases	40	75	35%
Cases involving U.S. as sanctioner			
1945-1990	26	52	33%
1945-1970	16	14	53%
1970-1990	10	38	21%
Unilateral U.S. sanctions			
1945-1990	16	39	29%
1945-1970	11	5	69%
1970-1990	5	34	13%

Source: Gary Clyde Hufbauer, Jeffery J. Schott and Kimberly Ann Elliott, *Economic Sanctions Reconsidered*, 2nd edition, revised. (Washington: Institute for International Economics, 1990.)

the presence of a large, well-organized opposition within South Africa were far more important. Moreover, in terms of external pressure, the purely private, risk-driven decision by large multinational banks to discontinue lending to South Africa had far more impact than the limited sanctions imposed by governments. Similar conditions do not occur often and are not present today in Burma or Nigeria, both ruled by regimes that are far more repressive and authoritarian than in South Africa where the enfranchised white business community added to the pressure to end apartheid.

Nor does more comprehensive analysis offer much hope that state and local sanctions could achieve their objectives, even if they resulted in broader national sanctions as in the South Africa case. In a study of 115 episodes from World War I through 1990, my colleagues and I at the Institute for International Economics found that sanctions contributed to even partial success in only about one-third of the cases analyzed. Many of these cases involved the United States acting alone. In an increasingly integrated international economy, however, unilateral economic sanctions inflict little pain on the nominal target country and have little impact on its policies. This same study showed that unilateral U.S. sanctions between 1970 and 1990 contributed to successful policy outcomes less than 15 percent of the time (see table 2).

State and local sanctions satisfy the urge to do something to punish repressive regimes, but even when imposed at the national level, they have little impact on the behavior of those regimes. Only if they receive broad support internationally do sanctions have any chance of succeeding.

Unfortunately, the impetus for international cooperation is diminished, not enhanced, by state and local initiatives. At the end of the day, taxpayers in Massachusetts, Maryland and elsewhere pay while the regimes in Nigeria and Burma go on undeterred.

The Senate's strange bedfellows

By John Isaacs

At its July 1997 summit in Madrid, NATO agreed that it would offer membership in the alliance to Hungary, Poland, and the Czech Republic. Following that vote, the alliance negotiated agreements with the candidates for membership, and those agreements were signed in mid-December. The next step in the process is for the governments of all 16 current NATO states to ratify the decision.

The Senate will probably begin grappling with the expansion issue in January, and the vote could come as early as March. Senate approval of enlargement is not, despite the administration's hopes, quite a done deal.

"An unlikely couple"

The players and politics of NATO enlargement differ from those of two other key treaties—the Chemical Weapons Convention, which was ratified last year, and the Comprehensive Test Ban Treaty, which will be brought forward later this year. All three measures require 67 votes, and all are important administration priorities. But there the similarity ends.

When it comes to NATO expansion, Republican leaders, including Majority Leader Trent Lott and Foreign Relations Committee Chairman Jesse Helms, are working hand and glove with the president. Together they concluded that the most advantageous time for a Senate vote would be early in the year, before the Senate has to consider the continued deployment of U.S. soldiers in Bosnia. The Senate Foreign Relations, Appropriations, and Budget Committees held preliminary hearings last fall to set the stage for quick action this spring.

In contrast, to win Senate approval of the chemical weapons treaty, the administration had to overcome years of delaying tactics by an antagonistic Jesse Helms and negotiate endlessly with a cagey Lott. Similar difficulties can be expected in scheduling the vote on the test ban treaty.

Another contrast is that the normal ideological lines are totally blurred on NATO enlargement. Helms and California Democrat Barbara Boxer are in favor, Virginia Republican John Warner and Minnesota Democrat Paul Wellstone are very critical. The arms control treaties, on the other hand, have produced the usual ideological cleavage.

The administration has organized early and well for the NATO campaign. It plucked seasoned executive branch veteran Jeremy Rosner from the think tank world to coordinate the effort. In contrast, it was several years before the administration took on an outside coordinator for the Chemical Weapons Convention campaign—and so far, the National Security Council has resisted entreaties to take on a test ban treaty czar.

The administration quickly realized that the Senate was focusing on the

The Senate's normal ideological lines are totally blurred on NATO enlargement.

costs of NATO expansion and who will pay. With France, Germany, and Great Britain expressing reluctance to pay an additional centime, pfennig, or pence, the administration prodded the NATO bureaucracy to devise lower cost estimates than the Pentagon's own much-criticized numbers. Sure enough, on November 13, with a straight face, NATO lowered the overall cost estimate from $27–35 billion to a measly $2 billion.

While some 50 critics, organized by Russian expert Susan Eisenhower, signed a July 1997 letter critical of NATO enlargement, Rosner and a

---

John Isaacs, a Bulletin *contributing editor, is president of the Council for a Livable World in Washington, D.C.*

brand-new coalition, the U.S. Committee to Expand NATO, came up with a list of 133 former officials—including eight previous secretaries of State—who endorsed the decision. The committee also ran full-page ads trumpeting those endorsements. Most endearing was a photo of Jesse Helms and Secretary of State Madeleine Albright holding hands, captioned: "An Unlikely Couple; A Common Cause."

The benefits of public apathy

The politics of NATO enlargement is moving in the administration's direction in other ways as well. Public opinion is largely supportive—if apathetic. A September 1997 Pew Research Center poll showed the American public behind the administration position 63 to 18 percent. On the other hand, only one in 10 of those polled could name even one of the three candidate countries. Those few who care strongly enough to pressure their senators tend to be "ethnic Americans" who identify with one of the proposed members.

Ironically, the policy elite is where you find those least happy with the administration's policy. The same Pew Research poll indicated that "experts in foreign affairs and security were the most dubious towards expanding NATO. Although a majority of foreign affairs and security experts favored NATO expansion, 44 percent of security experts and 39 percent of foreign affairs experts disapprove."

The NATO issue has engendered a hot and heavy debate among foreign policy elites and opinion leaders. But outside the op-ed pages, there has been little public debate or interest. Even Javier Solana, NATO's secretary general and chief salesperson, has found it impossible to get on Sunday talk shows.

An apathetic public gives the executive branch more latitude, and the administration could also benefit from longstanding tradition—not since the failure of the Treaty of Versailles at the end of World War I has the Senate rejected a treaty outright.

Hesitant critics

Expansion has a number of vocal supporters in the Senate. In addition to Helms and Lott, many senators endorsed NATO expansion early on. Kentucky Republican Mitch McConnell told the Senate Appropriations Committee on October 21 that he's been "on board for NATO expansion" since 1993. Supporters also include Maryland's Joseph Biden, the Foreign Relations Committee's ranking Democrat, and a number of midwestern senators who have many "ethnic American" constituents.

When Congress completed its first session in November, only Warner and fellow Republican Larry Craig of Idaho had publicly declared their opposition. Warner told the Senate on July 10, 1997, "I am not in favor of the expansion of NATO. It seems to me that the actions taken in Madrid are not in [NA-

The odd couple: Secretary of State Madeleine Albright and Jesse Helms, chairman of the Foreign Relations Committee, agree on expanding NATO.

TO's] best interests in the long term.... There may be a degree to which our tinkering with NATO and changing it in concept could begin to undermine American public support for NATO, and I think that would be a terrible loss."

Even Texas Republican Kay Bailey Hutchison, who rounded up 20 colleagues to sign a critical letter to the president, has yet to declare that she will vote no and organize others to do the same.

Right now, the administration clearly has the momentum, with some members who are uncomfortable with expansion nonetheless announcing their reluctant acquiescence.

Arkansas Democrat Dale Bumpers, for example, told an October 21 Senate Appropriations Committee hearing: "I am probably going to support this treaty, but with considerable misgivings. I would quote the [former] ambassador to Russia [George Kennan] when he said that he thought we were making a historic mistake.... And I think that could possibly carry a very heavy price for the United States in the future."

Still, the outcome is a long way from being settled. Intervening events could undermine the administration's best laid plans. Most notably, some senators are linking NATO expansion with Bosnia, which could threaten NATO's activities there. Like the Pentagon, the Senate is concerned that the commitment in Bosnia is open-ended, with no clear exit strategy. Some want to end the continued and expensive U.S. troop commitment to Bosnia. And if U.S. troops are withdrawn in June 1998, the NATO allies have said they will follow suit.

With friends like these . . .

A second complication involves the possible conditions or amendments that may be offered to the resolution of ratification. The Senate added 28—mostly benign—conditions to the Chemical Weapons Convention resolution of ratification. Depending on the nature of the conditions imposed on NATO expansion, they could smooth the way toward 67 votes—or they could break apart the pro-NATO coalition.

Expansion supporter though he may be, Jesse Helms has compiled a list of 10 conditions, some of which could be spoilers.

Lest the treaty become "an exercise in the appeasement of Russia," Helms

> **Obtaining a two-thirds Senate majority on any issue short of motherhood can be a daunting challenge.**

wants it made clear that the alliance's promises to refrain from stationing troops or weapons on new members' territories will not be honored, and that no "nuclear-weapons-free zones" will be popping up in Eastern or Central Europe. He also wants NATO's decision-making procedure to be free from U.N. or Russian influence, and he wants to make sure that Russia receives no concessions in any further negotiations on the Conventional Forces in Europe Treaty or the Anti-Ballistic Missile Treaty.

Others in the Senate who approve of the first group of new NATO members say privately they will draw the line if NATO offers membership to the Baltic States. Russia has threatened a fierce reaction if, as NATO appeared to promise in July, a second round includes Latvia, Lithuania, and Estonia, all former parts of the Soviet empire.

Provisions requiring the three new members and the other NATO member states to pick up the bulk of the costs could also cause significant problems. The Senate could delay the vote until NATO's final allocation of costs is made in June 1998, or it could add provisions requiring acceptance by all NATO members of their share of the budget. Then, too, on October 29, Michigan Democrat Carl Levin suggested on the Senate floor that he may offer an amendment to the original 1949 treaty to add a procedure for suspending members that do not live up to NATO's human rights and democracy standards.

At cross purposes?

Important differences remain among Senate supporters. Helms continues to view Russia as the enemy against which NATO should be directed. Despite the administration's protestation that enlargement is not directed against Russia, Helms wrote in the European edition of the July 9 *Wall Street Journal*, that "a central strategic rationale for expanding NATO must be to hedge against the possible return of a nationalist or imperialist Russia."

There is also disagreement over whether NATO should remain as a military alliance organized only to protect the soil of its members or whether it should take on a broader role. Former Clinton cabinet secretaries Warren Christopher and William Perry wrote in the *New York Times* last October 21: "Shifting the alliance's emphasis from defense of members' territory to defense of common interests is the strategic imperative."

Helms rejects this view. He argues for a military alliance, not a guarantor of democracy or economic reforms: "NATO's job is not . . . to build democracy and pan-European harmony." Adopting a broadened NATO mission "make[s] a better case for the alliance to disband."

John Ashcroft, a conservative Missouri Republican, asked in an October 7 Foreign Relations Committee hearing: "If NATO becomes an agency which addresses the interests of NATO nations wherever they might take place, is it to be a sort of limited U.N. that doesn't require quite as much consensus?"

Ultimately, obtaining a two-thirds Senate majority on any issue short of motherhood can prove a daunting challenge. While the administration has raced into the lead on NATO enlargement, the constitutional advice-and-consent barrier placed by the founding fathers insures that the battle will continue up to the final vote.

"Decisions made in Washington in the coming years will determine whether the revolution in military affairs stokes future arms races and proliferation problems... So far the American approach, while a logical response to vexing strategic problems, has not been shaped by concern for long-term political implications."

Racing Toward the Future: The Revolution in Military Affairs

STEVEN METZ

The Persian Gulf War may have signaled a historic change in the nature of armed conflict. By most indicators the Iraqi military that occupied Kuwait was proficient and well equipped with modern weaponry, especially tanks, artillery, and air defense systems. Battle-tested in a long war with Iran, it should have been a fearsome enemy for the United States–led coalition. Pundits and political leaders expected a bloody struggle. But once the war began, Saddam Hussein's forces were brushed aside with stunning suddenness and minimal human cost to the United States and its allies, leaving the world to ponder the war's meaning.

Initially, American military leaders saw Desert Storm as the payoff for years of accumulated improvement in training, personnel quality, doctrine, leadership, and equipment. Some analysts unearthed deeper lessons. Rather than attributing the outcome to evolutionary advancements in the United States military, they saw Desert Storm as the prologue to a fundamental transformation in the nature of warfare—a "revolution in military affairs," or RMA. This idea had such immense strategic and political implications that American military leaders, defense policymakers, and strategic analysts soon adopted it, changing the RMA concept from a theoretical construct to a blueprint for the armed forces of the twenty-first century.

Today the RMA has become the basis of most long-term thinking in the Defense Department and, increasingly, for the militaries of other advanced states. But the full implication of this is not yet clear; many dimensions of the RMA await analysis. For example, little thought has been given to how the RMA might affect arms races and weapons proliferation—a serious oversight. If armed conflict is undergoing historic and significant change, "traditional" arms races will persist into the next century even as new and very different ones take shape. The more these new problems are anticipated, the easier they will be to deal with. To assess the proliferation and arms control issues that will challenge world leaders 10 years from now requires tracing the evolution of thinking on the RMA and its effect on military strategy in the United States and around the world.

THE EVOLUTION OF AN IDEA

The concept of military revolutions grew from Soviet writing of the 1970s and 1980s, particularly a series of papers by Marshal Nikolai Ogarkov. When American defense analysts initially considered this idea, they focused on the technological dimension. One of the first major study groups in the United States labeled its final report *The Military Technical Revolution*.[1] But it quickly became clear that this was an overly narrow approach that understated the importance of concepts and organizations. The idea of a "military-technical revolution" soon evolved into the more holistic concept of a revolution in military affairs.

There is now a loose consensus among scholars, policymakers, and military strategists on the most salient aspects of RMAs. In simple terms, an RMA is a rapid and radical increase in the effectiveness of

---

STEVEN METZ *is Henry L. Stimson Professor of Military Affairs at the United States Army War College and a research professor at the college's Strategic Studies Institute, where he specializes in future warfare and changes in military technology. The views expressed in this essay are those of the author.*

[1] Michael J. Mazarr, et al., *The Military Technical Revolution: A Structural Framework* (Washington, D.C.: Center for Strategic and International Studies, March 1993).

military units that alters the nature of warfare and changes the strategic environment. RMAs result from mutually supportive changes in technology, concepts, and organizations; technological advancement alone does not make an RMA. Analysts also agree that RMAs are, by definition, strategically significant. States that understand and exploit them accrue geopolitical benefits; those that do not slide into military weakness.

Even given this simple conceptual base, writers differ on when RMAs have occurred in the past. Ironically, there is greater agreement on the nature of the current RMA. Scholars, military strategists, and defense policymakers acknowledge that what drives it is a vast improvement in the quality and quantity of information made available to military commanders by improvements in computers and other devices for collecting, analyzing, storing, and transmitting data. The United States Army, for instance, talks of "digitized" battle in which a commander would use an array of sensors and data-fusion technologies to obtain a near-perfect picture of the battlefield that would provide the location and status of all friendly and most enemy units, thus dispersing what has been called the "fog of war." Such a development would certainly represent a sea change in the nature of armed conflict. The presence (or absence) of accurate information has long shaped the conduct of warfare. If the RMA does lift the "fog of war," the results will be stunning, giving those armed forces that master the changes immense advantages.

The increasing quality and quantity of military information will have a number of corollary effects. One is an alteration of the traditional relationship between operational complexity and effective control. Accurate, real-time information and advanced, computer-based training and simulation models will allow more complex military operations than in the past. Simultaneous operations across one or more military theaters might soon be possible. At the same time, the relationship between accuracy and distance in the application of military force might change as extremely precise, standoff strikes become the method preferred by advanced militaries. The RMA could relegate the close-quarters clash of troops to history.

The RMA might change military strategy as well. Futurists Alvin and Heidi Toffler have argued that information is becoming the basis of economic strength, especially in what they call "Third Wave" states. During the "First Wave" of human development, production was primarily agricultural, so military strategies were designed to seize and hold territory or steal portable wealth. During the "Second Wave" industrial production dominated, which meant that war was often a struggle of attrition where belligerents wore down their enemies' capacity to feed, clothe, and equip armies. Following this logic, "Third Wave" warfare will seek to erode or destroy the enemy's means of collecting, processing, storing, and disseminating information.[2] Instead of using explosives to kill and destroy, the warrior of the future might fight with a laptop computer from a motel room, attacking digital targets with strikes launched through fiber-optic webs in order to damage or alter enemy information infrastructure and data resources. The opening words of the next global war might be "Log-on successful" rather than "Tora, Tora, Tora." From the perspective of arms control, it is a chilling thought that something as uncontrollable as a few thousand lines of computer code could become a dangerous weapon.

THE AMERICAN ORTHODOXY

No organization undertakes a revolution without a pressing incentive. This certainly holds for the United States military. The Defense Department is pursuing the RMA in response to two important post–cold war strategic trends. One is a decline in the American military force structure and budget without a concomitant decline in responsibilities and missions, which has generated a growing mismatch between means and ends. The other is what military and civilian leaders see as the American public's limited tolerance for the human toll of armed conflict. These two issues form the core dilemma of current United States national security strategy and drive the quest for the RMA.

During the wide-ranging reassessment of national security strategy in the early 1990s, people like Andrew Marshall, director of the Defense Department's Office of Net Assessment, and Admiral William A. Owens, former vice chairman of the Joint Chiefs of Staff, concluded that an American military built along the principles of the RMA could be smaller yet more powerful than the present one. To use jargon that has become a mantra within the military, the goal was to "leverage technology" to solve strategic dilemmas. By the mid-1990s the RMA had moved from the realm of theorists and military historians to the world of force structure planning and programming.

---

[2]Alvin and Heidi Toffler, *War and Anti-War: Survival at the Dawn of the 21st Century* (Boston: Little, Brown, 1993).

The RMA quickly entered the mainstream thinking of the American armed forces. Courses appeared at war colleges and staff schools, RMA-related articles became common in military journals, and military think tanks began to produce studies, reports, exercises, and war games. Institutions designed to develop, test, and refine RMA-related concepts emerged throughout the Department of Defense. Government labs explored technologies to make the RMA possible, especially in areas such as information gathering, assessment, and dissemination, nonlethal weapons, robotics, unmanned military systems, new materials, and new energy sources.

Other nations quickly joined the bandwagon. The Australian military hosted one of the first major RMA conferences outside the United States in Canberra, Australia, in February 1996. At the National Institute for Defense Studies in Tokyo, a series of RMA seminars attracted the attention of senior policymakers. The French have also begun exploration of the RMA.

Still, the United States military is clearly the leader in RMA thinking and continues to define the "orthodoxy." In 1996 this was codified in Chairman of the Joint Chiefs of Staff General John Shalikashvili's Joint Vision 2010, which is the best distillation of official United States thinking on the RMA and the future security environment. Joint Vision 2010 projects no revolutionary change in the global strategic environment over the next decade. The primary task of American armed forces, Shalikashvili contends, will continue to be to deter conflict and, if that fails, to fight and win the nation's wars. Power projection enabled by an overseas presence will remain the fundamental strategic concept, and the military forces of other nations still the primary foe.

Joint Vision 2010 does, however, anticipate great strides in the adoption of new technology, concepts, and organizations. It predicts that technology will allow even more emphasis on long-range precision strikes. New weapons based on directed energy will appear. Advances in low observable ("stealth") technologies will augment the ability to mask friendly forces from enemies. And improvements in information and systems integration technologies will provide decision makers with fast and accurate information. In combination, these technologies will allow increased stealth, mobility, and dispersion, and a higher tempo of operations, all under the shield of information superiority.

The opening words of the next global war might be "Log-on successful" rather than "Tora, Tora, Tora."

Four operational concepts form the heart of Joint Vision 2010. The first, *dominant maneuver,* would allow overwhelming force against an opponent by conducting synchronized operations from dispersed locations rather than from a few large bases or camps. The second key concept is *precision engagement.* This would be based on a "system of systems" that would allow United States forces to locate a target, attack it with great accuracy, assess the effectiveness of the attack, and strike again when necessary. In many cases, the strike systems themselves would be "stealthy." The third operational concept, *full-dimension protection,* entails protecting friendly forces from enemy information warfare, missile attacks, and other threats. The final concept is *focused logistics,* which fuses information, logistics, and transportation technology to deliver tailored logistics packages at all levels of military operations. If attained, these four concepts would give American forces full spectrum dominance over anticipated enemies in the first two decades of the twenty-first century, assuming such enemies cannot develop effective responses to American advances.

While largely excluded from Joint Vision 2010, there is one other important component of current American thinking on the RMA: a desire to use technology to make warfare "cleaner" by reducing the casualties and collateral damage normally associated with combat operations. To a great extent, this is a response to the global communications explosion that has expanded the audience for armed conflict beyond the participants. To be politically acceptable, military operations must minimize casualties. Precision conventional strikes are part of this, but even more radical change may be possible through explicitly nonlethal weapons such as acoustic, laser, and high-power microwaves; nonnuclear electromagnetic pulses; high-power jamming; obscurants, foams, glues, and slicks; supercaustics that erode enemy equipment; magnetohydrodynamics; information warfare; and soldier protection. The American military's interest in nonlethality has increased dramatically, but the full implications—especially for human rights and ethical limits on the use of force—await exploration.

STOKING A NEW ARMS RACE?

The military described in Joint Vision 2010 will be able to counter a traditional enemy relying on massed, armor-heavy formations in relatively open terrain. But, since Desert Storm showed the futility of pitting an old-fashioned military against a cutting-edge one in maneuver warfare, future opponents are unlikely to repeat Iraq's mistakes. Indeed, the world is unlikely to cede permanent military superiority to the United States. A few advanced nations may emulate the American version of the RMA, but those with the technological capacity to do so do not have the political incentive.

Most potential enemies will not have the scientific and technological resources to emulate the United States military and will instead seek asymmetric counterweights. Like guerrilla warfare in Vietnam, these may not give American enemies the ability to win battlefield victories, but they will allow them to raise the cost of the conflict, possibly to the point of paralyzing American policymakers. One example is the "Somali strategy," in which small groups of warriors armed with relatively low-cost weapons operate among civilians in an urban environment. The United States military envisioned in Joint Vision 2010 would have more trouble with such an opponent than with an Iraq- or North Korea-style enemy. Even more ominously, potential enemies may turn to terrorism against "soft" targets in the United States, perhaps using weapons of mass destruction, in order to deter American military action. Even though terrorism may not be the preferred method of fighting, enemies of the United States may feel that its military power leaves them no alternative.

Finally, information warfare is likely to stoke an arms race of its own. Even today there is sharp competition between computer hackers and virus-writers and businesses, networks, and law-abiding individuals. As armed forces become more information- and computer-dependent, this competition may shift to the military realm. Hacking, virus-writing, and crashing data information systems—as well as defending against enemy hackers and virus writers—may become core military skills, as important as the ability to shoot. In this particular arena, the American armed services are less clearly superior to potential enemies than in traditional military functions, so the spiral of response and counter-response is likely to be intense.

Marching Toward the Fringe

The RMA described in Joint Vision 2010 does not represent a fundamental transformation of armed conflict; it is more "hyper-evolutionary" than revolutionary. But it is possible to use existing trends to speculate on the direction armed combat may take beyond 2010 and imagine the problems that could emerge. For example, future armed conflict may involve little or no direct human contact. Advances in robotics and nanotechnology—the ability to manipulate and manufacture individual molecules—may soon allow the construction of tiny but "brilliant" military machines capable of complex decision making. This could turn warfare into a machine-on-machine struggle, with humans on the sidelines. Machines may become self-repairing, self-replicating, even self-improving. At some point, cyborgs—complex machines with some attributes of living organisms—may become feasible and the proliferation of militarily relevant genetic material a key issue for arms control.

Even more ominously, technology to manipulate human thoughts, perceptions, attitudes, and beliefs using electronic or chemical means might become feasible. This could entail direct "mind control," holograms, and "morphing" an individual by creating, manipulating, and transmitting a computer-generated image indistinguishable from a real one. It is easy to imagine the horror of such developments, but it is equally easy to understand how a beleaguered leader might decide that the immorality of psychotechnology is justified by a serious security threat (especially if the public has already become accustomed to such techniques through the entertainment and advertising industries). If one nation opens this Pandora's box and demonstrates substantial progress in psychotechnology, others will surely follow, unleashing another kind of arms race.

Finally, future warfare may also see changes in who fights, with the "privatization" of warfare made possible, perhaps even likely. If the current RMA allows the development of small but effective armed forces, powerful transnational mercenary corporations may arise. The same factors that led to the proliferation of mercenaries in the past—the expense of training and sustaining a military force, the sporadic need for one, and a moral disdain for the profession of arms—show signs of rebirth. In coming decades, high-tech, transnational mercenary corporations or the private armies of other transnational corporations may be able to challenge or defeat the armed forces of less advanced states.

Distant Rumblings

Only the historians of the future will know whether a full-scale RMA was under way in the 1990s. But for those living through these times—especially policymakers who must deal with arms control and proliferation—there is little doubt that there is at least a revolution in weaponry. This can be seen in the shifting valuation of weapons systems. In the past, valuation was based on the ratio of cost to destructiveness. Now what might be called "discernment"—accuracy and, increasingly, decision-making capacity—is equally important. To some extent, availability and usability will still structure the arms races of the early twenty-first century, but the technology-driven global dispersion of information, the advent of "brilliant" systems requiring less training, the development of highly realistic computer-based training systems, and the declining distinction between weaponry and other types of information technology will encourage proliferation and arms races. At the same time, information-based weapons systems will erode the concept of national arms industries, again complicating traditional state-centric arms control regimes.

Decisions made in Washington in the coming years will determine whether the RMA stokes future arms races and proliferation problems. Other nations are interested in the RMA, but only the United States has the money, technological prowess, and strategic incentive to embrace it. So far the American approach, while a logical response to vexing strategic problems, has not been shaped by concern for long-term political implications. Pursuit of an RMA is not the wrong policy, but pursuit of the RMA described in Joint Vision 2010 may generate unintended political and diplomatic side effects and lead to a more dangerous world rather than a more stable one.

In part, this problem is structural. Within the United States government, responsibility for military strategy and arms control policy is split. The Defense Department is charged with the former while the State Department and the Arms Control and Disarmament Agency oversee the latter. In terms of political power and influence, this is an uneven match. The architects of American military strategy are not oblivious to political and diplomatic concerns, but they must respond primarily to the nation's strategic dilemma. Their attention to the diplomatic and political impact of military strategy is minimal. (The National Security Council was designed to synchronize and integrate the disparate dimensions of United States national security strategy but has shown little inclination to shape long-term military strategy.)

Still, the American approach to the RMA could be recast so that long-term political and diplomatic considerations would receive greater emphasis. This would require redirecting the RMA from simply improving power projection. Seeking a radical improvement in the American military while the United States faces no powerful enemy raises suspicions. To many other states, the only logical reason for the United States to augment its military power in the current security environment is to pursue hegemony. So long as United States military strategy seeks power projection, other states will develop countermeasures to American military prowess, thus sparking arms races, whether symmetric or asymmetric. While this may be an acceptable risk, American policymakers and military strategists should at least explore the possibility of a less provocative variant of the RMA.

In addition, the United States should develop a coherent strategy to defend national information assets. Information systems are daily becoming more central to national life (and thus national security), but no government agency has clear responsibility for coordinating efforts to protect them. Enemies will recognize this vulnerability and attempt to use it to counter the American military, unleashing a spiral of escalation. The United States should also publicly eschew and condemn the development of any technology designed to manipulate human thoughts, beliefs, or perceptions. However alluring this "nonlethal" technology might appear at first glance, its danger is immense. Finally, the United States should expand the time horizons of its efforts to control arms races and proliferation. This would entail crafting regimes to control forms of military technology that, although technologically feasible, are not yet fielded. It is much easier to manage the development of a new form of technology than to control one that has matured to the point that powerful organizations have a vested interest in it.

The political difficulties of altering the current trajectory of the RMA should not be underestimated. In the short term, the RMA will benefit the United States by easing or alleviating some key strategic problems. The United States military of 2010 will be smaller than the current military, but it will also be more effective. In the long term, however, the RMA will create new problems for the United States by provoking asymmetric responses and fueling arms races. The record of the United States at forgoing short-term benefits for long-term gains offers little ground for optimism.

WHY SPY? THE USES AND MISUSES OF INTELLIGENCE

U.S. intelligence agencies should devote their resources to serious security threats, such as international terrorism and adverse political trends. Instead, the Clinton Administration has diverted their mission to economic espionage.

by Stanley Kober

WHEN PRES. CLINTON took office, his administration made several assumptions about foreign policy: first, that the Cold War was over; second, that during the Cold War, Washington had allowed political-military allies to take advantage of the U.S. in international trade; and third, that because of that indulgence, as well as the traditional American aversion to any sort of government guidance of the economy, the U.S. was losing its international competitiveness.

According to that view, international rivalry in the post-Cold War world was going to be economic, rather than political-military. Consequently, the Administration established the National Economic Council in the White House to give economic issues the same importance the National Security Council gives national security; the State Department estab-

Mr. Kober is a research fellow in foreign policy studies, Cato Institute, Washington, D.C.

22. Why Spy?

lished its own office to deal with economic issues; the Office of the U.S. Trade Representative became much more confrontational in foreign negotiations; and the Commerce Department established its "war room," whose very name summarized the new attitude toward international trade.

That change in focus also affected U.S. intelligence agencies. After all, if international trade and competitiveness were the new areas of battle, should not the intelligence agencies contribute to America's overall effort? Economic intelligence, Central Intelligence Agency director-designate R. James Woolsey said at his confirmation hearings in February, 1993, had become "the hottest current topic in intelligence policy."

Woolsey is gone, but the focus on economic intelligence survives. The *Los Angeles Times* reported in July, 1995, that "President Clinton has ordered the Central Intelligence Agency to make economic espionage of America's trade rivals a top priority." A month later, the London *Sunday Times* revealed that "the Foreign Office is voicing alarm over a strategy by the Central Intelligence Agency to spy on foreign companies, including British firms," adding that "the scheme has been devised by John Deutch, the new CIA director, who plans to ask American spies to recruit agents inside foreign businesses and use electronic eavesdropping to gather details of company operations." Indeed, in early 1995, the French government exposed an American economic espionage attempt, and shortly afterward, a similar effort against Japan was revealed by the U.S. press. Neither country took kindly to that treatment, and the French insisted that five U.S. citizens, four of them diplomats attached to the embassy, leave the country.

Although some economic espionage may be necessary when there is a clear national security connection (*e.g.*, tracking foreign arms sales), the assumptions that have guided the Clinton Administration are badly flawed. Perhaps worse, the Administration's assumptions about the international security environment are indicative of a failure to comprehend the dangerous world that has begun to emerge from the debris of the Cold War.

When the Cold War ended, it was widely believed that a new era of international cooperation had begun. The Gulf War seemed to confirm that impression, with former rivals uniting to oppose Saddam Hussein's aggression. Yet, the allied victory in that conflict has not deterred other wars, as the fighting that has accompanied the disintegration of Yugoslavia demonstrates. Indeed, the victory in the Persian Gulf has not even brought stability to that troubled region.

Simply put, the end of the Cold War has not led to a more peaceful world and, as the attacks on Americans in Saudi Arabia testify, the U.S. is the target of those who challenge the status quo. The failure of U.S. intelligence to anticipate such attacks is significant.

Intelligence agencies are America's eyes and ears in a dangerous world. Their purpose is to warn the nation of threats, so that the U.S. has time to take measures to protect itself. When their resources are diverted in an effort to improve American "competitiveness," they are less able to perform their security mission. In a world in which terrorists openly have declared war against the U.S., that mission should not be compromised.

There are several reasons for economic espionage. One identified by the White House is to "contribute where appropriate to policy efforts aimed at bolstering our economic prosperity" by "helping policymakers understand economic trends." However, economic trends are not secret. To rely on intelligence analysis to identify underlying trends that are, by definition, out in the open, is to place unwarranted faith in the cachet of secrecy. Since such trends can not be hidden, analysis of them will benefit from open discussion and should not be pushed behind closed doors. Nevertheless, three specific areas have emerged as the focus of economic espionage: stopping foreign practices, especially bribery, that hurt U.S. firms; halting thefts of American corporate secrets; and supporting U.S. negotiators in trade talks. Each of those areas may seem reasonable at first glance. Precisely because they seem reasonable, those issues have not received the scrutiny they deserve.

Stopping bribery. On July 18, 1994, CIA Director Woolsey addressed the Center for Strategic and International Studies in Washington on the future direction of intelligence. After that appearance, he was asked about the role of economic and commercial intelligence. His reply stressed the importance of using the intelligence agencies to win contracts for American firms by exposing bribery attempts by competitors:

"A number of countries in other parts of the world, including some of our oldest friends, are very much into the business of bribing their way to contracts that they can not win on the merits.... And when we find out about those ... we go not to the American corporation that's competing, but the Secretary of State, and he sends an American ambassador to see a president or a king, and he—that ambassador—says, `Mr. President,' or `Your Majesty, your minister in charge of construction is on the take, and you have a lot going with the United States, and we don't really take kindly to your operating that way.' And so rather frequently what happens—not always—is that the contract is rebid.... We calculate, really very conservatively, that several billion dollars a year in contracts are saved for American business by our conducting that type of intelligence collection."

It is not just ambassadors who play that role. In 1994, Pres. Clinton personally complained to the governments of Brazil and Saudi Arabia about bribes that French companies had paid to win contracts, which were then awarded to U.S. firms. Afterwards, the President praised the performance of the intelligence agencies: "You uncovered bribes that would have cheated American companies out of billions of dollars," he told CIA employees. It might seem churlish to object to that use of the intelligence agencies, but there are two concerns that have been overlooked and need to be addressed.

The first is the possibility that, when such representations are made, the source that provided the intelligence could be compromised. Any foreign government that receives such information is bound to launch an investigation to discover how it was obtained, and the results could be tragic. During the Bush Administration, Secretary of State James A. Baker III, responding to requests from Pres. Hafez Assad of Syria for facts about terrorists based in his country, turned over detailed information to support the U.S. case. Shortly afterward, agents who had infiltrated a terrorist organization in Syria were apprehended and executed by Syrian authorities. Although the State Department denied any cause and effect, the incident underlines the danger inherent in releasing classified information to foreign governments. Even if it does not put individuals at risk, sharing such information could jeopardize a source that might provide other information that was more crucial to America's national security.

The second concern is the manner in which evidence of corruption is utilized. To use it as U.S. officials did in Saudi Arabia and Brazil—as a way of obtaining business for American firms—is to cooperate in the corruption while nominally opposing it. After all, we are using evidence of corruption as leverage to benefit ourselves, rather than register opposition to corrupt practices. Although that is not as bad as actually paying bribes, it is questionable whether ordinary people will be impressed with the distinction.

The Clinton Administration may be repeating the American experience with Iran before the Islamic revolution. Iran under the Shah was a tremendous market for the U.S., but also was pervasively corrupt. When the Shah fell, in large part because of public indignation over the abuses of his regime, American interests also suffered because the U.S. had been his ally and therefore became a target of popular wrath. That episode demonstrates that widespread corruption should be viewed as an indicator that a regime is shaky and that U.S. reliance on such a regime for any purpose may be questionable, if not dangerous.

It is particularly disturbing that the lesson that should have been learned in Iran is being ignored with regard to Saudi Arabia. After all, it is not as if the warnings have not been present. "Businessmen gripe that some princes use their influence to grab government contracts and muscle in on successful enterprises," the *Washington Post* reported in December, 1994. The U.S. is the target of public anger because it fails to oppose such abuses. In November, 1995, a bomb exploded outside a U.S. training mission, killing five Americans. Saudi authorities were shocked when the bombers turned out to be Saudis acting without foreign assistance. "It was directed against the [ruling] Saud family," explained a Western diplomat, effectively underlining the closeness of the Saud-American link: to get at the Saud family, you attack Americans. Nevertheless, the warning signals went unheeded, and in June, 1996, 19 American military personnel were killed when their barracks in Saudi Arabia was destroyed by a truck bomb.

The other case in which evidence of corruption has been viewed purely as an economic issue is Brazil. One of the Commerce Department's "10 big emerging markets," Brazil has been identified by the CIA as a country on the brink of failure. Indeed, it is just one of several such major markets on the CIA's list.

The pertinent question raised by the Saudi episodes and the situation in Brazil is whether the Clinton Administration is using intelligence information properly. The existence of widespread corruption in a country is an important indicator of a potentially unstable regime. Information indicating instability should be viewed in connection with other information to give U.S. political leaders warning of situations that could affect national security. Viewing that information merely as a marketing tool risks jeopardizing American security and even, as the Saudi bombing incidents demonstrate, American lives.

A much better way to address the problem of international corruption is to lead the effort to stop it. People around the world are venting their disgust with corrupt leaders, and the U.S. is admired for its relative lack of corruption. "As governments seek to tighten laws to stamp out corruption, they would be wise to look at the U.S. experience," advises the European. It would be folly for the U.S. to do anything to undermine its natural leadership position.

Countering industrial espionage. Stopping the theft of American business secrets is a legitimate focus of espionage (or, more precisely, counterespionage) and a function of law enforcement. The problem of foreign commercial espionage should not be exaggerated, though. Testifying before the Senate Select Committee on Intelligence in August, 1993, Boeing Vice Pres. John F. Hayden estimated that, on a scale of one to 10 (least to most serious threat), foreign industrial espionage "is on the lower spectrum. Maybe a two." Similarly, Woolsey's predecessor as CIA director, Robert Gates, told the House Judiciary Committee in 1992 that "We lack the evidentiary basis for establishing any over-all trend toward increased economic espionage among advanced industrial countries." Despite such assertions, Clinton Administration officials have portrayed economic espionage as a dire threat.

In February, 1996, FBI Director Louis J. Freeh told Congress, "Types of U.S. government economic information, especially prepublication data, of interest to foreign governments and intelligence services as determined through FBI investigations include: U.S. economic, trade, and financial agreements; U.S. trade developments and policies; U.S. national debt levels; U.S. tax and monetary policies; foreign aid programs and export credits; technology transfer and munitions control regulations; U.S. energy policies and critical materials stockpiles data; U.S. commodity policies; and proposed legislation affecting the profitability of foreign firms operating in the United States."

Freeh's list suggests an overly broad definition of the economic espionage threat. There is, after all, nothing sinister about foreign governments wanting to know about legislation affecting the profitability of their countries' firms operating in the U.S.

The encryption controversy

What did come up in the committee hearing, however, was a complaint by several representatives of U.S. industry that the FBI and the National Security Agency, by insisting on weak encryption technology, were obstructing efforts by American businesses to protect their secrets from foreign intelligence operations. "At present, the U.S. government is not effective in assisting U.S. corporations to effectively defend themselves against economic espionage by foreign intelligence services," charged Geoffrey Turner of the Information Security program at SRI

International. "One area of current U.S. government policy, export controls of commercial cryptography, are [sic] in fact operating contrary to the true U.S. national security interest by impeding access of U.S. corporations to effective use of cryptography in international commerce."

That position was echoed by a representative of Microsoft Corp. "Government imposition of substandard information security systems threatens the continued growth and development of personal computers and the competitiveness of America's software companies," argued Nathan P. Myhrvold, vice president for advanced technology and business development. "We must make certain that our government doesn't deprive U.S. companies of protection against industrial espionage or limit the ability of U.S. software companies to compete internationally."

Despite its vocal concern about foreign industrial espionage, the Clinton Administration initially followed the path of its predecessor, ignoring the pleas of the very industries it insisted it was seeking to help. When a Congressionally mandated National Research Council study endorsed stronger encryption standards, the Administration dismissed the recommendation. In November, 1996, though, the Administration relented and loosened its encryption policy.

Assisting trade negotiators. On Jan. 26, 1995, French Interior Minister Charles Pasqua summoned U.S. Ambassador Pamela Harriman to his office and informed her that several embassy officials had been identified as spies engaged in economic espionage and would have to leave the country. Shortly afterward, news of the meeting "leaked" to the French press. U.S. officials, upset at the publicity, complained that Pasqua was using the scandal to bolster the presidential election campaign of Prime Minister Edouard Balladur.

Although both governments quickly acted to put the affair behind them, the incident reflected tensions that had been building for some time. According to the *Wall Street Journal,* a number of governments, including those of Britain and Germany, had begun to complain about the size of the U.S. intelligence contingent in their countries, but had refrained from taking action for fear of jeopardizing relations with their biggest ally. Instead, they "had been looking forward to France taking the lead on this," a former U.S. intelligence official related, "because France doesn't worry too much about U.S. sensitivities."

The charges coming from Paris must be taken with a grain of salt. Given France's own record of economic espionage, its public indignation did seem a little hypocritical. "It is an elementary blunder to think we're allies with countries like America," argues former French intelligence chief Pierre Marion. "When it comes to business, it's war." Marion openly boasts that his service was "able to obtain for the French company [Dassault] confidential documents from the American competition, which Dassault was then able to undercut."

In Britain, the Intelligence Services Act provides a statutory basis for spy agencies to support the country's "economic well-being," which one British newspaper interprets as a "green light for gathering commercial intelligence on trade competitors." Indeed, a former British intelligence official has alleged that Britain's equivalent of the U.S. National Security Agency has been used to gather information on foreign competitors and pass it on to British firms.

Even if other countries engage in economic espionage, what does the U.S. gain by imitating them? One of the principal objectives of the operation in Paris was to learn what the French position would be in negotiations under the General Agreement on Tariffs and Trade. Yet, as one retired CIA official observed, "I imagine that you could get the French position on GATT without spying on them."

Even if U.S. officials could not, what would be the problem? The purpose of trade negotiations is to broaden the choices available to consumers, not to protect one's own producers at the expense of everybody else's. The closed nature of one's own economy should not be used as a bargaining chip to pry open other economies. That attitude reflects a fundamental misunderstanding of the purpose of trade. The U.S., which considers itself a moral leader on issues of free trade, should be setting an example of the benefits of an open economy.

Viewed from that perspective, spying to discover another country's trade position becomes utterly irrelevant, if not counterproductive. Indeed, when it was revealed that the U.S. also had spied on the Japanese in the course of another set of trade negotiations, the reaction was one of bewilderment. "The U.S. is believed to have gained little or no advantage from the alleged action," the *Financial Times* reported. "Car industry officials found it hard to see how any espionage could have helped the U.S. negotiators."

As the *Financial Times* also noted, the Japanese government and people were upset by the revelations, thus pointing up a greater danger inherent in the use of economic espionage among democratic capitalist countries. The world still is a dangerous place, and it would be folly for the democracies to engage in nasty intramural squabbles. Yet, that is the risk economic espionage against other free societies poses. "This will not blow over in a matter of months; it will take several years, at least, before we can talk about serious cooperation again in intelligence matters," a U.S. official observed after the French fiasco. A French colleague agreed. "Right now, the mood is too poisoned to believe that we will ever be able to cooperate on anything as we did before, unless there is a major crisis that poses a serious threat to both governments."

Those crises now are occurring. Americans are familiar with terrorist bombings on U.S. soil and acts of violence against Americans in the armed forces abroad. The U.S. is not the sole target, however. France has been a victim as well. Intelligence collaboration between the two countries was critical in capturing the notorious terrorist, Carlos, who had murdered several French police officers, and both sides are represented in NATO's Implementation Force in Bosnia. Washington ought to consider that it may need the cooperation of Paris (or other Western capitals) to help deal with a mutual security threat at some point. The desired cooperation will be less likely to be forthcoming if Washington has created animosity through its policy of economic spying.

Refocusing

The focus on economic espionage ultimately reflects an underlying belief in the necessity of industrial policy. "It's essential we have some kind of national economic strategy, or we just won't be competitive," Secretary of Commerce Ron Brown argued. "Be it in telecommunications or aerospace, we intend to use the weight of the U.S. government to help U.S. industry." Since the intelligence agencies are part of the U.S. government, they are to play a role in implementing that strategy. "Winning the battle for 'competitiveness' in world marketplaces is a prime new agenda for American security policy," notes a 1996 study for the Twentieth Century Fund. "More aggressive industrial espionage is only one of many implications for intelligence policy that would follow from such a worldview."

Those who argue in favor of a national economic strategy maintain that the market is unable to predict the future and thus provide guidance about investment. "In the presence of increasing returns and spillover effects, the market can not signal to private agents the unintended outcome of their collective behavior," Laura D'Andrea Tyson, head of the National Economic Council, has written. "To put it differently, markets can not deliver information about or discount the possibility of future states of the world whose occurrences are externalities resulting from the interaction of the present decisions of behaviorally unrelated agents." Consequently, she has advocated "a change in the philosophy of U.S. trade policy from one of free trade to one of sophisticated intervention."

Markets are imperfect guides to the futures because the future is unpredictable. Thus, all investment involves risk. So, the question can not be: Who can predict it better? The relevant question is: Who should be accountable for the inevitable mistakes that result?

When people invest their own money, they are directly accountable for the risk they have assumed and personally feel the loss or gain. When government officials invest money, it is not theirs. If the investment is lost on a technology that does not work, they do not feel the loss, since the money does not come out of their pockets. The taxpayers probably will not feel it, either. In the first place, the connection is too tenuous. In addition, government officials are not going to publicize their mistakes. That is why, except for a limited sector of public goods, private investment (direct accountability) is economically preferable to government investment (indirect accountability).

Indeed, the concerns about American competitiveness in high technology that were voiced years ago now seem almost quaint. Instead of providing stable and highly paid employment, publicly funded firms overseas are in crisis. The assumption that such firms had an unfair advantage because they could operate at a loss has been disproved. In 1996, the French government announced a major shakeup in its defense sector, prompted by the need to make funds available to pay for social programs and to reduce government indebtedness. As part of that change, France's defense industries are to be put on a more commercial basis to make them more competitive and reduce the huge losses they have sustained. "The state feeds those firms the way a farmer tends his herds," a French banker at a large investment house observed about France's industrial policy. "Feeding one, then the other. But now the state no longer has the means." Even governments, it would appear, can not operate businesses at a loss indefinitely, and the effort to try simply weakens the competitiveness of their countries' firms by interfering with responses to commercial pressures.

Thus, to the extent that economic intelligence rests on the desire to support a national economic strategy, it should be rejected. That is not to say, however, that there is no role for economic intelligence. It should be focused on dealing with threats to national security. In this respect, two considerations stand out.

The first is economic indicators that could point to political instability in a foreign country. Indicators would include such factors as pervasive corruption, high inflation and/or unemployment, capital flight, a marked decline in national income, and growing income inequality. It is perfectly appropriate, even obligatory, for agencies of the U.S. government to monitor such developments, especially in regions where there is a significant American interest. Most of that information is publicly available, however, so, strictly speaking, gathering it is not economic *espionage*.

The other consideration is arms sales or transfers, not only because of the military implications, but because of what they signify about the intentions of the regimes that are buying and selling. For example, the CIA was aware of Saddam Hussein's efforts to acquire nuclear weapons technology by establishing dummy firms in Western countries well before he invaded Kuwait. The political implications of his actions were not appreciated fully, though, in large part because the Bush Administration saw Iraq primarily as a market it did not want to jeopardize.

The problem with economic intelligence is not so much with the intelligence agencies, but with their political masters, who do not understand how it should be utilized. Such intelligence is not a tool for leveling the playing field; it is input to the investigation and analysis that should be employed to identify adverse political developments or outright security threats before they turn urgent. Intelligence is most effective when it points out erroneous assumptions of official policy before those mistakes become serious. That means political leaders must be willing to listen to unpleasant information they would rather not hear. If they won't do that, no reform or redirection of the intelligence community is likely to be successful.

Justifying assumptions

Thus, the most urgent foreign policy question the Clinton Administration must address is whether its underlying hopeful assumptions are justified. The Administration still clings to the view that peace is breaking out all over, and any challenges can be handled by a brief display of American might.

There is an echo here of the argument that led to the disastrous American involvement in Southeast Asia. "Vietnam represents a test of American responsibility and determination in Asia," Sen. John F. Kennedy proclaimed in 1956. "If it falls victim to any of the perils that threaten its existence—communism, political anarchy, poverty, and the rest—then the United States, with some justification, will be held responsible." Having assumed that responsibility as a senator, Kennedy sought a showdown with communism in Vietnam as president. "If you were going to have a confrontation, the place to have it was in Vietnam," Ambassador William H. Sullivan subsequently explained. "People were looking at Vietnam as something that could be a more solid instrument for settling this thing."

In retrospect, the foolhardiness of that policy is clear. "I underestimated the tenacity of the North Vietnamese, and I overestimated the patience of the American people," former Secretary of State Dean Rusk admitted in 1973. Moreover, the tragedy of Vietnam is magnified by the realization that the intelligence agencies had tried to warn their political masters of the disaster ahead. "The intelligence analysis compiled by the CIA and the State Department in the spring of 1964 examined every possible kind of American intervention, and its conclusion was stalemate at best and war with China at worst," recalls Allen S. Whiting, former head of the East Asian Section of the State Department's Bureau of Intelligence and Research. "With that kind of agreement among the best Asian specialists of the two major analytic agencies of the U.S. government, one did not think that the president [Lyndon Johnson] would do it."

The irony is that Pres. Clinton, an opponent of the Vietnam War, now seems to be repeating the mistakes that led the U.S. into that conflict. "Somalia is a test case of whether we can help keep peace in the world without having to do it all ourselves," a Clinton Administration official explained in early 1993. Just as had been done in Vietnam, Washington underestimated the enemy and overestimated U.S. capabilities.

Despite the debacle in Somalia, the Administration is intent on demonstrating that the U.S. can keep peace in the world virtually by itself. America now is effectively responsible for maintaining the peace in the Persian Gulf, the Middle East, East Asia, and Europe. If Washington wants to accept those responsibilities, it had better be ready for the attacks that will come from people who challenge the *status quo*. "We must be prepared for the frequency and the scale of attacks on our Gulf—in the Gulf to increase," Secretary of Defense William Perry warned in a revealing slip of the tongue in 1996, emphasizing that "we do not want to simply sit and wait for terrorists to act. We want to seek them out, find them, identify them, and do what we can to disrupt or preempt any planned operation, and the key to this is better intelligence." Yes, it is, and that is why intelligence should have been focused on security matters all along, instead of being diverted into economic espionage on the assumption of a benign world.

Even if Washington adopts a more restrained policy, security threats inevitably will emerge from time to time. In a dangerous, turbulent, and unpredictable world, the intelligence agencies will be the first line of protection, and their effectiveness largely will determine how many Americans live or die.

To improve the effectiveness of the intelligence agencies, two things will be necessary. First, they should focus on genuine threats to national security, such as terrorism, and not on trade negotiations. Not only do such diversions represent a misuse of resources, the espionage spats between the U.S. and other democratic countries undermine their ability to deal with the dangers that confront them all.

Second, at the political level, the President and his advisers should view the intelligence agencies as institutions that are most valuable when they bring into question the premises of existing policy. That is, admittedly, a hard thing to do, but history demonstrates the consequences of refusing to believe intelligence that contradicts the views of the political leadership. Already, the intelligence agencies are flashing warning signals about some of the Administration's (and, it must be said, the Republican opposition's) policies.

The secrets of corporate America should be protected by the appropriate agencies of the U.S. government. However, the intelligence agencies should focus on their main mission—safeguarding the security of the American people.

Tin Cup Diplomacy

Hans Binnendijk

FIFTY YEARS AGO the United States entered a new international system armed with resources to meet the new challenge of communism. At the height of the Marshall Plan, for example, some 16 percent of the U.S. federal budget was dedicated to supporting Europe alone. Today we are again in the early stages of a new international system, but without a unifying challenge to raise foreign affairs resources much above 1 percent of the federal budget. Remarkably, with tin cup diplomacy and some triage, the United States has been able to deal fairly successfully with post-Cold War complexity. Our capabilities are now fraying, however, and international leadership cannot be sustained unless the resource slide is reversed.

Reductions in the international affairs budget have been deep, with constant dollar cuts of about 34 percent over the past decade, including a 14 percent cut in just the last two years. Defense expenditures have also fallen 34 percent since 1986. Expressed as a percentage of GNP, defense and international affairs spending together has dropped from 6.9 percent to 3.7 percent during this period. International affairs cuts have also been targeted at specific accounts. For example, the drop in international security assistance has been 74 percent over the decade, so deep that if aid to Israel, Egypt, and Turkey is excluded, the United States has basically given up security assistance as an instrument of foreign policy.

Hans Binnendijk is director of the Institute for National Strategic Studies at the National Defense University. The opinions expressed in this article are the author's alone.

Other areas particularly hard hit are the United Nations, information and exchange programs, and multilateral development aid.

Analysts disagree about the impact of the international affairs cuts. The Georgetown University Institute for the Study of Diplomacy concluded last year that resource problems are already harming the capacity of the United States to lead and that the national security capital built up during the Cold War is being depleted. The Heritage Foundation, on the other hand, has argued that some key accounts have increased and that no real harm has been done.

There is some truth to both sides of these apparently contradictory conclusions. Innovative U.S. approaches have masked the impact of reductions, especially in vital areas of the world. Passing the tin cup and designing ad hoc solutions have worked so far. In Central Europe, for example, the Partnership for Peace is a bargain at $100 million, while the United States intends to pay for less than 10 percent of the NATO enlargement bill. In Korea, U.S. creation of the Korean Peninsula Energy Development Organization helped halt North Korea's nuclear program, and Japan and South Korea are picking up more than 90 percent of the tab for it. In the former Soviet Union, Western disbursements of more than $20 billion since 1991 have been made primarily by international financial institutions. In the case of Mexico, the United States found an obscure account—the Exchange Stabilization Fund—to provide $20 billion in financing to deal with the 1994 financial crisis there. In the Zaire crisis, the United States promised to help the new leadership retrieve billions of Mobutu's stolen dollars as an incentive to stop the massacres—a skillful use of someone else's money. Only in the Middle East has the United States continued to pour aid funds in at pre-1990 levels. But when it came to Operations Desert Storm and Vigilant Warrior in the Persian Gulf, the United States again successfully turned to its allies to pay most of the bills.

According to a new book entitled *Who Needs Embassies?*, U.S. embassies in strategically significant countries have also managed, at least until now, to pursue critical U.S. interests successfully despite fraying caused by cutbacks.[1] The book examines recent U.S. operations in five key countries—Germany, South Korea, South Africa, Israel, and Guatemala—and concludes that despite policy successes, demands on these embassies are increasing dramatically even as they are being pinched financially. In addition, the State Department reports that thirty-one new missions or embassies have been created since 1991, mostly in countries formerly part of the Soviet Union or Yugoslavia. And the National Defense University's *Strategic Assessment 1996* shows that the number of U.S. personnel stationed in our embassies has actually increased from 15,000 to 19,000 during the past ten years.

But all this is misleading. What has been happening is that other U.S. agencies have stepped in overseas to help the often beleaguered State Department. Most of the increase in U.S. embassy personnel, for example, is from the military or from U.S. law enforcement agencies. In Mexico City, over thirty U.S. agencies are represented at the embassy, and seventeen work on counter-drug efforts. A Defense Department publication entitled "Foreign Military Interaction: Strategic Rationale" lists thirteen different defense engagement programs overseas, most of which have diplomatic purposes. The National Guard works closely with "sister states" in Central Europe, where it helps to implement the Partnership for Peace. And three new U.S.-run regional military education centers have been established for Europe, Asia, and Latin America.

Allied nations and other organizations are also filling some of the gaps left by the United States. In Bosnia, private voluntary organizations provide vital services that thirty years ago would have been performed by the U.S. government. In Haiti, Canadians and Pakistanis perform international policing functions that the United States left to them last summer. In North Korea, the International Atomic Energy Agency provides continuous on-site monitoring of nuclear material, and its teams include a substantial number of specialists from the U.S. Department of Energy. During the Cold War, of course, all treaty verification obligations were carried out directly by the United States, either through remote technical means, or, where agreed, treaty-specified U.S. on-site inspections. In El Salvador, our stabilizing influence has been partially replaced by the United Nations.

IF TIN CUP DIPLOMACY is working, why then the concern about budget cuts? Because while these activities may be useful, they cannot compensate fully and indefinitely for the shortfall in the core foreign affairs budget. In order to save key programs, State has had to sacrifice others. For example, *Who Needs Embassies?* notes that in order to support democratic transitions in countries such as Guatemala and South Africa, resources for other embassies in those regions have been sucked dry. To open the thirty-one new missions of the kind mentioned above, State had to close thirty-five other embassies and consulates. Some of the less important embassies that have stayed open suffer like our poorly constructed embassy in Guinea-Bissau. In what should become a classic cable, sent to Washington in February, the embassy sought guidance on pesticides to kill both the hundreds of rats that eat documents and the thousands of locusts that penetrate into the deepest security areas of the post. At the Agency for International Development (AID), planners will cut the number of overseas AID missions by more than half in order to save critical programs. And the U.S. Information Agency (USIA) is closing libraries by the dozen, giving rise to the concern that our friends see American librarians and development officers leaving just as Drug Enforcement Agency personnel arrive.

---

[1] Mary Locke and Casimir Yost, eds., *Who Needs Embassies?* (Washington, DC: Georgetown University Institute for the Study of Diplomacy, 1997).

Behind the façade of success, then, our basic foreign affairs infrastructure is eroding. The State Department has cut two thousand employees and USIA has cut 25 percent of its work force during the past four years, many of them experienced regional experts that are needed to deal with today's complex world. Half of State's computers and three-quarters of its phone systems are obsolete. The archaic State Department Wang computer system cannot read e-mail documents prepared in a Windows program. Some of our embassies, such as those I visited recently in China and South Korea, are apparent firetraps. Departing overseas personnel routinely leave their posts three to four months before their replacements arrive, in order to save money but at the expense of continuity. In other embassies, biographic files on key local figures are no longer kept up to date, so valuable information is sacrificed. There are not enough funds to enable political officers to travel often outside the capital city, and consequently reporting suffers. We now run the risk of developing diplomatic Alzheimer's disease.

International affairs budget cuts are also beginning to affect our ability to influence events and to practice preventive diplomacy. It is only because an unrivaled military stands behind the diplomatic tin cup that the United States retains any influence at all. Our Economic Support Fund, designed in 1977 to provide influence-generating economic aid, is now focused almost exclusively on Israel and Egypt. In the multilateral banks, we are losing our ability to block loans of which we do not approve and direct other loans to projects we support. In Panama, we may lose access to military bases critical to the counter-narcotics fight because we cannot afford security assistance. In Africa, declining foreign aid resources coincide with a marked increase in civil conflict in failed states.

The negative impact of these budget cuts has reached the point where constructive actions are now being taken in the administration, on Capitol Hill, and in the private sector to regenerate our capabilities. Negative budget trends may have bottomed out. The administration has agreed with Congress to undertake an ambitious merger of the State Department, the Arms Control and Disarmament Agency (ACDA), USIA, and AID. ACDA and USIA would become one with State, while AID would remain separate but would report to the secretary of state rather than the president. This would eventually result in greater efficiency and possibly some savings, but more importantly it has created a smoother relationship between the two branches of government on the question of foreign affairs resources. That cooperation is also evident in the deal made with Senator Jesse Helms to repay over three years $819 million owed in arrears to the United Nations. In exchange for authorizing the funds, Senator Helms extracted various useful UN reforms, and he intends to shave future American contributions to UN operations from 25 to 20 percent of the total bill, in order to bring U.S. dues in line with new international realities.

Secretary of State Madeleine Albright has also given higher priority to fixing the resources problem. She has initiated a much needed effort to explain to the American people the benefits of engagement overseas. She has convinced the President and the director of the Office of Management and Budget to increase the fiscal year 1998 international affairs request to Congress by $1.2 billion over last year's appropriation of $18.2 billion. Albright's State Department has created a new strategic planning system that for the first time sets out specific budget-driven policy goals, designs a strategy to implement them, and establishes indicators to judge progress. Ambassador Max Kampelman took the lead in stimulating private sector initiatives such as the "Advocacy of U.S. Interests Abroad" project, which, under the guidance of the Stimson Center, seeks to create a clearer national consensus on foreign policy goals and means.

Both efforts attest to the recognition that the pendulum has swung too far and that the foreign affairs budget has been cut too deep. Now is the time to sustain the new cooperation between the administration and Congress so that the United States can indeed lead the world into the twenty-first century.

Unit 5

Unit Selections

24. **Inside the White House Situation Room,** Michael Donley, Cornelius O'Leary and John Montgomery
25. **NATO Expansion: The Anatomy of a Decision,** James Goldgeier
26. **The White House Dismissed Warnings on China Satellite Deal,** Jeff Gerth and John M. Broder

Key Points to Consider

❖ Construct an ideal foreign policy-making process. How close does the United States come to this ideal? Is it possible for the United States to act in the ideal manner? If not, is the failing due to individuals who make foreign policy or to the institutions in which they work?

❖ What is the single largest failing of the foreign policy-making process? How can it be corrected? What is the single largest strength of the foreign policy making process?

❖ Does the foreign policy-making process operate the same way in all policy areas (human rights, foreign aid, military intervention, etc)? Should it? Explain.

❖ What changes, if any, are necessary in the U.S. foreign policy-making process if the United States is to act effectively with other countries in multilateral efforts?

❖ Should the United States try to be more like other countries in how it makes foreign policy decisions? If so, what countries should serve as a model?

Links — www.dushkin.com/online/

17. **Belfer Center for Science and International Affairs (BCSIA)**
    http://ksgwww.harvard.edu/csia/
18. **DiploNet**
    http://www.clark.net/pub/diplonet/DiploNet.html
19. **InterAction**
    http://www.interaction.org/
20. **Welcome to the White House**
    http://www.whitehouse.gov/WH/Welcome.html

These sites are annotated on pages 4 and 5.

The Foreign Policy-Making Process

In thinking about how to bring a halt to the fighting in Bosnia, bring about peace in the Middle East, respond to the refugee crisis in Rwanda, or stop human rights violations in China while at the same time improving trade relations with that country, we often slip into the habit of assuming that an underlying rationality is at work. Goals are established, policy options listed, the implications of competing courses of action are assessed, a conscious choice made as to which policy to adopt, and then the policy is implemented correctly. This assumption is comforting because it implies that policymakers are in control of events and that solutions do exist. Moreover, it allows us to assign responsibility for policy decisions and hold policymakers accountable for the success or failure of their actions.

Comforting as this assumption is, it is also false. Driven by domestic, international, and institutional forces, as well as by chance and accident, perfect rationality is an elusive quality. Often policymakers will knowingly be forced to settle for a satisfactory or sufficient solution to a problem rather than the optimum one. At other times, the most pressing task may not be that of solving the problem but of getting all of the involved parties to agree on a course of action—any course of action. This retreat from rationality has been very much evident as the Clinton administration struggled with the questions of formulating a policy toward China. Rather than proceeding in orderly steps of identifying goals and weighing options, the policy-making process lurched back and forth as conditions in China changed and political pressures for action on the part of the Clinton administration rose and fell.

While most Americans are willing to acknowledge that the give and take of the political process can have a negative effect on the quality of decisions arrived at, even when decisions are made out of the public spotlight, rationality can be difficult to achieve. This is true regardless of whether the decision is made in a small group setting or by large bureaucracies. Small groups are created when the scope of the foreign policy problem appears to lie beyond the expertise of any single individual. This is frequently the case in crisis situations. The essence of the decision-making problem here lies in the overriding desire of group members to get along. Determined to be a productive member of the team and not to rock the boat, individual group members suppress personal doubts about the wisdom of what is being considered and become less critical of the information before them than they would be if they alone were responsible for the decision. They may stereotype the enemy, assume that the policy cannot fail, or believe that all members of the group are in agreement on what must be done.

The absence of rationality in decision making by large bureaucracies stems from their dual nature. On the one hand, bureaucracies are politically neutral institutions that exist to serve the president and other senior officials by providing them with information and implementing their policies. On the other hand, they have goals and interests of their own that may not only conflict with the positions taken by other bureaucracies but may be inconsistent with the official position taken by policymakers. Because not every bureaucracy sees a foreign policy problem the same way, policies must be negotiated into existence, and implementation becomes anything but automatic. While essential for building a foreign policy consensus, this exercise in bureaucratic politics robs the policy process of much of the rationality that we look for in government decision making.

The readings in this unit provide insight into the process by which foreign policy decisions are made in Washington. The essay "Inside the White House Situation Room" provides an insider's account of how the national security decision-making process is organized to respond to international crises. Written for senior and mid-level intelligence professionals, this study delves into a little-studied facet of the foreign policy-making process. Relying heavily on interviews, James Goldgeier, in "NATO Expansion: The Anatomy of a Decision," traces the manner in which the government responded to President Clinton's decision to seek NATO enlargement. He gives special attention to the role that the bureaucracy and presidential advisers played in this decision. Finally, Jeff Gerth and John Broder, in "The White House Dismissed Warnings on China Satellite Deal," describe one of the most controversial decisions made by the Clinton administration. They reveal that national security considerations did not play a major role in the decision to grant a waiver to Loral Space & Communications to export a satellite to China.

Article 24

A National Nerve Center

Inside The White House Situation Room

Michael Donley, Cornelius O'Leary, and John Montgomery

> **"Just remember that there are many important people who work in the White House, and you're not one of them."**

Michael Donley was Deputy Executive Secretary of the National Security Council, 1987-89.
Cornelius O'Leary is a former Director of the White House Situation Room. **John Montgomery** is a former intelligence analyst at the National Security Council.

Go to the southwest gate of the White House complex, present the guard with identification, and state your business. If you are on the appointment list, an escort will be called. Walk up West Executive Avenue and turn right into the West Basement entrance; another guard will check your pass for White House access. Take the first right, down a few stairs. To the left is the White House Mess; on the right is a locked door.

Behind these layers of security is the White House Situation Room (WHSR), a conference room surrounded on three sides by two small offices, multiple workstations, computers, and communications equipment. The conference room is soundproofed and well appointed but small and slightly cramped. The technical equipment is up to date, though not necessarily "leading edge"; every square foot of space is functional. Visitors typically are impressed by the location and technology, but they are often surprised at the small size.

While it is widely known that important meetings are held here, the importance of the WHSR in the daily life of the National Security Council (NSC) and White House staff and its critical role in Washington's network of key national security operations and intelligence centers are less understood. This paper is intended to fill that void. We believe there is a longstanding need within middle and senior levels of the Intelligence Community (IC) for a basic understanding of NSC and White House functions and how current intelligence information is provided to key decisionmakers, including the President.

Mission, Organization, Functions

The WHSR was established by President Kennedy after the Bay of Pigs disaster in 1961. That crisis revealed a need for rapid and secure presidential communications and for White House coordination of the many external communications channels of national security information which led to the President.[1] Since then, the mission of the "Sit Room" has been to provide current intelligence and crisis support to the NSC staff, the National Security Adviser, and the President. The Sit Room staff is composed of approximately 30 personnel, organized around five Watch Teams that provide 7-day, 24-hour monitoring of international events. A generic Watch Team includes three Duty Officers, a communications assistant, and an intelligence analyst. The number and composition of personnel varies, depending on shift requirements and workload.

Sit Room personnel are handpicked from nominations made by military and civilian intelligence agencies for approximately two-year tours. This is a close, high-visibility work environment. Egos are checked at the door, as captured in the admonition of a former Sit Room Director to incoming Duty Officers: "Just remember that there are many important people who work in the White House, and you're not one of them." Personal characteristics count: an even temperament, coolness under pressure, and the ability to have a coherent, professional, no-advance-notice conversation with the President of the United States.

Sit Room functions are perhaps described best in the daily routine of activities. The day begins with the Watch Team's preparation of the Morning Book. Prepared for the President, Vice President, and most senior White House staff, the Morning Book contains a copy of the *National Intelligence Daily*, the *State Department's Morning Summary*, and diplomatic cables and intelligence reports. These cables and reports are selected based on their relevance to ongoing diplomatic initiatives and/or specific subject matter on the President's schedule. The Morning Book is usually in the car when the National Security Adviser is picked up for work. The morning routine also includes the *President's Daily Brief*, which is prepared by CIA, hand-delivered, and briefed by a CIA officer to the President and other NSC principals.[2]

In addition, the Watch Teams produce morning and evening summaries of highly selective material. These summaries, targeted on current interagency issues, are transmitted electronically to the NSC staff. Such summaries, which draw on a number of finished interagency products, field reports, and newswires, may also elicit requests for the original products. The Sit Room staff does not perform intelligence analysis or render the kind of formal interagency judgments found in National Intelligence Estimates. But it is important to recognize that, especially at the White House, there is always more intelligence information available than there is time for senior decisionmakers to read, and it falls to the Sit Room to boil that information down to its essential elements.

In a typical 24-hour day, the Sit Room will provide alerts on breaking events to NSC and White House personnel. Triggered by specific events

> "In all situations other than nuclear war or physical threats against the President, the Sit Room is in effect the 24-hour, one-stop shop for the White House staff."

and followed with consultations among operations and intelligence centers, the alert notification process results in a rapid series of phone calls to key officials. Responsibility for informing the President belongs to the National Security Adviser. Later, a written "Sit Room Note" will be prepared, summarizing the event with up-to-the-minute reports from other centers, perhaps including a photo, diagram, or map. At the direction of the National Security Adviser, such a note might be delivered by a Duty Officer directly to the Oval Office or the President's residential quarters. After hours, depending on their personal style or interest, the President or Vice President might call the Sit Room directly or drop by unannounced for a quick update.

The advent of 24-hour-a-day television news broadcasting as well as radio has added a new dynamic to warning and alert operations. Not only do Duty Officers pour over hundreds of incoming cables, but they also are constantly bombarded by on-site television broadcasts from the crisis area and newswire services pumping a steady volume of information destined for the morning front pages. The Duty Officer's task is to ensure that the President and National Security Adviser are informed not only of the current situation but also how the situation is being portrayed by the media. Less-than-objective images can sometimes place the Duty Officer in a position of having to produce "negative" intelligence to put the event into con-

text. Occasionally, it may even prove necessary to tell the principal that the events as portrayed by the press are incorrect.

While the advancements in telecommunications have placed more pressure on the watch standers, they have also simplified the exchange of information among participating agencies. The same satellites that allow news reporting from the field also enable crisis-support elements to extract information from remote databases, provide for timely reporting, and, in some cases, engage in video teleconferencing.

Another typical Sit Room activity is arranging the President's phone calls and other sensitive communications with foreign heads of state. This includes coordinating the timing of such calls at each end, providing interpreters where necessary, and ensuring appropriate security and recordkeeping. In this function, the Sit Room coordinates closely with the White House Communications Agency, which supplies communications technicians to the Watch Teams.

The importance of the Sit Room's communications function cannot be overstated. In all situations other than nuclear war or physical threats against the President, the Sit Room is in effect the 24-hour, one-stop shop for the White House staff. It is also the funnel through which most communications, especially classified information, will pass when the President is not in residence. It is an essential link, providing the traveling White House with access to all the information available from Washington's national security community.

Essential Relationships

There are two essential relationships that the Situation Room has to maintain if it is to be successful in providing timely information to the Oval Office. The most important relationship is with the NSC's Executive Secretary, who reports directly

5 ❖ THE FOREIGN POLICY-MAKING PROCESS

to the National Security Adviser and the Deputy.

As statutory head of the NSC staff, the Executive Secretary is the primary point of contact for the White House Staff Secretary and is the key player in moving national security information to and from the Oval Office.[3] National-security-related memorandums from departments and agencies to the President are transmitted through the NSC's Executive Secretary for staffing to the appropriate office. When staffing is complete, finished packages for the National Security Adviser or the President are sent back up the chain through the Executive Secretary. When the President makes a decision or approves a course of action, the Executive Secretary formally communicates the decision to affected departments and agencies. Thus, virtually all national security correspondence passes through the Executive Secretary.

> **This intimate knowledge of the President's schedule makes the Sit Room unique among Washington-area operations and intelligence centers.**

For this reason, the Sit Room has often been administratively assigned to the Office of the Executive Secretary. With inclusion of the Sit Room, the Executive Secretary becomes the focal point for all information going to the National Security Adviser, from the deliberative ("slow paper") policy process to fast-moving perishable intelligence and crisis information. As coordinator of the President's national security schedule, the Office of the Executive Secretary also has an enormous reservoir of policy and operational information at its fingertips. It is through this key relationship that the Sit Room will first hear of a proposed Presidential trip abroad or a potential call to a foreign head of state.

A second essential connection for the WHSR is its relationship with the National Security Adviser, formally known as the Assistant to the President for National Security Affairs. He and the Deputy are the officials most "in the know," and they are in frequent and direct contact with NSC principals and key subordinates. Because of the Sit Room's role in the alert process, its position as the funnel for national security information when the President is traveling, and its 24-hour capability, a close working relationship with the National Security Adviser usually develops. For the system to work at its best, a special trust has to be established among the National Security Adviser, the Executive Secretary, and the Sit Room Director.

This trust is especially important in establishing the thresholds for warning and alert after hours and providing advance notice of future events. Upon the death of a foreign head of state, for example, it may not be necessary to awaken the National Security Adviser or the President in the middle of the night. If there are no threats to American citizens involved and no action for the President to take, perhaps a "wake-up" notification at 5 a.m. would suffice. Similarly, it is not unusual for the Sit Room Director to be included in sensitive interagency meetings before initiation of military operations or for the National Security Adviser to instruct the Sit Room that a special "Eyes Only" message should be brought directly upstairs. Establishing such trust can be developed only through close and routine personal interactions.

Through daily interaction with the Executive Secretary and National Security Adviser (including the Deputy), and routine access to the schedules and agendas of interagency meetings, the Sit Room Director is able to provide effective operational guidance to Watch Teams. The teams are then in a better position to assess the value and importance of incoming cables and newswires in the context of long-range policy issues under discussion at the highest levels, as well as fast-breaking crises that will demand Presidential attention. This intimate knowledge of the President's schedule makes the Sit Room unique among Washington-area operations and intelligence centers.

Support to the NSC Staff

The NSC staff is organized into regional and functional directorates located in the Old Executive Office Building (OEOB). A directorate is headed by a Senior Director, who is appointed by the President to coordinate and oversee Presidential policy in a particular area. A Senior Director's counterpart at State or Defense would be at the Assistant Secretary level. The Senior Director supports the National Security Adviser, in effect coordinating the interagency policy agenda in a given area. The directorates are best described as a mile wide and an inch deep because they usually consist only of a Senior Director assisted by two to four directors. On a day-to-day basis, the Sit Room supports the NSC directorates by electronically routing nearly 1,000 messages to staff members; scanning cables, newswires, and press reports; and monitoring CNN for fast-breaking events.

It is important that the NSC's Directorate for Intelligence Programs not be confused with Sit Room operations. The Intelligence Directorate oversees interagency intelligence policies and programs such as covert action Findings, counterintelligence, major procurement projects, and the interagency intelligence budget; it has no responsibility for production, dissemination, or coordination of current intelligence.[4]

Direct Sit Room contact with the NSC staff increases markedly during crises. In some cases, such as Iraq's invasion of Kuwait and the 1991 coup attempt against President Gorbachev, it is not unusual for the Senior Director to move into the Sit Room to be closer to the crisis and take advantage of the on-duty staff and its communications services. This approach, however, has limitations: Sit Room Watch Teams may lack the specific regional expertise appropriate to the crisis; Sit Room spaces are cramped and not suited physically to accommodate longer term crisis operations; and Watch Teams have a continuing responsibility to monitor other global events.

Intelligence Support to Policymakers

Efforts to strengthen intelligence support to policymakers have a long history. Every administration seems to reach its own modus vivendi, squaring expectations with realities between the policy and intelligence communities. As in the creation of the Sit Room itself, postcrisis evaluations often are catalysts for change. Many adjustments in organization, process, and personnel have been made over the years in response to the problems perceived at the time. We describe below a model that was used successfully in the late 1980s to strengthen intelligence support at the NSC Senior Director and Interagency Working Group level.

In the late 1980s, the connectivity of the Sit Room to the NSC staff benefited from the assignment of several regional and functional intelligence analysts to the Sit Room staff. These analysts worked for the Sit Room Director but had offices in the OEOB and were assigned to the NSC's regional and functional directorates. Their job was to provide tailored current intelligence support to the staff and to serve as a focal point for Sit Room support in the directorates. Though a recent casualty of personnel cutbacks, this approach was developed after several years of trial and error focused on improving internal and external intelligence support for the National Security Adviser and the NSC staff.

Use of intelligence analysts to provide daily intelligence augmentation to NSC directorates was previously considered necessary to keep up with even the normal volume of relevant intelligence and cable traffic. At the same time, resulting from their close association with the policy staff, intelligence analysts also garnered an insider's perspective on interagency policy deliberations. This perspective strengthened the Sit Room's ability to anticipate specific intelligence requirements. During crises, the Senior Director would have a familiar face who would coordinate intelligence support in the Sit Room and who would know where to find key information in the IC. In turn, the Sit Room Watch Team would be augmented by appropriate functional or regional expertise from an intelligence analyst familiar with current interagency policy deliberations. It proved on many occasions to be a useful marriage.

Use of on-scene intelligence analysts was also a valuable means for the IC to enhance its support to the White House. With insights gained through daily interaction with the NSC directors, the analysts communicated the precise current needs of the directorates to the IC's production elements. The analysts served as a soundingboard for IC-initiated studies and would discuss with NSC directors the gist of draft or just-published studies, often resulting in requests for deskside briefings. Finally, the analysts were responsible for framing the bulk of the issues included in the Sit Room's *Weekly Emphasis List,* which was often exchanged with other agencies.

Again, it is important not to confuse the role of the Sit Room Watch Team or intelligence analysts with the role of other, more senior players in the interagency intelligence process. The interagency process includes National Intelligence Officers (NIOs), who are responsible for coordinating the preparation and adjudication of formal interagency National Intelligence Estimates in support of the policy community. NIOs are often included in senior-level interagency meetings and provide feedback and tasking to the IC. Whereas the NIO is focused on *future* (although sometimes near-term) requirements for collection, production, and analysis, the Sit Room analyst was focused on ensuring access to *today's* information already available in the Community, and on effecting close coordination at the working level.

This model worked for several reasons: It supported (rather than competed with) the senior policymakers' role as crisis managers; the Sit Room's role as the NSC focal point for current intelligence was reinforced; midcareer analysts were careful not to intrude on NIO responsibilities; and the process worked the same way with the same people in both routine and crisis environments.

Interagency Connections

In addition to providing current intelligence support to the NSC staff in important regional and functional areas, the Sit Room has a more independent role to play as an operations and intelligence center. There is a constant need for daily coordination on

> **"**
> **Perhaps the most distinguishing feature of the Sit Room is its proximity to the President. As in real estate, the operative principles are location, location, and location.**
> **"**

current issues with other centers, especially at the Defense and State Departments and CIA. This coordination takes place largely out of view of the NSC staff and leadership, but is nonetheless critical to the effectiveness of the interagency system. When less formal coordination has been found inadequate, formal interagency groups have been chartered by the President or National Security Adviser to strengthen connectivity among operations and intelligence centers, improve the flow of information, develop common practices and procedures where possible, and coordinate hardware and software decisions concerning interagency communications systems.

Sit Room responsibilities sometimes extend beyond intelligence and national security functions. Maintaining connectivity with the Federal Emergency Management Agency, the Departments of Justice, Transportation, Commerce, and other agencies, the Sit Room is frequently the initial point of White House notification for domestic disasters, including everything from earthquakes, fires, and floods to Haitian refugees and Federal prison riots. The periodic inclusion of Coast Guard and other Federal agency personnel as Sit Room Duty Officers has sometimes proved helpful in these crises, because the Sit Room may be called upon to facilitate initial coordination of crisis response within the White House until an appropriate interagency task force is formed.

Comparisons With Other Washington-Area Centers

Perhaps the most distinguishing feature of the Sit Room is its proximity to the President. As in real estate, the operative principles are location, location, and location. To be sure, the President gets most important intelligence advice and inputs from the Director of Central Intelligence, NIOs, and other key officials. But these officials cannot be at the White House 24 hours a day. The Sit Room often is the "first phone call" when senior White House officials are looking for the latest intelligence information, and it plays a key role in synthesizing cables and intelligence products originated by other agencies.[5]

A second feature is that the Sit Room is both an operations and intelligence center for the White House. These activities are divided in most departments and agencies. In the Department of Defense, for example, the National Military Command Center is colocated but separate from the National Military Joint Intelligence Center. Likewise, in the State Department and at CIA headquarters, operations and intelligence activities are separated. In the White House, this means that the relationship between policy development and current intelligence can be extremely close.

The close connectivity between intelligence and policy also means that the White House is not a passive consumer of intelligence. Even at the national level, information has an "operational" and sometimes "tactical" dimension. Diplomatic and intelligence cables may be closely correlated with Presidential events, perhaps allowing a glimpse of the talking points of a foreign head of state only hours or minutes before he meets with the President.

A third feature is the small size of the Sit Room staff. By all measures, the Sit Room is the smallest of the Washington-area operations and intelligence centers. This has come to mean a relatively junior staff. Senior Duty Officers are perhaps O-3, or GS-12 or 13 equivalents, as compared to O-6 or GS-15 equivalents elsewhere. Limitations of size and depth, however, can in part be offset by quality personnel, high standards of performance, the Sit Room's interagency character, excellent technical support, and the motivation that comes with working inside the White House.

In addition to the Sit Room's inherent limitations stemming from the small size of its staff, it lacks many advantages of a large intelligence agency. But the Sit Room does not need such advantages to fulfill its mission, and it should not be considered a peer competitor for influence in the IC. The implications of the Sit Room's proximity to the President, moreover, should not be underrated. Despite its limitations, the Sit Room by virtue of its location has greater access and potential impact on White House officials than any of

> **Sit Room personnel provide some of what little continuity exists within the NSC staff, and they are often able to observe potential gaps in the complex, fast-moving crisis management process.**

Washington's other operations and intelligence centers.

Implications for Leadership

A better understanding of the role of the WHSR has important implications for NSC leadership and for the intelligence agencies which supply both information and personnel to the NSC staff, including the Sit Room.

There is a need within the NSC for continuing education and dialogue among staff and leadership about the role and potential of the Sit Room in support of NSC activities. An orientation to Sit Room operations should be mandatory for incoming NSC staff officers. Likewise, an orientation to the NSC and interagency process should be mandatory for incoming Sit Room Duty Officers.

In addition, the National Security Adviser, Executive Secretary, and Sit Room Director should nurture in their personal interactions a routine concept of operations for crisis management. The enemy in crises is confusion and "ad hocracy"; responsibilities and expectations need to be as clear as possible. Sit Room personnel provide some of what little continuity exists within the NSC staff, and they are often able to observe potential gaps in the complex, fast-moving crisis management process. Routine and open dialogue with key NSC officials is essential for getting the most from the Sit Room staff.

The messages for the IC are equally clear. First, departmental and agency Watch Teams should be better educated about who works at the Sit Room and what they do. Operations and intelligence center personnel need to know that access is sometimes more important than rank. When a Sit Room Duty Officer phones, even though he or she may be junior in rank or grade, take the call and get the answer. Do not view the Sit Room as an institutional threat; support the White House in any attempt to find information and accept that the deadlines imposed, however unreasonable, will be for good reason. The IC should be confident that Sit Room information requests are for legitimate purposes and will not be mishandled.

Second, send your best people and treat them well when they return. Personnel nominated to serve as Sit Room duty officers should have operations/intelligence center experience. These are junior-to-midlevel personnel going to an outside assignment—not always regarded as a career-enhancing move. But the destination is crucial; these junior personnel may have more contact with senior officials than certain agency directors. Personal screening of nominations by the leadership of supporting agencies is called for, as well as personal debriefings. In addition, look for opportunities to augment the Sit Room staff or NSC directorates with mid- to senior-level intelligence analysts during periods of intense activity or crisis.

When Sit Room Duty Officers return to your agency for their next assignment, ensure that the personnel system makes the most of their experience. Promotion boards do not always recognize the signature of the National Security Adviser or his Deputy on personnel evaluation or promotion recommendation forms. Take a close look at planned career progression, and concentrate on placement that takes advantage of the White House experience and enlarges the individual's Sit Room-attained knowledge of the IC.

Conclusion

Greater knowledge about the role of the WHSR has the potential for several beneficial effects within the IC. These include strengthening current intelligence support within the NSC staff and the White House; improving the timeliness of intelligence support during crises; enhancing the quality of individual agency products in support of national leadership; and better internal use of department and agency personnel with White House experience. In current intelligence and crisis support, the Situation Room is well positioned at the working level to assist in bridging the needs of the policy and intelligence communities. IC effectiveness would be improved with better understanding of how the White House works, how the President gets information, and how decisions are made.

NOTES

1. Bromley Smith, "Organizational History of the National Security Council During the Kennedy and Johnson Administrations," p. 51. Unpublished monograph, courtesy of the NSC staff.

2. Further unclassified background on the *President's Daily Brief* can be found in: "PDB, the Only News Not Fit for Anyone Else To Read," *The Washington Post*, 27 August 94, p. 7.

3. 50 U.S.C. 402, Sec. 101(c)

4. An example of the coordination and oversight functions performed by the NSC's Intelligence Directorate may be found in David G. Major's article, "Operation 'Famish': The Integration of Counterintelligence into the National Strategic Decisionmaking Process," *Defense Intelligence Journal*, Vol. 4, No. 1, spring 1995.

5. For a broader and fuller treatment of the White House–CIA relationship, see Robert M. Gates, "An Opportunity Unfulfilled: The Use and Perceptions of Intelligence at the White House," *Washington Quarterly*, winter 1989.

James M. Goldgeier

NATO Expansion: The Anatomy of a Decision

In deciding to enlarge the North Atlantic Treaty Organization (NATO) Bill Clinton's administration followed through on one of its most significant foreign policy initiatives and the most important political-military decision for the United States since the collapse of the Soviet Union. The policy has involved a difficult tradeoff for the administration between wanting to ensure that political and economic reform succeeds in Central and Eastern Europe and not wanting to antagonize Russia, which has received billions of dollars to assist its transition to a democratic, market-oriented Western partner. Skeptics of the NATO expansion policy within the government also worried about its costs, its effect on the cohesiveness of the Atlantic Alliance, and the wisdom of extending security guarantees to new countries. How did President Clinton, often criticized for a lack of attention to foreign policy and for vacillation on important issues, come to make a decision with far-reaching consequences for all of Europe at a time when NATO faced no military threat and in the context of diminishing resources for foreign policy?

This article analyzes the process the U.S. government followed that led to this major foreign policy initiative. I have based my findings largely on interviews I conducted in 1997 with several dozen current and former U.S. government officials, from desk officers deep inside the State and Defense Departments all the way up to President Clinton's top foreign policy advisers.[1] The interviews reveal that the administration decided to expand NATO despite widespread bureaucratic opposition, because a few key people wanted it to happen, the most important being the president and his national security adviser, Anthony Lake. Other senior officials—particularly those in the State Department—became important supporters and implementers of NATO expansion, but Lake's intervention proved critical early in the process. Keenly interested in pushing NATO's expansion as part of the administration's strategy of enlarging the community of democracies, Lake encouraged the president to make statements supporting expansion and then used those statements to direct the National Security Council (NSC) staff to develop a plan and a timetable for putting these ideas into action. The president, once convinced that this policy was the right thing to do, led the alliance on this mission into the territory of the former Warsaw Pact and sought to make NATO's traditional adversary part of the process through his personal relationship with Russian president Boris Yeltsin.

Rather than being a story of a single decision, this policy initiative came about through a series of decisions and presidential statements made during three key phases of the process in 1993 and 1994. During the summer and fall of 1993, the need to prepare for Clinton's January 1994 summit meetings in Brussels pushed the bureaucracy into action. The product of this bureaucratic activity was the October 1993 proposal to develop the Partnership for Peace (PFP), which would increase military ties between NATO and its former adversaries. In the second phase, which culminated in his January 1994 trip to Europe, Clinton first signaled U.S. seriousness about NATO expansion by saying the question was no longer "whether" but "when."

The final phase discussed here encompasses the period from April to October 1994, when key supporters of NATO expansion attempted to turn this presidential rhetoric into reality. At the end of this period, the newly installed assistant secretary of state for European affairs, Richard Holbrooke, bludgeoned the bureaucracy into understanding that expansion was presi-

---

James M. Goldgeier is an assistant professor of political science at The George Washington University. He is currently writing a book about U.S. foreign policy decision-making.

dential policy, and an idea that had been bandied about for a year and a half finally started to become reality.

Phase One: Bureaucratic Debate and Endorsement of the PFP

In the first few months of his administration, President Clinton had not given much thought to the issue of NATO's future. Then, in late April 1993, at the opening of the Holocaust Museum in Washington, he met one-on-one with a series of Central and Eastern European leaders, including the highly regarded leaders of Poland and the Czech Republic, Lech Walesa and Vaclav Havel. These two, having struggled so long to throw off the Soviet yoke, carried a moral authority matched by few others around the world. Each leader delivered the same message to Clinton: Their top priority was NATO membership. After the meetings, Clinton told Lake how impressed he had been with the vehemence with which these leaders spoke, and Lake says Clinton was inclined to think positively toward expansion from that moment.

At the June 1993 meeting of the North Atlantic Council (NAC) foreign ministers in Athens, Greece, U.S. secretary of state Warren Christopher said enlarging NATO's membership was "not now on the agenda." But Christopher understood that NATO needed to assess its future, and with White House endorsement, he pushed his fellow foreign ministers to announce that their heads of state would meet six months later, in January 1994.[2] This announcement set in motion a process back in Washington to discuss the contentious issue of expansion. At the White House, Lake wrote in the margins of Christopher's statement, "why not now?", and his senior director for European affairs, Jenonne Walker, convened an interagency working group (IWG) to prepare for the January 1994 meeting in Brussels and to recommend what the president should do there. The working group involved representatives from the NSC staff, the State Department, and the Pentagon. According to several participants, Walker informed the group at the start that both the president and Lake were interested in pursuing expansion.

On September 21, 1993, nine months into the Clinton administration, Lake gave his first major foreign policy speech, in which he developed ideas on promoting democracy and market economies that Clinton had enunciated during his campaign. Clinton had stressed the theme that democracies do not go to war with one another and thus that U.S. foreign policy strategy should focus on promoting democracy. Lake had helped to develop this approach, which leading campaign officials saw as a foreign policy initiative behind which different wings of the Democratic party could rally. In the 1993 speech, Lake argued that "the successor to a doctrine of containment must be a strategy of enlargement—enlargement of the world's free community of market democracies." And he added, "At the NATO summit that the president has called for this January, we will seek to update NATO, so that there continues behind the enlargement of market democracies an essential collective security."[3]

Although Lake tried rhetorically to push the process along, the bureaucracy greatly resisted expanding the alliance. Officials at the Pentagon unanimously favored the Partnership for Peace proposal developing largely through the efforts of Gen. John Shalikashvili and his staff, first from Shalikashvili's perch as Supreme Allied Commander in Europe and then as chairman of the Joint Chiefs of Staff. PFP proponents sought to foster increased ties to all the former Warsaw Pact states as well as to the traditional European neutrals, and to ensure that NATO did not have to differentiate among its former adversaries or "draw new lines" in Europe. Every state that accepted its general principles could join the PFP, and the countries themselves could decide their level of participation. Many officials viewed the partnership as a means of strengthening and making operational the North Atlantic Cooperation Council (NACC), which had been NATO's first formal outreach effort to the East, undertaken in 1991. From the Pentagon's standpoint, it did not make sense to talk about expansion until after NATO had established the type of military-to-military relationships that would enable new countries to integrate effectively into the alliance. Several participants in the IWG say that Pentagon representatives made clear that both Secretary of Defense Les Aspin and General Shalikashvili opposed expansion and, in particular, feared diluting the effectiveness of NATO.[4] As NSC staffer and PFP supporter Charles Kupchan would write after leaving the government, "The partnership was deliberately designed to enable member states to put off questions of formal enlargement and of NATO's ultimate disposition in post-Cold War Europe."[5]

In addition to concern about NATO's future military effectiveness, the bureaucracy also feared that expansion would antagonize Russia and bolster nationalists and Communists there. Many State Department debates at this time focused on this fear, and views on expansion there were more divided than those in the Pentagon. In September, Yeltsin had written a letter to Clinton and other NATO heads of state backtracking on positive remarks he had made in Warsaw on Polish membership in NATO and suggesting that if NATO expanded, Russia should be on the same fast track as the Central Europeans. Then, in early October, Yeltsin's troops fired on his opposition in Parliament, and it appeared to many that the political situation in Russia was deteriorating.

During this period, a small group at the State Department—including Lynn Davis, the under secretary for arms control and international security affairs, Thomas Donilon, the chief of staff, and Stephen Flanagan, a member of the Policy Planning Staff—advocated a fast-track approach to expansion. This group argued that in January 1994, NATO should lay out criteria, put forward a clear timetable, and perhaps even offer "associate membership" to a first set of countries. At a series of lunches with Secretary Christopher, organized to present him with the pros and cons of expansion, these individuals pressed him to move the process forward as quickly as possible, saying, as one participant recalls, that NATO should "strike while the iron is hot."

Flanagan had served on the Policy Planning Staff in the previous administration and had first publicly floated ideas about expansion in an article in *The Washington Quarterly* in spring 1992, arguing that NATO would have to address the membership issue "at some point." "No one is under any illusion," he wrote, "that the membership issue will go away as long as NATO is perceived by Eastern states as the bedrock institution of European security."[6] He laid out the basis for what would become a key element of the NATO expansion strategy: putting the onus for not drawing closer to the West on those countries themselves. As Flanagan wrote, "Any European states outside the Alliance would not be excluded by a geostrategic gambit; rather states would exclude themselves from the new collective security pact by their failure to realize or uphold the expanded Alliance principles."[7]

Flanagan, Donilon, and Davis worried that without the prospect of membership in a key Western institution, Central and Eastern Europe would lose the momentum for reform. NATO and the European Union (EU) were the premier institutions in Europe, and the EU, absorbed in the internal problems associated with the Maastricht Treaty, would clearly postpone its own expansion. These officials wanted to encourage states such as Poland and Hungary to continue on the path of reform—to adopt civilian control of the military, to build a free polity and economy, and to settle border disputes—by providing the carrot of NATO membership if they succeeded.

This pro-expansion group also drew on compelling arguments from two other government officials. Charles Gati, a specialist on Eastern Europe serving on the Policy Planning Staff, had written a memo in September 1993 arguing that the new democracies were fragile, that the ex-Communists were likely to gain power in Poland, and that if NATO helped Poland succeed in carrying out reforms, it would have a huge impact on the rest of the region. Donilon took this memo straight to Christopher, who found the reasoning impressive. When the ex-Communists did win parliamentary elections in Poland weeks later, Gati's words carried even greater weight.

The other argument came from Dennis Ross, the special Middle East coordinator for the Clinton administration, who had been director of policy planning under Secretary of State James A. Baker III. Given his involvement in the German unification process and the development of the NACC, Ross attended two of the Christopher lunches on NATO. During one, he reminded the group that critics had believed that NATO could not successfully bring in a united Germany in 1990, but it did, and without damaging U.S.-Soviet relations. He suggested that NATO involve Russia in the expansion process rather than confront its former enemy. Ross argued that the previous administration's experience with German unification offered good reason to believe that the current administration could overcome problems with Russia.

Inside the State Department's regional bureaus dealing with Europe and with the New Independent States (NIS), however, bureaucrats expressed tremendous opposition to a fast-track approach and in a number of cases to any idea of expansion. Many who worked on NATO issues feared problems of managing the alliance if Clinton pushed ahead with this contentious issue. Those who worked on Russia issues thought expansion would undermine reform efforts there.

In these State Department debates, the most important proponent of a much more cautious and gradualist approach to expansion was Strobe Talbott, then ambassador-at-large for the NIS. Talbott proved important for two reasons: As a longtime friend, he had direct access to Clinton, and as a former journalist, he could write quickly, clearly, and persuasively. Christopher asked Talbott and Nicholas Burns—the senior director for Russian, Ukrainian, and Eurasian Affairs at the NSC—to comment on the fast-track approach. He and Burns argued to both Christopher and Lake that Russia would not understand a quick expansion, which would impair the U.S.-Russia relationship and, given the domestic turmoil in Russia in late September and early October, might push Russia over the edge.

> **Lake wrote in the margins of Christopher's statement, "Why not now?"**

One Saturday in mid-October, when Talbott was out of town, Lynn Davis forcefully argued to Christopher at a NATO discussion lunch that NACC and the PFP were simply not enough. When Talbott returned that afternoon and learned about the thrust of the meeting, he quickly wrote a paper reiterating the importance of a gradual approach to expansion. The next day, he delivered a memo to Christopher, stating, "Laying down criteria could be quite provocative, and badly timed with what is going on in Russia." Instead, he suggested, "Take the one new idea that seems to be universally accepted, PFP, and make that the centerpiece of our NATO position." Talbott argued that the administration should not put forward any criteria on NATO membership that would automatically exclude Russia and Ukraine, and that the administration could never manage the relationship if it did not offer Russia the prospect of joining the alliance at a future date. He firmly believed that Clinton should mention neither dates nor names in Brussels.[8]

By Monday morning, October 18, Christopher had decided to support the gradual rather than fast-track approach, which meant that any agreement among leading officials would place the policy emphasis on the PFP. Among Clinton's top foreign-policy advisers, Lake sought to push ahead with expansion, Aspin and Shalikashvili sought to delay consideration of expansion and instead supported the PFP, and Christopher fell

> **The bureaucracy resisted expanding the alliance.**

somewhere in between, open to gradual expansion but concerned about Russia's reaction. At the White House later that day, Clinton endorsed the consensus of his principal foreign policy advisers that, at the January summit, the alliance should formally present the PFP, and he should announce NATO's intention eventually to expand. This decision reflected the consensus that had emerged from the bargaining within agencies and in the IWG, which had easily agreed on the PFP, but which could not agree on issues such as criteria, a timetable, or "associate membership" status. In the end, the IWG agreed on what its principals in turn could accept: to put forward the PFP and to say something general about NATO's eventual expansion.

The consensus emerged because, as with many decisions, opponents and proponents of expansion had different interpretations of what they had decided, and this ambiguity created support for the decision throughout the bureaucracy. Vociferous opponents of NATO expansion believed the administration's principals had decided to promote the PFP while postponing a decision on enlargement. Those in the middle, who could live with expansion but did not want to do anything concrete in 1994, also saw the October decision as consistent with their preferences. Finally, the decision that Clinton should comment on expansion pleased proponents of near-term enlargement, as they believed such a statement would help to move the process along on a faster track.

The October 18 meeting would be the last of its kind on NATO expansion for another year. Given the meeting's ambiguous outcome—the foreign policy principals had not given the president a timetable to endorse—confusion reigned concerning the policy's direction. For the moment, the decision to develop the PFP was the Clinton administration's NATO outreach policy.

Yet from the moment the participants went their separate ways observers could tell they interpreted the decision differently. Secretary of State Christopher's entourage, on its way to Budapest to brief the Central Europeans (and then on to Moscow to explain the policy to Yeltsin), said the January summit would send the signal that NATO's door would open at some future date (and apparently even State Department officials on Christopher's plane disagreed about how to present the decision). The senior official conducting the airborne press briefing stated, "We believe that the summit should formally open the door to NATO expansion as an evolutionary process."[9] Meanwhile, Secretary of Defense Aspin and his advisers, attending the NATO defense ministers' meeting in Travamünde, Germany, to gain alliance endorsement of the PFP, emphasized that NATO would not enlarge soon. According to one report, Lake called Aspin in a pique saying the secretary of defense had veered from the script.[10]

Phase Two: The President Speaks

After mid-October, administration officials knew the president would say something about NATO enlargement on his trip to Europe in January. But no one was sure how much he would say and how specific he would be. After all, the bureaucratic wrangling had produced a decision that the president should emphasize the PFP while delivering a vague statement that NATO could eventually take in new members.

> **Advocates worried that Central and Eastern Europe would lose the momentum for reform.**

The first official statement prior to the summit came from Secretary Christopher at the plenary session of the Conference on Security and Cooperation in Europe (CSCE) in Rome on November 30. Noting that the United States was proposing a Partnership for Peace, he also stated, "At the same time, we propose to open the door to an evolutionary expansion of NATO's membership."[11] Two days later, at the NAC ministerial in Brussels, he said, "The Partnership is an important step in its own right. But it can also be a key step toward NATO membership."[12]

Meanwhile, prominent figures from previous administrations pressured Clinton to be more forthcoming on expansion at the summit. Former secretary of state Henry Kissinger complained in an op-ed piece that the PFP "would dilute what is left of the Atlantic Alliance into a vague multilateralism," and he called for movement to bring Poland, Hungary, and the Czech Republic into some form of "qualified membership." Former national security adviser Zbigniew Brzezinski urged NATO members to sign a formal treaty of alliance with Russia and to lay out a more explicit path to full NATO membership for the leading Central European candidates. Former secretary of state James Baker also made the case for a "clear road map" with "clear benchmarks" for the prospective members.[13]

During this time, Brzezinski had been meeting with Lake to share ideas about his two-track approach to expansion, and he also invited Lake to his home to meet a number of Central and Eastern European leaders. Since the debate at the White House focused more on "whether" than concretely "how," these meetings with Brzezinski helped Lake to clarify his own thinking and emphasized to him the importance of keeping the process moving forward. Significantly, Brzezinski argued that Russia would be more likely to develop as a stable, democratic presence in Europe if the West removed all temptations to reassert imperial control and precluded Russia's ability to intimidate its former satellites.

In late December, Lake's staff members, who were in general opposed to moving expansion onto the near-term agenda, presented him with the draft briefing memoranda for the different stops on the president's upcoming trip to Europe. Several of his staffers say he threw a fit on seeing the initial work, because the memos emphasized the Partnership for Peace. According to Nicholas Burns, Lake wanted a presidential statement in January that would leave no doubt about the policy's direction.

But high-level opposition to any push toward expansion continued to color the agenda. The Pentagon appeared unanimously to share the view that the policy should be sequential; countries would participate in the PFP for a number of years and then the alliance might start addressing the issue of expansion. General Shalikashvili, at a White House press briefing on January 4, emphasized the value of the Partnership for Peace as a way of ensuring that the alliance create no new divisions in Europe, and he suggested postponing discussions of membership to a future date:

> I think it is important that everyone understand—and I hope that our newfound friends in the East will understand that the reason that partnership is defined as it is, is to avoid at all costs the establishment of a new line, a new division that in turn, then, would create new tensions and fuel new conflicts.

But, he added, in words that Clinton would make much more significant a week later, "It is useful to remember that we are talking so much less today about whether extension of the alliance [should take place], but so much more about how and when." Pentagon officials, however, had a much different view of what "when" meant than did proponents of expansion at the NSC and State, believing the PFP should operate for several years before the alliance began thinking about expansion.

Prior to the summit, even Clinton still seemed unsure of how far he wanted to go. The strong showing of nationalists and Communists in the December 1993 Russian parliamentary elections had sent shockwaves through the administration. On January 4, Clinton said in an exchange with reporters at the White House,

> I'm not against expanding NATO. I just think that if you look at the consensus of the NATO members at this time, there's not a consensus to expand NATO at this time and we don't want to give the impression that we're creating another dividing line in Europe after we've worked for decades to get rid of the one that existed before.[14]

This was hardly the signal the Central Europeans had hoped to receive.

Just prior to his trip, Clinton sent Polish-born General Shalikashvili, Czech-born U.S. ambassador to the UN Madeleine Albright, and Hungarian-born State Department adviser Charles Gati to Central Europe to explain the administration's policy and to quell criticisms stemming from this region prior to the summit. Albright argued forcefully to the Central European leaders that the Partnership for Peace would provide the best vehicle for these countries to gain future NATO membership, and she reiterated that it was not a question of whether, but when.

In Brussels, Clinton said that the PFP "sets in motion a process that leads to the enlargement of NATO." According to Donilon, Lake wanted the president to make a more forceful statement in Prague to give a clear impetus to expansion. Sitting around a table in Prague prior to Clinton's remarks, Lake, Donilon, and presidential speechwriter Robert Boorstin wrote the statement that Clinton agreed to deliver. Echoing what Albright had told the Central Europeans, the president said, "While the Partnership is not NATO membership, neither is it a permanent holding room. It changes the entire NATO dialogue so that now the question is no longer whether NATO will take on new members but when and how."[15]

To proponents such as Lake, this statement was a clear victory, and it laid the basis for moving the process along. He wanted the alliance to address the "when" as soon as possible. For expansion skeptics, to whom "when" meant after the PFP had created a new military environment in Europe, the president's words meant nothing specific and reflected, they believed, the outcome of the October 18 decision; they concluded that although the president had stated that expansion was theoretically possible, the administration would not undertake any actual effort to expand the alliance anytime soon. Their failure to recognize the importance of the president's remarks—at least as Lake and other expansion proponents interpreted them—would lead to their surprise later in the year that the process had been moving forward.

Administration critics would later suggest that Clinton supported expansion purely for political purposes, to woo voters of Polish, Czech, and Hungarian descent. Numerous foreign policy officials in the administration, who deny that domestic political considerations came up in their meetings on expansion, hotly disputed this claim. Lake says that although everyone knew the political context of the NATO enlargement debate, he never had "an explicit discussion" with the president about the domestic political implications of expansion.

> The key proponent of a cautious approach was Strobe Talbott.

Domestic politics probably played a more complicated role in this policy decision than a simple attempt to court ethnic votes in key midwestern and northeastern states. First, for several political reasons, Clinton needed to demonstrate U.S. leadership. His administration's policy in Bosnia was failing miserably, and this failure overshadowed every other foreign policy issue at the time. Second, even if ethnic pressures did not drive the decision, Clinton would have alienated these vocal and powerful domestic constituencies had he decided against expanding NATO; Republicans thus would have gained another issue to use in congressional elections later that year. If domestic politics did not drive the decision, they gave it more resonance for the White House, and both parties certainly used the policy for political purposes; Clinton's speeches in places like Cleveland and Detroit in 1995–96 provide clear evidence of the perceived value of NATO expansion to those communities, and the Republicans included NATO expansion as a plank in their Contract with America during the 1994 congressional campaign.

The bureaucratic decision-making process had not advanced much between October 1993 and the president's trip to Europe in January 1994. But regardless of where the bureaucratic consensus remained, Clinton had opened the door for expansion with his forceful remarks in Brussels and Prague. This in turn gave Lake the impetus he needed, and because of his proximity and access to the president, for the moment he could move the process along without having to gain the backing of the rest of the bureaucracy.

Phase Three: From Rhetoric to Reality

For several months after Clinton's pronouncements in January, neither his advisers nor the bureaucracy paid much attention to NATO expansion, largely because of the crises in Bosnia that winter and because of the attention they paid to getting the PFP up and running. In early spring, the NATO expansion process began moving forward again, at Lake's instigation. In April, Lake held a meeting with his deputy, Samuel R. "Sandy" Berger, and one of his staffers, Daniel Fried, a specialist on Central and Eastern Europe, to discuss how to follow up on the president's January remarks and to prepare for the president's trip to Warsaw that July. Lake asked for an action plan on enlargement, and when Fried reminded him of the bureaucracy's continued strong opposition, Lake replied that the president wanted to move forward and Lake therefore needed an action plan to make it happen.

To write the policy paper, Fried brought in two old colleagues: Burns at NSC and Alexander Vershbow, then in the European bureau of the State Department but soon to become the NSC's senior director for European affairs. Fried had known Vershbow since they were both graduate students together at Columbia University and valued his expertise on NATO. Fried had known Burns since the two worked on Central European issues at the State Department during the tumultuous events of 1989. Despite his NSC portfolio on Russian affairs, Burns was not opposed to NATO expansion, which pleased Fried; Burns in turn appreciated that Fried accepted a gradual approach and understood that the strategy had to include a place for Russia. Unlike the authors of many policy papers that need approval, or clearance, from key actors at each of the relevant agencies, this troika worked alone, thus sidestepping the need for bureaucratic bargaining. Before the president's Warsaw trip, Lake invited Talbott and State Department Policy Planning director James Steinberg to the White House to discuss the draft paper with Fried and Burns. Talbott sought assurances that the proposed process would be gradual, consistent with the policy he had pushed the previous October.

Many people believe Talbott opposed enlargement during this time, especially because most of the Russia specialists outside government vehemently opposed expanding NATO. Talbott clearly opposed making any immediate moves and emphasized that the process must be gradual and include rather than isolate Russia. But many of Talbott's colleagues say that once he became deputy secretary of state in February 1994 and more regularly considered the broader European landscape and the needs of the Central and Eastern Europeans, he warmed to expansion. (Several of Talbott's colleagues argue that he opposed expansion, lost, and then sought to ensure that both the expansion track and the NATO-Russia track would proceed in tandem.) Talbott encouraged Christopher to bring Richard Holbrooke back from his post as ambassador to Germany to be assistant secretary of state for European affairs in summer 1994, both to fix the Bosnia policy and to work on NATO expansion. By the following year, Talbott had become one of the most articulate Clinton administration spokespersons in favor of the NATO expansion policy.

By summer, the NSC and State Department positions had converged. Thinking in more gradual terms than Lake had been pushing earlier in the year, the troika's views now coincided with the consensus that had developed in the State Department. The efforts to begin figuring out a way to develop a timetable for both the expansion track and the NATO-Russia track led to a major push in summer and fall 1994 to get an expansion policy on firmer footing.

In Warsaw in July, Clinton spoke more forcefully on the issue than many in the bureaucracy would have preferred, just as he had done in Brussels and Prague earlier in the year. In an exchange with reporters after his meeting with Lech Walesa, he said, "I have always stated my support for the idea that NATO will expand.... And now what we have to do is to get the NATO partners together and to discuss what the next steps should be."[16] By emphasizing the need to meet with U.S. allies, the president gave a green light to those who wanted a concrete plan.

Two months later, addressing a conference in Berlin, Vice President Al Gore proved even more outspoken, saying,

> Everyone realizes that a military alliance, when faced with a fundamental change in the threat for which it was founded, either must define a convincing new rationale or become decrepit. Everyone knows that economic and political organizations tailored for a divided continent must now adapt to new circumstances—including acceptance of new members—or be exposed as mere bastions of privilege.[17]

Holbrooke apparently had major input on this speech, and one staffer for the Joint Chiefs says the vice president's remarks gave the military its first inkling that the administration's NATO policy had changed since January. Senior military representatives objected to the draft text of Gore's remarks, but to no avail.

Despite his inclination toward expanding the alliance, Clinton understood concerns about Russia's reaction. After all, Clinton's foreign policy had centered in part on U.S. assistance for the Yeltsin government's reform program, and he did not want to undercut Yeltsin before the 1996 Russian presidential election. In late September, Yeltsin came to Washington, and Clinton had a chance to tell him face to face that NATO was potentially open to all of Europe's new democracies, including Russia, and that it would not expand in a way that threatened Russia's interests. At a White House luncheon, Clinton told Yeltsin that he had discussed NATO expansion with key allied leaders, and he made sure Yeltsin understood that NATO would not announce the new members until after the Russian and U.S. 1996 presidential elections. At the same time, Clinton wanted to ensure that any advances in the process that might take place in the meantime—during the NATO ministerials—would not surprise the Russian president.

With Holbrooke coming back to the State Department and with Vershbow and Fried both now special assistants to the president at the NSC, expansion proponents had gained more power within the bureaucracy than they had during the previous autumn. Lake successfully circumvented bureaucratic opposition to get Clinton to make forceful statements that expansion would occur. His troika had continued to update its action plan throughout the summer and fall, and by October 1994 its strategy paper proposed the timeline that the alliance eventually followed: a series of studies and consultations designed to lead to a membership invitation to the first group and a NATO-Russia accord in 1997. But concerns about the military dimension of expansion still existed in the Pentagon, without whose efforts to address the nuts and bolts of expanding the military alliance the decision could not have moved from theory to practice.

For their next task, proponents had to convince skeptics within the administration that the president was serious. A year earlier, one State Department official had said of the Clinton foreign policy team, "They make decisions and then they have absolutely no idea of how to get the bureaucracy to implement those decisions.... There is no enforcer."[18] For NATO expansion, the enforcer would be Holbrooke, the newly installed assistant secretary of state, whom Christopher had brought back to the department at the urging of Talbott, Donilon, and Under Secretary for Political Affairs Peter Tarnoff.

Holbrooke held his first interagency meeting on NATO expansion at the State Department in late September, almost immediately after taking office. He wanted to make clear that he would set up and run the mechanism to expand NATO, because the president wanted it to happen. Holbrooke knew that most Pentagon officials preferred concentrating on making the PFP work rather than moving ahead with expansion, and he wanted to make sure everyone understood that he was taking charge. His opportunity came at this meeting when the senior representative from the Joint Chiefs of Staff (JCS), three-star Gen. Wesley Clark, questioned Holbrooke's plans to move forward on the "when" and "how" questions of expansion. To the Pentagon's way of thinking, no one had yet made a decision that would warrant this action. Holbrooke shocked those in attendance by declaring, "That sounds like insubordination to me. Either you are on the president's program or you are not."[19]

According to participants, Deputy Assistant Secretary of Defense Joseph Kruzel, one of the key figures in developing the PFP program, argued that the issue had been debated in October 1993 and the decision at that time, the last formal meeting on the subject at the highest levels, was *not* to enlarge. Other Pentagon officials in attendance argued that only the "principals" could make this decision, and thus another meeting needed to be held at the highest level. Holbrooke responded that those taking this view had not been listening to what the president had been saying. The skeptics simply could not believe that Holbrooke was resting his whole case on remarks Clinton had made in Brussels, Prague, and Warsaw. Former defense secretary William Perry still refers to Holbrooke as having "presumed" at that point that the administration had decided to enlarge NATO, whereas Clinton had made no formal decision to that effect.

After this dramatic outburst, Holbrooke asked Clark to set up a meeting to brief this interagency group on what they would need to do to implement the policy. Through this request, Holbrooke enabled the Joint Chiefs of Staff to voice their concerns but also forced them to begin acting on the issue. At the Pentagon two weeks later, a team with representatives from both the Office of the Secretary of Defense (OSD) and the JCS presented to the interagency group the full range of military requirements each country would need to meet to join NATO. The JCS briefer pointed, for example, to the 1,200 Atlantic Alliance standardization agreements the former Warsaw Pact armed forces would have to address to become compatible with NATO. Holbrooke, now playing "good cop," responded by saying that this briefing was exactly what the group needed, and he invited them to work with him to make the process a smooth one. This briefing would, in fact, serve as the basis both for the briefing to the NAC later in the fall and for the NATO study conducted the following year.

Because Pentagon officials did not believe the administration had ever made a formal decision, Perry recalls that he called Clinton and asked for a meeting of the foreign policy team to clarify the president's intentions. At the meeting, Perry presented his arguments for holding back and giving the PFP another year before deciding on enlargement. He wanted time to move forward on the NATO-Russia track and to convince Moscow that NATO did not threaten Russia's interests, before the alliance moved ahead on the expansion track. Instead, the president endorsed the two-track plan that Lake and his staff, as well as the State Department, now pushed—the plan that ultimately led to the May 1997 signing of the NATO-Russia Founding Act and the July 1997 NATO summit in Madrid inviting Poland, Hungary, and the Czech Republic to begin talks on accession to full NATO membership.

The Ambiguity of the Decision

Like so many decision-making processes, the NATO expansion process was not at all clearcut. The best evidence of its ambiguities comes from asking participants a simple question: "When did you believe that the decision to expand NATO had been made made?" Their answers demonstrate that what you see depends on where you stand; attitudes toward the decision affected individuals' views of what was happening. Most supporters, including Lake, cite the period between the October 1993 meeting of the principals and Clinton's trip to Europe in January 1994. The answers of opponents, on the other hand, generally range over the second half of 1994, depending on when they finally realized the president was serious. One State Department official who opposed expansion said that when he objected to language circulating in an interagency memo on the issue in August 1994, a colleague told him it was the same language the president had used in Warsaw the previous month. At that point, he says, he understood that the policy had moved from theory to reality. Others, such as Perry, did not start to believe that expansion was on the table until after the Holbrooke interagency meeting in September 1994. In support of this last interpretation, Brzezinski pointed out at the time that until Clinton *answered* the questions "when" and "how," rather than simply *asking* them, the United States had no decisive plan for Europe.[20]

These interpretations vary so widely because the president and his top advisers did not make a formal decision about a timetable or process for expansion until long after Clinton had started saying NATO would enlarge. The when, who, how, and even why came only over time and not always through a formal decision-making process. In January 1994, when the president first said that he expected the alliance to take in new members, no consensus existed among his top advisers on the difficult questions of "when" and "how." Clinton's advisers could as reasonably believe that his remarks amounted to no more than a vague statement that NATO might someday expand as they could believe that the president wanted to begin moving forward *now*. Whereas proponents of expansion took his statements as a signal to begin planning how to put theory into practice, the president did not make an explicit decision in the presence of his top foreign policy advisers until nearly a year later, and some opponents therefore choose to believe that the course was not set until that meeting.

Readers may find it unsatisfying that I have not uncovered either *the* moment of decision or the president's ulterior motive. Truthfully, however, most policies—even those as significant as this one—develop in a more ambiguous fashion. This process was hardly unique to the Clinton administration. White House meetings often result in participants, as well as those they inform, having conflicting understandings of what the administration has decided. Policy entrepreneurs use presidential statements to push forward an issue that remains highly contentious in the bureaucracy. Each step alone seem trivial. But cumulatively, they can result in momentous policies.

As for motive, Walesa and Havel may well have made a huge impression on a president open to emotional appeals. Still, given that Clinton cared so much about the fate of Russian reform, Walesa's appeal to bring Poland and other Central European nations into the West could hardly have been sufficient. Rather, Clinton's motive was probably more complex, and he probably had only a vague idea of when he himself made the formal commitment to expand NATO. For Clinton, the appeal by the Central Europeans to erase the line drawn for them in 1945, the need to demonstrate U.S. leadership at a time when others questioned that leadership, the domestic political consequences of the choice, and his own Wilsonian orientation toward spreading liberalism combined by the second half of 1994—if not earlier—to produce a presidential preference favoring expansion.

Much more work remained to be done, including working with allies, developing the NATO-Russia track, and eventually seeking Senate ratification. Without the 1995 Dayton Accords that ended the fighting in Bosnia, NATO may not have sustained the process underway in 1994. But once Clinton spoke out in favor of NATO expansion in January 1994, expansion supporters within the administration had what they needed to begin to turn rhetoric into reality.

The author would like to thank Michael Struett for his research assistance; and both the Institute for European, Russian, and

5 ❖ THE FOREIGN POLICY-MAKING PROCESS

Eurasian Studies and GW's Columbian School of Arts and Sciences for funding.

Notes

1. Many of the individuals I interviewed spoke on condition of anonymity.
2. For information on Secretary Christopher's intervention at the June 1993 NAC meeting, see *U.S. Department of State Dispatch* 4, no. 25, p. 3.
3. Anthony Lake, "From Containment to Enlargement," *Vital Speeches of the Day 60* (October 15, 1993), pp. 13–19.
4. Author interviews with IWG participants William Perry, Ashton Carter, Graham Allison, and other U.S. government officials.
5. Charles A. Kupchan, "Strategic Visions," *World Policy Journal* 11 (Fall 1994), p. 113.
6. Stephen J. Flanagan, "NATO and Central and Eastern Europe: From Liaison to Security Partnership," *Washington Quarterly* (Spring 1992), p. 142.
7. Ibid, p. 149.
8. For quotations from the Talbott memo, see Michael Dobbs, "Wider Alliance Would Increase U.S. Commitments," *Washington Post*, July 5, 1995. pp. A1, 16; Michael R. Gordon, "U.S. Opposes Move to Rapidly Expand NATO Membership," *New York Times,* January 2, 1994, pp. A1, 7.
9. The official is quoted in Elaine Sciolino, "U.S. to Offer Plan on a Role in NATO for Ex-Soviet Bloc," *New York Times,* October 21, 1993, pp. A1, 9.
10. Elaine Sciolino, "3 Players Seek a Director for Foreign Policy Story," *New York Times,* November 8, 1993, pp. A1, 12; Stephen Kinzer, "NATO Favors U.S. Plan for Ties with the East, but Timing is Vague," *New York Times,* October 22, 1993, pp. A1, 8.
11. *U.S. Department of State Dispatch,* December 13, 1993.
12. Ibid.
13. See Henry Kissinger, "Not This Partnership," *Washington Post,* November 24, 1993, p. A17; Zbigniew Brzezinski, "A Bigger—and Safer—Europe," *New York Times,* December 1, 1993, p. A23; and James A. Baker III, "Expanding to the East: A New NATO," *Los Angeles Times,* December 5, 1993, p. M2.
14. Remarks by the president in a photo op with Netherlands prime minister Ruud Lubbers, January 4, 1994, *Public Papers* (1994), pp. 5–6.
15. On the Brussels statement of January 10, 1994, see U.S. Department of State Dispatch Supplement, January 1994, pp. 3–4; for the Prague remarks, see Clinton, *Public Papers* Book I (1994), p. 40.
16. For his exchange with reporters in Warsaw after meeting with Walesa on July 6, 1994, see Clinton, *Public Papers* (1994), p. 1206.
17. *U.S. Department of State Dispatch,* September 12, 1994, pp. 597–598.
18. See Mary Curtius, "Mass. Man is Clinton's Invisible Adviser," *Boston Globe,* September 18, 1993, p. 4.
19. Quoted in Dobbs, "Wider Alliance." Confirmed by author interviews with numerous officials who attended the meeting.
20. Zbigniew Brzezinski, "A Plan for Europe," *Foreign Affairs* 74 (January/February 1995), pp. 27–28.

The White House Dismissed Warnings on China Satellite Deal

By JEFF GERTH and JOHN M. BRODER

WASHINGTON, May 31—The caution signs were evident that the application by Loral Space & Communications to export a satellite to China earlier this year was anything but routine.

Justice Department prosecutors warned that allowing the deal could jeopardize possible prosecution of the company for an earlier unauthorized technology transfer to Beijing. The Pentagon reported that Loral had provided "potentially very significant help" to China's military rocket program. And senior White House aides cautioned that the deal was certain to spark opposition from critics of the Administration's nonproliferation and human rights policies toward China.

But the White House pressed ahead, concerned about the financial costs to Loral of delaying approval of the deal and certain that it could defend the decision against subsequent criticism.

Rarely is the public given a detailed glimpse inside the White House decision-making process on a matter of national security as sensitive as the export of a satellite to China. These records ordinarily remain sealed for years, buried under the Government's strict regime of secrecy.

But documents produced by the White House 10 days ago in response to a demand from Congress provide an unusually rich account of the evolution of a Presidential decision in which numerous warning signals were raised and then dismissed.

According to the records, the February decision by President Clinton to approve the Loral satellite launching was treated as an urgent matter not because of its importance to the national security, but because the company was facing heavy fines for delay.

Concerns about European competition for the satellite business and fears that denying the deal would damage the United States-China relationship overrode words of caution from other Government agencies.

The presumption throughout was that the deal would be approved, as had 19 previous applications under Presidents Clinton and Bush. The documents reflect the White House staff's search for a defensible rationale for the decision.

Federal and Congressional investigators are now examining what led the President to risk political embarrassment by creating the perception that he might be letting Loral—headed by the Democratic Party's largest campaign contributor—off the hook in a serious criminal inquiry into whether Loral executives helped China's missile program.

Decision Traced To a Satellite Crash

Samuel R. Berger, the national security adviser, had a preemptive answer in the decision memorandum he forwarded to the President on Feb. 12. The memo briefly notes the Justice Department's concerns and refers to the possibility that Loral might have significantly aided China's military rocket program.

But he urged the President to approve the deal regardless.

"In any case," Mr. Berger wrote, "we believe that the advantages of this project outweigh this risk, and that we can effectively rebut criticism of the waiver."

Mr. Clinton approved it with his distinctive backward check mark six days later.

Since 1989, the export of American satellites for launching on Chinese rockets has been suspended as a result of sanctions imposed after the killings in Tiananmen Square. A deal can go forward only if the President concludes that the export is in the national interest and issues a waiver.

President Bush approved all nine waiver requests that reached his desk; President Clinton routinely followed the practice in his first four years in office, signing 10 waivers with little internal debate or external controversy.

But the waiver Mr. Clinton signed on Feb. 18 was not routine. The roots of his unusual decision trace back two years when a Chinese rocket carrying a Loral satellite crashed into a village seconds after liftoff, killing and injuring dozens of civilians.

A few months later, Loral led an outside review team to help the Chinese figure out what happened. The company says its officials did nothing wrong. But Loral also acknowledged serious mistakes in a June 1996 disclosure to the State Department, including an admission that it allowed the Chinese to see its lengthy review of the rocket mishap without prior Federal approval. Such technological assistance to the Chinese requires prior Government approval, which Loral had not received.

At virtually the same time that Loral made its disclosure to the Government, the company was seeking another Presidential waiver for a satellite. Its chairman, Bernard L. Schwartz, donated $100,000 to the Democratic Party four weeks before the waiver application was approved in early July 1996 by Mr. Clinton.

It is not known whether Loral's help for the Chinese was mentioned in the memorandum that went to the President because the White House has not released documentation on that decision.

It is known that the State Department had already alleged in a letter to satellite industry executives that there had been a violation of American export control laws in the accident review.

But as of July 1996, no criminal inquiry was yet under way. The Justice Department began its investigation only after the Pentagon completed an assessment of the accident review in May 1997.

That is the same month Loral applied for its most recent waiver, for the Chinasat 8 satellite.

Company's Concerns Reach White House

The first notice to the White House of unusual problems with the Chinasat 8 waiver application came in an early January memorandum from the State Department detailing the factors for the President to consider.

Although couched in careful bureaucratic language, the State Department document made it clear that this was no routine export license application.

The State Department pointed out that China's transfer of missile technology to Iran might prohibit the export of the Loral satellite or any other satellites or related items.

"Moreover," the State Department memo stated, "information about unauthorized defense services provided by Space Systems/Loral and another U.S. firm to China's Long March 3B Launch Vehicle" could lead to imposition of harsh sanctions against the company.

But the State Department and other agencies nonetheless recommended granting the waiver, because the deal would enhance the United States' leadership in commercial telecommunications, provide an incentive for China to adhere to international nonproliferation rules and improve trade ties with Beijing.

After virtually no debate at the White House, the State Department memorandum was rewritten as a decision paper for the President.

The State Department's concern about technology transfers to Iran appeared nowhere in the decision document, but a new element is inserted in the first and in most subsequent drafts. The President must act quickly, the draft states; any delay will cost Loral money.

"Due to severe contractual penalties which Loral will incur if it cannot begin technical discussions with the Chinese by next week, we recommend that you take action on this issue by January 20," read the first draft of the Presidential memorandum, dated Jan. 13.

A day earlier, Loral officials had made known to the White House their frustration at the slow Government response to their waiver application, which was submitted in May 1997.

A Loral letter found in White House files stated that unless the approval is granted within a week, the launching, scheduled for November, would be delayed by several months, costing the company at least $6 million. Any such delay would give the Chinese grounds for canceling the project, which would cost Loral $20 million, the company warned.

"Our competitors in Europe," Loral officials complained, "do not suffer delays due to export licensing or legal complications."

The company's concerns clearly were heard at the White House.

A senior aide at the National Security Council, Maureen E. Tucker, repeatedly pressed for a rapid decision in forwarding early drafts of the Presidential decision paper to associates at the council.

She described the memorandum and accompanying documents as "a very quick turnaround package for which I am seeking your clearance by tomorrow," she wrote on Jan. 13.

By Jan. 20, one frustrated aide scrawled on a draft of the memo, "Needs to go to POTUS today!!" POTUS is the White House jargon for President of the United States.

But the waiver request was held up by questions from Mr. Berger, who asked his legal aides to research the status of the Justice Department investigation and determine whether it would bar approval of the waiver.

Tellingly, Mr. Berger asked Gary Samore, the National Security Council's top weapons proliferation expert, in a handwritten note if the approval can be granted in phases "to get over immediate crunch."

Mr. Berger did not ask whether Loral's cooperation with the Chinese after the 1996 accident would require denial of the export license. Instead, he wonders in the note to Mr. Samore where there is "anything we can hang our hat on to characterize Loral's 'offense.'"

Mr. Berger's aides sought advice from officials at the State Department, who informed them that Loral's offenses appear to be "criminal" and "knowing." Ms. Tucker was told that the Pentagon investigated Loral's assistance to the Chinese after the 1996 missile explosion and concluded that the company provided "potentially very significant help" to Beijing's ballistic missile program.

Behind Decision To Grant a Waiver

The White House counsel Charles F. C. Ruff told a Security Council lawyer that the Justice Department's investigation mattered less than maintaining close diplomatic and business relations with China.

"Issue is not [underlined twice] impact on DOJ litig(ation)," the Security Council deputy counsel Newell Highsmith wrote in notes of his conversation with Mr. Ruff, "but whether bilateral U.S.-China concerns and economic factors outweigh risk of political embarrassment."

A principal argument behind Mr. Clinton's decision was that it would be unfair to penalize Loral by denying it a license if it was under investigation but had not been charged with any crimes.

The export law allows the President to deny a license if the license seeker has been indicted or if there is "reasonable cause to believe" the license seeker "has violated" United States export control laws. The White House documents show that some White House and State Department officials believed the latter, but Administration officials say they relied on a 1993 State Department memo which said that companies will be denied licenses only after indictment.

"In an ideal world we would wait until this matter is resolved," Malcolm R. Lee, a National Security Council aide, told other White House officials in an electronic message a month before the President's decision, referring to the pending Justice Department inquiry. But, Mr. Lee added, "that is impracticable."

A senior Administration official, speaking not for attribution, said that waiting for the results of the Justice Department investigation could delay the satellite launching for months, if not years.

And, the official added, "There were some imperatives to get a timely decision because of the penalties facing the company."

But the company acknowledges that no such penalties have been imposed and the launching is still scheduled for November, as it has been for the last year.

"We believe we will not incur penalties because we can work around the problem," a Loral official said late last week.

Pentagon Troubled By Loral's Role

The President did not receive a detailed assessment of the potential damage to American security caused by Loral's help to China in determining the cause of the 1996 launching failure. The Pentagon was troubled by Loral's technological assistance because the rocket science involved in putting a satellite into orbit is similar to that needed to deliver a nuclear warhead.

The Pentagon, relying on Air Force missile and intelligence experts, did not find grave damage but did conclude that the United States national security had been harmed, according to Administration officials.

A White House official said that the National Security Council never received the Pentagon report, which was prepared to assist the State Department. "We did the best we could in the memo for the President in describing what we understood to be the allegations," the official said. "We didn't beat around the bush."

White House aides overcame the major impediment to the waiver—the concern of Justice Department prosecutors that it would jeopardize any possible prosecution—by relying on the fact that "the Department had every opportunity to weigh in against the waiver at the highest levels and elected not to do so," as Mr. Ruff, the White House counsel, wrote on Feb. 13.

But Justice Department officials say that Mr. Ruff, in his discussion with Robert Litt, the top aide to the Deputy Attorney General, asked only about the impact of the waiver on possible prosecution—not whether the department opposed the waiver.

It is not known how the Justice Department would have answered that question.

Unit 6

Unit Selections

27. **Globalization and Its Discontents: Navigating the Dangers of a Tangled World,** Richard N. Haass and Robert E. Litan
28. **For a New, Progressive IMF,** Robert Borosage
29. **Foreign Aid,** Carol Graham
30. **Bogotá Aid: To Fight Drugs or Rebels?** Diana Jean Schemo and Tim Golden

Key Points to Consider

- Which type of international system, global free trade or regional trading blocs, is in America's national interest? Explain.

- Who is the more important trading partner for the United States—Japan, Europe, or Mexico? Defend your answer.

- Select a country in need of foreign aid. What type of foreign aid strategy should the United States pursue toward it? How does this compare with current U.S. foreign aid programs?

- What types of foreign policy goals can be advanced using economic means?

- What type of policy should the United States adopt in trying to help countries facing currency crises? Should it work through the IMF or act unilaterally?

- Can foreign aid be used in the fight against drugs? If so, what type of strategy should be adopted?

Links www.dushkin.com/online/

21. **International Monetary Fund (IMF)**
    http://www.imf.org/
22. **United States Agency for International Development**
    http://www.info.usaid.gov/
23. **United States Trade Representative**
    http://www.ustr.gov/
24. **World Bank**
    http://www.worldbank.org/

These sites are annotated on pages 4 and 5.

U.S. International Economic Strategy

As in so many areas of American foreign policy, the selection of U.S. international economic strategies during the cold war seems to have been a rather straightforward process and the accompanying policy debates fairly minor compared to the situation that exists today. At the most fundamental level, it was taken for granted that the American economy would best be served by the existence of a global free trade system. The lengthy Depression of the 1930s and the accompanying rise to power of extremist governments in Germany, Italy, and elsewhere had discredited the competing policy of protectionism. A consensus existed that, for such a system to work, America's active involvement and leadership were essential. To that end, international organizations were set up whose collective task it was to oversee the operation of the postwar international economic order. Foremost among them were the General Agreement on Tariffs and Trade (GATT), the International Monetary Fund (IMF), and the International Bank for Reconstruction and Development (the World Bank).

It was also widely accepted that many states would not be able to resist pressure from the Soviet Union or from domestic communist parties, due to the weak state of their economies and military establishments. Thus, containing Communism would require foreign aid programs designed to transfer American economic and military expertise, goods and services, and financial resources to key states. Finally, containing Communism was seen as requiring economic strategies of denial. Lists were drawn up of goods that U.S. firms were prohibited from selling to communist states because they could contribute to the strength of their military establishments.

Over time, problems arose in all of these areas. Events of the 1960s and 1970s shook the international economic system at its political and economic foundations. Among the most prominent were the growing U.S. balance of payments deficits growing out of the Vietnam War; the completed economic recoveries of Germany and Japan; President Richard Nixon's decision to take the United States off the gold standard and allow the exchange rate to fluctuate; and oil price hikes led by the Organization of Petroleum Exporting Countries (OPEC). It was now clear that there was nothing automatic about the operation of a free trade system. The institutions created after World War II have struggled to meet the challenges presented by the increased attractiveness of regional trading blocks, the recognition that economic issues intersect with environmental and democratization problems, and the lingering effects of large-scale developing world debt.

Foreign aid programs also became controversial. Unable to foster economic growth and development that would remove the need for continued U.S. foreign aid, these programs increasingly came to be seen as entitlement programs. Moreover, many began to question America's ability to pay for such programs, given the declining health of the American economy. A concern for the state of the American economy also led to feelings of disenchantment with policies designed to deny American products to the Soviet Union and its allies. With many of its allies selling "denied" technology to the Soviet Union, these policies were costing American companies access to markets and costing American workers jobs.

The end of the cold war, then, did not in a single stroke undermine America's international economic strategy. It did bring into sharp relief the strategy's growing ineffectiveness and open up the policy process to the possibility of new solutions. As the debates over the North American Free Trade Agreement (NAFTA), foreign aid to the Soviet Union, establishing the World Trade Organization, and "bailing out" countries whose currencies suffer a sudden and dramatic drop in value such as happened in Mexico, Russia, and Asia make clear, a consensus has not yet taken hold within the American political system on what type of international economic strategy to pursue. For some, the solution lies in reaffirming the commitment to making a global free trade system work. For others, the solution lies with embracing a policy framework centered on the creation of a system of regional trading blocs. Also at issue is the degree to which the government should allow market forces to dictate the direction of the American economy and the extent to which it should intervene to promote certain economic sectors and protect others from foreign competition.

The readings in this section highlight several important dimensions to U.S. international economic policy. Richard Haass and Robert Litan, in "Globalization and its Discontents," review three fundamentally different strategies for participating in the global economy. They argue that the best advice for governments is not to try and fight globalization but to learn to manage it. Robert Borosage, in "For a New, Progressive IMF," provides us with a critical commentary on the workings of the International Monetary Fund (IMF) and its efforts to bolster the collapsing Asian economies.

The last two essays examine U.S. foreign aid policy. Carol Graham, in "Foreign Aid," asserts that it is time to ask some hard questions about the effectiveness of foreign aid, particularly: would economic performance in the recipient states have been worse without aid; how is the United States allocating aid; do economic aid policies produce growth; and do better economic conditions facilitate the implementation of better aid policies? Perhaps no aspect of America's foreign aid program is as controversial as that designed to fight drug trafficking. Diana Jean Schemo and Tim Golden examine the issues involved in this policy area in "Bogotá Aid: To Fight Drugs or Rebels?" They conclude that the distinction between the two is breaking down and creating problems for U.S. foreign policy.

Globalization and Its Discontents

Navigating the Dangers of a Tangled World

Richard N. Haass and Robert E. Litan

The period immediately following the Second World War, which produced the Marshall Plan, NATO, and the U.S.-Japan security treaty, is rightly regarded as foreign policy's golden era. But it also saw the birth of comparably successful economic institutions—such as the International Monetary Fund, the World Bank, the General Agreement on Tariffs and Trade—designed to promote long-term prosperity through stable exchange rates, worldwide development, and open trade. Today these institutions are increasingly subject to criticism. The IMF, for instance, has come under attack for imposing drastic conditions in its "rescues" of Mexico in 1995 and Asia today. The World Trade Organization, formed in 1995 as the result of American calls for a body to resolve market-access disputes, has been attacked in this country for usurping America's sovereignty. And doubts abound about the role of development banks in an era of massive direct foreign investment.

The gap between the legacy of Bretton Woods and the economic and political demands of the modern world is growing. Much of this change is driven by rapid advances in, and thus lower costs of, communications, information flows, and travel. Official policy, much of it American, has played its part by reducing barriers to the movement of goods and capital across national boundaries. The result has been more intrusive and intense economic interaction—including the explosive growth of world capital markets, which led to the demise of fixed exchange rates—between a large and growing number of entities outside government control, a phenomenon that has come to be called "globalization."

But globalization has its problems. In some quarters it is seen as having caused the rapid flows of investment that moved in and out of countries as investor sentiment changed and were behind the Mexican and Asian financial crises. In the United States it is blamed for job losses, increasing income inequality, and stagnant or deteriorating real wages. Domestic discontent with globalization thwarted the passage last year of legislation that would have granted the president "fast track" authority to negotiate trade arrangements that Congress could not modify.

Globalization has become a target. Its dangers must be navigated successfully or the United States and others may be compelled to backtrack, diminishing the free movement of goods, services, and capital, which would result in slower growth, less technological innovation, and lower living standards.

RICHARD N. HAASS, Director of the Program in Foreign Policy Studies at the Brookings Institution, is the author of *The Reluctant Sheriff: The United States after the Cold War*. ROBERT E. LITAN, Director of Brookings' Program in Economic Studies, is coauthor of *Globaphobia: Confronting Fears about Open Trade*.

FREE-MARKET FOREIGN POLICY?

In this new world, poor economic policy-making, corrupt banking practices, dishonest accounting, and unrealistic currency alignments can have an impact on societies far removed. Although the United States, with its vast internal market, is considerably less "globalized" than other industrialized countries, millions of American jobs and billions of dollars are tied to economic developments elsewhere.

If there is consensus on the diagnosis, there is none on the prescription. There are at least three fundamentally different approaches to addressing the problems of the global economy.

The first embraces the free market and would abandon IMF-like rescue packages. It is motivated by the belief that the IMF lulls governments, investors, and lenders into recklessness. Emboldened by the prospect that the IMF will come to their rescue, they are free to act irresponsibly. In the words of George Shultz, William Simon, and Walter Wriston, IMF "interference will only encourage more crises." Mexico, in this view, led to Asia.

The laissez-faire, free-market approach looks good in the abstract because markets reward sound investments and regulatory practices and punish poor ones. In principle, it can provide incentives for investors to avoid overly risky investments and for governments to adopt prudent policies. To international free marketeers, safety nets destroy this incentive.

But this critique goes too far. Governments submitting to IMF rescue plans must often agree to wrenching reforms—not the kind of experience that invites other governments to be reckless. Similarly, investors in equity markets in Mexico and Asia were hit by depressed local stock prices and heavily devalued local currencies. The only parties that emerged relatively unscathed, and thus for whom the free market critique has some relevance, were certain creditors: holders of Mexican government debt during the Mexican crisis and banks in the recent Asian crisis.

The solution to this problem is not to remove the IMF—the international lender of last resort—but to develop ways to warn banks and other creditors that they will suffer in the event of a future crisis. During the Depression, Americans learned the cost of not having a functioning lender of last resort: a wave of bank and corporate failures, aggravated by a shortage of liquidity that the Federal Reserve failed to provide. The international equivalent of having no Fed is standing idly by while currencies plummet, countries run out of foreign exchange, trade and investment come to a halt, and crises in one region spread to others.

A hands-off approach would risk transforming limited crises into something much more costly. More than economics is at stake. Years of punishment by the marketplace are simply not acceptable when immediate strategic interests are involved, as they are, for example, in Mexico or South Korea. For better or worse, the United States cannot afford the collapse of countries vital to its national interest.

GOVERNING GLOBALIZATION

The second approach to taming the dangers of globalization could hardly be more different. It suggests the creation of new institutions to lend structure and direction to the global marketplace, complementing what is seen as the constructive but inadequate roles of the IMF and other bodies. For example, George Soros, arguing that "international capital movements need to be supervised and the allocation of credit regulated," has recommended creating the international equivalent of the United States' Fannie Mae, which guarantees residential mortgages for a fee. He calls for the establishment of an "International Credit Insurance Corporation" that would guarantee private sector loans up to a specified amount for a modest charge, while requiring that the borrowers' home countries provide a complete financial picture in order for them to qualify.

Henry Kaufman, a Wall Street economist, would go even further, creating a

"Board of Overseers of Major International Institutions and Markets" that would set minimum capital requirements for all institutions, establish uniform accounting and lending standards, and monitor performance. It would even discipline those who did not meet these criteria by limiting the ability of those who remained outside the system to lend, borrow, and sell.

Governments are sure to resist supranational bodies that so fundamentally challenge their sovereignty. Moreover, except for extreme crises when an IMF-like rescue is warranted, it is difficult to understand why international officials could determine how much credit to allocate better than the market. There is more than a little irony in applying the "Asian model" of centralization to the international economy just when the model has been so thoroughly discredited.

A third approach, which would leave the basic architecture of the international economy alone but still do some "remodeling," would involve a number of reforms designed to structure and discipline financial operations and transactions. This managed approach would eschew the heavy hand of international regulation but aim to maintain the element of risk essential to capitalism without removing the safety net provided by the IMF. This approach is closest to the manner in which the United States dealt with the savings and loan and banking crises of the 1980s: enacting legislation requiring shareholders to maintain a larger financial commitment to their banks while making it more difficult for regulators and policymakers to bail out large, uninsured depositors who could previously count on being protected. The challenge for the international community is to introduce the equivalent of the U.S. reforms at both the national and international levels.

Such reforms are already being worked on at the behest of the IMF. They include improving the supervision of financial institutions, instituting Western-style accounting practices in banks and corporations, and opening up markets to foreign investment. To ensure that these reforms are carried out, some other international body, such as the Bank for International Settlements or perhaps a nongovernmental organization, should issue regular "report cards" on individual countries' progress. In addition, the IMF must press countries to be forthcoming with accurate information about key financial data, including their current account positions, foreign exchange reserves, and short-term indebtedness to foreign creditors. Banks and investors will favor countries that are positively rated, and penalize or avoid those that are not. Governments and institutions will introduce desirable reforms lest they lose out.

More transparency and information is necessary but not sufficient for markets to avoid excesses. The challenge is to find effective ways of addressing the free market critique. A possible solution is for the IMF to condition its assistance on countries' penalizing all lenders of foreign currency in the event IMF intervention is required. In particular, the model legislation that each country could adopt would require (as long as an IMF rescue is in effect) that creditors automatically suffer some loss of their principal when their debt matures and is not rolled over or extended. This approach would discourage the sudden outflow of maturing debt when countries can least afford it. The threat of automatic loss in the event a country experiences economic crisis could underscore to banks and other creditors that their money is at risk and that they can no longer count on the IMF to bail them out. Creditors would respond, of course, by insisting on higher interest rates for borrowers with opaque or poorly capitalized balance sheets. But that is precisely the point: the price of loans should better reflect the risk of not getting repaid.

The Asian crisis demonstrates the need for more formal bankruptcy codes and mechanisms for restructuring the balance sheets of heavily indebted firms without necessarily shutting them down. Existing international institutions can assist countries in this area, as well as in strengthening bank supervision and accounting standards, but there is no need to establish a new international bankruptcy court or to vest existing international institutions with such powers. The United States has a bankruptcy code and process that handles insolvency of firms located here, even when they have foreign creditors. There is no reason why other countries cannot do the same thing.

THE HOME FRONT

To paraphrase former House Speaker Tip O'Neill, all economics is local. Policies promoting unfettered trade and investment will be rejected by Congress unless steps are taken to build a firm domestic political base. Once again, there are three approaches to choose from, running the gamut from laissez faire to heavy regulation. A pure market approach—one that would let the chips (and the workers) fall where they may—would be neither fair nor politically sustainable. Some sort of safety net is both desirable and necessary. At the same time, it would be foolish to try to insulate Americans from all of globalization's effects. It is impossible to protect jobs rendered obsolete by technological change and foreign competition. What lies between is a managed approach that helps workers cope with the consequences of globalization. It would both change and supplement existing programs and policies.

Since 1962, American policymakers have provided extended unemployment insurance to workers who can prove they were displaced primarily because of international trade. But this discourages workers from looking for employment, channeling them toward government training programs with little proven success. Moreover, it does not compensate workers for the cuts in pay they take even after finding new jobs. A more effective program would pay workers a portion of the difference between their wages at their previous and new jobs. This kind of earnings insurance would encourage workers to take new jobs even if they paid less, and offer the only real training that works—on the job. Workers could also be provided with benefits—health insurance, pensions, training, and unemployment insurance—that they could take with them when moving to a new employer.

Some will argue that portable benefits and earnings insurance are not enough. But globalization is a reality, not a choice. "You can run but you can't hide" might serve as the mantra for the age.

Those who urge us to hide by resurrecting barriers to trade and investment, with the ostensible aim of insulating Americans from the forces of globalization, would abandon America's commitment to the spread of markets and democracy around the world at precisely the moment these ideas are ascendant. Moreover, the potential economic and political cost would be enormous, depriving Americans of cheaper and in some cases higher quality goods and services, as well as denying them the opportunity to work at better paying jobs that depend on exports.
to manage it, which will require creative policies both at home and abroad. It is ironic: the age of globalization may well be defined in part by challenges to the nation-state, but it is still states and governments—by the practices they adopt, the arrangements they enter into, and the safety nets they provide—that will determine whether we exploit or squander the potential of this era.

FOCUS ON THE MULTILATERALS

FOR A NEW, PROGRESSIVE IMF

THE IMF SHOULD TEMPER, NOT FEED, SPECULATIVE FRENZIES, PROTECT WORKERS

By Robert Borosage

Treasury Secretary Robert Rubin has enlisted the Business Roundtable and other corporate lobbies to press the Congress for $18 million in borrowing authority to bolster the International Monetary Fund in the wake of the Asian financial collapse. Despite the secretary's sterling reputation, the business community's impressive clout, and nearly universal editorial approval, Rubin is having a hard time rounding up the votes.

As the emergency room doctor for the global economy, the IMF faces charges of malpractice and questions about its license. The fund intercedes when countries face currency crises. Many critics argue the fund is more quack than cure. In Asia, the IMF has received withering criticism for imposing remedies that have little to do with the source of the crisis, thereby making it worse. But the debate about the fund is part of a far broader struggle over regulating the global economy, a policy and political debate likely to frame a good portion of our politics over the next decades.

The crisis is Asia is, in cause and in effect, a global crisis. The Asian tigers — Thailand, Indonesia, Korea — have been shaken by the bursting of a classic speculative bubble. The bubble was inflated by profligate short-term loans to and equity speculation in Asian companies, with U.S., European and Japanese banks and investment houses central participants in the folly. Despite ritual assurances — just a "glitch in the road" said President Clinton last fall — the crisis is much more serious than initially expected. Currencies and stock markets have plunged throughout Asia. Initial IMF bailout plans proved inadequate in South Korea, Indonesia, Thailand and the Philippines. Bankruptcies and layoffs have just begun. Food riots are spreading in Indonesia. Over a million workers are facing layoffs in Korea. Analysts fear that aftershocks of the crisis may yet shake Russia, Brazil and other developing nations. The impact in the industrial nations is just beginning to be felt. Japan — already in recession and with a banking system burdened by bad debts — will face greater pressure from lost markets and bankrupt investments in Asia, and greater competition in export markets from the Asian tigers. China — facing slower growth amid a wrenching reduction of wasteful state enterprises — will also contend with greater competition for export markets. If China devalues or Japan allows the yen to depreciate as many fear, it could trigger another round of competitive devaluations, and global deflation.

Robert Borosage is the co-director of the Campaign for America's Future, a new organization that seeks to insert a populist economic agenda into the debate about the nation's future. He earlier served as the director of the Institute for Policy Studies.

IMF policies bail out speculators, while imposing austerity on the poor and creating unnecessary recessions.

The impact on Europe and the U.S. has yet to be measured, but, as Jeffrey E. Garten, dean of the Yale School of Management, notes, "It's simply not credible that a third of the world can suddenly go from dynamic growth to widespread recession without affecting our own economy." Even if current efforts to staunch the hemorrhaging are successful, U.S. exports to the region — which constitute 30 percent of the total — will decline. Exports elsewhere will face tougher competition. Our markets will be flooded with lower-priced goods. Conservative estimates predict a trade deficit increased by $50 to 100 billion in the current year. Rule of thumb estimates suggest over one million workers will lose their jobs over the next 18 months. Wages and profits will be under pressure as corporations struggle to meet the competition.

The most knowledgeable are the most alarmed. Barton Biggs, the chairman of Morgan Stanley Asset Management, warns that the "U.S. economy inevitably will begin to be hollowed out and the protectionist outcry begin. World-wide competitive devaluation, trade wars and deflationary tendencies could result in a synchronized global slowdown recession and simultaneous bear markets in Western stock markets. A vicious circle could develop." Even Chairman of the Federal Reserve Alan Greenspan, a man not given to rhetorical excess, has warned of the dangers of generalized "deflation."

Representatives of the Clinton administration and the International Monetary Fund have labored to blame the crisis primarily on Asia's "crony capitalism." And it is true that authoritarian regimes in East Asia, as Korean President Kim Dae Jung has argued, lived a "lie." But crony capitalism isn't new. Indeed, the Asian tigers received lavish praise from the World Bank and the IMF for getting the "fundamentals right" — high savings rate, low inflation, balanced budgets. They were the sole countries in the world to enjoy year after year of significant growth, lifting living standards for their people.

What burst in Asia was a classic speculative bubble.

Deregulation — dismantling capital and currency controls without the regulation needed to monitor the risk — opened a flood of short term, speculative money, predicated on the general assumption that growth would continue indefinitely. But when China devalued in 1994 and the yen lost 40 percent of its value in dollars, East Asian exports faced new competition. When growth slowed, nervous speculators started to get out, and the bubble burst.

The IMF then stepped in to try to stem the crisis. But the IMF has been as much part of the problem as part of the solution. The fund helped create the bubble by pushing the Asian nations to end controls on capital accounts and currency flows before sensible banking regulations were in place. It helped feed the bubble by bailing out speculators from profligate loans in Mexico and elsewhere, creating what Treasury Secretary Rubin calls the "moral hazard" of gamblers encouraged to bet ever more recklessly, confident their losses will be covered on the down side. It helped attract more investors into the bubble by lavishly praising the Asian economic management that it now condemns for rampant corruption and crippling debt. And when the crisis began, the fund marched in — and by its own admission in Indonesia and Thailand — helped spread the panic rather than relieve it.

Numerous experts have criticized the IMF standard bailout program for reinforcing the very dynamics that caused the crisis. As Jeff Uscher, the editor of *Grant's Asia Observer*, writes, the fund bails out the speculators, giving them back "100 cents on the dollar," thus feeding the speculative fever for another round. It enforces austerity on the countries involved, boosting interest rates, demanding spending cutbacks, requiring sale of assets to foreign investors at firesale prices, forcing countries to export their way out of the crisis. The fund's package seems particularly inappropriate to the Asian countries where the problem was not in the public sector — these are countries with balanced budgets and high savings rates — but in private profligacy. Even Joseph Stiglitz, chief economist of the World Bank, publicly criticized the fund for pushing the Asian nations into unnecessarily severe recessions.

The IMF and Congress

Ironically, the strongest opposition to the administration's IMF request is based in the Republican party. The social conservatives of the Republican right turned against globalization long before the Asian crisis. Pat Buchanan railed against the North American Free Trade Agreement, the World Trade Organization and fast-track trade authority. Conservative activist Gary Bauer led the religious right into the battle against most favored nation status for China. Much of the Republican class of 1994 — what one Republican pollster called the "black helicopter crowd"— is generally suspicious of global institutions — from the United Nations to the "pointy headed bureaucrats" at the WTO. Last year, social conservatives blocked an emergency $3.5 billion supplemental that Treasury sought for the IMF by attaching an anti-abortion rider to it.

Now, the protectionist right is joined by mainstream Republican free traders. The Heritage Foundation, the libertarian Cato Institute, and much of the American Enterprise Institute — all supportive of fast track — have come out against refunding the IMF. They have been joined by surprising allies in the establishment like former Secretary of State George Shultz and former Citibank head Walter Wriston.

The free traders argue that the IMF interferes in workings of the free market which otherwise would work out the financial crisis. Markets require punishment of the improvident to discipline speculators and entrepreneurs. Thus, speculators shouldn't be bailed out of bad loans; improvident borrowers should be forced to take their losses. Republican presidential candidate Steve Forbes argues that the IMF should be "told to take a hike," and that "bailing out investors and speculators ... unwittingly encouraged speculative money flows elsewhere."

Democrats, on the other hand, generally favor public intervention and strong international institutions. They argue that markets "work out" these crises through deflation and depression. Since the 1930s, civilized nations have considered that too big a risk. Thus House Minority leader Richard Gephardt, who led the fight against fast track, has worked with the administration to round up support for the IMF request. But while progressives in the Democratic Party support *an* IMF, most of them strongly oppose *this* IMF.

For them, expanding the IMF without dramatic reforms is perverse. It's like giving a full gas can to an admitted arsonist in order to forestall future fires. In the Asian conflagration, they argue, the IMF may not have lit the match, but it helped provide the tinder, supply the gas and cheer on those who were playing with fire. And once the smoke appeared, the IMF shouted fire, adding to the panic.

Moreover, support for the IMF is not an easy vote. As Rep. Barney Frank noted, "no one in New Bedford is urging me to vote $18 billion to the IMF." Many union activists, mobilized around NAFTA and the fast-track debates, oppose IMF funding, as do the environmental and consumer groups that led the fight against fast-track. The AFL-CIO has not mobilized union opposition, but it has conditioned its support on structural reforms of the IMF, including support for worker rights.

So progressive Democrats — led by David Bonior, Barney Frank, Bernie Sanders and others — have been pushing for reform of the IMF and the international system as a price of their support (though it seems that in March Bonior for one had reached a compromise with the administration that would allow him to support IMF funding). They've introduced amendments demanding that the fund's work be opened to outsiders, that it practice the transparency it preaches to others. They insist that the fund's programs measure their impact on workers and the environment, and take concrete steps to further basic worker rights and environmental protections. They want the fund to stop promoting an export-oriented growth strategy, and start laying the conditions for what economist Lester Thurow calls a "shift to a strategy of internal growth." They urge Secretary Rubin and the president to press Japan and Germany to stimulate their economies to provide a global stimulus, alleviating the deflationary effects of the Asian collapse.

Treasury Secretary Rubin concedes much of this critique, has warned of the "moral hazard" of bailing out speculators, and called for reform of the "architecture" of the global financial system. In meetings of finance ministers, Treasury representatives have pushed for finding

The IMF may not have ignited the Asian conflagration but it has cheered on those who were playing with fire.

ways to "bail speculators in" — not bail them out — of financial collapses.

But like Saint Augustine who implored God to rid him of sin, but not yet, Rubin is for reform, but not yet. He wants the Congress to pass the IMF funding first. A U.S. vote of confidence, he says, is vital to help staunch the crisis, warning that failure to act may shake markets here and abroad.

The threat is more effective than true. The IMF has more than enough capital to handle the next crisis and can borrow virtually unlimited amounts. No other country is racing to ante up the new request for expanded quotas. Clearly the treasury secretary is using the crisis to drum up support for IMF expansion. But he doesn't want to dramatize the seriousness of the Asian collapse for fear of spooking the markets once more. Federal Reserve Chair Alan Greenspan's testimony in March — when he balanced fears of inflation with warnings of potential deflation — demonstrates how carefully the financial leaders are treading.

With millions of Americans invested in an already overpriced stock market, Rubin's warning has political force. Legislators, headed into an election in a time of prosperity, have no desire to be tagged with responsibility if the market falls. Many observers assume that, at the end of the day, Congress will pass the IMF funding, rather than risk being blamed if the market does crash.

At the Davos, Switzerland, meetings of world leaders this spring, AFL-CIO President John Sweeney argued that the Asian crisis marks an historic turning. "The long effort to build a global market has succeeded. ... The question now is how to put sensible boundaries on the market that already exists. How to make the market work for the majority and not simply for the few." Sweeney's views might have been hard for the corporate executives in the audience to swallow, but they were seconded by George Soros, the billionaire hedge fund operator whose success gives his word great clout.

Global trade and corporations are hardly new. But the growing integration of a global market is a relatively recent achievement. It is only in the last two decades that countries have dismantled currency and capital controls, and opened markets to foreign investment. President Clinton, like President Bush before him, made the construction and celebration of this global market a centerpiece of his "economic strategy." The administration has pushed for the ratification of the World Trade Organization, the North American Free Trade Agreement. It has opened negotiations on a Multilateral Agreement on Investment. It has encouraged the IMF to seek greater authority over liberalizing capital flows. It has sought fast-track trade authority to facilitate negotiation of a free trade accord with Latin America, among other trade agreements.

As a result, financial flows to favored countries in the developing world have skyrocketed since 1990, with the vast majority coming from the private sector of banks and investors. Mutual funds and pension funds began to allocate more of their portfolio to overseas investments. Whereas public sources provided the bulk of financial flows in 1990, by 1996 the flows increased sixfold and over 85 percent came from private sources — banks, investment houses, corporations, etc. Each day over $1 trillion dollars is exchanged in foreign transactions, with merely a small fraction needed for the real economy — financing trade, supporting direct investment. The remainder is short-term, hot speculative money — gambling in a casino economy.

Investment banker and former Treasury official Roger C. Altman compares the force contained in the new global financial market to that of nuclear weapons: "The markets have emerged as the ruling international authority, more potent than any military or political power." The Mexican collapse in 1994 might be considered an initial test of the power of this force. And it is truly a perverse historic irony that it would first detonate over Asia. In the sudden collapse of the Asian tigers, Altman warns, "we saw what a worldwide collapse might look like." The world's central bankers and investors continue to fear that the Asian market collapse will go global. It is essential that this new potent force be brought under better control.

Needed: A New Internationalism

Even before the Asian detonation, the struggle to put rules around the global marketplace had begun. Human rights campaigns against child labor led companies to cobble together "codes of conduct" for their subcontractors to protect themselves from consumer reaction. Labor unions began working across national borders in organizing and negotiating efforts. Environmentalists have continued to push global agreements to limit despoliation. Consumers issued alarms as uninspected imported foodstuffs poisoned children in Michigan and elsewhere.

In the aftershock of the Asian collapse, these citizen groups are joined by more enlightened business leaders. Financier George Soros calls for radical reform of the global financial system, warning that the "private sector is ill-suited to allocate international credit. It provides either too much or too little." Morgan Stanley's Barton Biggs calls for measures to "control macro traders who today almost rule the world."

For years, efforts to regulate the global system have been scorned as "protectionist." But efforts to build rules around the global market — to enforce labor rights and environmental protections, to regulate food and drug standards, to slow currency and capital flows — aren't efforts to shut down the market, but to save it from its own excesses. This is a new internationalism vital to the global market.

Thus, progressives should be insisting that IMF replenishment be conditioned on structural reforms, both of the fund and of U.S. policy generally. The central reform demands are clear.

Enforcement of internationally established labor rights — the right to organize, to bargain collectively, to strike — is essential. Labor rights help temper the "race to the bottom," where companies play countries off one against the other, forcing competitive devaluations, suppression of workers, elimination of sensible regulation to attract capital. Economically, the growth of inequality, the suppression of wages in the North from competition and in the South, often by brute force, is raising the specter of inadequate demand, and global deflation. Protection of labor rights gives workers in each nation a better chance to capture a fair share of the returns they generate. As their wages go up, they can afford to buy more of other nations' products. This is essential not only for human rights, but for continued economic growth.

Yet, the World Trade Organization protects property rights, but not worker rights. The IMF often forces — as it has in Korea — the dismantling of worker protections as a condition for its aid. Replenishment of the fund should be conditioned on the fund's agreement to report on the effects of its programs on workers and worker rights, and requiring that it seek to enforce core labor rights.

Second, the speculative frenzies of the global financial markets must be tempered. The fund seeks permission to change its charter to gain a mandate to push for further dismantling of capital and currency controls. Congress should insist that the U.S. representative oppose any such expansion.

Instead, the Congress should require the Treasury to put together a plan for regulating short-term capital flows. At the very least, the fund must be required to make speculators pay part of the price of their own folly as part of any rescue plan. Treasury should explore renewed support for national controls on speculation, like those imposed by Chile on short-term foreign currency loans and investment. George Soros has called for a global version of the Federal Deposit Insurance Corp., a public institution funded by private banks and investment houses that would set limits on the levels of insured debt nations could assume. Nobel laureate James Tobin has pushed for a small tax on global transactions, that would make short-term speculation more costly. These might be considered first steps towards moving to a new Bretton Woods, an international agreement to re-regulate currencies.

Third, the IMF must be opened up. Its past efforts should be open to independent review. Its conditionality agreements should be published and open to outside criticism. Democrats on the House Banking Committee have pushed for an independent citizen committee — including representatives from labor, business and consumer groups — to review IMF activities. This is the prerequisite for a larger debate about the extreme laissez-faire potions that the IMF prescribes as an all-purpose remedy.

Environmentalists and consumers have focused more of their attention on the World Trade Organization and the World Bank. But they want the fund to assess the environmental and consumer impact of the conditions that the IMF enforces on countries in distress. When a country is in crisis, the fund's objective is to stabilize currencies and regain the confidence of international investors. But the dismantling of environmental and consumer protections ought not be part — directly or indirectly — of the package created to appeal to investors. Environmentalists have also been the most vocal about the need for debt relief for developing nations, lifting the debt burden that too often gives them no choice but to join the "race to the bottom."

> *The IMF has more than enough capital to handle the next crisis and can borrow virtually unlimited amounts.*

Not all of these core reforms will be gained in the current debate over the IMF. If conservatives continue to oppose any funding, then the administration will have no choice but to obtain a majority from the center and the left, opening the possibility for progressives to insist on significant reform as a precondition for support. Whatever happens, the IMF debate and the Asian crisis mark historic turning. In many ways, the debate parallels the American experience at the beginning of this century. Then capital and communications built national companies, production and distribution networks. The centralization triggered populist resentment from local farmers and small businesses, from workers and consumers. Muckrakers exposed corporate abuses. Middle class progressives, combined with some of the more enlightened corporations, emerged to push for reform — the minimum wage, eight-hour day, union rights, food safety laws, banking and currency reform, etc. It took decades — two world wars and a great depression — but eventually progressives built the mixed economy that provided greater security for more working people.

Today, the companies and communications have gone global. In the global North, a populist response is building among labor, environmental, human rights and consumer movements. (It takes reactionary as well as reformist forms — as illustrated by Pat Buchanan in the U.S., Jean Marie Le Pen in France or the fundamentalist and nationalist movements building across the developing world.) Now it is vital that a movement for progressive reforms of the global marketplace begin. The debate over the IMF — and the reform pledges exacted as a price of funding — may well mark the beginnings of a new age of reform.

FOREIGN AID

CAROL GRAHAM

At a time when the entire foreign affairs budget is under fire, it is more important than ever to address the question of whether foreign aid is effective. Official development assistance, or ODA, as the foreign assistance component of the foreign affairs budget is called, is roughly half of that budget, and is arguably the part about which the public is most skeptical.

The United States, once the world leader in global aid, is now in fourth place after Japan, Germany, and France in terms of absolute amounts. In terms of percentage of GDP with 0.1 percent of American GDP allocated to ODA, the United States is well at the bottom of all industrialized nation donors. This clearly imperils U.S. leadership not only in international financial institutions such as the World Bank, but also in the aid debate more generally. Washington is increasingly being seen as unwilling to pay its global dues.

It is time to ask some hard questions about foreign aid. What do we know about it? Does it work? Is it effective? There has been much debate in recent years. I'd like to try to sum up what we know about aid effectiveness—and what we don't.

One reason for the extensive debate over aid is that so many diverse objectives drive its allocation that it is hard to evaluate how effective it is. While economic growth is clearly not the sole objective of foreign assistance, it's one of the few areas where empirical evidence permits evaluation. Growth is also important because without growth it is difficult, if not impossible, to achieve all the other goals—security, human rights, democracy—attributed to aid.

Recently the debate has been heightened by a series of studies that have found a negative relationship between conditioned aid flows and economic growth, particularly in low-income countries in Africa. These same studies, however, are also finding that the broader policy orientation that aid seeks to promote—market-friendly, open economic policies with prudent macroeconomic management—is producing strong results in countries worldwide. And the experience of many Asian countries

Carol Graham is a visiting fellow in the Brookings Foreign Policy Studies program. She is the author, with Michael O'Hanlon, of "Making Foreign Aid Work," which appeared in the July/August 1997 issue of Foreign Affairs.

and, more recently, many Latin American countries confirms that appropriate policies do yield good results.

These findings raise three questions about aid flows. First, is aid ineffective, or would poor economic performers have fared worse without aid? Second, how effective is conditionality in its current form? How are we allocating aid, and how is it working? And third, what is the causal relationship? Do policies produce growth, or do better initial economic conditions facilitate the implementation of better policies?

CAN AID SLOW GROWTH?

What accounts for the negative correlation between aid flows and growth performance? Africa, for example, receives 10 times more aid per capita than Latin America or East Asia and yet performs far worse by most or all economic measures. There are several explanations, and I don't want to oversimplify the issue, but one point is clear. By removing a hard budget constraint, aid inflows to a country can impede formation of a domestic consensus on the need for difficult economic reforms. Recent research on economic crisis undertaken at the World Bank suggests that countries that enter high-inflation crises tend to implement more complete reforms and then enjoy higher average growth rates than countries that just muddle along at "medium" inflation rates. What happens is that aid flows are often cut off in countries with very high inflation rates but continue in countries with medium inflation rates. These aid flows protect countries from the full costs of bad economic policies, often preventing the onset of deeper crisis and the important policy learning experience that is often critical to successful economic reform. Countries often have to hit bottom to get a domestic consensus on the need for economic reforms. Of course, allowing countries to enter acute crisis is hardly an acceptable policy recommendation. And to complicate the issue further, it's also important to note that in some cases aid has actually helped develop a consensus in favor of market reforms. For example, in Poland in 1989 the promise of foreign aid as something that the reform team could deliver was critical to the election of that team and the undertaking of market reform.

Both the timing and the role of aid flows in the implementation of policy reforms is still being widely debated. But what we clearly do know is that financial aid to countries where there is no consensus at all in favor of reform has a negative impact.

STOPPING THE FLOW OF INEFFECTIVE AID

How and why has so much aid continued to flow under such conditions? Conditionality, which is how aid is appropriated for the most part, is usually applied "ex ante," that is, borrowing countries must meet certain conditions to be eligible for a loan and then must continue to meet those conditions along the way as aid is disbursed. But despite a marked increase in conditional lending in the past decade, and also an increase in the number of conditions on each loan, conditionality has not been particularly effective in attaining borrower compliance. The higher number of conditions actually seems to decrease borrower ownership of reforms. It creates a vicious cycle: weak compliance with conditions prompts donors to impose more conditions, increased conditions make it yet harder for the recipient to comply, thus increasing the incentive not to comply, and so on. On the donor side, meanwhile, the incentive structure rewards continued lending rather than halting financial flows in response to breaches in compliance. Ultimately multilateral institutions are lending institutions, and they must lend to remain operational. It's their raison d'être. So the average loan officer at the World Bank or the Interamerican Development Bank has a lot more incentives to disburse loans on time than to enforce strict compliance among recipients of those loans.

As a result, many countries continue to receive loans even though they have bad records at both compliance and policy reform. It's increasingly evident, at least to those who observe it closely, that we have to move to more selective lending, with less focus on detailed conditions and more focus on building overall agreement on a policy package. At the very least we really have to stop lending to countries with major slippage on conditions.

While the shift to more selective lending makes intuitive sense, it also entails substantial risk. For example, withdrawing funds, particularly from many poor countries in Africa, may well spur the adoption of policy reforms in some, but in others it will cause performance to deteriorate even further, and at a relatively high human cost. At the least, one would need to maintain humanitarian and technical assistance. There could also be other costs to lending more selectively. A lot of the lending that takes place now is undertaken to enable debtor countries to pay back loans. For example, when heavily indebted countries default on loans, somebody is going to have to pay the cost. So a shift to selective lending must be taken with care, and while budget cutters would like to see it as a way of saving money, in the short term a shift toward more selective and more effective lending would actually increase costs.

THE CHICKEN OR THE EGG?

The final question is whether policies or initial conditions determine a country's economic performance. One school of thought is that poor countries perform badly on the macroeconomic front because of their weak initial conditions: a very poor country's performance is almost predetermined regardless of the level of aid. But some recent research refutes this view. Jeffrey Sachs and Andrew Warner of Harvard University did a study of the effects of policy as against those of initial economic conditions on economic performance. Using a sample of more than 100 countries, they found that countries that follow standard, market-oriented policies, and in particular maintain open trading regimes, have an overwhelming tendency to grow faster and converge with wealthier countries, regardless of initial conditions. Indeed, they had trouble finding a single case where a poor country

> Uncertainty about foreign aid effectiveness, uncomfortable enough at any time, is particularly worrisome when the foreign affairs budget is under fire.

that protected property rights and maintained economic openness did not grow. Very few of the countries that pursued poor policies, meanwhile, grew at equivalent rates. One that did was China. In fact, one reason why China is growing is that half of its economy actually functions with the market policies that produce growth in all the other countries. In any event, we have increasing evidence besides the Sachs and Warner study that good policies produce growth performance and poor policies do not, and that initial conditions are not a predetermining factor.

We need to know more about how aid can better support the adoption of appropriate policies. We have a sense that the answer lies in a more selective aid strategy, but the debate over the appropriate timing and level of aid flows is unresolved. Such uncertainty about aid effectiveness, uncomfortable enough at any time, is particularly worrisome when the foreign affairs budget is under fire.

Bogotá Aid: To Fight Drugs or Rebels?

By DIANA JEAN SCHEMO and TIM GOLDEN

WASHINGTON—Concerned about the growing power of leftist rebels in Colombia, the Clinton Administration is expanding its support for Government forces fighting in the hemisphere's longest-running guerrilla war.

United States officials say the aid is aimed at stanching the flow of illegal drugs from Colombia, and will only go after the insurgents where they protect the production of heroin and cocaine. The officials say they have no intention of getting mired in Colombia's internal conflict.

Officials say more United States training and equipment are going to shore up basic deficiencies in the tactics, mobility and firepower of the Colombian military, rather than for operations directed at the drug trade. Faced with a string of rebel victories, including a devastating ambush of Colombian troops in March, American generals have embarked on an ambitious effort to help reorganize the Colombian Army.

According to senior American officials, the Clinton Administration has also been considering options that officials said include additional military training, providing more sophisticated helicopters and matériel, and creating a high-tech intelligence center that would be run by American officials on Colombian soil.

The limits of American involvement in Colombia are still largely set by the constraints on military, intelligence and foreign-aid spending in the aftermath of the cold war. Compared with the billions of dollars poured into Central America during the 1980's, the hundred million or so that the United States now spends annually on Colombia remains relatively modest.

Yet Administration officials have begun to describe Colombia as another grave strategic risk. If the rebels and the drug traffickers bond more closely, the officials warn, both could become greater threats to the region. Colombia's troubles could spill across its borders toward the Venezuelan oil fields, America's chief source of imported petroleum, or into Panama, home to the vital Panama Canal.

Colombia's stability, they contend, is a responsibility from which the United States cannot run.

"This is not a one-night stand," said the commander of United States military forces in Latin America and the Caribbean, Gen. Charles E. Wilhelm. "This is a marriage for life."

Such admonitions come at an especially delicate political moment in Colombia, where a new President will be chosen in a run-off election on June 21.

While Washington's concerns about the country have risen in the last year, Colombian leaders were cutting their military spending and suggesting a new willingness to negotiate with the insurgents. Business groups are pressing for peace talks with the rebels, and last month thousands of Colombians rallied against the violence. Both the candidates who emerged from the first round of presidential elections on Sunday have said they would make new efforts to reach a settlement.

The evolving United States policy is also the subject of a growing debate, one almost as sharp in the Administration as outside it.

At one end are officials who cannot consider the Colombia plans without seeing Central American ghosts. They point to cases in which more than a dozen Colombian Army units given anti-drug training by the United States were later linked to serious human rights violations in the fight against the rebels.

At the other end are officials who believe that even the most ambitious policy proposals are inadequate, and that whatever the final Administration plan, political sensitivities will insure that it falls well short of Colombia's needs.

"We're afraid to use the 'I' word," said an official who is influential in the Colombia policy's design. "We should be able to say with a straight face, and without feeling like we have to go to confession, that there is an insurgency problem in Colombia that threatens the stability of the country."

More quietly, other voices in the Government are challenging important arguments at the source of Washington's alarm.

For instance, Administration officials have argued that a boom in the cultivation of coca in southern Colombia has brought the guerrillas a dangerous windfall. They say the rebels, by in effect renting their forces to protect those who grow coca and refine cocaine, have been able to pay for new recruits, better weapons and more aggressive strikes against the Government.

But intelligence officials have said that there is scant evidence of a major change in the insurgents' relationship with the traffickers, and that the impact of Colombia's coca boom on the availability of drugs in the United States is probably not great.

Background
From 1990, Aid Rose To Highest in Region

Since the end of the cold war and the waning of civil conflicts elsewhere, Colombia has emerged as the largest recipient of United States military assistance in the hemisphere.

The aid began to rise in 1990, with the Bush Administration's "Andean strategy," a five-year, $2.2 billion plan to try to stop the cocaine plague at its source. American officials believed that with global security threats shifting after the Soviet Union's demise, soldiers and intelligence agents could find a worthy new adversary in the bosses of Colombia's cocaine trade. And as such efforts gathered momentum in the early 1990's, they focused largely on the bosses themselves.

The expanding American role also coincided with a turn in the region's oldest guerrilla war.

Starting in 1990, several guerrilla groups agreed finally to lay down their arms. Some 7,000 more, mostly of the Revolutionary Armed Forces of Colombia (known by its initials in Spanish as the FARC) and the National Liberation Army, rejected the peace.

César Gaviria, then Colombia's President, attacked the holdouts as "deranged fanatics who have not read in the newspapers the sorry story of the end of Communist totalitarianism." Confident that history was on his side, he doubled military spending and increased the size and authority of the armed forces.

The guerrillas and their supporters also came under new assault by rightwing paramilitary forces that often worked with Government troops. In many cases, drug traffickers have also armed the paramilitaries against the insurgents; victims of the squads have included thousands of peasants and unionists, and hundreds of the rebels who gave up their guns.

By the mid-1990's, the remaining insurgents had dug in militarily and begun shoring up their finances. They stepped up ransom kidnappings, extortion and the protection of coca fields, jungle laboratories and clandestine airstrips.

The collaboration of some guerrilla fronts with the drug trade became the central plank of Government propaganda campaigns against them. It also began to emerge as a justification for the difficulty that officials had in keeping American aid from going to Colombian units that fought mainly against the insurgents.

"They're guarding drugs, they're moving drugs, they're growing drugs," the White House drug-policy director, Gen. Barry R. McCaffrey, said in 1996, adding that he was "uneasy" with American efforts to restrict Colombia's use of advanced UH-60 Blackhawk helicopters that it was then buying from the United States. "They're a narco-guerrilla force, period."

Beginning in 1994, Congress required the Clinton Administration to verify that United States military aid would go only to troops that "primarily" carried out anti-drug operations. In March 1996, the Administration reacted to evidence that President Ernesto Samper had taken money from Cali traffickers by cutting off almost all American aid to Colombia except what was designated to fight drugs, a step known as decertification.

Yet according to many officials, the Pentagon quietly distinguished itself by finding creative ways around the restrictions. "We refused to disengage," said a Pentagon official who spoke on the condition that he not be identified.

Over all, United States anti-drug aid granted to the Colombian military and police rose from $28.8 million in 1995 to at least $95.9 million in 1997, according to State Department figures. Military sales to Colombia jumped from $21.9 million to $75 million over the same period, largely on the Colombian Army's purchase of the six Blackhawks.

Unlike the early stages of the civil war in El Salvador, when whole battalions were flown to American bases for training, the Pentagon's efforts to overhaul Colombian forces have been conducted mainly in Colombia by small teams of special-forces trainers.

Administration officials describe the curriculum as heavy doses of anti-drug tactics with some counterterrorism, hostage-rescue and medical training thrown in. But military officials familiar with the programs said they concentrated less on weak links in the cocaine trade than on shortcomings of the Colombian Army.

One instance of the vague definition of "counter drug" preparation are the courses that United States Army trainers, drawn largely from the Seventh Special Forces Group at Fort Bragg, N.C., often lead in the Pentagon's Joint Combined Exchange Training.

Working with Colombian units, Defense Department officials said, the teams teach skills as basic as marksmanship and jungle maneuvers. At the end of a course, the trainers will typically plan a "graduation" attack on the guerrillas and then wait at their base while the students carry it out.

Another program, Joint Planning Assistance and Training, often involves the preparation of psychological operations against guerrillas and drug traffickers. Still other teams analyze military intelligence information to help the Colombian Army to plan its operations.

The Colombian military is also adding to its drug-interdiction role under a new, American-financed program to intercept the river boats that traffickers are increasingly using to move refining chemicals and partly refined coca paste into and around southern Colombia.

United States officials do not deny that many of the Colombian units they train go back into battle against the rebels. The Colombian Army has no forces dedicated entirely to fighting drugs, and the use of American-trained troops is left up to Colombian commanders.

By 1994, both the General Accounting Office and the Defense Department had found that the light-infantry skills taught in anti-drug training were easily adapted to fighting the rebels. When the United States Embassy in Bogotá reviewed the matter in 1994, officials said they discovered that anti-drug aid had gone to seven Colombian brigades and seven battalions that had been implicated in abuses or linked to right-wing paramilitary groups that had killed civilians.

Conditions subsequently imposed by Congress sought to cut off aid to any Colombian units involved in human rights violations. But some American-trained forces have continued to be accused of abuses, and Colombian prosecutors are investigating reports that a massacre of suspected rebel sympathizers last year around the southern village of Mapiripán was carried out by a paramilitary squad flown into the nearby military air field at San José del Guaviare, the staging base for American-supported anti-drug operations in the region.

Guerrillas
Rebels and Traffickers In a 'Coca Republic'

Administration officials say there is no sure way to keep the anti-drug battle from running into the guerrillas, given what has taken place over the last couple of years.

In response to an aggressive Government campaign against coca cultivation and transportation in neighboring Peru, the officials say, the traffickers have joined some major rebel fronts to create a virtual coca republic. Peasants who support the insurgents are planting more coca, FARC units are protecting more drug crops and labs, and Government authority has eroded across the region.

Military officials including General Wilhelm, the commander in chief of the United States Southern Command, said drug profits and other income are financing the guerrillas' purchase of more and perhaps more sophisticated communications equipment and weaponry. Intelligence officials said there was now some guerrilla activity in perhaps 700 of the country's 1,071 municipalities. And they estimate the insurgents' strength at as many as 18,000 combatants—10,000 or 11,000 in the FARC, 7,000 in the National Liberation Army—up from as few as 8,000 fighters six years ago.

"The threat is intensifying," General Wilhelm said in an interview. "We are seeing, basically, an undermining of governance at the grass-roots level. In a sense, I see a nation divided."

More vivid than the C.I.A.'s estimates of rising coca cultivation, however, have been American intelligence reports on the decrepitude of the Colombian Army.

In March, a force of 400 to 600 FARC guerrillas crushed an army unit near the southern village of Billar, killing 67 soldiers and capturing about 30 more, according to Pentagon figures. Officials said it was probably the most serious defeat of Government forces since the guerrillas took up arms in the mid-1960's, but only one of a series of battles they have lost in the last 18 months.

And military analysts said the Colombian Army was probably weaker than it looked. As many as half of its 121,000 soldiers are deployed to protect cities, oil pipelines and other fixed targets. A classified Defense Intelligence Agency assessment first reported by The Washington Post speculated that if current trends continued unchanged, the armed forces could be defeated within five years.

Congressional Republicans cast the situation in even more dire terms.

"The frightening possibilities of a narcostate just three hours by plane from Miami can no longer be dismissed," Representative Benjamin A. Gilman of New York, chairman of the House International Relations Committee, said at a recent hearing.

Prodded insistently by Mr. Gilman and a small group of other powerful Republican lawmakers, the Administration recently announced what the acting State Department anti-narcotics chief, R. Rand Beers, called "an ambitious new strategy to attack narcotics trafficking in Colombia on all fronts."

Mr. Beers, who helped draft the Andean strategy 10 years ago, said the State Department would start by adding at least $21 million to its anti-drug aid program to Colombia this year. In part, the money is to finance an expanded campaign to eradicate drug crops and destroy laboratories in the southern Colombian departments of Putumayo and Caquetá.

Because the rebels have such a strong presence in the region, officials say, those efforts will require greater help from the Colombian Army to the national police. But while American officials have often announced such collaboration in the past, it has consistently foundered on the rivalry that has long existed between the army and the police.

United States officials have already begun to work with the Colombian Air Force to intercept drug flights, and will provide night-vision equipment for its planes. Colombian military officials have also said they would like to buy armored attack MH-1 Cobra helicopters, and a Defense Department official predicted that the Pentagon would support such a request.

General Wilhelm, the Southern Command chief, insisted that the United States was not sending the sort of advisers that it once stationed with military units in countries like El Salvador and Vietnam. But he also made it plain that he himself has become a crucial adviser to the Colombian high command.

After the Colombian military commander, Gen. Manuel José Bonett, presented his own strategy plan in January, General Wilhelm and his aides began picking it apart, highlighting a number of problems. General Wilhelm has since worked with Colombian commanders on a sweeping overhaul of the armed forces, and ordered a "comprehensive" review of American training.

Additionally, a small group of Southern Command analysts have embarked on a side-by-side comparison of Colombia's experience to that of Peru, where leftist guerrillas protected coca growers for years.

With the waiver of Colombia's decertification penalties this spring, Administration officials said their basic question was not whether they would increase aid to Colombian forces, but how and by how much.

Policy
Will U.S. Be Drawn Into War on Rebels?

Administration officials have played down fears that the United States is being drawn deeper into Colombia's guerrilla war. The Pentagon recently said it would tighten safeguards meant to keep aid from going to forces involved in human rights abuses, and promised new scrutiny of the "joint combined exchange training" in particular.

Under an agreement signed in August, Colombian military units can receive American support only after their rosters have been screened to determine that they do not harbor troops known to have violated human rights with impunity. Officials said only two batallions of the Colombian Army have qualified so far, and both of those have had to be assembled from other forces.

Another key condition cited by United States Embassy officials is that American aid can be used only in a designated region of Colombia where the ties between drug producers and guerrillas are held to be so close that any rebel unit could be fairly considered the traffickers' ally.

There was no question that the definition of the zone was broad: "the box," as it was described by American diplomats, encompassed almost the southern half of the country. Yet officials said the area was not big enough for the Pentagon, which has quietly refused to acknowledge its limits.

"In terms of geography, the use of the resources, I'm personally not aware of any restrictions," General Wilhelm said.

So far, Administration policies on Colombia have received nothing like the scrutiny given United States policies for Central American in the 1980's, and aid conditions have often been only loosely applied.

ADDING IT UP
U.S. Backing
The United States support for Colombia's military and police operations shot up last year.

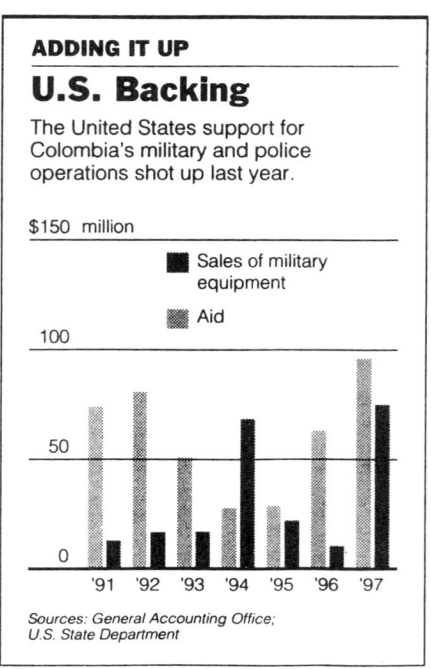

[Bar chart showing Sales of military equipment and Aid from '91 to '97, with values ranging from 0 to $150 million]

Sources: General Accounting Office; U.S. State Department
The New York Times

For instance, the Colombian military was required to pledge in writing that it would use the six Blackhawk helicopters it bought in 1996 largely for anti-drug operations with the national police. But American officials said they knew of no such operations since the helicopters arrived in early 1997. The Administration has since been fighting Congressional demands that it give three more Blackhawks directly to the police.

Some policy analysts question the new alarm about Colombia because they say the drug threat is overblown. The quality of Colombian-grown coca is so low, they argue, that it cannot offset the declines in cultivation in Peru.

Intelligence analysts also raise questions about the rebel-trafficker alliance that has been at the core of the policy makers' concern.

According to a 1996 report by intelligence and law-enforcement agencies, the rebels' ties to the drug trade are extensive. But a declassified summary of the report says that while guerrilla fronts sell protection "in virtually all departments where traffickers operate," only a few rebel fronts "probably are involved more directly in localized, small-scale drug cultivation and processing."

Officials said there was a consensus among the United States intelligence agencies that the insurgents' role in the drug trade had not grown or changed substantially since the report was issued.

A FARC spokesman who uses the alias Leonardo García contended that the rebels did not protect coca fields to make money so much as to defend peasants with whom they are allied.

"The idea is simply to label us as delinquents, to reject us as people with a political struggle," the spokesman said in an interview in New York. "It's a way to legitimize a military intervention."

There is little question that the evolving United States policy has focused less on the close relationship that Colombian traffickers have with many right-wing paramilitary groups. The problem of such apparent partisanship, critics of the policy argue, is that it may get in the way of the settlement that United States officials say they would like to help bring about.

After the kidnappings of several American citizens by the guerrillas, Washington refused to deal with the insurgents at all. And while the rebels recently announced their willingness to negotiate with a new President, they have also threatened to attack American military personnel.

Although Colombian history has demonstrated that it is easier to talk peace than to produce it, political pressure for an end to the war clearly has grown. "We're talking about land reform, about dealing with oil policy, about constitutional reforms," said the head of the Government's peace commission, Daniel García Peña. "Today, people understand that these social and political questions the guerrillas raised have to be put on the table."

Unit 7

Unit Selections

The Use of Military Power
31. **Inventing Threats,** Carl Conetta and Charles Knight
32. **Responding to Terrorism,** David Tucker

Arms Control
33. **Paring Down the Arsenal,** Frank von Hippel
34. **The New Arms Race: Light Weapons and International Security,** Michael T. Klare

Key Points to Consider

❖ List the five most serious national security threats that could face the United States in the next 5 years. How likely is each to happen? How prepared is the United States military for dealing with each of them?

❖ Does arms control have a future? Has arms control contributed to making the United States more secure, or has it weakened U.S. security?

❖ How should we think about nuclear weapons in the post–cold war world? What is their purpose? Who should they be targeted against? What dangers must we guard against?

❖ How should the United States protect itself from terrorist attacks?

DUSHKIN ONLINE Links — www.dushkin.com/online/

25. **The Commission on Global Governance**
    http://www.cgg.ch/
26. **Counter-Terrorism Page**
    http://counterterrorism.com/
27. **Federation of American Scientists (FAS)**
    http://www.fas.org/
28. **Human Rights Web**
    http://www.hrweb.org/
29. **U.S. Arms Control and Disarmament Agency (ACDA)**
    http://www.acda.gov/

These sites are annotated on pages 4 and 5.

U.S. Post–Cold War Military Strategy

During the height of the cold war American defense planners often thought in terms of needing a two-and-a-half war capacity: the simultaneous ability to fight major wars in Europe and Asia plus a smaller conflict elsewhere. The principal protagonists in this drama were well known: the Soviet Union, China, and their developing world allies. The stakes were also clear. Communism represented a global threat to American political democracy and economic prosperity. It was a conflict in which both sides publicly proclaimed that there could be but one winner. The means for deterring and fighting such challenges included strategic, tactical, and battlefield nuclear weapons; large numbers of conventional forces; alliance systems; arms transfers; and the development of a guerrilla war capability.

The political-military landscape of the post–cold war world presents defense strategists with a far different set of challenges than did that of the cold war. However, the extent to which the new international order requires rethinking the basic premises and assumptions that produced American cold war military strategy is only now beginning to be fully realized. The influence of cold war thinking and traditional American national security concerns was very much in evidence in the Pentagon's Defense Planning Guidance Report of 1992, which described seven different paths to war that might be traveled by the end of the decade. They included an Iraqi invasion of Kuwait and Saudi Arabia, a Russian invasion of Lithuania, a North Korean attack on South Korea, coups in Panama and the Philippines, and the reemergence of a hostile superpower. For each of these paths, the Pentagon study identified a U.S. response force and projected the amount of time it would take U.S. (and allied) forces to secure a military victory.

Absent from the Pentagon's list was any reference to war emerging from conditions in Africa, Eastern Europe, Central Asia, the Indian subcontinent, or Latin America. Yet, these are the areas (Bosnia, Somalia, Rwanda, Haiti, Cuba) where calls for the use of American force have been heard or where U.S. forces have actually found themselves pressed into service. Moreover, the manner in which they have been used bears little resemblance to that anticipated by cold war military planners.

Change is present, however. Military planners now speak of a two-war capacity by which they mean the ability to conduct two Bosnia and Somalia operations simultaneously. The summer of 1994 also saw "peace maneuvers" held at the Joint Readiness Training Center at Fort Polk where infantry troops undertook a large-scale field exercise designed to resemble a real-life peace enforcement operation. Even with this new sensitivity to the altered conditions under which U.S. military forces will be placed into combat, the "hows" and "whys" that will govern this process will continue to provoke controversy.

However, one thing has become abundantly clear: the use of military force will be very much a part of the post–cold war international system. Between them, the Bush and Clinton administrations have sent American troops abroad more often than occurred during the combined presidencies of Richard Nixon, Gerald Ford, Jimmy Carter, and Ronald Reagan. The first set of essays in this unit examines the range of conflict situations that will confront American forces abroad and some of the key issues in formulating military strategy.

Carl Conetta and Charles Knight, in "Inventing Threats," urge caution in planning for and carrying out military undertakings. They assert that in this new era of uncertainty Pentagon planners have moved from threat-based planning to capability-based planning and in the process "let their imaginations run riot."

A military undertaking at the opposite end of the spectrum, terrorism and nuclear deterrence, is the subject of the next essay. David Tucker, in "Responding to Terrorism," reviews and critiques the different policies that the United States has used to combat terrorism and concludes by presenting his own recommendation.

With changes in the nature of the military threats confronting the United States has come a change in the arms control agenda. The old arms control agenda was dominated by a concern for reducing the size of U.S. and Soviet nuclear inventories. A much broader agenda exists today and it is one with many more players.

Two readings contribute to our understanding of the arms-control issues now confronting the international community. Focusing on the very existence of nuclear weapons, Frank von Hippel calls for taking U.S. missiles off high-alert status and making deep cuts in U.S. nuclear stockpiles. Then, Michael Klare speaks to a new phenomenon in world politics in his report, "The New Arms Race: Light Weapons and International Security." No longer does the transfer of large-scale and sophisticated weapons represent the sole conventional weapons arms-control problems. The growth of ethnic conflict has created situations where the transfer of small and light weapons now has the potential for altering regional balances of power.

Inventing threats

By Carl Conetta & Charles Knight

With real enemies not menacing enough, defense planners have learned to let their imaginations run riot.

IT WAS A REMARKABLE ADMISSION FOR a chairman of the Joint Chiefs: "I'm running out of demons. I'm down to Kim Il Sung and Castro."

The context for Gen. Colin Powell's 1991 remarks to Congress was the dissolution of the Warsaw Pact and America's recent victory in the Gulf War. When the Soviet Union collapsed soon after, an article in *Aerospace Daily*, a leading defense industry newsletter, recalled Powell's remarks and predicted: "Pentagon Budget Headed for $150 Billion—Half Current Level—By 1996."

But what a difference a few years can make. When he unveiled the "Quadrennial Defense Review" last May, Defense Secretary William Cohen warned that "new threats and dangers, harder to define and more difficult to track, have gathered on the horizon." Contrary to *Aerospace Daily*'s forecast, Secretary Cohen sees keeping the Pentagon budget at $250 billion or slightly more—about 77 percent of the 1991 level.

Breaking with reality

The quadrennial review seeks to lead the United States into the next century with a defense budget only 23 percent lower than the average for the Cold War period of 1976–90. Despite Secretary Cohen's warning, however, there is no profusion of actual threats to justify this course. The preservation of high levels of spending instead reflects a novel way of thinking and talking about military requirements.

Beginning with efforts at the Rand Corporation during the late 1980s, the focus of defense planners has shifted from "the clear and present danger" of Soviet power to the intractable problem of "uncertainty." Along with this shift has come a new type of Pentagon partisan—the "uncertainty hawk."

The uncertainty hawks forsake "threat-based" planning for new methods variously called "adaptive," "capability-based," or "scenario-based" planning. These methods seek to release planning from the "tyranny of scenario plausibility," as Rand analyst James Winnefeld puts it.[1] Any hypothetical danger that seems remotely "possible" is deemed worthy of attention. In this approach, the concrete assessment of interests, adversaries, and trends matters less than does the unfettered exercise of "worst case" thinking.

A fixation on uncertainty colors all of the major post–Cold War policy blueprints—the quadrennial review, the 1993 "Bottom Up Review," and even the independent National Defense Panel report, "Transforming Defense," which was issued in December. Lost in these documents, however, is any real appreciation of America's profound post–Cold War security windfall.

Puzzling evidence

No nation even approximates America's current combination of size, stability, economic vitality, military prowess, and geographic insulation. The strength of America's allies further reinforces its substantial security margin.

The countries of the Organization for Economic Cooperation and Development—the "West"—now account for three-quarters of the world's economic activity. And these states, along with other long-time American allies, account for 72 percent of world military spending. In contrast, current and potential adversary states—including Russia and China—account for 18 percent.

Another measure: Despite its absolute reduction in military spending, the U.S. share of worldwide military spending increased from 27.5 to 32 percent between 1986 and 1995. In 1986, the United States spent only two-thirds as much on defense as did "potential threat states" (the Warsaw Pact states, China, Cuba, Iran, Iraq, North Korea, Libya, Syria, and Vietnam). In 1995, it spent 76 percent more than the group.

Western dominance is also reflected in the arms trade. The U.S. share of the arms export market grew from 22

Carl Conetta and Charles Knight are co-directors of the Project on Defense Alternatives at the Commonwealth Institute in Cambridge, Massachusetts. Project analyses are on the Web (http://www.comw.org/pda).

to 49 percent from 1986 to 1995. Meanwhile, the aggregate share of all NATO countries grew from 44 to 78 percent. This change occurred in the context of a 55 percent contraction in the market. Thus, not only has the general diffusion of military power slowed dramatically, it has come substantially under the control of the United States and its allies.

But recent official Defense Department analyses miss both the forest and the trees. With the collapse of Soviet power and the return of U.S. defense spending to pre-Reagan levels, threat assessment has taken a great leap backward. The 1993 Bottom Up Review set the post–Cold War standard, promoting the image of regional "rogues" wielding huge arsenals of armored vehicles and combat aircraft.

But all tanks are not equal, as the Gulf War demonstrated. Quality makes a difference. Consider North Korea, which is invariably held up as a potential foe. A simple "bean count" of the North Korean arsenal adds up to almost 4,000 tanks and more than 700 combat aircraft.

However, a 1995 study by the Brookings Institution, which used a Pentagon methodology that takes quality into account, cut the challenge down to size. It showed the North Korean military as possessing the equivalent of less than 4.5 U.S. heavy divisions and 2.5 fighter wings—about 1,500 tanks and 250 fighters. And even this calculation overlooked America's war-winning advantages in troop quality; logistics; and communications, intelligence, and information systems.

Twilight of the rogues

Rather than redress the shortcomings of the Bottom Up Review, last year's quadrennial review compounds them. Notably, it fails to revise the estimated strengths of regional foes, despite their having suffered four years of decline.

In contrast, the National Defense University's "Strategic Assessment 1997," which is not an official document, observes that the Korean situation was "significantly different at the end of 1996 than it was in 1993." Surveying the poor state of the armed forces and economies of both North Korea and Iraq, the assessment concludes that the United States most likely will face "declining military challenges in both areas, especially in Korea."

Turning to Iran, the other *bête noire* of U.S. planners, the assessment similarly finds that Iran's conventional forces "on the whole are not improving" and their "ability to conquer ground is deteriorating." The Iranian military, the assessment suggests, has not recovered from the Iran-Iraq war, nor has the Iranian economy recovered from the 1979 revolution. Economic stagnation and sanctions together have held Iran's planned $10 billion military modernization program to less than 40 percent of its goals.

The concurrent decline of North Korean, Iraqi, and Iranian power is not merely fortuitous. Stripped of superpower patronage, these nations stand exposed to global trends that disfavor rigid and narrow economies. The military ascent of these states, and others like them, was dependent on a circumstance that no longer exists—the East-West Cold War.

The masque of uncertainty

Against the evidence—of a diminished and diminishing threat—uncertainty hawks describe the strategic environment as turbulent, allowing for few, if any, reliable forecasts.

"The real world defies prediction," says Rand's Winnefeld.[2]

"The new strategic landscape is not rigid and linear, but highly fluid and unpredictable," says David Abshire, president of the Center of Strategic and International Studies.[3]

These visions of uncertainty and instability lie at the core of both the quadrennial review and Transforming Defense. Similarly, "Joint Vision 2010" frames its force development program with the observation that "accelerating rates of change will make the future environment more unpredictable and less stable."

The agnosticism of the uncertainty hawks extends not only to the specifics of discrete future events, such as the presidential succession in Russia or the role of the mullahs in Iran, but also to the general character and magnitude of possible threats. Uncertainty envelops events and trends equally. Even with regard to its future national interests, goes the prevailing mantra, the United States is groping in twilight, if

"Wild card" scenarios can gain credibility in the telling.

not in the dark.

"Uncertainty is a dominating characteristic of the landscape," wrote Paul Davis, editor of a 1994 compendium of Rand Corporation planning studies, "New Challenges for Defense Planning." "Most striking is the fact that we do not even know who or what will constitute the most serious future threat."

The new planning methods supposedly tame uncertainty by varying assumptions about America's future national interests, the identity and number of possible threats, the character and magnitude of these threats, how fast they could develop, and how quickly the United States could respond. The result is a vast array of hypothetical scenarios that serve to define requirements.

Winnefeld argues that in addition to breaking free from plausibility, planners must consider "discontinuous scenarios . . . in which there is no plausible audit trail or storyline from current events."[4]

Among the "non-standard" scenarios that Rand analysts favor are defending the Ukraine or the Baltics against Russia, civil wars in Russia and Algeria, a variety of wars with China, contention with Germany, and wars aligning Iraq and Syria against Turkey, and Iraq and Iran against Saudi Arabia.

Along these lines, the quadrennial review uses unnamed "wild card" scenarios to help define requirements. Although it describes the scenarios as individually improbable, the review asserts that, given the whole set, there is a better than even chance that one or more will occur.

Of course, to prepare for "one or

more" wild cards, the United States would have to hedge against the whole pack. One of the Pentagon's wild cards may be a scenario involving war in 2015 with China and North Korea—the Navy recently used that scenario to test the cost-effectiveness of its planned replacement for today's cruisers and destroyers.

Playing with wild cards

Simulations—including nonstandard ones—can aid planning. But to what end? And to what effect? Exploring "wild cards" to identify warning signs or to define limits is one thing. Using them to establish force structure or modernization requirements is quite another.

Conflict scenarios, both wild and tame, can gain more credibility in the telling than they deserve. Cognitive researcher Massimo Piattelli-Palmarini calls this the "Othello Effect," referring to the trail of plausible but false suppositions that led Othello to murder his wife, Desdemona.

We have seen the Othello Effect writ large in the development of the two-war concept, the principal driver of U.S. defense policy since the end of the Cold War. The "need" to retain the ability to fight and quickly win two near-simultaneous major regional wars has kept defense spending high, and will continue to do so in the future.

Although both the 1993 and 1997 defense reviews link the two-war requirement to Korean and Persian Gulf scenarios, these were also described as merely illustrative. Officially, the two-war requirement is generic. As the quadrennial review puts it: "We can never know with certainty when or where the next major theater war will occur," or "who our next adversary will be."

The issue, however, is not the ability of the United States to predict events, but its willingness to clarify and weigh interests—at least when it comes to sending hundreds of thousands of Americans to war.

Outside Europe, only the Korean peninsula and the Persian Gulf qualify as areas in which perceived U.S. interests, vulnerable allies, and significant threats might converge to compel *very* *large-scale* U.S. intervention. Recognizing this helps to contain both uncertainty and military requirements. Similarly, stricter attention to risk factors would put into perspective the supposed need for a capability to fight two wars *simultaneously*.

Since 1945 the United States has fought three major regional conflicts—one every 15 or 20 years. Whether the future holds more major wars or fewer, two-war contingencies will occur much less often than single-war contingencies—even if war in one region boosts the chances of an attack elsewhere.

A "second war capability" might cost America two-thirds as much as the first—perhaps $50 billion a year. But it would serve its full purpose only a fraction as often. Is it worth spending $3 trillion dollars over 60 years to meet a double war contingency that might occur only once, if at all?

Of course it would be worth spending that kind of money—if delaying a full response to the second war would entail a catastrophic loss for the nation. But what possible regional war scenario could fit that description? Where are the adversaries and interests of sufficient magnitude to justify the expense?

The quadrennial review holds tenaciously to the two-war strategy as originally conceived, but cracks are appearing elsewhere. The December 1997 National Defense Panel report, for instance, calls the entire concept into question. Noting that "the current posture minimizes near-term risk at a time when danger is [already] moderate to low," the panel suggests that the two-war construct "may have become a force-protection mechanism—a means of justifying the current force structure."

However, the panel does not hold out any hope of budget reductions. Instead, it seeks to redirect more resources toward preparing for the putative security challenges of the post-2010 world. These are gathered under the headings of "Asymmetric Warfare," "Military-Technical Revolution," and a "Re-emergent Peer Competitor."

Asymmetric warfare

Both 1997 defense reviews and Joint Vision 2010 suggest that the West's foes may turn to unconventional methods and weapons to sap or circumvent Western strengths. The quadrennial review, for instance, speaks of "increasingly sophisticated asymmetric challenges involving the use of chemical, biological, and possibly nuclear weapons; attacks against the information systems of our forces and national infrastructure" as well as insurgency, terrorism, and environmental destruction. Joint Vision 2010 asserts that "our most vexing future adversary may be one who can use rapid improvements in its military capabilities that provide asymmetrical counters to U.S. strengths, including information technologies."

The Vietnam War amply illustrated the potential of asymmetric warfare—and its limits as well. Although masters of unconventional war, the North Vietnamese and their Viet Cong allies were dependent for success on the shield and support of a superpower—the Soviet Union—as well as neighboring China. Outside similar circumstances, the potential of asymmetric methods is limited.

In the post-Soviet era, few if any "non-peer" nations would plan or attempt a major military confrontation with the United States, although they might blunder into it, as Iraq did in 1990. Still, none can afford to set aside the funds needed to indulge dare-the-superpower fantasies, even by asymmetric means. Primarily, what will shape the armed forces of regional powers and developing nations in the coming decades will be local challenges such as old-fashioned cross-border threats and internal insurgencies.

The real core of the asymmetric warfare threat involves the spread of cheap ballistic missiles and weapons of mass destruction. This poses a real, but well-defined potential threat—mostly to U.S. regional operations. Compared to former Soviet capabilities, the threat is quite limited. And all of the recent defense reviews implicity acknowledge this by recommending that only a small part of U.S. military forces and investment be devoted specifically to meeting this challenge.

To find a more sophisticated and comprehensive threat, scenario writers must work backwards from perceived Western vulnerabilities. "What would it take to defeat the United States?" is the question that animates their visions of asymmetric warfare. But the fact that we can spot theoretical "windows of vulnerability" does not mean that real-world foes could climb through them.

Technology diffusion

When uncertainty hawks turn to assess the danger of technology diffusion, the actual capabilities and efforts of potential foes matter less than formal access to the military marketplace. The National Defense Panel, for instance, sees the future as providing "all nations with more or less equal access to defense-related technologies."

Similarly, Joint Vision 2010 leaves no doubt about where this leads: "Wider access to advanced technology along with modern weaponry . . . and the requisite skills to maintain and employ it will increase the number of actors with sufficient military potential to upset existing regional balances of power."

What is lacking in these analyses is any general evidence of a rising curve of technological competence among our likely adversaries. Russell Travers, an analyst with the Defense Intelligence Agency, surveyed the modernization efforts of U.S. allies and adversaries alike in a Spring 1997 *Washington Quarterly* article, concluding that the idea that America is in danger of losing its technological superiority "does not hold up." Similarly, in a 1994 *Foreign Affairs* article, Ethan Kapstein of Harvard University's Olin Institute wrote that "by the early twenty-first century, the United States will be the sole producer of the world's most advanced weaponry." This is because "rising costs and declining defense budgets are putting pressure on the world's inefficient defense producers, and most of them are collapsing under the strain."

The plain fact is that all but a handful of nations lack the capacity to build, buy, integrate, support, and effectively use cutting-edge military systems in significant quantities. Nonetheless, the use of formal "market access" models to gauge the diffusion problem treats anyone's technology as though it were everyone's. Thus, every advance in American capabilities motivates the next. This suggests a continuous, solitary arms race in which the United States labors to outdistance its own shadow. In the end, technical feasibility alone defines requirements.

As with asymmetric warfare, the real core of the diffusion threat is the potential proliferation of medium-range missiles and weapons of mass destruction. The prospect of any more intensive technological competition than this hinges on the emergence of a major new rival to the United States.

The threat with no name

The quadrennial review sees the rise of a peer competitor as improbable before 2015. However, like the Bottom Up Review before it, it hedges against an earlier-than-expected arrival. To help decide near-term policy, it relies on simulations of war in 2014 with what might be called a "half-way peer"—a regional great power with armed forces significantly larger and more capable than those of Iraq, Iran, or North Korea.

The plausibility of this scenario depends on its details, which the review typically neglects to provide. Who is this threat? Why are we fighting it? What capabilities have planners given it? Even setting these questions aside, fighting simulated contests 17 years in advance begs the issue of how best to prepare for challenges that do not exist today and may not exist tomorrow.

The regional great powers and peer competitors that currently enthrall planners are only hypothetical constructs. Separating hypothesis from reality would be a process of emergence. Superpowers do not take shape easily or quickly. Their advent takes time and involves an extraordinary convergence of circumstances and trends—political, economic, geographical, and military. Tracking these provides a way to gauge the real danger of peer emergence.

Meeting the challenge of a peer rival, should one begin to gestate, would involve a race between its emergence and the ability of the United States to reconstitute sufficient additional military power. Given its incomparable military-industrial base, the United States would enjoy a unique advantage in any such competition. Today's huge gap between the United States and any potential rival defines America's strategic reaction time—its margin of safety.

But not for uncertainty hawks. They argue that the historical example of Nazi Germany's rapid ascent makes a reconstitution strategy untenable. But today's armed forces take much longer to develop than those of the 1930s.

> **The quadrennial review imagines a war in 2014 with an unidentified "half-way peer."**

Combat vehicle and aircraft development, for instance, takes three to five times as long.

And even in the 1930s, for that matter, major threats did not spring up full grown. By 1928 Germany's manufacturing output was already 50 percent of the combined total of France, Great Britain, and Russia. Its per capita output was much higher. By 1935 Germany was leading the world in military spending.

The prime candidates for future peer rival status are Russia and China. A dozen years of dedicated investment might resuscitate a significant portion of the Russian armed forces. But the emphasis is on the "might." Russia's military is in ruins. And, Russia would have to rehabilitate its economy and governing structures before it could begin to rebuild its military strength.

The Chinese "threat" is even more iffy. If China's economy holds out, it might in 30 years be able to mount a Soviet-style challenge. Meanwhile, China is just beginning to inject 1980s technology into select portions of its armed forces. The National Defense University's "Strategic Assessment 1997" surmises that China's military in 1996 was "probably two decades away from challenging or holding its own against a modern military force." Paul Goodwin of the National War College puts "the window for China becoming one of the world's major military powers ... at somewhere between 2020 and 2050."

Surveying the prospects worldwide, Russell Travers, the Defense Intelligence Agency analyst, concludes that "no military or technical peer competitor to the United States is on the horizon for at least a couple of decades."[5]

Certain force

Uncertainty has breathed new life into declining and hypothetical threats. And current policy prescribes that the U.S. military do more than simply respond or prepare to respond to these threats. The quadrennial review proposes an expanded peacetime role for the Pentagon in shaping the strategic environment. "Environment shaping" is meant to encompass all the diffuse ways, apart from crisis response, that the U.S. military might protect and promote U.S. interests. Key to environment shaping are overseas presence, military assistance programs, and military-to-military contacts.

An important environment-shaping goal for the Pentagon is to discourage military competition with America and stem the emergence of hostile regional hegemons. As the quadrennial review sees it, the United States can stop difficult relationships from evolving into military contests by projecting a sense of overwhelming and unbeatable American power. And it can stem arms races by winning them in advance.

Of course, this assumes that countries will not view such preemptory moves as reason enough to gear up their own military efforts. Strategic Assessment 1997 warns that this type of toughest-kid-on-the-block dissuasion is a "two-edged sword" because it may "lead others to believe that their interests are at risk, in which case they may decide they have no choice other than the use of force."

Current U.S. defense policy embraces a uniquely high standard for defense sufficiency: the maintenance of U.S. military superiority over all current and potential rivals. As Defense Secretary Cohen states, with remarkable hyperbole: "Without such superiority, our ability to exert global leadership and to create international conditions conducive to the achievement of our national goals would be in doubt."

Tunnel vision

There is no escape from uncertainty, but there is relief from uncertainty hysteria. It begins with recognizing that instability has boundaries—just as turbulence in physical systems has discernible onset points and parameters. The turbulence of a river, for instance, corresponds to flow and to the contours of the river's bed and banks. It occurs in patches and not randomly.

Despite uncertainty, statements of probability matter. They indicate the weight of the evidence—or whether there is any evidence at all. Uncertainty hawks would flood our concern with a horde of dangers that pass their permissive test of "non-zero probability."

In so doing they establish an impossible standard of defense sufficiency: absolute and certain military security. Given finite resources and competing ends, something less will have to do. Strategic wisdom begins with the setting of priorities—and priorities demand strict attention to what appears likely and what does not.

The world may be less certain and less stable today than during the Cold War, but it also involves less risk for America. Risk is composed of equal parts probability and utility—chances and stakes.

With the end of global superpower contention, America's stake in most of the world's varied conflicts has diminished. So has the magnitude of the military threats to American interests. This permits a sharper distinction between interests and compelling interests; turbulence and relevant turbulence; uncertainties and critical uncertainties. And these distinctions will pay dividends whenever the country turns to consider large-scale military endeavors, commitments, and investments.

U.S. defense policy documents speak of military threats, however uncertain. But they fail to deal with the opportunity cost of continuing high defense expenditures. In a world in which economic issues have displaced military issues as the central focus of global competition, the failure to take a hard look at opportunity costs is critical.

A recent Rand Corporation paper argued against reduced defense spending on the basis that "the U.S. defense burden is now quite low by historical standards."[6] Defense Secretary Cohen likewise accentuates the post–Cold War decline in the proportion of gross national product that America devotes to defense.

But it is a peculiar parochialism that compares today's defense investment rate with that of the Reagan era while ignoring comparisons between the United States and its economic competitors. The United States continues to invest far more of its national product in defense than its allies, far more than the world average, and far more than its chief economic competitors. U.S. defense policy is oblivious to the strategic opportunity costs of high levels of military spending. And it is this lapse that gives license to the speculative methods and overweening goals of the uncertainty hawks.

In disregarding the requirements and consequences of increased global economic competition, present policy makes an unacknowledged bet about the future. The Soviet Union is gone and no comparable military challenge to the West exists, except as a distant possibility. Nonetheless, say the hawks, the American prospect depends as much as ever—if not more so—on the specifically military aspects of strength. Of this, the uncertainty hawks are certain.

1. James Winnefeld, *The Post–Cold War Sizing Debate: Paradigms, Metaphors, and Disconnects* (Santa Monica: Rand, 1992) p. viii.
2. Ibid, p. 5.
3. David Abshire, "Toward an Agile Strategy," *Washington Quarterly*, Spring 1996, p. 43.
4. Winnefeld, p. 15.
5. Russell Travers, "A Strategic Breathing Space," *Washington Quarterly*, Spring 1997, p. 107.
6. Paul K. Davis, et al., "Adaptiveness in National Defense: The Basis of a New Framework," Rand Issue Paper, August 1996.

David Tucker

Responding to Terrorism

Terrorism is back. Over the years, it has waxed and waned. Having reached high points in the early and late 1970s and again in the mid-1980s, and a low point in the late 1980s and early 1990s, it is now again on an upswing. Domestic terrorism—the bombings of the World Trade Center in New York and the Federal Building in Oklahoma City—caused a significant loss of life. Fear of international terrorism has shadowed our involvement in Bosnia, restricting our scope of activities. A poison gas attack in the Tokyo subway in 1995 highlighted what many fear is the growing willingness of terrorists to use weapons of mass destruction, while reminding us of our own vulnerability to such attacks. Two bombings at U.S. military facilities in Saudi Arabia in 1995 and 1996 took the lives of 24 Americans, strained our relations with the Saudis, called into question our ability to maintain our presence in this vital area, and, as we implemented additional security measures, added significantly to the cost of this presence. Terrorism has undermined, if not destroyed, a major U.S. foreign policy initiative, the Middle East peace process. Globally, U.S. casualties from terrorism have increased in the mid-1990s. The resurgence of terrorism and fears for the future recently led Secretary of Defense William Cohen to list terrorism as one of his principal concerns.[1]

David Tucker is on the staff of the assistant secretary of defense for special operations and low-intensity conflict and is the author most recently of *Skirmishes at the Edge of Empire: The United States and International Terrorism* (Praeger, 1997).

As attacks on Americans and the attention paid them have increased, officials have reportedly conducted the same debates about how to respond to terrorism that their predecessors had 10 years ago, when terrorism was last at a high point. Once again, they have debated the relative merits of preemptive attacks, covert action, economic sanctions, military retaliation, and diplomacy, and whether to target the states that sponsor terrorist attacks or the organizations and individuals that carry them out—all of this, apparently, with little or no reference to our nearly 25-year experience combating terrorism.[2] But this experience should not be ignored. If we are to handle terrorism effectively in the future, at whatever level it threatens us, we should learn from what we have done before. Not only will doing this improve our ability to deal with terrorism, it will also tell us something about how we must operate in the post-Cold War world.

How the United States Has Responded to Terrorism

Over the years, the United States has combated terrorism in nine ways. It has negotiated international legal conventions, implemented defensive measures, addressed the causes of terrorism, followed a policy of making no concessions to terrorists' demands, imposed economic sanctions, retaliated militarily, prosecuted suspected terrorists (in some cases, following extradition or rendition from another country or seizure overseas), preempted terrorist attacks, and disrupted terrorist organizations. Today, "no concessions," prosecution, and economic sanctions remain the principal weapons we employ against terrorism, but all three present problems.[3] We will begin to develop wisdom in combating terrorism only when we can recognize these problems.

OPTION 1: THE POLICY OF NO CONCESSIONS

Policymakers use as their principal argument to support the policy of no concessions the belief that paying ransom or making other concessions only encourages more terrorism. Moreover, for fear of granting terrorists standing in the international community or among their peers, some analysts argue that a policy of no concessions should exclude even talking with terrorists. Former president Ronald Reagan, for example, announced that although his administration would honor the terms of the agreement Jimmy Carter's administration reached with Iran during the 1979 hostage crisis, it would not have negotiated with the Iranians in the first place. However strictly they interpret it, those who support a policy of no concessions do so for the same reason: If we make concessions, they say, the terrorists win and will only demand more, while other groups will follow their example and pick on the nationals of any government that gives in.

> Terrorists do not necessarily make demands because they want them met.

But terrorists do not necessarily make demands because they want them met, and terrorist groups do not necessarily have the same fundamental motivations and modus operandi; hence they may not respond to external stimuli in the same ways. Some terrorists benefit from violent acts even if their targets do not yield to their demands. Rather than immediate concessions, terrorists may seek publicity or the destruction of a society's sense of security and order. The Tupac Amaru seizure of the Japanese ambassador's residence in Lima appears to have been a case where the terrorists acted not only to force the government to meet demands but also to gain recognition and public standing following a period when they had lost both. That terrorists do not need to have demands met explains in part why we see terrorist acts like the World Trade Center bombing, in which demands do not play a central role.

In fact, conceding to terrorists may have no direct correlation with the level of violence. British firmness during the seizure of the Iranian embassy in London in 1980 and U.S. firmness following the kidnaping of Brig. Gen. James Dozier in Italy 1981 did not prevent the subsequent kidnaping of Britons and Americans in Lebanon. Nor did publicity concerning Washington's effort to trade arms for hostages with Iran in the mid-1980's lead to an increase in terrorist attacks or hostage-taking. Again, when the Colombian government—which earlier had taken a hard line with terrorists and responded forcibly to terrorist attacks—made concessions to terrorists in the early 1980s, terrorism began to decrease. Indeed, studies have concluded that refusing to make concessions may not limit terrorism, despite what proponents of "no concessions" claim.[4]

Less effective in combating terrorism than its proponents claim, "no concessions" is also less relevant than it was when first articulated as a policy in the 1970s. Then, terrorism constituted part of struggles for so-called national liberation; Palestinian terrorism was the archetype. Negotiating with terrorists in these cases undermined the legitimacy of governments the United States wanted to protect. Therefore, we rightly resisted negotiating. Now, however, states sponsor terrorism directly. The United States works with or makes deals with these state sponsors, because we could not secure our regional or more general interests otherwise. Our relations with Iraq when we hoped to make it a counter to Iran or with Syria during the ongoing Middle East negotiations exemplify the degree to which we will deal with a state sponsor of terrorism if doing so serves our interests.

> The United States should not adopt a rigid policy of no concessions.

For several reasons, then, the United States should not adopt a rigid policy of no concessions. It may not work in every case and is less relevant in fighting modern-day terrorism. Besides, making concessions may even help us catch a terrorist: The *Washington Post* and *New York Times* conceded to the Unabomber's demand to publish his 35,000-word manifesto, because federal officials thought that doing so might lead to a suspect; according to media reports, it did. As a practical matter, therefore, policymakers will make exceptions—and concessions—when they have good reasons to do so. We should not worry that this will make us look weak. A flexible policy to which we can adhere consistently will work better and make us look stronger than a rigid policy we consistently violate.

OPTION 2: PROSECUTION

Washington has always used prosecution as the principal response to terrorist acts committed in the United States. For several reasons, it has come increasingly to rely on the same response in dealing with terrorist acts committed against Americans or their property outside the United States. Those who have worked to combat terrorism generally agree that apprehending terrorists outside the United States deters terrorism or makes it more difficult for terrorists to carry out their plans, primarily because it complicates their travel. They must be careful where they set foot and what kind of documentation they use—and as international terrorists require mobility to work, this significantly disrupts their activities.

Further, prosecuting specific acts, such as killing, hijacking, or hostage taking, rather than focusing on the contentious political issues that surround these acts, removes an impediment to interstate cooperation. In addition, Washington's counterterrorism actions have greater credibility when the government bases its claims about a terrorist act on the exacting standards of U.S. criminal procedure and on evidence that can be used in a public judicial process rather than on intelligence that we cannot make public without compromising sources and methods. Finally, we may have no other available response than to arrest individual terrorists and bring them to trial if the connection between the terrorists and their sponsors does not suffice to allow us to retaliate against the latter.

As an example of successful prosecution, one may note the case of Pan Am Flight 103, destroyed in a midair explosion over Lockerbie, Scotland, in 1988. After a three-year investigation, the U.S. and British governments indicted two Libyans for the bombing. The two governments, with the help of France—whose airliner, UTA 772, Libyans bombed over Niger in 1989—then persuaded the United Nations (UN) Security Council to endorse a series of demands on Libya based on the indictments. When Libya failed to meet these UN demands, the United States and Great Britain persuaded the Security Council to impose sanctions on Libya. Although this legal process has unfolded slowly, it has kept pressure on Libya since 1991. During this time, as far as we can tell and apparently in response to legal pressure and sanctions, Libya has ceased to sponsor international terrorist attacks. It continues to support terrorist groups, attacks Libyan dissidents, and retains its capacity to commit other terrorist acts, but the legal process so far has effectively countered Libyan terrorism directed at the United States and its allies.

The judicial approach has led to arrests and prosecutions in other cases as well. In 1996, after Pakistan turned over Ramzi Yousef to the United States, a federal court in New York City convicted him, as the man behind the 1993 bombing of the World Trade Center in New York, of a conspiracy to bomb U.S. passenger planes in East Asia. After the FBI seized Omar Mohammed Rezaq in Nigeria, a U.S. district court convicted him of air piracy in connection with the hijacking of an Egyptian airlines flight in 1985 that resulted in the death of a U.S. citizen and the injury of two others. An Asian country turned over Tsutomu Shirosaki to the United States for trial in connection with a mortar attack on a U.S. embassy in 1986. In 1997, the FBI arrested Mir Aimal Kansi in Pakistan on charges that he murdered two Central Intelligence Agency (CIA) employees outside the agency's headquarters in 1993.

Despite the general enthusiasm for prosecuting terrorists, supporters of the judicial response admit its limitations. The United States can conduct foreign criminal investigations only with the cooperation of the governments involved. Exercising extraterritorial legal authority without permission would likely damage our relations with other countries, and it could also weaken the international cooperation necessary to combat terrorism. Finally, in some cases our powerful forensic abilities may be useless. Had the bomb aboard Pan Am Flight 103 exploded while the plane was over deep ocean, authorities might have faced insuperable challenges to investigating the crime scene. The difficulties investigating the explosion aboard TWA flight 800 when its pieces fell into waters off Long Island, New York, highlight this problem.

Although proponents of the judicial approach present these political and practical restrictions as only minor limitations, this approach is less effective than its supporters tend to acknowledge. To avoid political disputes over what may or may not be legitimate uses of force for political reasons, prosecution focuses our attention on individual terrorists and thus does not affect the traditional core of the terrorist threat: state sponsorship. Moreover, the effectiveness of the sanctions against Libya in the Pan Am 103 case resulted not from a judicial process, but from a political process at the United Nations and in foreign capitals that got UN members to agree to act against Libya—a political process that has not always worked to U.S. advantage in other cases. Washington found it difficult to get international agreement to impose sanctions against Syria in 1986–1987, for example, and the administration faced constant pressure, even inside the government, to lift them. For similar reasons, the UN has hesitated to impose meaningful sanctions on Sudan for its support of terrorism.[5] The judicial process, then, provides limited leverage against terrorism and depends largely on an international political process that it does little to shape.

Furthermore, the judicial approach can prove misleading. First, by emphasizing the criminality of terrorism, it may make us less able to respond flexibly—some might say cynically—to the irreducible political core of terrorism. Second, in adopting the judicial approach, we set the burden of proof for overseas action as high as that for domestic action, an impractical standard that will hinder our counterterrorism activities abroad. Proponents of the judicial response claim that we can, in effect, pick and choose when and where to use the standard, but given our attachment to the rule of law, the domestic judicial standard may become the only standard. Where it cannot be applied—in cases where, for example, the forensic evidence is inconclusive—we may come to believe that we have no justification for action.

This problem has a long history. Even before the legal response became so important in our counterterrorism efforts, we faced political pressure to find a "smoking gun" before responding forcibly to a terrorist attack. The Reagan administration, for example, sought such evidence before U.S. forces launched the raid on Libya. With increasing reliance on the judicial approach, this attitude may become even more pronounced. For example, while the Clinton administration deliberated its response to the Iraqi assassination attempt on former President Bush, the *Washington Post* reported that

> intelligence analysis... [based on circumstantial evidence] had been considered adequate proof of complicity in previous U.S. policy deliberations, but officials said senior Clinton administration policymakers—a group dominated by lawyers—indicated from the outset they wanted to act only on the basis of evidence that would be sufficient to produce a courtroom conviction.[6]

According to another press account, President Clinton asked the Federal Bureau of Investigation (FBI) and the attorney general to take the lead in investigating the alleged assassination attempt, involving the State Department and the National Security Council (NSC) only in the very final stages of the decision-making process.[7] A similar attitude seems to prevail in the case of possible Iranian involvement in the bombings of U.S. military bases in Saudi Arabia. This makes the emphasis on prosecution a dangerous double-edged sword. If detailed forensic investigation gives credibility to U.S. government responses to terrorist acts, [t]hen the absence of such an investigation or its inconclusive results will detract from this credibility and may make officials hesitant to act, thus restricting our scope of international action.

The judicial approach is a double-edged sword for another reason: It establishes a precedent we may not want other nations to follow. The Iranian death sentence against novelist Salman Rushdie, for example, is an application of Iranian law outside its borders, similar to the application of our counterterrorism laws outside ours. Some will object that there is no moral equivalence between the United States applying the law to terrorists and Iran condemning Rushdie for exercising his right to free speech. Indeed, any right-thinking democrat rejects such an equivalence. But this only highlights the problem with applying a country's laws overseas: If we assert our right to do this, we can deny the right of other nations to do so only by arguing that their laws are inferior to ours—or even illegitimate. Inevitably, by making this case we will have to insist on moral and political distinctions between nations that, for the sake of diminishing the causes of war, have been excluded for the most part from legitimate international discourse for more than 300 years. This can hardly enhance our security.

OPTION 3: ECONOMIC SANCTIONS

"No concessions" and prosecution therefore prove problematic and less effective methods of responding to terrorism than the U.S. government claims. But economic sanctions—a government's decision deliberately to curtail or cease customary economic or financial relations so as to coerce another government—is *less* problematic and *more* effective as a response to terrorism than generally assumed.

In 1973, the United States used economic sanctions for the first time, to punish Libya for sponsoring international terrorism. Since then, in combination with Libya's own economic mismanagement and corruption, the array of U.S.- and UN-imposed sanctions has seriously weakened Muammar Qadaffi's regime, even though the sanctions have not touched the core of Libya's economy: its ability to export oil. The sanctions have produced this effect, moreover, at relatively little cost to the United States. Likewise, economic sanctions helped to change Syria's behavior. The United States last imposed economic sanctions on Syria in 1986 following a particularly vicious terrorist attempt. Since then, according to the State Department, Syria has not sponsored any terrorist attacks, although it continues to provide safe-haven and training facilities for terrorists.

Of course, economic sanctions alone cannot explain this change in Syria's behavior. The collapse of the Soviet Union and changes in Middle East politics have also played important roles. But for a country like Syria, with a weak economy and little in the way of valuable resources, sanctions—especially multilateral ones such as those imposed in 1986—can inflict serious economic damage. In the view of diplomats who have dealt with the Syrians on terrorism, sanctions had a significant influence in stopping Syrian-sponsored attacks. And even in Iran, sanctions have had an effect, impairing Tehran's ability to get the long-term financing its oil and natural gas industry needs.[8]

Imposing economic sanctions places fewer moral, political, and, often, economic costs on the United States than using military force would, while producing better results than diplomatic démarches alone. But sanctions are far from an ideal policy tool. They are more effective if imposed multilaterally, but the time it takes to organize such a sanctions regime can allow the targeted country to adjust to the impending sanctions, weakening their effect. Unilateral U.S. sanctions will likely become increasingly less effective as global economic integration increases and the U.S. economy becomes a smaller part of the world economy. Finally, sanctions are a blunt instrument; as we have seen in the cases of Iraq and Haiti, they may hurt only the little people and not their leaders, who are their real targets. This increases the difficulty of sustaining them over a long period of time.

> **Economic sanctions are more effective as a response to terrorism than is generally assumed.**

Reconsidering Other Methods

The limited effectiveness of the three methods the U.S. government currently considers most useful in fighting terrorism suggests that we look at the six others we have used to see what help they might offer. I will discuss the most oft-considered tactic, military force, at length, and then consider more briefly each of the other five: treaties and conventions, addressing the causes of terrorism, defensive measures, preempting terrorist attacks, and disrupting terrorist groups.

OPTION 4: MILITARY FORCE

On April 15, 1986, U.S. Air Force and Navy jets attacked targets in Libya as retribution for both the bombing of a Berlin discotheque on April 5 that killed 2 and injured 64 Americans, and other, earlier Libyan actions. This was the first use of military force by the United States to combat terrorism. Its primary purpose was to deter future acts of Libyan-sponsored terrorism against the United States. It was also intended to indicate to the world the intensity of U.S. resolve to deal with this kind of violence.

Generally speaking, the raid achieved its secondary more than its primary purpose. As far as we know, after an initial outburst of revenge attacks, Qadaffi did not sponsor an attack on Americans for roughly 12 months after the raid. Following this hiatus, and excluding a spate of anniversary attacks in 1988, five of which took place in April and one of which allegedly was the bombing of Pan Am Flight 103 in December, Libyan terrorist attacks against Americans returned to their typical level of one or two a year. Sanctions and political pressure following the investigation into the bombing of the Pan Am flight probably explain, at least in part, the absence of Libyan-sponsored attacks on Americans since 1990. The most telling statistic concerning the raid, however, is that Libyan-sponsored terrorist attacks killed and injured more Americans after the raid than before—*not* counting those killed in the Pan Am bombing.[9] If the Reagan administration launched the raid primarily to deter Qadaffi from killing Americans, it failed in that purpose.

The raid met more success in achieving its secondary purpose: proving U.S. resolve. According to diplomats in charge of our counterterrorism policy at the time, this proof of our seriousness got the attention of the Europeans and made them more willing to cooperate in efforts to combat terrorism by imposing sanctions on state sponsors (such as those imposed on Syria) and by expelling from European countries the "diplomats" from countries that supported terrorist activities, undoubtedly curtailing terrorist operations. According to records made public since the collapse of the Warsaw Pact, the raid also impressed the East Germans, who cited it in discussions with Palestinian terrorists when trying to persuade them to curtail their terrorist activities.[10] In these ways, the raid probably saved American lives and thus contributed indirectly to its primary purpose. Even so, the number of lives saved by the indirect effects of the raid do not likely outnumber those lost in the Pan Am bombing and other Libyan-sponsored terrorist operations launched after the raid.

On balance, then, our experience with Libya calls into question the utility of using military force to combat terrorism. Indeed, the economic and political pressure that Great Britain, the United States, and France could organize through the UN in response to the bombings of Pan Am Flight 103 and UTA Flight 772—rather than the U.S. military reprisal for the Berlin bombing—seems finally to have stopped Qadaffi's attacks on Americans.

Generally stated, using military force to combat terrorism will always involve an asymmetry of both force and opportunity between the United States and countries that sponsor terrorism. The activities of the United States and its citizens around the world present many more lucrative targets to terrorists than they or their sponsors present to us. More important, terrorists and their sponsors accept the killing of innocents, making them much less restrained than we are in the use of violence. Our military activity may kill innocents, as it did in the raid on Libya, but we do not deliberately target them.

Moreover, we place other constraints on our use of force. A raid on Libya's oil production capabilities would have been a devastating blow to Qadaffi, but the Reagan administration ruled out such an option in favor of attacks on targets associated with terrorism, since this would fit within the international legal understanding of self-defense. Finally, coercing good behavior—our objective when we combat terrorism—may require applying the coercion again and again, which the United States has difficulty doing, given our official and public attitudes toward the use of force. When Qadaffi launched his attacks on the second anniversary of the raid, for example, we did not respond with military force. In any violent confrontation outside of a conventional military engagement, then, we are likely to be at a disadvantage.

OPTION 5: NEGOTIATING TREATIES AND CONVENTIONS

Establishing international norms for dealing with terrorism helps to focus attention on terrorism and encourages like-minded countries to work together. It does not necessarily overcome political differences or the self-interest that guides national decision-making, however, which limits the utility of the resulting treaties and conventions. For example, in January 1994, the French prime minister cited his country's national interests while ignoring the Swiss government's request to extradite two suspected terrorists. Whenever the United States criticizes continued German contacts with Iran, which have included discussions between intelligence officials, the Germans defend these contacts by referring to Germany's economic interests.[11]

OPTION 6: ADDRESSING TERRORISM'S CAUSES

The U.S. government has sought to combat terrorism by addressing its socioeconomic and political roots. But no one has clearly proven what specifically causes terrorism. Both poverty and the unequal distribution of wealth, for example, often thought to cause terrorism, exist in areas free from political violence. Where poverty and terrorism coexist, economic growth might remove this cause of violence, but economic growth can also threaten traditional ways of life and thus *generate* terrorism; much of the fundamentalist religious rebellion around the world exemplifies this dynamic. Moreover, encouraging the establishment of democracy so that grievances may find peaceful expression does not necessarily decrease terrorism. The Soviet Union did not have a problem with terrorism, but Russia does, and Spain's terrorist problem also worsened as it democratized. Encouraging economic growth and democracy may help resolve some conflicts only to generate new ones or create new opportunities for the violent expression of old ones.

OPTION 7: DEFENDING AGAINST TERRORISM

For more than 25 years, the U.S. government has taken steps to make its personnel and facilities overseas harder targets for terrorists to hit. These defensive measures have had notable effects. By following proper procedures with appropriate seriousness, U.S. personnel overseas have made themselves and the facilities in which they work demonstrably more secure than they were before these programs began. In 1980, terrorists launched 177 attacks on U.S. diplomats, military personnel, and other U.S. government officials; in 1995, 10. Terrorists have not stopped targeting Americans, of course, and greater security measures for U.S. officials overseas has probably only deflected some attacks to easier targets, such as American businesspeople or other civilians, or compelled terrorists to devise more sophisticated or lethal means of attack. Still, it is a positive development that America now conducts its official business overseas with more security from terrorist attack than it once did. This success has come at a price, of course, in dollars and personnel resources, costs that will increase in response to the Saudi bombings, and the imposition of these costs constitutes some degree of success for terrorists and their sponsors.

OPTION 8: PREEMPTING TERRORISM

Whereas addressing the causes of terrorism works, if at all, only in the long term, a country can take short-term steps to stop, or preempt, a specific terrorist act. Americans often think of preemption in terms of lethal force or believe it to be a euphemism for assassination. But preempting a terrorist attack might require nothing more than warning another country that a terrorist group is planning to use its territory, or organizing a police raid that arrests suspects before they can carry out a terrorist attack.

More than any other method of combating terrorism, preemption requires specific, accurate, and timely intelligence. A warning to the wrong country or the arrest of the wrong suspects will not stop a terrorist attack. Accurate intelligence is even more important if a situation requires lethal force. We can apologize to another country for a false warning and free mistakenly arrested suspects, but we cannot raise the dead.

OPTION 9: DISRUPTING TERRORISTS

Whereas addressing terrorism's causes has only limited effectiveness and preemption has only limited application, disruption offers a middle ground. Disrupting terrorist activity means targeting a terrorist organization and taking measures not to stop a particular operation but to render all its activities more difficult and, eventually, to make the organization ineffective. Unlike addressing causes, disruption allows us to focus our resources on targeting a specific group. Unlike preemption, disruption does not require that we act before a specific attack takes place, and it thus allows for the gradual buildup of intelligence that permits accurate targeting. In the mid-1980s, the United States conducted a successful campaign to disrupt the Abu Nidal Organization (ANO), one of the most deadly terrorist groups. As reported in a series of newspaper articles, this campaign combined public diplomacy with diplomatic and intelligence initiatives to shut down ANO operations.

As with all the methods we have examined, disruption has its weaknesses. Like preemption, disruption depends critically on intelligence. And it tends to work best against well-developed organizations, like the ANO, that have a significant infrastructure. Groups that do not present such a target prove more immune to disruption.

How the United States Should Respond

As this survey suggests, we should not single out any one—or even three—of the methods we have used to combat terrorism as the most important. To some degree, all suffer from limited effectiveness and applicability, or both. For this reason, success has come when we have combined them and taken advantage of circumstances.

Libya's current restraint, for example, is the result of relentless diplomatic pressure, sanctions, public diplomacy, disrupting its terrorist operations, and direct and indirect military action (such as the raid in 1986 and support to Qadaffi's opponents in Chad). This campaign took advantage of such circumstances as falling oil prices (Qadaffi kept supporting terrorism as oil revenues declined but his support became more circumscribed and deprived him of money for other purposes), the disappearance of a powerful ally (the pre-Gorbachev Soviet Union), and the inefficiencies of Libya's domestic arrangements, which have prevented it from adapting well to external pressures.

Our success combining counterterrorism methods suggests in turn that we find additional ways to combine these methods. Carefully targeted sanctions combined with the discreet use of military force may prove more effective than our current tactic of using sanctions and force successively. If the trend toward more independent groups backed by wealthy individuals or religious sects continues, finding and prosecuting individuals will remain an important way to combat terrorism. But, under certain circumstances, we might usefully supplement this approach with disruptive techniques including sabotage, legal proceedings, and information welfare, to attack the assets of the individuals and sects that support terrorism. If the likelihood of terrorist use of weapons of mass destruction increases, we may become willing to accept measures currently deemed too risky.

Combining methods will not by itself increase our effectiveness against terrorism. We must employ these methods in a strategy that counters terrorism slowly but relentlessly. The horror and shock at a terrorist attack may encourage calls for immediate violent revenge, but this will seldom be an effective response: The asymmetry between the terrorists and their victims will always place us at a disadvantage in the use of violence. As a result, the United States should use conventional military force sparingly in combating terrorism, emphasizing instead public diplomacy, diplomatic and economic pressure, the discreet use of force, and, when possible, prosecution. Such an approach will prevent us getting involved in a tit-for-tat exchange that we will likely lose.

More generally still, our efforts against terrorism will be no more successful than our overall foreign policy and national security strategy. Those devoted to fighting terrorism sometimes forget that the purpose of combating terrorism is to enhance our security and that combating terrorism is only part of this broader effort, because terrorism is not the greatest threat we face. We should remember, especially as calls for stronger action against terrorism mount, that imposing sanctions, using military force, or snatching a terrorist from the streets of a foreign capital—any effort we make to combat terrorism—should be undertaken only if in striking a blow against terrorism it does not undermine our overall well-being.[12] In particular we must recall, as we contemplate how to respond to terrorism, that without the cooperation of our allies and other nations, we would have a much more difficult time combating terrorism, and preserving our security. Integrating counterterrorist efforts into our overall foreign policy and security strategy should also allow us to moderate our attachment both to the policy of no concessions and to an overly legalistic approach to combating terrorism.

Finally, this survey should encourage us. The different methods we use to combat terrorism did not develop all at once or arbitrarily. We have developed and adapted our methods as terrorism has changed. We should be able to do so as terrorism changes in the future.

This record should encourage us not only about our ability to combat terrorism in the post-Cold War world but also about our more general prospects in this world. We must now accommodate ourselves to a geopolitical situation that does not play to our strengths. For the time being, we have no grand reasons to go to war, and we confront few if any threats that the arsenal of democracy can overwhelm with decisive force—the two traditional U.S. ways of responding to threats. Nor as time passes will we have the economic or military weight to tip the balance of power in our favor singlehandedly. The threats and problems we confront with military resources diminishing and our weight in the world declining will likely be smaller and more difficult to assess and counter.

To prevent the slow but sure erosion of our security in this world, we will need patience, a willingness to accept partial and inconclusive results, an ability to absorb setbacks, and the determination to employ policies that take time. Maintaining favorable balances of power will require allies and thus an ability to accept compromise and ambiguity and a willingness to act for something less than the establishment of worldwide democracy. Because these new attitudes so starkly contrast with our past behavior, several authoritative commentators have suggested that the United States will have difficulty adapting and may not be able to do so.[13] Our campaign against international terrorism is at least somewhat reassuring in this regard, however, because for the past 25 years, under administrations of both parties, with only occasional lapses, we have fought terrorists and their sponsors using the modern equivalent of Roman methods of siege warfare, which one of these commentators argues we should emulate.[14] We have been patient, accepted inconclusive results, suffered setbacks, but struggled on. We have worked with allies, applied sanctions, practiced other economic forms of statecraft, undertaken slow but steady criminal investigations, engaged in diplomatic cajolery, gathered intelligence, and operated clandestinely. We have, in the case of terrorism, pursued our goals with the persistent application of diplomacy and force that the United States was supposed to be incapable of achieving. To the extent that the problems we now confront resemble terrorism—in its indirect, slow, but persistent method of attack—we can learn and draw some consolation from our history of combating it.

The views expressed here are the author's and not those of the Department of Defense or the U.S. government.

Notes

1. Patrick Pexton, "Cohen Focuses Sights on Terrorism," *Navy Times*, September 22, 1997, p. 4.
2. David B. Ottaway, "U.S. Considers Slugging It Out With International Terrorism," *Washington Post*, October 17, 1996, p. A25.
3. *Patterns of Global Terrorism: 1996* (Washington, D.C.: Department of State, 1997), p. iv.
4. Richard Clutterbuck, "Negotiating with Terrorists," *Terrorism and Political Violence* 4 (Winter 1990), p. 285; *The Impact of Government Behavior on Frequency, Type, and Targets of Terrorist Group Activity*, (McLean, Va.: Defense Systems, Inc., December 15, 1982), pp. 6–55, 56; Martha Crenshaw, "How Terrorism Declines," *Terrorism and Political Violence* 3 (Spring 1991), pp. 74, 79.
5. John M. Goshko, "UN Remains Reluctant to Impose Tough Sanctions on Sudan for Terrorist Links," *Washington Post*, November 24, 1996, p. A32.
6. R. Jeffrey Smith, "Iraqi Officer Recruited Suspects in Plot Against Bush, U.S. Says," *Washington Post*, July 1, 1993, p. A18.
7. "Commander for a Day," *Economist*, July 3, 1993, p. 25.
8. Thomas W. Lippman, "U.S. Economic Offensive Against Iran's Energy Industry Is Bearing Fruit," *Washington Post*, March 3, 1997, p. A8.
9. David Tucker, *Skirmishes at the Edge of Empire: The United States and International Terrorism* (Westport, Conn.: Praeger, 1997), p. 97.
10. "Stasi Assistance for PLO 'Terrorists' Alleged," *Die Welt*, April 16, 1991, p. 3; in *Foreign Broadcast Information Service, West Europe*, June 27, 1991, p. 29.
11. Sharon Waxman, "France's Release of Iranians Triggers Swiss Complaint," *Washington Post*, January 1, 1994, p. A15; Steve Vogel, "Allies Oppose Bonn's Iran Links," *Washington Post*, November 6, 1993, p. A18; "EU Nations' Envoys Going Back to Iran," *Washington Post*, April 30, 1997, p. 15.
12. As an example of increasing calls for a stronger response to terrorism, see David Morgan, "Gingrich Backs Preemptive Acts on Terror," *Philadelphia Inquirer*, August 21, 1966, p. 11.
13. Henry Kissinger, "We Live in an Age of Transition," *Daedalus* 124 (Summer 1995), p. 103; Samuel P. Huntington, "America's Changing Strategic Interests," *Survival* 33 (January–February 1991), p. 16; Edward Luttwak, "Toward Post-Heroic Warfare," *Foreign Affairs* 74 (May/June 1995), pp. 109–122.
14. Edward Luttwak, "Toward Post-Heroic Warfare," pp. 116–118.

PARING DOWN THE ARSENAL

By Frank von Hippel

It's time to pull missiles off hair-trigger alert and get on with deep cuts in nuclear stockpiles.

THE HELSINKI SUMMIT IN MARCH gave a much needed impulse—albeit a modest one—to the long-dormant nuclear arms reduction process. There had been no negotiations since the second Strategic Arms Reduction Treaty (START II) had been signed four years earlier. Although the treaty had been ratified by the U.S. Senate, it had not been ratified by the Russian Duma, where opposition was intense.

By the time the summit convened, it looked as if the treaty might simply unravel, the victim of lingering Cold War–era distrust. But President Boris Yeltsin said at the conclusion of the summit that enough progress had been made to "prepare grounds so that the Duma could positively look at ratifying START II."

That progress included a commitment by President Bill Clinton to begin negotiating a START III agreement after the Duma ratifies START II. The aim of START III, according to Clinton and Yeltsin, would be to reduce the ceiling on the number of deployed strategic warheads on each side to 2,000–2,500 by the end of the year 2007. In contrast, START II called for a limit of 3,500 deployed strategic warheads by 2003.

Frank von Hippel is a professor of public and international affairs at Princeton University. In 1993–94, he served as assistant director for national security in the White House Office of Science and Technology Policy.

The presidents also agreed to "explore possible measures relating to long-range nuclear sea-launched cruise missiles [SLCMs] and tactical nuclear systems." The U.S. military is concerned that Russia retains over 10,000 nuclear warheads while Russia's military is concerned about the remaining hundreds of U.S. bombs deployed in Europe and the lingering SLCM launch capabilities of U.S. attack submarines.

Clinton and Yeltsin also agreed to integrate into the START III process exchanges of information about *total* U.S. and Russian stockpiles of strategic warheads (deployed and nondeployed) and about the elimination of excess warheads. Confidence-building "transparency" arrangements, such as on-site inspections, also would be negotiated.

Finally, Clinton succeeded, after three and a half years of effort, in getting Yeltsin to agree to a dramatic loosening of the terms of the 1972 Anti-Ballistic Missile (ABM) Treaty. That frees the United States to continue to develop and produce mobile long-range land-, sea-, and air-based anti-missile systems for "theater defense." These systems can have virtually unlimited capabilities as long as they are not *tested* against strategic ballistic missiles and are not deployed against Russia's strategic missiles.

While Yeltsin and Clinton reaffirmed the "fundamental significance" of the ABM Treaty to strategic stability and the possibility of further reductions in strategic offensive arms, Yeltsin's decision to go along with U.S. theater missile defense plans may eventually impede future arms-reduction efforts. Analysts in Moscow will continue to point out that mobile U.S. theater defenses could be quickly redeployed as national defenses. Indeed, U.S. missile-defense enthusiasts have already proposed using the navy's upper-tier missile defense system for that purpose.

But if the ballistic-missile-defense problem can be contained, then deeper cuts and other steps to reduce the nuclear danger would be possible. Given the political will, it would be possible, over the course of the next 20 or 25 years, to get the U.S. and Russian nuclear arsenals down from about 10,000 warheads apiece to, say, 200 warheads apiece—and still preserve the principle of nuclear deterrence.

The ultimate objective should be the elimination of all nuclear weapons. But that is still beyond the horizon. Meanwhile, debate over the requirements of elimination should not be allowed to delay the deep reductions that must come first.

Russia's nightmares

At the Joint Summit press conference, Yeltsin, when asked whether the Duma would now ratify START II, responded: "I expect that the State Duma will make a decision based on my advice." This may be the case, but it is not certain.

To understand how the balance might be swayed in the Duma by the Helsinki agreements, it is useful to examine the way in which those agreements dealt with the four main concerns that lay behind the Duma's opposition:

■ **Start II limits were too high to allow Russia to maintain parity with the United States.** START II requires Russia to eliminate most of its land-based multiple-warhead missiles at a time when many of its ballistic missile submarines and bombers are reaching their design lifetimes. As a result, when the START II limits on deployed warheads would come into force at the end of 2003, Russia would probably be able to deploy fewer than 3,000 strategic warheads on its permitted strategic weapon systems. By the year 2010, it would probably be able to deploy fewer than 2,000.

The U.S. START III proposal deals with much of this problem—although the whole issue could have been avoided if President Bush had agreed to the 2,000 warheads proposed by President Yeltsin five years ago.

■ **The United States has a breakout advantage.** The U.S. Defense Department has deliberately structured its proposed START II reductions (in the words of its public report on the "Nuclear Posture Review") to preserve an "upload-hedge" option. That means the United States would be able to deploy twice as many warheads as permitted by START II "should political relations with Russia change for the worse [and/or] START I and START II not be fully implemented."

Both the United States and Russia have about 7,000 strategic warheads deployed today. But because of the very different impact of START II on the two forces, a rapid upload option would not be available to Russia.

The treaty requires Russia to eliminate about 280 land-based ballistic missiles carrying about 2,600 warheads. Because of obsolescence and lack of funds, Russia is also expected to retire 12 submarines and 68 bombers carrying about 1,600 warheads for a total reduction of about 4,200.

In contrast, START II requires the United States to eliminate only 50 MX missiles carrying 500 warheads. The United States also expects to retire four submarines carrying 768 warheads for a total of about 1,200. Most of the remaining U.S. reductions are to be accomplished by "downloading" 500 Minuteman III land-based missiles from three to one warhead each; downloading 336 Navy Trident II missiles from eight to five warheads each; and converting 95 B-1 bombers, which can carry 16 warheads each, to non-nuclear roles.

If the United States ever chose to abrogate START II and upload, it could redeploy stored warheads onto the previously downloaded Trident II and Minuteman III missiles as well as the B-1 bombers. As a result, in the year 2010, for instance, the number of U.S. deployed strategic warheads could still be built back up to about 7,000, while Russia would be able to field only about 1,600.

The impact of the Helsinki summit agreement on this concern will not be clear until the shape of the START III forces are negotiated. However, the proposal to exchange information on stored strategic warheads provides a possible handle on the upload problem.

■ **The United States might deploy a national ballistic-missile defense system.** The Republican congressional leadership continues to press for a commitment to deploy nationwide defenses against ballistic missiles by 2003. This would be done—if necessary—by using the "supreme national interests" escape clause in the ABM Treaty.

Although ballistic missile defense enthusiasts describe their idea as providing a "thin" defense against an accidental or unauthorized launch or against an attack from a rogue nation, many Russian analysts see it differently.

From a Russian perspective, it looks as if the United States could quickly upgrade a thin defense into a system that could serve as a shield from behind which the United States might launch a first strike in a crisis confrontation. Russian analysts also believe that the elimination of Russia's land-based multiple-warhead missiles under START II would make the U.S. missile defense task much easier. For now, the Clinton administration does not believe that there is adequate justification for deployment of a national missile defense. But the administration has agreed to develop hardware that could be deployed by 2003, if a go-decision were made by the year 2000.

On a parallel track, the administration is developing mobile long-range interceptor missiles and space-based sensors for "theater" missile defense. Domestic and Russian analysts alike note that such hardware could become part of a national defense.

As already noted, the Helsinki summit agreement sent a mixed message in response to concerns about the future of the ABM Treaty. Clinton pledged U.S. adherence to the treaty and Yeltsin dropped Russian objections to U.S. theater missile defense programs, which could provide the future wherewithal for a rapid breakout from the treaty.

• **NATO is expanding toward Russia.** Largely at the urging of the United States, NATO is expected to announce in July that it will admit Poland, Hungary and the Czech Republic. NATO's military expansion into the buffer area created by the voluntary Soviet withdrawal has created outrage in Russia across the political spectrum.

The North Atlantic Council announced in December 1996 that NATO members have "no intention, no plans, and no reason" to move its nuclear systems east. At the Helsinki summit, Clinton added, "nor do they foresee any future need to do so." He also agreed to include this language in a new agreement that would be signed by the leaders of all the NATO countries, as well as by Russia. And Clinton assured Yeltsin that NATO does not intend to build up forces permanently stationed in Eastern Europe. Indeed, NATO offered to renegotiate the Conventional Forces in Europe Treaty to formalize this commitment.

For now, these commitments will

help assuage Russian concerns about NATO's short-term expansion plans. In the future, these concerns are likely to focus principally on whether NATO will move to expand all the way up to Russia's border by admitting the Baltic States and perhaps even Ukraine.

Nuclear dangers

Many Western leaders, political and military, are still quietly exultant over having "won" the Cold War and are dismissive of Russia's security concerns. That's a mistake. If nuclear dangers are to be further reduced, Russia's concerns must be dealt with. The Helsinki summit was a good start. But it was not enough, by itself, to calm the waters in Moscow.

There is the danger that Russia—if not reassured by further actions and commitments that the West's intentions are benign, will attempt to deal with its concerns about the continuing high state of readiness of U.S. forces, conventional and nuclear, by attempting to maintain a large portion of its own deteriorating strategic forces on high alert. And Russia may attempt to deal with the abysmal state of its conventional military forces by retaining thousands of tactical nuclear weapons.

Such Russian responses would magnify two of the greatest dangers posed by Russia's deteriorating nuclear forces: the possibility of mistaken or unauthorized launch of strategic missiles, and of leakage of tactical nuclear weapons into the international black market.

A third threat, which will develop if the United States and Russia do not go much further in reducing their nuclear confrontation, will be to the nonproliferation regime. In 1995, in exchange for an agreement by the non-weapon states to an indefinite extension of the Nuclear Non-Proliferation Treaty (NPT), the United States and Russia (and the other weapon states) committed themselves to "systematic and progressive efforts to reduce nuclear weapons globally, with the ultimate goal of eliminating those weapons."

The NPT is the legitimating authority for international actions to stop clandestine nuclear programs such as those mounted by Iraq and North Korea. But if the nuclear powers—particularly the United States and Russia—ignore their NPT obligation to work toward nuclear disarmament, the treaty may become a dead letter.

The United States, which emerged from the Cold War as the only true superpower, must take the lead in launching new initiatives to reduce these dangers by achieving an agreement with Russia to quickly take most **nuclear weapons off alert [see "Dealerting"] and by negotiating additional deep cuts beyond START III.**

Finally, the United States should join China in adopting a no-first-use nuclear policy, and it should press Russia, Britain, and France to join in. That would go a long way toward strengthening the nuclear nonproliferation regime. After all, how can the role of nuclear weapons be de-emphasized elsewhere if the world's most powerful nation insists that *its* security requires it to reserve the option of using nuclear weapons first?

During the Cold War, the U.S. first-use policy was directed primarily at the Soviet Union, the assumption being that nuclear weapons might be needed to counter a massive Soviet conventional attack on Western Europe.

Today, the Soviet threat is gone. But U.S. think-tank warriors are endlessly creative. Now the possibility that a "rogue state" might use chemical or biological weapons is often cited as the principal justification for preserving a first-use option.

It would be much more supportive of the nonproliferation regime for the United States to push for universal adherence to the Chemical Weapons Convention, which it has signed but—as of early April—not ratified. Similarly, the United States ought to deal with the objections of its biotech industry to greatly strengthening verification provisions for the biological weapons ban.

Warhead control

If the United States and Russia are to move seriously toward deep reductions, they will also have to move toward greater openness regarding the numbers of *non-deployed* warheads; they will have to come to grips with tactical nuclear weapons; and they will have to hammer out some difficult verification issues.

Reserve warheads. No nuclear arms limitation agreement has ever limited nuclear warheads *per se*. The Strategic Arms Limitation Treaties (SALT I and II) and the Intermediate-Range Nuclear Forces Treaty limited launchers and delivery vehicles. START I and II, in addition, limited the numbers of *deployed* warheads and bombs.

As deployed forces become smaller, however, stored warheads become a greater concern. As previously noted, reserve warheads in the United States already worry Russia because of the large upload capacity of the planned U.S. START II forces. Similarly, the U.S. military frets over the very large stockpiles of tactical nuclear warheads that Russia still retains.

One reason for keeping a small number of warheads and bombs in reserve is to provide a source of spares (in case a problem develops with an individual warhead) and to provide samples for destructive examination for the effects of aging.

But a common argument for preserving a large number of bombs and warheads, as the United States plans to do, is to provide backups in case all the weapons of a given *type* develop a disabling defect. In a de-alerted posture, it would be unreasonably provocative, however, to maintain a large stockpile of reserve warheads in addition to the stockpile of de-alerted warheads that had been removed from their launchers.

If the de-alerted warheads included warheads of a different type that could be placed on the same launchers as the deployed warheads, they could serve as spares as well as a reserve for re-enlarging the deployed force, if needed.

The de-alerted warheads could be widely dispersed, so that they would not be tempting targets for a possible first strike. If the START Treaty could be amended to allow it, they might, for instance, be stored in former ICBM silos that had been partially filled with concrete so they were no longer deep enough to hold missiles.

With such arrangements, the United States and Russia could agree to dismantle all stored strategic warheads in

> ## The Deep Cuts Study Group
>
> Frank von Hippel's essay draws heavily—although it may differ in detail—from the preliminary findings of a study carried out by the Deep Cuts Study Group.
>
> The members of the group: Von Hippel and Harold Feiveson, Princeton University; Bruce Blair and Janne Nolan, the Brookings Institution; Jonathan Dean, the Union of Concerned Scientists; Steve Fetter, the University of Maryland; James Goodby, Stanford University; George Lewis and Theodore Postol, the Massachusetts Institute of Technology.

excess of treaty limits (2,000–2,500 for START III, for example) and place the recovered fissile material under international safeguards.

Tactical warheads. The United States is reducing its tactical nuclear arsenal to about 1,000 warheads. According to Robert S. Norris and William M. Arkin of the Natural Resources Defense Council, the tactical nuclear stockpile will consist of about 600 B61 bombs and about 350 sea-launched cruise missiles. (See the *Bulletin*'s "NRDC Nuclear Notebook, July/August 1996.)

Russia's approximately 18,000 remaining pre-1991 tactical nuclear warheads will have reached the end of their design lives by about 2003. Thereafter, the size of Russia's tactical nuclear stockpile will be determined by the amount of its post-1991 production.

There seems to be very little new Russian warhead production thus far, because the warhead assembly facilities have been busy dismantling the Cold War stockpile. That suggests that there is an opening for a U.S.-Russian agreement to limit their stockpiles of tactical nuclear weapons to lower levels—to 500 each, for example.

Better yet, why not eliminate them entirely? Reducing the number of U.S. tactical nuclear bombs now deployed in NATO countries to zero is said to be politically difficult because their presence symbolizes the U.S. commitment to defend its NATO allies from nuclear attack. In turn, that commitment is said to make it unnecessary for countries such as Germany to acquire their own nuclear deterrents.

And yet, the United States provides a nuclear guarantee to Japan without basing nuclear weapons there, and it continues to provide such a guarantee to South Korea, although it has withdrawn all nuclear weapons from that country.

A possible compromise would be to leave it up to the individual nuclear powers to decide on the mix between tactical and strategic warheads within a fixed limit. Under that arrangement, the price of keeping a tactical nuclear warhead would become the loss of a strategic warhead.

Verification. Presidents Clinton and Yeltsin have repeatedly agreed in joint summit statements on a desire to make their warhead stockpiles and reductions more "transparent." Their most detailed statement, issued after their May 1995 Moscow summit, affirmed "the desire . . . to exchange detailed information on aggregate stockpiles of nuclear warheads [and] stocks of fissile materials . . . on a regular basis" and "to negotiate . . . a cooperative arrangement for reciprocal monitoring of storage facilities of fissile materials removed from nuclear warheads and declared to be excess to national security requirements."

U.S. and Russian technical experts have conducted joint demonstrations of external radiation measurements that could be used to confirm that sealed containers hold stored plutonium objects of the approximate mass and size expected of "pits" extracted from dismantled nuclear warheads.

However, the implementation of this and other proposed transparency agreements awaits the conclusion of an "Agreement of Cooperation" on the bilateral protection of the classified data that would be revealed through such measurements.

Unfortunately, as Russia became increasingly disillusioned about its security partnership with the United States—and indeed public cooperation with the United States became a political liability for Russian officials—Moscow became unresponsive to U.S. proposals to complete the agreement. It is to be hoped—but not at all assured—that these negotiations will be revived after the Helsinki summit.

In their May 1995 "Joint Summit Statement," Clinton and Yeltsin also agreed on the principles of irreversibility of stockpile reductions: no new civilian nuclear material will be used for weapons and, once fissile material removed from nuclear warheads is declared excess, it will not again be used in weapons.

At the April 1996 summit of the Group of Seven Industrialized Nations in Moscow, the United States, Russia, Britain, and France joined in a pledge that such irreversibility would be made verifiable by "the placing of fissile material designated as not intended for defense purposes under IAEA [International Atomic Energy Agency] safeguards . . . as soon as it is practicable to do so."

The United States has already placed about 10 metric tons of highly enriched uranium and two tons of plutonium under IAEA safeguards at three Energy Department sites at Oak Ridge, Hanford, and Rocky Flats. However, the United States expects to maintain a very large stockpile of weapon-grade uranium for future use as fuel in U.S. and British naval-propulsion reactors.

If this naval-fuel stockpile were placed under IAEA safeguards, materials would have to be withdrawn from safeguards in the future—a bad precedent. This problem could be mitigated by a multilateral agreement that all new naval nuclear reactors would be fueled with non-weapons-usable uranium enriched to less than 20 percent uranium 235. (The U.S. Navy, however, is not enamored of that idea, because the reactors would need larger cores to achieve the same interval between refuelings.)

Another factor complicating the placing of fissile materials from excess weapons under IAEA safeguards is that these materials are mostly in the form of weapons components. The designs of these key components are considered secret by both the United States and Russia.

There has been some discussion among the United States, Russia, and the IAEA regarding the possibility of applying non-intrusive safeguards to these components, which would protect the secret information. However, such procedures would still reveal the average amounts of plutonium and highly enriched uranium in warheads—information that some U.S. weapons designers insist should be kept secret for nonproliferation reasons.

And in Russia, the Ministry of Atomic Energy reportedly considers the isotopic composition of its weapon-grade plutonium to be classified, although the United States does not classify such information.

If such obstacles cannot be overcome, excess fissile materials should be converted to standard ingots, cans of oxide, or other non-classified forms that could be placed under international safeguards. This should be done as soon as it can be assured that the processing will be done without any of the material being stolen.

Getting on with reductions

It now appears that START III negotiations will take place, and they will lead to an agreement that limits deployed strategic warheads to 2,000–2,500 each for the United States and Russia. While START III reductions are under way, the Deep Cuts Study Group, of which I am a member, believes the United States and Russia should reach a START IV agreement that would make deeper reductions to about 1,000 strategic and—at most—100 tactical warheads each, *with stored warheads and warhead components counted in the total.*

That would be a dramatic reduction indeed, considering that both sides seem to be planning to keep 10,000 or so *total* warheads, even though START II limits each of them to fewer than 3,500 *deployed* strategic warheads.

Before reductions to the 1,000-warhead level could be implemented, however, the remaining declared weapon states—Britain, France, and China—would have to be recruited into the disarmament process—at least to the extent of committing not to build up their nuclear arsenals and to exchanging declarations regarding the sizes of their warhead and fissile-material stockpiles.

A global ban on the production of fissile material for weapons and a global agreement to strictly limit stockpiles of weapons-usable fissile materials also would have to be achieved by this stage.

A fissile cutoff. A global ban on the production of fissile material for warheads would cap the size of the potential nuclear-warhead stockpiles of the declared and threshold weapon states, thereby preventing others from building up while the United States and Russia are reducing. All five declared nuclear weapon states have indicated their willingness to join in a fissile cutoff and have also indicated they are not currently producing fissile materials for weapons.

However, Israel and India are believed to still be building up their stockpiles of weapons plutonium, and India—supported by many of the non-weapon states—insists on linking the fissile cutoff to negotiations on "time-bound" nuclear disarmament. Pakistan (the third "threshold" state) wants a linkage to reductions to equal stockpiles. As a result, more than three years after the unanimous vote at the United Nations to pursue a fissile-materials-cutoff treaty, negotiations have not begun.

A possible compromise first step that would achieve the sought-for linkage between the production cutoff and disarmament would be for the threshold states to join the production moratorium on the condition that the weapons states continue their stockpile reductions.

It would probably be necessary to strengthen the credibility of the production-halt declarations with bilateral and multilateral transparency measures and the shutdown of facilities considered too sensitive for intrusive inspections.

Limitations on weapons-usable fissile materials. As nuclear-warhead arsenals become smaller, other stockpiles of weapons-usable materials will become matters of concern, even if they are under international safeguards. China is already worried that Japan could quickly convert its stockpile of IAEA-safeguarded civil plutonium into a large nuclear arsenal.

Much larger stockpiles of separated civil plutonium have accumulated elsewhere. France and Britain each have stockpiles at their commercial reprocessing plants of about 50 metric tons—the equivalent of about 10,000 nuclear warheads. Russia has accumulated about 30 tons at its commercial reprocessing plant. And India has a small but growing stockpile of separated civil plutonium.

Civilian use of plutonium increases the threat of nuclear theft as well as nuclear proliferation. Further plutonium separation should therefore be halted and excess civilian and weapons stocks disposed of.

That will be difficult to achieve, however, given the financial, career, and intellectual investments that have been made in the separation of plutonium and its recycle as nuclear fuel.

There is also another (but still not widely understood) factor that is even more important in sustaining the uneconomic activity of plutonium separation. Commercial spent fuel reprocessing continues largely because the nuclear utilities of some countries, notably Germany and Japan, use it to "export" their radioactive waste disposal problems. (In fact, they only delay the problem rather than solving it, because reprocessing contracts specify that the separated fission-product waste must eventually be returned to the country of origin.)

If the United States were to take the lead in establishing a set of international spent-fuel storage facilities, storage would be seen by many nuclear utilities as an attractive alternative to reprocessing.

Such an effort, however, would somehow have to overcome the inevitable environmental and safety objections that so far have blocked almost all efforts to site national spent-fuel storage facilities.

Deep cuts

In the third stage, reductions would have to become fully multilateral, with Britain, France, and China joining in the negotiations and verification of all warhead and fissile-material stockpiles.

If this were done, reductions to 200 warheads each for the United States, Russia, China, and Western Europe could be achieved by the year 2020. (This assumes that Britain and France would be willing to have their nuclear forces treated as a single West European force.)

A 200-weapon stockpile does not necessarily mean 200 *deployed* weapons, however. The Deep Cuts Study Group believes that each region would need only 10 to 20 deployed weapons; the remainder would be in storage. Ten survivable warheads would still be a terrifying deterrent. A single 450-kiloton Trident II warhead, for example, could destroy an urban area of 200 square kilometers—roughly the size of Washington or St. Louis.

We do not, however, endorse the idea of targeting urban populations—even though such a policy would be no more immoral than today's policy of targeting *thousands* of military targets with the full knowledge that tens of millions of civilians would die as a "collateral" effect.

There would be no need to target cities to have a strong deterrent. Any kind of nuclear retaliation would be devastating. For example, major military bases or key economic facilities such as refineries could be attacked in retaliation for a nuclear strike.

We also assume that, if the nuclear powers could agree on a plan involving reductions to such small numbers of strategic warheads, they could also agree to eliminate tactical nuclear weapons. Alternatively, tactical nuclear weapons could be included in the permitted 200-warhead forces.

Difficulties

The "threshold" nuclear states—Israel, India, and Pakistan—will have to be engaged at some point in the deep-reductions process. Otherwise, it will come to a halt.

As a start, the threshold states should join in a moratorium on fissile-material production and then a formal cutoff treaty. They should also put any nuclear-weapons-usable fissile material that they have produced for civilian purposes under IAEA safeguards. These measures would cap the potential sizes of their arsenals.

At a later stage, they could join in the reductions process by placing agreed amounts of their remaining stocks of unsafeguarded fissile material under international safeguards. Or, consistent with their current policies of keeping their nuclear deterrents undeployed—that is, "in the closet"—one or more of the threshold states might be willing to put all its nuclear materials in a national storage facility that was subject to international perimeter-portal monitoring to verify that the material was not removed.

The form of the material (which might even be weapons components) would not be subject to international inspection, and it would have to be understood that, in a crisis, the owning country would have both the power and the right to order the international monitors to depart.

As for the five declared nuclear powers, there are many uncertainties that could make an agreement on low numbers of weapons difficult. Consider, for instance, the huge quantities of fissile materials that were produced over the decades by the United States and the Soviet Union.

There have been considerable losses at various stages of the production process. As a result, the weapons states cannot even prove to *themselves* that ton-quantities of fissile material have not been hidden away. In February 1996, for example, the United States made public a complete accounting of its plutonium production and use and found that the cumulative "inventory difference... between the quantity of nuclear material held according to the accounting books and the quantity measured by a physical inventory... for the 50-year period from 1944 to 1994 is 2.8 tonnes."

These inventory differences were attributed to inaccurate predictive codes for production reactors; materials trapped in production facilities (in pipes, for instance); measurement uncertainties—especially for plutonium in difficult-to-assay waste—unmeasured losses in accidental spills; "recording, reporting, and rounding errors"; and so on. The Energy Department believes that there have been no thefts and that there are no hidden stockpiles. But it would be difficult to prove that to the satisfaction of another government suspicious about possible cheating.

Such concerns could be reduced if the United States and Russia—and later, all nuclear weapon and threshold states—launched (as first suggested four years ago by Steve Fetter of the University of Maryland) a joint "nuclear archaeology" project to reconstruct the production and disposition history of their nuclear materials, using all available records, interviews with key active and retired personnel, and physical measurements at production facilities.

In the end, however, reductions of the magnitudes proposed here may only be possible when political leaders realize that survivable weapons systems capable of launching just a few warheads are an adequate deterrent even against threats from states armed with much larger nuclear forces.

At the height of the Cold War, when the Soviet Union was threatening to cut off Berlin, a very small and not very survivable Russian force was more than adequate to deter U.S. nuclear planners from proposing a first strike to a desperate U.S. leadership.

For his 1983 book, the *Wizards of Armageddon*, Fred Kaplan interviewed participants in the U.S. nuclear planning process during the 1961 Berlin crisis. He learned that intelligence analyses indicated that the Soviet strategic forces were in "awful shape" in 1961—warheads had not been loaded onto missiles, bombers were not on alert, and almost all of the nuclear submarines were in port. The Soviet early-warning network was riddled with gaps, which would have made it difficult for the Soviets to detect a "less-than-massive U.S. bomber attack," especially if the bombers flew low.

That year, war over Berlin seemed possible, even likely, and White House and Pentagon officials searched for a way to stand firm while—in President Kennedy's words—avoiding "humiliation or holocaust." After all, writes Kaplan, if the Soviets went all out in capturing and defending Berlin with conventional forces, they would win. Berlin was an isolated enclave behind the "Iron Curtain" that divided Europe. If it came to war, the United States would have to use nuclear weapons.

The Pentagon prepared a detailed strike plan with information on the precise location of Soviet nuclear targets. The data were fed into a mathematical model, which indicated that a counterforce attack was feasible and could be carried out with high confidence.

Nevertheless, the study also indicated that a few Soviet bombs and missiles would survive. If the Soviets retaliated with nuclear weapons, two to three million Americans would die, under best-case assumptions. In the worst case, as many as 10 to 15 million would perish, along with many millions of Europeans. Writes Kaplan:

"If ever in the history of the nuclear arms race, before or since, one side had unquestionable superiority over the other, one side truly had the ability to devastate the other side's strategic forces, one side could execute the Rand counterforce/no-cities option with fairly high confidence, the autumn of 1961 was that time. Yet approaching the height of the gravest crisis that had faced the West since the onset of the Cold War, everyone said 'No.'"

What is needed

Technically, there is no absolute obstacle to the staged reductions proposed here. However, as demonstrated by the analysis of the history of the Pentagon's Nuclear Posture Review by Janne Nolan of the Brookings Institution, there will not be a deep-cuts policy as long as the development of the policy is left to the nuclear targeteers.

The failure of the Nuclear Posture Review should be contrasted with the high-level process in which President Bush, his national security adviser, the secretary of defense, and the chairman of the Joint Chiefs of Staff were personally involved in August and September 1991. That process quickly resulted in a decision to initiate a parallel U.S.-Soviet process to eliminate army nuclear weapons and to store or destroy all the nuclear weapons then on surface naval ships.

If the Clinton administration wants to remove U.S. and Russian missiles from their launch-on-warning postures and to initiate a deep cuts process, its national security team will have to engage these issues with similar intensity. Bill Clinton is said to hunger for a prominent place in the history books. No other issue presents a finer opportunity, either for him or for the world.

Article 34

> "Because of the global upsurge in ethnic and sectarian conflict, policymakers have become more attuned to the role played by [light] arms in sparking and sustaining low-level warfare and have begun to consider new constraints on trade in these munitions... Although heavy weapons sometimes play a role, most of the day-to-day fighting is performed by irregular forces armed only with rifles, grenades, machine guns, light mortars, and other 'man-portable' munitions."

The New Arms Race: Light Weapons and International Security

MICHAEL T. KLARE

For most of the past 50 years, analysts and policymakers have largely ignored the role of small arms and other light weapons in international security affairs, considering them too insignificant to have an impact on the global balance of power or the outcome of major conflicts. Nuclear weapons, ballistic missiles, and major conventional weapons (tanks, heavy artillery, jet planes) are assumed to be all that matter when calculating the strength of potential belligerents. As a result, international efforts to reduce global weapons stockpiles and to curb the trade in arms have been focused almost exclusively on major weapons systems. At no point since World War II have international policymakers met to consider curbs on trade in light weapons, or to restrict their production.

Recently, world leaders have begun to take a fresh interest in small arms and light weapons. Because of the global upsurge in ethnic and sectarian conflict, policymakers have become more attuned to the role played by such arms in sparking and sustaining low-level warfare, and have begun to consider new constraints on trade in these munitions. "I wish to concentrate on what might be called 'micro-disarmament,'" United Nations Secretary General Boutros Boutros-Ghali declared in January 1995. By that, he explained, "I mean practical disarmament in the context of the conflicts the United Nations is *actually dealing with*, and of the weapons, most of them light weapons, that are actually killing people in the hundreds of thousands" (emphasis added).

This focus on the conflicts the United Nations is "actually dealing with" represents a major shift in global priorities. During the cold war, most world leaders were understandably preoccupied with the potential threat of nuclear war or an East-West conflict in Europe. Today policymakers are more concerned about the immediate threat of ethnic and sectarian warfare. While such violence does not threaten world security in the same catastrophic manner as nuclear conflict or another major war in Europe, it could, if left unchecked, introduce severe instabilities into the international system.

This inevitably leads, as suggested by Boutros-Ghali, to a concern with small arms, land mines, and other light munitions; these are the weapons, he notes, that "are probably responsible for most of the deaths in current conflicts." This is true, for instance, of the conflicts in Afghanistan, Algeria, Angola, Bosnia, Burma, Burundi, Cambodia, Kashmir, Liberia, Rwanda, Somalia, Sri Lanka, Sudan, Tajikistan, and Zaire. Although heavy weapons sometimes play a role, most of the day-to-day fighting is performed by irregular forces armed only with rifles, grenades, machine guns, light mortars, and other "man-portable" munitions.

SMALL ARMS, GLOBAL PROBLEMS

The centrality of light weapons in contemporary warfare is especially evident in the conflicts in Liberia and Somalia. In Liberia, rival bands of guerrillas—armed, for the most part, with AK-47 assault rifles—have been fighting among themselves for

---

MICHAEL T. KLARE *is a professor of peace and world security studies at Hampshire College and director of the Five College Program in Peace and World Security Studies. He is the author of* Rogue States and Nuclear Outlaws: America's Search for a New Foreign Policy *(New York: Hill and Wang, 1995).*

> **Light Weapons in Worldwide Circulation**
>
> ASSAULT RIFLES:
> - Russian/Soviet AK-47 and its successors
> - U.S. M-16
> - German G3
> - Belgian FAL
> - Chinese Type 56 (a copy of the AK-47)
> - Israeli Galil (also a copy of the AK-47)
>
> MACHINE GUNS:
> - U.S. M-2 and M-60
> - Russian/Soviet RPK and DShK
> - German MG3
> - Belgian MAG
> - Chinese Type 67
>
> LIGHT ANTITANK WEAPONS:
> - U.S. M-20 and M-72 rocket launchers
> - U.S. Dragon and TOW antitank missiles
> - Russian/Soviet RPG-2 and RPG-7 rocket-propelled grenades (and Chinese variants, Types 56 and 69)
> - French-German MILAN antitank missiles
>
> LIGHT MORTARS:
> - Produced by many countries in a variety of calibers, including 60 mm, 81 mm, 107 mm, and 120 mm.
>
> ANTIPERSONNEL LAND MINES:
> - U.S. M-18A1 "Claymore"
> - Russian/Soviet PMN/PMN-2 & POMZ-2
> - Belgian PRB-409
> - Italian VS-50 and VS-69
> - Chinese Types 69 and 72
>
> SHOULDER-FIRED ANTI-AIRCRAFT MISSILES:
> - U.S. Stinger
> - Russian/Soviet SAM-7
> - British Blowpipe
> - Swedish RBS-70

control of the country, bringing commerce to a standstill and driving an estimated 2.3 million people from their homes and villages. In Somalia, lightly armed militias have been similarly engaged, ravaging the major cities, paralyzing rural agriculture, and at one point pushing millions to the brink of starvation. In both countries, UN-sponsored peacekeeping missions have proved unable to stop the fighting or disarm the major factions.

The widespread use of antipersonnel land mines (small explosive devices that detonate when stepped on or driven over) is a common feature of many of these conflicts. These munitions, which can cost as little as $10 apiece, are planted in roads, markets, pastures, and fields to hinder agriculture and otherwise disrupt normal life. An estimated 85 million to 110 million uncleared mines are thought to remain in the soil of some 60 nations, with the largest concentrations in Afghanistan, Angola, Cambodia, and the former Yugoslavia. Each year some 25,000 civilians are killed, wounded, or maimed by land mines, and many more are driven from their homes and fields.

There are many reasons why small arms, mines, and other light weapons figure so prominently in contemporary conflicts. The belligerents involved tend to be insurgents, ethnic separatists, brigands, and local warlords with modest resources and limited access to the international arms market. While usually able to obtain a variety of light weapons from black-market sources or through theft from government arsenals, they can rarely afford or gain access to major weapons systems. Furthermore, such forces are usually composed of ill-trained volunteers who can be equipped with simple infantry weapons but who lack the expertise to operate and maintain heavier and more sophisticated equipment.

Logistical considerations also mitigate against the acquisition of heavy weapons. Lacking access to major ports or airfields and operating largely in secrecy, these forces must rely on clandestine and often unreliable methods of supply that usually entail the use of small boats, pack animals, civilian vehicles, and light planes. These methods are suitable for delivering small arms and ammunition, but not heavy weapons. Tanks, planes, and other major weapons also require large quantities of fuel, which is not easily transported by such rudimentary methods.

The character of ethnic and sectarian warfare further reinforces the predominance of light weapons. The usual objective of armed combat between established states is the defeat and destruction of an adversary's military forces; the goal of ethnic warfare, however, is not so much victory on the battlefield as it is the slaughter or the intimidation of members of another group and their forced abandonment of homes and villages ("ethnic cleansing"). In many cases a key objective is to exact retribution from the other group for past crimes and atrocities, a task best achieved through close-up violence that typically calls for the use of handheld weapons: guns, grenades, and machetes.

While the weapons employed in these clashes are relatively light and unsophisticated, their use can result in human carnage of horrendous proportions. The 1994 upheaval in Rwanda resulted in the deaths of as many as 1 million people and forced millions more to flee their homeland. Similarly, the fighting in Bosnia is believed to have taken the lives of 200,000 people and has produced millions of refugees.

Although the availability of arms is not in itself a cause of war, the fact that likely belligerents in internal conflicts are able to procure significant supplies of light weapons has certainly contributed to the duration and intensity of these contests. Before the outbreak of violence in Rwanda, for example, the Hutu-dominated government spent millions of dollars on rifles, grenades, machine guns, and machetes that were distributed to the army and militia forces later implicated in the systematic slaughter of Tutsi civilians. In Afghanistan, the fact that the various factions were provided with so many weapons by the two superpowers during the cold war has meant that bloody internecine warfare could continue long after Moscow and Washington discontinued their supply operations. The ready availability of light weapons has also contributed to the persistence of violence in Angola, Kashmir, Liberia, Sri Lanka, and Sudan.

The widespread diffusion of light weapons in conflict areas has also posed a significant hazard to UN peacekeeping forces sent to police cease-fires or deliver humanitarian aid. Even when the leaders of major factions have agreed to the introduction of peacekeepers, local warlords and militia chieftains have continued to fight to control their territory. Fighting persisted in Somalia long after American and Pakistani UN peacekeepers arrived in 1992, leading to periodic clashes with UN forces and, following a particularly harrowing firefight in October 1993, to the withdrawal of American forces. Skirmishes like these were also a conspicuous feature of the combat environment in Bosnia before the signing of the Dayton peace accords, and remain a major worry for the NATO forces stationed there today.

Even when formal hostilities have ceased, the diffusion of light weapons poses a continuing threat to international security. In those war-torn areas where jobs are few and the economy is in ruins, many demobilized soldiers have turned to crime to survive, often using the weapons they acquired during wartime for criminal purposes or selling them to combatants in other countries. During the 1980s, South African authorities provided thousands of guns to antigovernment guerrillas in Angola and Mozambique; these same guns, which are no longer needed for insurgent operations, are now being smuggled back into South Africa by their former owners and sold to criminal gangs. Some of the guns provided by the United States to the Nicaraguan contras have reportedly been sold to drug syndicates in Colombia.

MAIMING PROGRESS

It is no longer possible to ignore the role of small arms and light weapons in sustaining international conflict. Although efforts to address this problem are at an early stage, policymakers have begun to consider the imposition of new international constraints on light weapons trafficking. The UN, for example, has established a special commission—the Panel of Governmental Experts on Small Arms—to look into the problem, while representatives of the major industrial powers have met under the auspices of the Wassenaar Arrangement (a group set up in 1996 to devise new international controls on the spread of dangerous military technologies) to consider similar efforts. Despite growing interest, movement toward the adoption of new controls is likely to proceed slowly because of the many obstacles that must be overcome. (Only in one area—the establishment of an international ban on the production and use of antipersonnel land mines—is rapid progress possible.)

One of the greatest obstacles to progress is the lack of detailed information on the international trade in small arms and light weapons. Although various organizations, including the United States Arms Control and Disarmament Agency (ACDA) and the Stockholm International Peace Research Institute (SIPRI) have long compiled data on transfers of major weapons systems, no organization currently provides such information on light weapons. Those who want to study this topic must begin by producing new reservoirs of data on the basis of fragmentary and anecdotal evidence. Fortunately, this process is now well under way, and so it is possible to develop a rough portrait of the light weapons traffic.[1]

---

[1] Three basic sources constitute a provisional database on the topic: Jeffrey Boutwell, Michael T. Klare, and Laura W. Reed, eds., *Lethal Commerce: The Global Trade in Small Arms and Light Weapons* (Cambridge, Mass.: American Academy of Arts and Sciences, 1995); Michael Klare and David Andersen, *A Scourge of Guns: The Diffusion of Small Arms and Light Weapons in Latin America* (Washington, D.C.: Federation of American Scientists, 1996); and Jasjit Singh, ed., *Light Weapons and International Security* (New Delhi: Indian Pugwash Society and British-American Security Information Council, 1995).

SUPPLY AND DEMAND

There is no precise definition of light weapons. In general, they can be characterized as conventional weapons that can be carried by an individual soldier or by a light vehicle operating on backcountry roads. This category includes pistols and revolvers, rifles, hand grenades, machine guns, light mortars, shoulder-fired antitank and anti-aircraft missiles, and antipersonnel land mines. Anything heavier is excluded: tanks, heavy artillery, planes, ships, and large missiles, along with weapons of mass destruction.

Small arms and light weapons of the types shown in the table on page 174 can be acquired in several ways. All the major industrial powers manufacture light weapons of various types, and tend to rely on domestic production for their basic military needs. Another group of countries, including some in the third world, has undertaken the licensed manufacture of weapons originally developed by the major arms-producing states. The Belgian FAL assault rifle has been manufactured in Argentina, Australia, Austria, Brazil, Canada, India, Israel, Mexico, South Africa, and Venezuela, while the Russian/Soviet AK-47 (and its variants) has been manufactured in China, the former East Germany, Egypt, Finland, Hungary, Iraq, North Korea, Poland, Romania, and Yugoslavia. All told, about 40 countries manufacture at least some light weapons in their own factories. All other nations, and those countries that cannot satisfy all of their military requirements through domestic production, must rely on the military aid programs of the major powers or the commercial arms market.

Historically, the military aid programs of the United States and the Soviet Union were an important source of light weapons for developing nations. In addition to the major weapons supplied by the superpowers to their favored allies, both Moscow and Washington also provided vast quantities of small arms, grenades, machine guns, and other light weapons. Today, direct giveaways of light weapons are relatively rare (although the United States still supplies some surplus arms to some allies), so most developing nations must supply their needs through direct purchases on the global arms market.

Unfortunately, there are no published statistics on the annual trade in light weapons. However, the ACDA has estimated that approximately 13 percent of all international arms transfers (when measured in dollars) is comprised of small arms and ammunition. Applying this percentage to ACDA figures on the value of total world arms transfers in 1993 and 1994 would put global small arms exports at approximately $3.6 billion and $2.9 billion, respectively (in current dollars). Adding machine guns, light artillery, and antitank weapons to the small arms category would probably double these figures to some $6 billion per year, which is about one-fourth the total value of global arms transfers.

Further data on the sale of small arms and light weapons through commercial channels are simply not available. Most states do not disclose such information, and the UN Register of Conventional Arms (an annual listing of member states' arms imports and exports) covers major weapons only. However, some indication of the scope of this trade can be obtained from the information in *Jane's Infantry Weapons* on the military inventories of individual states. The FAL assault rifle is found in the inventories of 53 third world states; the Israeli Uzi submachine gun is found in 39 such states; the German G3 rifle in 43 states; and the Belgian MAG machine gun in 54 states.

For established nation-states (except those subject to UN arms embargoes), the commercial arms trade provides an ample and reliable source of small arms and light weapons. For nonstate actors, however, the global arms market is usually closed off. Most countries provide arms only to other governments, or to private agencies that employ or distribute arms with the recipient government's approval. (Such approval is sometimes given to private security firms that seek to import firearms for their own use, or to gun stores that sell imported weapons to individual citizens for hunting or self-defense.) All other groups, including insurgents, brigands, and ethnic militias, must rely on extralegal sources for their arms and ammunition.

THE OTHER ARMS MARKETS

Nonstate entities that want weapons for operations against the military forces of the state or against rival organizations can obtain arms in three ways: through theft from government stockpiles; through purchases on the international black market; and through ties to government agencies or expatriate communities in other countries.

Theft is an important source of arms for insurgents and ethnic militias in most countries, especially in the early stages of conflict. The fledgling armies of Croatia and Slovenia were largely equipped with weapons that had been "liberated" from Yugoslav government arsenals. Weapons seized from dead or captured soldiers also figure prominently in the arms inventories of many insurgent forces. Thus the mujahideen of Afghanistan relied largely on captured Soviet weapons until they began receiving arms in large quantities from outside sources. Many of the guerrilla groups in Latin America have long operated in a similar fashion.

For those insurgent and militia groups with access to hard currency or negotiable commodities (such as diamonds, drugs, and ivory), a large variety of light weapons can be procured on the international black market. This market is composed of private dealers who acquire weapons from corrupt military officials or surplus government stockpiles and ship them through circuitous routes—usually passing through a number of transit points known for their lax customs controls—to obscure ports or airstrips where they can be surreptitiously delivered to the insurgents' representatives. Transactions of this sort have become a prominent feature of the global arms traffic, supplying belligerents around the world. The various factions in Bosnia, for example, reportedly obtained billions of dollars in arms through such channels between 1993 and 1995. Many other groups, including the drug cartels in Colombia and the guerrilla groups in Liberia, have also obtained arms in this fashion.

Finally, insurgents and ethnic militias can turn to sympathetic government officials or expatriate communities in other countries for weapons (or for the funds to procure them from black-market suppliers). During the cold war, both the United States and the Soviet Union—usually operating through intelligence agencies like the CIA and the KGB—supplied weapons to insurgent groups in countries ruled by governments allied with the opposing superpower. At the onset of the 1975 war in Angola, for example, the CIA provided anticommunist insurgents with 20,900 rifles, 41,900 anti-tank rockets, and 622 mortars; later, during the Reagan administration, the United States supplied even larger quantities of arms to the contras in Nicaragua and the mujahideen in Afghanistan. The KGB also supplied insurgent groups with arms of these types, often routing them through friendly countries such as Cuba and Vietnam.

Superpower intervention has largely ceased with the end of the cold war, but other nations are thought to be engaged in similar activities. The Inter-Services Intelligence (ISI) agency of Pakistan is believed to be aiding in the covert delivery of arms to antigovernment insurgents in Kashmir. Likewise, the government of Iran has been accused of supplying arms to Kurdish separatists in Turkey, while Burkina Faso has been charged with aiding some of the guerrilla factions in Liberia. Expatriate groups have also been known to supply arms to associated groups in their country of origin. Americans of Irish descent have smuggled arms to the Irish Republican Army in Northern Ireland, while Tamil expatriates in Canada, Europe, and India are thought to be sending arms (or the funds to procure them) to the Tamil Tigers in Sri Lanka.

A DUAL STRATEGY FOR ARMS CONTROL

What are the implications of all this for the development of new international restraints on light weapons trafficking? We are dealing with two separate, if related, phenomena: the overt, legal transfer of arms to states and state-sanctioned agencies, and the largely covert, illicit transfer of arms to insurgents, ethnic militias, and other nonstate entities. While there is obviously some overlap between the two systems of trade, it is probably not feasible to deal with both through a single set of controls.

Any effort to control the light weapons trade between established states (or their constituent parts) will run into the problem that most government leaders believe the acquisition of such weaponry is essential to the preservation of their sovereignty and therefore sanctioned by the United Nations charter. Many states are also engaged in the sale of light weapons and would resist any new constraints on their commercial activities. It is unlikely, therefore, that the world community will adopt anything resembling an outright ban on light weapons exports or even a significant reduction in such transfers.

This does not mean that progress is impossible. It should be possible to insist on some degree of international transparency in this field. At present, governments are under no obligation to make available information on their imports and exports of light weapons. By contrast, most states have agreed to supply such data on major weapons systems, for release through the UN Register of Conventional Arms. Although compiling data on transfers of small arms and light weapons would undoubtedly prove more difficult than keeping track of heavy

---

For those...with access to hard currency or negotiable commodities (such as diamonds, drugs, and ivory), a large variety of light weapons can be procured on the international black market.

weapons (because small arms are normally transferred far more frequently, and with less government oversight, than heavy weapons), there is no technical reason why the UN register could not be extended over time to include a wider range of systems. Including light weapons in the register would enable the world community to detect any unusual or provocative activity in this area (for example, significant purchases of arms and ammunition by a government that is supposedly downsizing its military establishment in accordance with a UN-brokered peace agreement) and to respond appropriately.

The major arms suppliers could also be required to abide by certain specified human rights considerations when considering the transfer of small arms and light weapons to governments involved in violent internal conflicts. Such sales could be prohibited in the case of governments that have suspended the democratic process and employed brutal force against unarmed civilians. An obvious candidate for such action is Burma, whose military leadership has usurped national power, jailed pro-democracy activists, and fought an unrelenting military campaign against autonomy-seeking minority groups. Human rights considerations have already figured in a number of UN arms embargoes—such as that imposed on the apartheid regime in South Africa—and so it should be possible to develop comprehensive restrictions of this type.

Finally, the world community could adopt restrictions or a prohibition on the transfer of certain types of weapons that are deemed to be especially cruel or barbaric in their effects. The first target should be the trade in antipersonnel land mines. President Bill Clinton called for a worldwide ban on the production, transfer, and use of such munitions in May 1996. Many other leaders have promised to support such a measure, but more effort is needed to persuade holdout states to agree. In addition to land mines, a ban could be imposed on bullets that tumble in flight or otherwise reproduce the effects of dumdum bullets (a type of soft-nosed projectile that expands on impact and produces severe damage to the human body). Bullets of this type where outlawed by the Hague Convention of 1899, but have reappeared in other forms.

STOPPING BLACK-MARKET TRAFFIC

An entirely different approach will be needed to control the black-market traffic in arms. Since such trafficking violates, by definition, national and international norms regarding arms transfers, there is no point in trying to persuade the suppliers and recipients involved to abide by new international restraints on the munitions trade. Instead, governments should be asked to tighten their own internal controls on arms trafficking and to cooperate with other states in identifying, monitoring, and suppressing illegal gun traffickers.

As a first step, all the nations in a particular region—such as Europe or the Western Hemisphere—should agree to uniform export restrictions and establish electronic connections between their respective customs agencies to permit the instantaneous exchange of data on suspect arms transactions. These measures should prohibit the export of arms to any agency or firm not subject to government oversight in the recipient nation, and the use of transshipment points in third countries that do not adhere to the uniform standards. At the same time, the law enforcement agencies of these countries should cooperate in tracking down and prosecuting dealers found to have engaged in illicit arms transfers. Eventually these measures could be extended on a worldwide basis, making it much more difficult for would-be traffickers to circumvent government controls.

It is unrealistic, of course, to assume that these measures will prevent all unwanted and illicit arms trafficking—there are simply too many channels for determined suppliers to employ. Nor should airtight control be the goal of international action. Rather, the goal should be to so constrict the flow of weapons that potential belligerents (including nonstate actors) are discouraged from achieving their objectives through force of arms and seek instead a negotiated settlement. Such controls should also be designed to reduce the death and displacement of civilians trapped in conflict areas, and to impede the activities of terrorist and criminal organizations.

Obviously, it will not be possible to make progress so long as policymakers view the trade in small arms and light weapons as a relatively insignificant problem. Educating world leaders about the dangerous consequences of this trade in an era of intensifying ethnic and sectarian conflict is a major arms control priority. Once these consequences are widely appreciated, it should be possible for the world community to devise the necessary controls and make substantial progress in curbing this trade.

Unit 8

Unit Selections

35. **Closing the Gate: The Persian Gulf War Revisited,** Michael Sterner
36. **Rethinking N+1**

Key Points to Consider

❖ Which events are most important to learn from, successes or failures? In studying the past, what should policymakers look for? List the three most important events in the cold war that policy makers should learn from.

❖ How can we improve the ability of the government to learn from the past?

❖ Looking back over the Clinton administration, how would you rate its ability to learn from the past?

❖ Which of post–cold war American foreign policy initiatives will be most studied in the future?

❖ What are the lessons of the Persian Gulf War for American foreign policy?

❖ Identify a major foreign policy event from each decade of the cold war that holds important lessons for the future. Justify your choices.

DUSHKIN ONLINE Links

www.dushkin.com/online/

30. **The Bulletin of the Atomic Scientists**
    http://www.bullatomsci.org/
31. **DefenseLINK**
    http://www.defenselink.mil/
32. **United States Institute of Peace (USIP)**
    http://www.usip.org/

These sites are annotated on pages 4 and 5.

Historical Retrospectives on American Foreign Policy

American foreign policy tends to be present- and future-oriented. It is the present that defines the foreign policy challenges that must be met and provides policymakers with opportunities to be seized. It is in the present that policymakers struggle to pass legislation, adjust policies to available resources, and make choices against a backdrop of incomplete information and conflicting interpretations of the national interest. The legitimacy of future-oriented thinking in these circumstances is readily acknowledged. The goal is not just to meet American foreign policy goals today but also tomorrow, next year, and the next decade. The obvious problem is that the future does not provide a concrete standard against which to evaluate policy. People are free to read what they will into the future, and the future they see will differ from person to person depending upon such things as their view of human nature, their faith in the ability of science and technology to solve environmental and social problems, and how much importance they give to chance and accident.

It is different with the past. The past both attracts and repels us, and for that reason its place in policy deliberations is less secure. We are drawn to the past by a desire to avoid repeating its failures and the hope of duplicating its successes. We want no more Vietnams, Bosnias, or Somalias, but we do wish for another Marshall Plan. We often turn our backs to the past out of the conviction that the present and future bear little resemblance to it.

The relationship of the past to the present and future affects much of the controversy over the nature of the post–cold war international system. Just how different is it from the cold war international system or earlier ones? Can a leader such as Saddam Hussein be equated with Hitler, or is that analogy misleading and dangerous? What insights can we gain from the way the cold war competition between the United States and Soviet Union was played out? How different is the mass exodus from Cuba in 1994 from those that occurred during the cold war? Can we respond to it the same way; should we adopt a different policy? Answering such questions is difficult because despite its more concrete nature, the past can be an elusive database to work from.

One reason for this is that our understanding of the past is never complete or final. New information is constantly coming forward that requires us to rethink established truths and entertain new explanations for why an event occurred. This is especially true in the case of American foreign policy. Not only are many of the most crucial decisions made in small group settings and surrounded in secrecy with only fragmentary information being made available through the press, but virtually the entire history of the cold war has been written from an American perspective and with American sources. As Russian archives open up, we can expect to see a new wave of cold war studies. Second, the past does not lend itself to a single interpretation. Just as with the future, different philosophical, conceptual, or strategic starting points will yield different insights and lessons. Third, it is not always clear where to look for lessons. The debate over whether the United States should send troops to Bosnia produced an abundance of historical parallels. Vietnam, Beirut, Somalia, and Grenada have all been cited by political commentators as the proper starting point for thinking about this policy problem.

The two readings in this section are concerned with achieving a better understanding of the past so that American foreign policy might enjoy successes in the present and future. The first essay addresses recent American foreign policy initiatives. In "Closing the Gate: The Persian Gulf War Revisited," Michael Sterner looks at the question of whether there was anything that might have been done militarily to alter the political outcome of the war. The second essay, and the last one in this volume, revisits one of the perennial problems in world politics over the past half century: what to do about nuclear proliferation. In "Rethinking N+1," Brad Roberts asserts that the world has changed greatly since U.S. foreign policy first addressed this problem. He argues that the old answer of providing security guarantees to would-be nuclear powers as a way of preventing nuclear proliferation has lost much of its relevance.

Article 35

> As the Persian Gulf War fades into memory, a revisionist reading of the war's aims and strategy has gained critical favor among those who see it as having been the last best hope for relieving the Middle East of Saddam Hussein. In response to this reinterpretation, Michael Sterner examines whether "there is anything the coalition did not do militarily that could have changed the political outcome of the war. To answer that we need to look not only at what coalition forces might have done, but at what the impact of those actions would likely have been in Iraq."

Closing the Gate: The Persian Gulf War Revisited

MICHAEL STERNER

As soon as it became apparent that the Persian Gulf War had not resulted in the ouster of Saddam Hussein, a host of articles, books, and other commentary began to appear second-guessing American war aims and Washington's decision to bring the war to an end. At the very least—so the argument went—the Bush administration had ended the war prematurely, allowing significant Iraqi forces to escape, which Saddam was then able to use to suppress the Shiite and Kurdish uprisings. Some critics faulted Washington's war goals from the outset, saying it should have pressed the war to the point of unconditional Iraqi surrender, or at least have occupied Iraqi territory to impose much tougher terms on Baghdad.

All this commentary has been generated by the disparity between one of the most complete battlefield victories in military history and the problematic political results that have been the war's legacy. Six years after the war's end, Saddam's repressive regime is still in power; the contest of wills between the Iraqi leader and the coalition victors has not ended but has merely been transferred to the UN Security Council; regional security has been only half achieved, requiring the United States to maintain large forces for rapid deployment to the Gulf; and Washington is faced with the dilemma that economic sanctions are hurting the Iraqi people more than Saddam's regime. It is not surprising that so many have rushed in to explain this discordant result.

Much of the commentary is more a cri de coeur than a systematic analysis. *New York Times* columnist William Safire declared on January 13, 1992, that George Bush had "snatched defeat from the jaws of victory." In a January 9, 1996, interview on the PBS program *Frontline*, former British Prime Minister Margaret Thatcher came up with the epigrammatic but hardly profound comment that "There is the aggressor, Saddam Hussein, still in power. There is the president of the United States, no longer in power. I wonder who won?" Even as good an analyst as Jeffrey Record clearly goes over the top when he says in his 1993 book, *Hollow Victory*, that the Gulf War "was a magnificent military victory barren of any significant diplomatic gains."

The initial postwar debate has been revived

MICHAEL STERNER *is a retired diplomat who served as ambassador to the United Arab Emirates and as deputy assistant secretary of state for Near East and South Asian affairs.*

recently by the publication in 1995 of *The General's War*, by Michael Gordon and Bernard Trainor, and by the 1995 memoirs of former Chairman of the Joint Chiefs of Staff General Colin Powell and Arab Forces commander General Khaled bin Sultan. Gordon, a *New York Times* correspondent, and Trainor, a retired Marine general now at Harvard, offer one of the best accounts of the war. They do not waste time on the we-should-have-marched-to-Baghdad argument—recognizing that this option was never in the cards—but make two judgments that deserve serious consideration: that the United States ended the war too soon, allowing much of the Iraqi Republican Guard to escape with its heavy equipment; and that, as they noted in a February 1, 1995, *Charlie Rose Show* interview on PBS, American willingness to withdraw unconditionally from Iraqi territory deprived the United States of "the opportunity to create the conditions to overthrow Saddam Hussein."

Yet Gordon and Trainor, along with most other critics of the way the war ended, rather breezily leave it at that, failing to explain how, in bringing the war to an "optimal" military close, conditions would have been created that would have led to the overthrow of Saddam. The crucial question is whether there is anything the coalition did not do militarily that could have changed the political outcome of the war. To answer that we need to look not only at what coalition forces might have done, but at what the impact of those actions would likely have been in Iraq.

SETTING WAR AIMS

Iraq's invasion of Kuwait on the morning of August 2, 1990, took Arab and Western governments by surprise. The first concern in Western capitals was to erect a defense of Saudi Arabia against a possible continuation of Iraq's move southward. But on the day of the invasion, the UN Security Council condemned Iraq's action and demanded its unconditional withdrawal; this immediately raised the question of what the United States, as Western leader, would do to put teeth into this resolution. Pondering this, President Bush proceeded to Aspen, Colorado, for a previously scheduled conference, where he met with British Prime Minister Thatcher. Thatcher urged a tough response, but as she herself records, found Bush already disposed to be very firm.

In this respect the president appears to have been well out ahead of some of his senior advisers. Colin Powell records in *My American Journey* surprise and admiration at how quickly Bush made up his mind that Iraq would have to be ejected from Kuwait, whatever it took.[1] On August 5, Bush told reporters that "this will not stand, this aggression . . ." Three days later, in an address to the nation, the president set forth American objectives: 1) the immediate, complete, and unconditional withdrawal of Iraqi forces from Kuwait; 2) the restoration of Kuwait's legitimate government; 3) the security and stability of Saudi Arabia and the Persian Gulf; and 4) the safety and protection of Americans abroad.

Achieving the third objective could reasonably be supposed to require the destruction of Iraq's warmaking capability over and above Iraq's eviction from Kuwait; nevertheless, it is notable that the statement did not contain a call for Saddam Hussein's replacement, or any other intervention in Iraqi internal affairs. This program of clearly defined and limited goals remained remarkably constant throughout the following months. Richard Haass, the administration's Middle East adviser on the National Security Council, said in a June 10, 1996, interview with this author that while it became tactically necessary for coalition forces to invade Iraqi territory to carry out a war plan that ensured Iraq's overwhelming military defeat, this did not change the political strategy. "The elimination of Saddam was a war hope but never a war aim." In his memoir, Colin Powell says that "In none of the meetings I attended was dismembering Iraq, conquering Baghdad, or changing the form of government ever seriously considered. We hoped that Saddam would not survive the coming fury. But his elimination was not a stated objective. What we hoped for, frankly, in a post-war Gulf region, was an Iraq still standing, with Saddam overthrown."

In public comments before, during, and after the war, Bush expressed the hope that the Iraqi people would overthrow Saddam Hussein, but this never became a United States policy objective. Powell, among others, regretted the tendency on the part of the president to personalize American war aims, and worried—correctly as it turned out—that it would raise expectations that might prove impossible to fulfill.

---

[1]Powell was initially very cautious about setting forth objectives that might require the use of United States military force when it was unclear whether there would be public support for it. He is quoted by Gordon and Trainor in *The General's War* as saying, at a meeting with Defense Secretary Dick Cheney on August 2, "I don't see the senior leadership taking us into armed conflict for the events of the last twenty-four hours. The American people don't want their young dying for $1.50 gallon [sic] oil . . ."

Several factors combined to solidify the decision to keep United States war aims carefully limited. Extending the war to include political objectives in Iraq would have been vigorously opposed by all of the Arab coalition members and most of the European members as well.[2] American policymakers were also aware that intervention in Iraq would have radically altered Arab public opinion about the conflict. Expelling Iraq from Kuwait had the support of a significant segment of the Arab public that would have turned against the United States had there been an attempt to invade Iraq with the purpose of installing a new government. Moreover, American sponsorship would have been a long-term political liability for a new Iraqi government.

Certainly the most compelling reason to avoid intervention in Iraqi internal affairs would have been the profoundly altered nature of the mission undertaken by the United States. Instead of a mission that could have had a clear ending (the expulsion of the Iraqis from Kuwait), the United States would have undertaken one that would have required the invasion and occupation of Iraq. This held excellent prospects of bogging down American forces for an indefinite period, without any assurance that the end result would not be a splintering of Iraq along ethnic and religious lines—which was not perceived as being in the United States interest. There would also have been the problem of seeking congressional support for a wider war; it must be remembered that the Senate approved military action for even the administration's limited war objectives by a margin of only a few votes. From the numerous memoirs and interviews since the war, it is apparent that senior United States policymakers from the president on down were aware of these considerations, and that they found them compelling.

THE 100-HOUR WAR'S END

The ground war strategy that General Norman Schwarzkopf and his planners devised called for a thrust directly north from Saudi Arabia by United States marines and Arab forces that would "fix" the Iraqi forces in Kuwait in battle, while two United States army corps, including British and French divisions, swung far to the west and north through Iraqi territory to cut off the Iraqi lines of retreat and engage Iraq's Republican Guard divisions, which were positioned just north of the Iraq-Kuwait border. The only flaw in this outstandingly successful plan was that progress in the eastern sector was so rapid that it exposed the flank of the advancing forces, causing Schwarzkopf to push forward the launching of the two western corps by nearly 24 hours. Then, as the conflict turned into an Iraqi rout, it was feared the "left hook" would not arrive in time to engage the Republican Guard divisions before most of them had been withdrawn northward across the Euphrates River.

> *"The elimination of Saddam was a war hope but never a war aim."*

Even so, after the four days of fighting between February 24 and 27, 1991, the results were overwhelmingly impressive: Kuwait City had been liberated; most of the Iraqi divisions in Kuwait had been overrun with minimal resistance; some 82,000 Iraqi soldiers had been captured; in tank battles on February 26 and 27, several of the Iraqi Republican Guard heavy divisions had been badly mauled; and United States forces were astride the main road between Basra and Baghdad, and within 25 miles of Basra itself. All this had been accomplished with an almost miraculously low allied casualty rate (260 killed, of whom 146 were American).

Although postwar interviews and memoirs have tossed the ball back and forth as to who was most anxious to end the fighting, there is no basic disagreement among the participants about how the decision was reached. According to Schwarzkopf's account, he received a call mid-afternoon February 27 from Powell, who said it was time to give thought to a cease-fire, adding that people at home were beginning to be upset by reports of unnecessary slaughter of fleeing Iraqi troops along Kuwait's "Highway of Death." (That day's *Washington Post*, for example, had carried a story with the headline, "'Like Shooting Fish in a Barrel,' US Pilots Say.") Schwarzkopf says he told Powell he would like to have another day to finish the job. "The five-day war. How's that sound?"

---

[2] In his memoir, *Desert Warrior*, General Khaled bin Sultan says, "The Syrians told me very clearly, and the Egyptians somewhat more tactfully, that they could not consider entering Iraq, nor indeed could any Arab troops including our own."

At 9 P.M. in Riyadh (1 P.M. EST), Schwarzkopf gave a briefing to reporters at which he said the coalition's objectives had basically been achieved. He claimed 29 Iraqi divisions had been rendered completely ineffective and, pointing to a map where the remaining Iraqi forces south of the Euphrates were located, said, "The gates are closed. There is no way out of here." Pressed on this by a reporter, Schwarzkopf said he did not mean that no one was escaping, but that the gate was closed on Iraq's "military machine."

In Washington, shortly after Schwarzkopf's briefing, a meeting of Bush and his senior advisers on the war was convened. Powell told the group about the battlefield results. There was general agreement that the war's objectives had largely been achieved, and concern was expressed that the war not be pursued to the point of needless slaughter. Powell expressed the view that the time was coming to end the war. According to Powell's account, he suggested "tomorrow" and the president said, "Why not today?" A call was placed to Schwarzkopf in Riyadh. Powell told him the president was thinking of going on the air at 9 P.M. EST (5 A.M. Riyadh time) to announce a suspension of hostilities, and asked if he had any problem with that. Schwarzkopf, after some thought, said he had none, but wanted to check with his commanders. He did so, and reports in his memoir that "nobody seemed surprised."[3]

In Washington the war council met again at 5:30 P.M. and reached a final decision: the United States would announce a "suspension of offensive combat operations" for midnight EST, or 8:00 A.M. February 28 on the battlefield. The change from the earlier time of 5:00 A.M. was evidently made entirely for PR reasons; the extra three hours allowed the administration to refer to a "100-hour war" (Schwarzkopf comments sardonically, "I had to hand it to them: they really knew how to package an historic event," but acknowledges the change made little difference on the battlefield).

The White House wanted to add the stipulation that those Iraqi forces left in the "Basra pocket" would have to abandon their equipment and walk home. When this was conveyed to Schwarzkopf, a member of his staff pointed out that it would be impossible to enforce this without keeping up allied attacks. Schwarzkopf says, "He was right, of course. There was a considerable amount of armored equipment—perhaps two divisions worth—pushed up against the pontoon bridges at Basra..." Schwarzkopf told this to Powell, still at the White House meeting, who says, "We were all taken slightly aback," but no one felt it changed the basic equation. As Powell puts it, the Iraqi army's back was broken; there was no need to fight a war of annihilation. All participants agree that no dissenting views were expressed at the meeting.[4]

National security adviser Brent Scowcroft later said in an interview that he had misgivings about ending the war prematurely, but admits he did not voice them at the time. Schwarzkopf told David Frost in an interview after the war that "frankly, my recommendation had been, you know, continue the march..." but quickly backed down when an angry Colin Powell reminded him that he had every opportunity to press this view during the February 27 discussions, but did not. (In his memoirs, Schwarzkopf says he basically agreed with the White House decision and does not mention the Frost interview.)

The CIA estimates that at the time of the suspension of hostilities Iraq had lost, to all causes, 75 percent of the tanks it had in the Kuwait Theater of Operations (KTO), more than 50 percent of its armored personnel carriers (APCs), and nearly 90 percent of its artillery. Since about half of Iraq's prewar armed forces had been in the KTO, the magnitude of this disaster can easily be judged.

Even so, the CIA estimate also notes that almost 50 percent of the Republican Guard's major combat equipment in the KTO escaped destruction and remained under Iraqi control. As the Iraqis prepared for another day of battle on February 28, the remnants of four Guard armored and infantry divisions were drawn up in defensive positions west and south of Basra in the hope of delaying the allied advance so that more Iraqi units could escape northward. There is little question that much of their equipment could have been destroyed or captured

---

[3]This does not square entirely with an interview given to Gordon and Trainor by Lieutenant General Calvin Waller, the deputy commander of allied forces in the Gulf, who said he forcefully told Schwarzkopf at the time that ending the war so soon was a mistake. It does, however, accurately reflect the view of Lieutenant General John Yeosock, the commander of the Third Army. While Yeosock had earlier told Schwarzkopf he would have preferred another day to "finish the job," when informed of the White House's decision he thought it was "a reasonable call." "If I had felt strongly otherwise, I would have fought Norm about it." Lieutenant General John Yeosock, telephone interview with author, July 1, 1996.

[4]This summary of events draws from Gordon and Trainor, the memoirs of Powell and Schwarzkopf, and Richard M. Swain, *"Lucky War": The Third Army in Desert Storm* (Ft. Leavenworth, Kans.: U.S. Army Command and General Staff College Press, 1994).

in another day of fighting. The troops and plans were in place that could have done so, and allied air power would have pounded Iraqi units trying to get across the bridges over the Shatt al Arab waterway.

But it is important to emphasize that the *total* destruction of the Guard units was never an attainable option. At least some of the Guard (probably mainly infantry units) had already been withdrawn across the Euphrates by the time hostilities had ceased. Moreover, equipment isn't everything, and was perhaps not even the most important thing for the Guard's next job, suppressing internal unrest. Gordon and Trainor point out that the Guard had saved its command headquarters units, which enabled it to quickly organize the remnants of the Guard field force into cohesive units. Even after the devastation of another day of fighting, this leadership cadre could well have been among the survivors.

Furthermore, had the Guard units defending Basra withdrawn into the built-up areas of Basra and Zubair, they would have posed a dilemma for the allies. The coalition had no intention of engaging in street-to-street fighting in Iraqi cities, a proposition that would certainly have entailed a higher rate of allied casualties, not to mention many Iraqi civilian casualties. While the allies might have been able to bottle up some Republican Guard units in Basra by cutting off all escape routes north, there would have been no way to compel them to surrender or abandon their equipment without a prolonged blockade.

THE TALKS AT SAFWAN

American handling of the cease-fire talks that took place under a tent at Safwan on March 3, 1991, has added further fuel to the revisionist charge that the allies "gave away" the peace. In his memoir, Schwarzkopf, who conducted the talks for the coalition, says he regrets his decision to allow the Iraqis to fly armed helicopters when the Iraqis said they needed these flights because of the damage done to their transportation system. To be fair to Schwarzkopf, most of this criticism was made later when the role that Iraqi helicopter gunships played in the suppression of the uprisings in the south became known. Once the decision had been reached to end the fighting, Schwarzkopf believed his job was to get allied prisoners of war back, establish clear cease-fire lines to avoid further clashes with the Iraqis, and begin as soon as possible to evacuate American soldiers for their triumphant welcome back home. Understandably, he would have felt that if anything beyond this had been required,

it was up to Washington to give him instructions. But beyond receiving approval for his own suggested military agenda, Schwarzkopf received no instructions from Washington to use the United States position on the battlefield as leverage to support political objectives in the postwar situation.

It is thus unrealistic to blame Schwarzkopf for having assured the Iraqis prematurely of American willingness to evacuate Iraqi territory. This was an important point for the Iraqis, and had it not been granted the implementation of other conditions of the cease-fire that were important to the allies would have been complicated. What, exactly, could the allies have achieved by continuing to occupy Iraqi territory? United States willingness to withdraw could not have been used as leverage to prevent Baghdad from suppressing the southern Shiite and northern Kurdish uprisings; Saddam would have waited the United States out, especially when he sensed that above all Washington wanted to bring American troops home as soon as possible.

> *The uprisings had no chance when they failed to spread to Baghdad and the central Sunni towns, the political nerve center of the country.*

THE KURDISH AND SHIITE UPRISINGS

The first incidents of rebellion in Iraq took place in the southern Sunni towns of Abu'l Khasib and Zubair immediately after the suspension of hostilities. They were touched off by disaffected and angry Iraqi troops straggling northward from the battlefield. Gunshots, and in some cases tank rounds, were fired at posters of Saddam; these incidents quickly generated more widespread demonstrations on the part of the civilian population. The uprising spread rapidly to other cities and towns in the south: Basra on March 1; Suk al-Shuyukh on March 2; Nassiriya, Najaf, and Kufa on March 4; Kerbala on March 7.

The best analysis of the uprisings is an article in the May–June 1992 issue of *Middle East Report* by Falah Abd al-Jabar, a London-based Iraqi journalist with good connections to the Iraqi opposition, who had also talked with participants in the uprisings. Abd al-Jabar writes that "a detailed account of what happened in each city is impossible, but reports in various outlawed Iraqi publications speak of a series of events remarkably similar in every case. Masses would gather in the streets to denounce Saddam Hussein and Ba'thi rule, then march to seize the mayor's office, the Ba'th Party headquarters, the secret police (mukhabarat) building, the prison and the city's garrison (if there was one). People shot as they went at every poster or wall relief of the dictator. As the cities came under rebel control, the insurgents cleaned out Ba'thists and mukhabarat."[5]

But, beyond these outbursts of rage at the apparatus of state control, the uprisings seemed to go nowhere. Although rebels were in control of these towns for several days, their leadership was fragmented and ineffective. Refugees fleeing south continued to report "chaotic conditions" in the towns under rebel control. No effort appears to have been made to restore order and organize a defense against the suppression that was inevitably to come. There was no evident communication between the rebel leadership in the various towns (ironically the air war's devastation of the Iraqi communications system made this even more difficult) and no apparent effort to convey what was happening in the south to the segments of the Baghdad population that might also have been ready to revolt.

As Abd al-Jabar points out, the revolt in the south was at a critical disadvantage. "First, it was close to the front lines where Republican Guard units were still stationed. Second, while the conscripted military was ripe for rebellion, it was politically immature. And thirdly, the Islamists, in the euphoria of apparent early success, joined in and raised a disastrous slogan: Ja'fari [Shiite] rule." Abd al-Jabar also notes that the Iraqi political opposition was surprised by the uprisings and totally unprepared to offer leadership.

The sectarian aspect was probably the most critical factor. Iraqi Shia who had fled to Iran during the Iraq-Iran War began to come back across the border, some displaying pictures of the Ayatollah Ruhollah Khomeini and Iraqi opposition figure Muhammad Bakr al-Hakim, who had organized the "Supreme Assembly of the Islamic Revolution in Iraq" in 1982 and was now based in Iran. Iran's behavior during the crisis was in fact quite cautious, and the role of the Iraqi exiles was limited—they did not start the uprisings, nor were they the majority element—but their attempt to co-opt the revolt in the name of Islam was enough to give the rebellion a sectarian character. This undermined the appeal of the uprising in the politically important central Sunni-dominated part of the country and, as Abd al-Jabar says, "provided an opportunity for Saddam to garner domestic support and regain implicit if undeclared international support." The sectarian aspect was underscored when uprisings began in the Kurdish region a few days later.

Meanwhile, the Iraqi military command reorganized the surviving elements of the Republican Guard and used them to restore control in the south. By all accounts they went at this with a vengeance. A Jordanian photographer reported seeing Guard tanks in the streets of Basra on March 4 "destroying everything in front of them." Reprisals were swift and brutal. Refugees reported fierce fighting for several days, but the tide turned rapidly. By March 7 loyalist troops were reported to be in control of Basra; after heavy shelling by government forces the rebellion was quelled in Kerbala on March 12 and in Najaf the next day. A further break for Saddam was that the rebellion in the Kurdish areas did not begin until after suppression of the southern revolt was well under way (the first reports of unrest in the north appeared in the international press March 7). While reinforcements in the form of two Guard brigades (a force of about 7,500 men) were sent from the northern part of the country and apparently participated in the sieges of Kerbala and Najaf, the basic job of suppression was performed by Republican Guard troops that had been in the Kuwait theater during the Gulf War. According to one analyst, the Iraqi command succeeded in putting together, out of the remnants of the Gulf War forces, about five effective divisions with some 50,000 to 60,000 troops.[6]

The uprisings had no chance when they failed to

---

[5] The phrase "cleaned out" should not be misunderstood; hundreds of government security and Baath Party personnel were killed in the fighting or executed by the rebels after summary trials in the cities they took over.

[6] Roland Danreuther, *The Gulf Conflict: A Political and Strategic Analysis*, Adelphi Paper no. 264 (London: Institute for International and Strategic Studies, 1991–1992).

spread to Baghdad and the central Sunni towns, the political nerve center of the country. Although Teheran radio broadcast reports of massive demonstrations in Baghdad, there has never been independent confirmation that any disturbances took place there.

The uprising in the south posed an uncomfortable dilemma for the United States. Washington did not want to appear to be standing by with folded arms as Saddam put down the rebellion with ruthless efficiency; at the same time, the administration was determined not to be sucked back into military involvement in Iraq. As Lawrence Freedman and Efraim Karsh have pointed out in their 1992 study, *The Gulf Conflict,* Saddam was astute in the days right after the war in accepting without dispute the immediate postwar Security Council resolutions and in scrupulously observing the terms of the cease-fire, thus reinforcing the coalition powers' disposition to call it a mission accomplished and go home.

Also reinforcing the tendency toward nonintervention was the sketchiness of the intelligence available to Washington. No one really knew who the leaders of the uprisings were, how much support they had, or what the Iranian role was. Richard Haass says policymakers were concerned about the reports of Iranian involvement and the "dismemberment of Iraq; we didn't want to see an Islamic Republic established in the south." Colin Powell goes further in saying, "Nor, frankly, was their [the rebels] success a goal of our policy," and he indicates his agreement with a telegram by Charles Freeman, the American ambassador in Saudi Arabia at the time, which said, "It is not in our interest to destroy Iraq or weaken it to the point that Iran and/or Syria are not constrained by it." Much of the retrospective commentary has been clothed in these geopolitical terms, but the most powerful considerations at the time were a strong bias against becoming re-engaged with Iraq, no matter what the perceived benefits, and a very unclear picture as to what any form of intervention could accomplish. The result was an embarrassing two weeks of belligerent warnings to the Iraqis accompanied by determined inactivity.

Was there anything the United States could have done to help the rebels? It certainly could have used its airpower to suppress the helicopter gunships. But, undeniably effective as the helicopters were in helping to quell the rebellion, their absence would probably not have made the difference between failure and success for the uprisings. The problem for the United States and its allies was that, having decided that they were not prepared to commit ground forces to establish, if necessary, a protectorate for the south, any half-measures raised the question, "How far do we go if the last half-measure fails? And what does a failed intervention do to allied interests in the region?" The Bay of Pigs experience certainly comes to mind as a cautionary precedent.

TWENTY-FOUR HOURS IN THE BALANCE

Compared with the meticulous planning that characterized preparations for the Persian Gulf War—especially the decision to concentrate overwhelming force to make sure the allied victory was a complete one—United States decision making to end the war had a decidedly ad hoc quality to it. Some allowance must be made for the "fog of war"—in particular the difficulty of getting timely and accurate battlefield damage assessments—and the surprising rapidity of the Iraqi collapse. Even so, once the main objective of liberating Kuwait had been achieved, Washington decision makers seemed to lose interest in the information that was available about the condition of the Iraqi army. Instead, they were preoccupied with the adverse publicity of the "Highway of Death" media reports, and with an overwhelming sense of relief that such a brilliant military victory had been achieved at so little cost.[7] Why press one's luck with another day of fighting? The mood at the political level was reinforced by the military high command's determination to make this war turn out differently from the Vietnam experience, with its ill-defined objectives, incremental reinforcements, and waning public support. In this atmosphere, even the news that the gate wasn't really closed on the Republican Guard was brushed aside.

One must respect the enormous responsibility that any president bears in making a decision that would add even a few names to those that were already on the allied casualty list, and it is certainly to the credit of George Bush and Colin Powell that they were thinking humanely about Iraqi casualties as well. It is also true that the stated objectives of the war were achieved by the morning of February 28. We can accept that the ouster of Saddam

---

[7]President Bush has stressed the adverse publicity aspect in postwar statements, most recently, for example, in an article written for the German newspaper *Welt am Sonntag* (Hamburg) on September 22, 1996: "If we had continued the war one more day, just to destroy more tanks and to kill more pitiful soldiers retreating on the highway toward Basra with hands raised, public opinion would have immediately turned against the coalition."

Hussein was indeed only a "war hope" and not a war aim.

But Bush had voiced hope of Saddam's ouster often enough, and any thought given to the postwar situation would have concluded that the survival of the Saddam regime would make the American objective of regional stability far more difficult to achieve. Policymakers at the time could not have known that a rebellion in the southern cities was about to break out. But from their own postwar testimony they were hoping for a coup of some sort, probably from within the armed forces. Recognizing the role the Republican Guard played in supporting the regime, it would have been logical to make sure maximum damage had been inflicted on the Guard. This, indeed, had been Powell's and Schwarzkopf's objective in planning the war from the beginning. From what policymakers knew at the time, continuing the war for another 24 hours to achieve that objective would have made sense. It was in part the universal conviction in Washington that no political leader could survive the catastrophe that had been inflicted on Saddam that made them casual about relating military results to Iraq's internal political situation.

But, from what we now know about the uprising that did take place, and about the internal situation in Iraq, it is hard to make the case that another day of fighting would have made the difference between Saddam's survival and ouster. No doubt the task of suppression would have taken somewhat longer if the regime had been deprived of the use of heavy armor and helicopters; but the ultimate outcome of a battle between battered but still disciplined troops and a rebellion that was disorganized and lacking in overall leadership or any plan of action beyond taking revenge on local officials was never in doubt. As Defense Intelligence Agency historian Brian Shellum put it in an interview, well-led soldiers with rifles in trucks—and Saddam had plenty of those—would have been enough in the end to do the job. And as another analyst has written—and this is at the heart of the matter—what Saddam had to do in the ashes of defeat was to maintain the nerve of the inner ruling group,[8] and he managed to do it.

[8]Danreuther, op. cit., p. 63.

Rethinking N+1

Brad Roberts

IN APRIL 1961, one of the seminal think-pieces on proliferation appeared. This was Albert Wohlstetter's famous *Foreign Affairs* article analyzing the so-called "N + 1" problem. This formulation was Wohlstetter's way of characterizing the next incremental addition to the existing number of nuclear weapons states. In an elegant analysis focused mainly on the nuclear problem in Europe, he argued that the U.S. nuclear umbrella was the answer to the security needs of NATO's potential next nuclear states. He argued further that disarmament would only fuel Soviet ambitions, but that export controls and modest arms control measures had a role to play in limiting nuclear diffusion.

In this, as in so many other areas, Wohlstetter's ideas helped to shape his generation's thinking about the proliferation problem. But wholly new factors have arisen over the past four decades, and we need to think differently about the issue because the problem itself has changed. We can best see how it has changed by taking separately the two parts of Wohlstetter's simple "N + 1" expression.

First is the "N" factor: the number of existing nuclear-armed states. Today, the policy debate remains focused on the challenge of preventing those two or three states most desirous of joining that number from achieving their ambition. Now, as then, nuclear proliferation presents risks of major importance for international stability and U.S. security. The emergence of a nuclear-armed Iraq, Iran, or North Korea would be deeply unsettling, both regionally and globally. So too would be the leakage of nuclear weapons materials, technology, or expertise to both state and non-state actors. Stopping such proliferation remains a top policy priority, as it was in 1961.

But the nuclear dynamic is more complicated than suggested by "N + 1." There is also an "N - 1" phenomenon. The number of states opting *out* of the nuclear weapons business (South Africa, Ukraine, Belarus, Kazakhstan, Argentina, and Brazil) is *roughly double* the number working to get in. Moreover, the emergence since 1961 of de facto nuclear weapons states outside the superpower strategic framework (Israel, India, and Pakistan) has not so far changed the world in any fundamental sense, largely because their purposes are understood to be essentially defensive.

The proliferation phenomenon has been further complicated by the increased prominence of elements of the problem other than the nuclear one. Chemical weapons proliferated rapidly in the 1980s, in a process driven largely by their use in the Iran-Iraq war. A spate of biological weapons proliferation followed. But here too the trends are not straightforward. Implementation of the new Chemical Weapons Convention of 1997 is leading to a decrease in the number of states

---

Brad Roberts is a member of the research staff at the Institute for Defense Analyses and author of *Weapons Proliferation and World Order After the Cold War* (Kluwer Press, 1996).

armed with such weapons (India and South Korea, for example, have signed the treaty and have promised to destroy their chemical weapons). In the biological area, there seems to be no increase in the number of states possessing or seeking such weapons since the number peaked at about a dozen in the early 1990s. If Iraq's biological warfare program is any indication, the proliferation of the 1990s may not be so much horizontal as vertical—in other words, the problem is now one of an increasing number and quality of such weapons *among* already existing possessors, rather than an increase in the *number* of possessors.

Then there is the rest of the proliferation problem: ballistic missiles, cruise missiles, advanced conventional weaponry, small and light arms, new supplier nations, new risks of non-state actors gaining access to nuclear/biological/chemical weapons (NBC) or technologies. And there is even a new category of concerns over the proliferation of the science and technology base, and the dual-use technologies that go along with it.

To understand these increasingly complex phenomena, analysts continue to reach into the conceptual tool kit assembled by Wohlstetter and others in an earlier generation. But what drove nuclear proliferation in the 1950s and 1960s—major power competition—does not drive the proliferation trends of the 1990s, which result more from the asymmetric strategies of regional powers. Nor does the debate about the consequences of proliferation as framed by Wohlstetter, Kenneth Waltz, and their colleagues capture the full range of present experience. If, for example, as Waltz argued, nuclear proliferation might be stabilizing if it strengthens deterrence among hostile powers, what are we to make of the secret Iraqi biological arsenal that was evidently intended to be used not as a deterrent but as a means of retribution?

IF THE PROBLEM has changed, so too must policy. This brings us to the second part of Wohlstetter's short formula: the "+ 1" part. With a singular focus on the small number of developed states then considering the desirability of independent national "nuclear strike forces", Wohlstetter prescribed a strategy "to abate, delay or control nuclear diffusion", one encompassing an American nuclear guarantee to Europe and integrated alliance nuclear planning, with a bit of arms and export control on the side.

Today, policy must continue to be effective in dealing with the states with nuclear ambitions. These are now typically American adversaries, not allies, a fact that dislodges the centrality of a U.S. nuclear guarantee in non-proliferation strategy. But policy must also be effective in dealing with the increasingly multifaceted nature of the proliferation problem. Toward this end, many more tools of policy have been created. Supplier restraints in the nuclear domain have been supplemented by similar restraints in the chemical, biological, missile, and conventional weapons domains. Non-proliferation has been supplemented by counter-proliferation. The non-proliferation benefits of arms control are also now more widely appreciated. Despite this profusion of policy instruments, however, their focus remains the "+ 1" problem, which is to say preventing states with weapons ambitions from achieving their aims.

But the diffusion of materials, technologies, and expertise that have both normal commercial and military uses—especially in the areas of mass casualty weapons—has made the policy agenda far more complex. Thanks to this "dual-use" phenomenon, most states now have the ability to make chemical and biological weapons (CBW), and to do so relatively quickly. Many more states than actually possess nuclear weapons have the ability to make them. A key question is what these states with latent weapons capabilities will choose to do with those abilities. Might they hedge against an uncertain future by cultivating those capabilities, perhaps to the point of acquiring virtual arsenals? Might they turn potential into actual possession? If one or two states in a particular region were to do so, would it touch off a domino effect within and beyond that region? How can the risks of a wildfire-like weaponization among states with latent technical capabilities be minimized, as they respond simultaneously to a worsening security environment by stepping up the readiness ladder?

ANSWERS TO THESE questions must begin with the recognition that not all potential proliferators have the same motives, or find themselves in comparable circumstances. There are three reasonably distinct types of states whose behavior will matter to the long-term success of non-proliferation: the determined, the dabblers, and the disinterested.[1]

Those states *determined* to possess nuclear, biological, and/or chemical weapons are generally desperate to gain the strategic and operational leverage presumed to derive from them. This is the category most in the public mind today, and not surprisingly so. Examples include the de facto nuclear weapons states plus Iraq and North Korea.

The *dabblers* are those states exploring their weapons potential but that lack an immediately compelling strategic need. They cultivate a scientific base and would move to weapons production and stockpiling under certain circumstances. Examples here are hotly debated, but certainly include Iran and Taiwan. The states that plunged into CBW work following Iraq's examples in the 1980s and 1990s may also be dabblers.

The *disinterested* states are those with neither the programs nor the ambitions to exploit their latent capabilities for weapons purposes. Sometimes those capabilities are substantial. In the nuclear domain, Germany and Japan are prime examples. In the chemical and biological domains, any developed country has a substantial latent ability. Why do so many refrain from exploiting their weapons potential? External guarantees play a role for some. So too does history and politics. Some simply calculate that developing such capabilities would cause more security problems than it would solve.

Let us now look at these three categories more closely, in reverse order.

The disinterested category—happily constituting the vast majority of countries of the world—rarely gets the attention of the non-proliferation community, but these states deserve to be a part of the policy picture for several reasons. First, their latent capability might eventually be translated into weapons prowess—which could have far-reaching consequences, especially if the country in question were a major power such as Germany or Japan. Second, some of these states are what Sandy Spector has called repentant proliferants—that is, states that over the last few decades have formally forsworn nuclear weapons programs after taking initial—and sometimes substantial—steps in that direction. Usually the reversal has followed lengthy debate over what best serves their national interest. (South Africa and Ukraine, after all, make a much more credible case for the virtues of nuclear non-possession than does the rhetoric of those that determinedly continue to be nuclear weapons states.) Third, some are states that have prospered even in a generally insecure international environment without resort to *any* major armaments programs. Costa Rica is perhaps the best example here, and a model for others—after all, it has no military forces and did not create them even when its neighbors Nicaragua and Panama were in deep crisis.

There are yet other reasons to fit these states into the non-proliferation equation. Many of them are the recipients, conduits, and even generators of militarily sensitive technologies. Because they are so numerous, their participation in the international effort to prevent those technologies from reaching states with weapons ambitions is essential. Relatedly, the weapons-disinterested states must be active in the promulgation of the international norms about weapons and war and in the implementation of the multilateral treaty regimes embodying these norms. Without their participation, the international consensus against proliferation would be limited to a few countries mostly in the developed world.

The dabblers are states reported or reputed to have weapons development programs, but not compelling reasons for actually acquiring the weapons. These states are not motivated by immediate fears for their national survival. Some may have substantial weapons programs that have gained momentum largely on the basis of domestic political and bureaucratic factors. Some of these programs seem to have paused at certain thresholds related to weaponization, serial production, or declaratory policy, and today face an uncertain future as national leaders debate the evolution of national military capabilities—a process obviously contingent on political perceptions and external factors. Because states do not publicize these programs, it is difficult to gauge

---

[1] Editor's note: Used here in the primary (though often considered incorrect) *Oxford English Dictionary* meaning of "disinterest": "Absence of interest, unconcern."

how numerous they may be. But they deserve to be in the non-proliferation equation because changes in security conditions can give rise to rapid movement toward unconventional weapons capabilities on their part. The speed with which such developments could occur is itself a source of worry, for there is nothing like an acute perception of time pressure to evoke a series of bad judgments.

Yet the policy debate focuses almost entirely on the third category—the determined proliferators. These are states whose leaders appear absolutely determined to achieve an unconventional weapons capability, or to continue improving one already attained, and who do so despite high costs and risks, due to some perceived overwhelming national interest.

In the U.S. policy debate, each tool of policy is scrutinized for what it contributes to preventing the success of the determined proliferator. Very often, the relevance and contributions of each tool to the other two categories of states is ignored. Arms control approaches are not likely to be especially effective for dealing with the determined proliferator, but they are valuable for enlisting the weapons-disinterested states as political partners in the non-proliferation effort, and indispensable for creating incentives for the contingent proliferator to abandon programs lacking an overriding strategic purpose. Export control approaches have a similar role in imposing costs on the dabblers and promoting cooperation among like-minded states, even if they are not always reliable in keeping sensitive technologies out of the hands of proliferators. Counter-proliferation, which is to say the strengthening of the U.S. ability to fight and prevail in regional wars in which aggressors threaten or use NBC weapons, is essential for creating yet more disincentives for the dabblers and the determined proliferators. It is also essential for reassuring those whose disinterest in acquiring NBC counters of their own depends to some extent on credible U.S. guarantees.

However much we may long for the tidiness embodied in Wohlstetter's "N + 1" concept, it is beyond our power to recreate the world of 1961. Enlisting the disinterested states and creating incentives for the dabblers to abandon their programs, or at least to remain under the threshold of weaponization, are as important to the long-term success of non-proliferation as is preventing North Korea, Iraq, and Iran from achieving their nuclear ambitions.

Yet the government as a whole still lacks an agenda that effectively encompasses the many facets of the proliferation problem. To be sure, it has an agenda—and as argued above, an increasingly broad one. Lots of bureaus, agencies, and departments are working the proliferation problem with myriad programs and policies. But there are signs that all this effort is not particularly well orchestrated. For example, absorption of the Arms Control and Disarmament Agency into the Department of State has reinforced the tendency to narrow the non-proliferation emphasis to the "rogue states", and to submerge arms control and non-proliferation issues in relations with the dabblers and disinterested states into the larger bilateral dialogue. As another example, the disputes about weapons programs in Iraq and North Korea graphically illustrate the fact that government is better at creating anti-proliferation instruments than at enforcing them. On the more positive side, after an early bureaucratic feud that left the impression that the effort to prevent proliferation was going to be abandoned in favor of an effort to cope with its consequences militarily, there is now widespread agreement that counter-proliferation and non-proliferation are complementary.

A more integrated and effective strategy cannot be won simply by creating new organizational structures or appointing a new proliferation czar. The chief deficiency of policy is not bureaucratic but political. Everyone working the problem in government understands that preventing proliferation is important but there is no generally accepted sense of why and how all the pieces of policy are supposed to fit together. The principles and purposes of U.S. policy remain set out in largely Wohlstetter-like terms. This reinforces the tendency to equate proliferation policy with nuclear non-proliferation. It also reinforces the tendency to treat non-proliferation as a discrete and separable policy problem, when in fact it cuts across large segments of American foreign and defense policy and can be dealt with effectively only as an integral component. Policy could be made more effective if someone in the bully pulpit would restate the principles and purposes of policy, define the components of American strategy, and identify the synergies among policy instruments. Without such a strategic perspective, there is no way to decide where proliferation fits in U.S. priorities in any given instance, how to handle conflicting policy interests as they arise, or how to determine sensible budgetary allocations among the various agencies.

The absence of a strategic perspective also brings with it a political cost. Without a sense of why and how the elements of policy fit together, individual pieces are vulnerable to poaching. Each piece has its strong critics (often with views firmly rooted in Cold War-vintage strategic perspectives). Some see arms control as a sellout of the national interest; others see counter-proliferation as an abandonment of the pure principle of non-proliferation. Some argue that the proliferation problem has been exaggerated, and that American power is sufficient in its "unipolar moment" to pay less rather than more attention to proliferation; others, contrarily, think things are so bad that we should jettison non-proliferation efforts altogether and instead prepare urgently for a world in which such weapons are widely proliferated and actually used.

But U.S. interests are best served by husbanding all of the tools of policy that have been developed over the years because, again, particular tools are relevant to different parts of the problem. The synergies among these tools, too, may be as important as the contributions they can make singly. Arms control is necessary if export controls are to be effectively coordinated among the growing number of supplier states. Arms control regimes can also help legitimize certain types of enforcement actions against proliferators, including coercive actions. Counter-proliferation capabilities are needed to deter, defeat, and punish the users of weapons of mass destruction and thus to deny them the coercive value of threats deriving from those weapons.

It is legitimate to ask whether the United States is capable of pursuing so comprehensive an agenda in an era of increasing partisanship over foreign policy. The attack on administration policy has been continuous. Not obliged to offer a strategic perspective of their own, administration critics can subject every instrument of policy to the hardest test (the determined proliferator test), and shine a bright light on its shortcomings. They have made a lot of headway. On balance, this sort of bureaucratic potshotting works against the national interest by weakening the political foundations necessary for implementing negotiated instruments, enforcing existing obligations, and building the right kinds of military forces at the same time. American leadership of the non-proliferation effort is no longer taken for granted by our historic partners in this process—and certainly not by some of our most dangerous potential opponents.

Re-reading Albert Wohlstetter's 1961 article reminds one of how much the world has changed over four decades. It is a reminder that potential proliferators are not few but many, as most states have been empowered by economic and technical developments to build quickly high-leverage weaponry with impressive strategic reach. It is also a reminder of the diminishing capacity of the United States to achieve non-proliferation results internationally by extending a security guarantee or two, or by orchestrating a few trade restraints.

Perhaps there is virtue in the necessity of engaging ever broader international coalitions in the fight against proliferation, for the best way to prevent states from hedging against uncertain futures is to enlist them in creating stable ones. Recognizing that necessity points to new leadership requirements for a United States whose place and role have changed, but whose leadership remains essential to the larger international effort. On the necessity of American leadership in this portentous policy area, a re-reading of Wohlstetter's article also reminds us of what has not changed over the years, and is not likely to either.

Index

A

Abu Nidal Organization (ANO), 194
Acheson, Dean, 77
Adams, John Quincy, 108, 110–111
Afghanistan, 83, 93, 204, 205, 206, 208
"Africa Crisis Response Initiative," 89
Africa, prospects of, and U.S. policy, 88–89
African Growth and Opportunity Act, 88–89
African National Congress, 81
Agency for International Development (AID), 142, 143
Albright, Madelaine, 73, 75, 106, 129, 143, 156
Algeria, 77, 79, 82–83, 204
American hegemony, 8–13, 14–20
American Israeli Public Affairs Committee (AIPAC), 102, 103
American Jews, Netanyahu and, 99–107
Angola, 204, 205, 206, 208
Anti-Ballistic Missile (ABM) Treaty, 197
apartheid, 80, 209
Arafat, Yasir, 85, 86, 99, 106
Argentina, 207
Armenia, 54
Arms Control and Disarmament Agency (ACDA), 143
arms sales, 185, 197–203, 204–208; military technology and, 131–135
Ashcroft, John, 130
Asian financial crisis, 167, 168–169, 170–172
Asia-Pacific Economic Cooperation (APEC), 80, 81
Aspin, Les, 155
Atlantic Alliance, 65, 70
Australia, 207
Austria, 207
Azerbaijan, 54, 55

B

Begin, Menachem, 100
Belarus, 45
Berger, Samuel R., 73, 75, 157, 161, 162–163
Blum, Fred, 104–105
"Board of Overseers of Major International Institutions and Markets," 168
Bolivia, 84
Bosnia, 72–76, 93, 95, 96, 97, 109, 142, 204, 206, 208
Boutros-Ghali, Boutros, 205
Brazil, 79, 82, 84, 138
Britain, 24, 53, 68, 77, 139, 199, 201
Brzezinski, Zbigniew, 14, 156, 159
Bumpers, Dale, 130
Burkina Faso, 208
Burma, 25, 126, 127, 204, 209
Burns, Nicholas, 154, 157
Burundi, 204
Bush, George, 26, 44, 46–47, 48, 66, 72, 93, 95–96

C

Cambodia, 58, 204, 205
Canada, 24, 81, 207, 208
capitalism, 22
Central Intelligence Agency (CIA), 21, 137, 139, 150
Chechnya, 25
Chemical Weapons Convention (CWC), 48, 128, 130
Chile, 81
China, 26, 27, 49, 50, 58, 61, 62, 77, 83, 84, 171, 177, 187–188, 199, 201, 202, 207; export of satellite technology to, 161–163
Chirac, Jacques, 73
Christopher, Warren, 73, 153, 154–156, 158
Clark, Wesley, 158
Clinton, Bill, 8, 12–13, 23, 45, 46, 47–48, 51, 58, 65, 67, 70, 72–73, 74–75, 78, 79, 85, 86, 87, 88–89, 96, 97, 98, 99, 100, 101–102, 105–106, 112, 115, 138, 140, 155, 156, 157, 158, 161–163, 173–174, 178–179, 192, 197, 198, 200, 203, 209
CNN effect, 95
Coca-Cola, 38
Cohen, William, 184
Colombia, 25, 178–181
Commonwealth of Independent States (CIS), 54
Communist Party, Russian, 53, 54
Comprehensive Nuclear Test Ban (CTB), 48
Conference on Security and Cooperation in Europe (CSCE), 68, 155–156
Conservative Jews, 100, 103–104
Constitution, U.S.: economic sanctions by state and local governments, 125–127; International Criminal Court and, 122–124
consumer protection, IMF and, 175
Conventional Forces in Europe (CFE) Treaty, 48, 198
conventions, as response to terrorism, 194–195
Cooperative Threat Reduction (CTR) program, 45
Croatia, 207
Cuba, 208
culture, American culture in global, 30–41
Cyprus, 82
Czech Republic, 51, 56, 198

D

Davis, Lynn, 153, 154
Dayton Peace Agreement, 74–76
De Geofproy v. Riggs, 123
Defense Department, "threat-based" planning of, 184–188
democracy, 22, 68, 176; global culture and end of, 35
Democratic Party: globalization and, 117, 118; IMF and, 172–173
determined proliferators, nuclear weapons and, 222, 223
Disney, 39
Dodik, Milorad, 76
Dole, Robert, 16
dominant maneuver, military technology and, 133
Donilon, Thomas, 153, 154
drug trafficking, 25, 70; rebels and, in Colombia, 178–181
dumdum bullets, 209

E

East Timor, 80
economic intelligence, 136–140
economic sanctions: as response to terrorism, 192–193; use of, by state and local governments, 125–127
Ecuador, 80
Egypt, 77–78, 83, 84, 207
Eighth Amendment, 123
Eisenhower, Dwight, 77
Eisenhower, Susan, 128–129
El Salvador, 77, 84
embassies, tin cup diplomacy and, 142, 143
encryption technology, 138–139
environmental issues, 83, 117; IMF and, 175
Estes, Howell, III, 73
Ethiopia, 83, 84
ethnic issues, 204, 205
European Community (EC), 65, 67–68, 70, 82
export laws, China satellite deal and, 161–163

F

Falwell, Jerry, 101
Fifth Amendment, 123
Finland, 207
First Wave, Toffler's theory of the, 132
Flanagan, Stephen, 153–154
focused logistics, military technology and, 133
fog of war, 132
foreign aid, 176–177
Founding Act on Relations, 50, 51
Fourth Amendment, 123
France, 24, 32, 82, 139, 140, 176, 199, 201
Freeh, Louis J., 138
full-dimension protection, military technology and, 133
fundamentalism, Islamic, 80, 82, 97

G

Gates, Bill, 39–40
General Agreement on Tariffs and Trade (GATT), 96, 117–188, 126, 139
Georgia, 54–55
Germany, 22, 24, 53, 54, 65, 66, 68, 92, 176, 201, 207, 222

225

global culture, American culture and, 30–41
globalization: dangers of, 166–169; as non-debate in U.S., 113–119
Golan Heights, 97
Goldberg, J. J., 100, 103
Gorbachev, Mikhail, 149
Gordon, Michael, 213, 216
Gore, Al, 158
Government Procurement Agreement (GPA), 126
Greece, 82, 108
Group of Seven (G-7), 200
guerrilla warfare, 134

H

Haass, Richard, 213, 218
Haiti, 77, 84, 93, 95, 96, 109, 111, 142
Havel, Vaclav, 159
Helms, Jesse, 128, 129, 130, 143
Holbrooke, Richard, 152–153, 157, 158
human rights, 68, 77, 176, 207
Hungary, 51, 156, 197, 206
Huntington, Samuel, 9
Hussein, Saddam, 93, 94, 135
Hutchinson, Kay Bailey, 130

I

Implementation Force (IFOR), 75
In re Yamashita, 123
India, 63–64, 79, 83, 201, 202, 207, 208
Indonesia, 79, 80–81, 82, 171, 172
intelligence, economic, 136–140
Intelligence Services Act, 139
Interamerican Development Bank, 177
International Atomic Energy Agency (IAEA), 200, 201
"International Credit Insurance Corporation," 167
International Criminal Court (ICC), 122–124
International Monetary Fund (IMF), 47, 82, 166, 167, 168; reform of, 170–175
Iran, 97, 135, 185, 190, 192
Iraq, 82, 97, 109, 111, 134, 149, 199, 207, 222. *See also* Persian Gulf War
Ireland, 208
Iron Curtain, 203
Islam, 25, 80, 81, 83. *See also* fundamentalism, Islamic
isolationism, 93
Israel, 26, 77, 80, 85–87, 97, 201, 202, 207; Netanyahu and, 99–107
Italy, 82

J

Jackson, Jesse, 89
Japan, 22, 24, 26, 27, 32, 66, 77, 81, 84, 94, 96, 171, 176, 201, 222; security alliance between U.S. and, 57–62
Java, 80

Jewish Agency, 104
Jewish Community Federation (JCF), 104
Jews. *See* American Jews; Conservative Jews; Orthodox Jews; Reform Jews
Joint Combined Exchange Training, 179
Joint Vision 2010, 133, 134, 135, 185, 186, 187
Jordan, 80
Justice Department, export of satellite technology to China, and, 161, 162

K

Kagan, Robert, 14, 15, 16–17
Kaplan, Fred, 202–203
Kashmir, 63, 64, 83, 204, 206
Karadzic, Radovan, 75
Kaufman, Henry, 167–168
Kazakhstan, 45, 55
Kennan, George, 92; on American principles, 108–112
Kennedy, John F., 140, 202
Khomeini, Ayotollah Ruhollah, 217
Kissinger, Henry, 77, 156
Kosovo, 76
Kurds, 216–217
Kuttner, Robert, 33
Kuwait, 26, 77, 80, 135, 149. *See also* Persian Gulf War

L

labor rights, IMF and, 174–175
Lake, Anthony, 23, 75, 152, 154, 156, 157, 158, 159
Lebanon, 26, 96, 97, 109
Liberia, 204, 206, 208
Libya, 82, 191–192, 193, 195
light weapons, 204–208
Lisbon Protocol, 45
Livingston, Bob, 102
Loral Space & Communications, 161–163
Lott, Trent, 128, 129
Luce, Henry, 16

M

Macedonia, 82
Mali, 83
Mandelbaum, Michael, 97
Marcuse, Herbert, 33–34
Marshall, Andrew, 132
Marshall Plan, 69, 71
Marx, Karl, 24
Maryland, economic sanctions of, 125, 126, 127
Massachusetts, economic sanctions of, 125, 126, 127
McWorld, American culture in global culture and, 30–41
media, 94–95
Mexico, 25, 79, 141, 167, 207
Microsoft, 39–40, 139
military force, as response to terrorism, 193
military issues: after cold war, 197–203, 204–208; technology and, 131–135

mines, 205
Mladic, Ratko, 74
Morocco, 82
Moscovitz, Bernard, 105
Mozambique, 206
Mubarak, Hosni, 79, 80
Myanmar. *See* Burma

N

"N+1" problem, nuclear weapons and, 220–224
National Security Act, 21
nationalism, 83
Netanyahu, Benjamin, 85, 86–87, 99–107
New Israel Fund, 104
Nicaragua, 208
Nigeria, 124, 126
Nixon, Richard, 77
no concession, policy of, as response to terrorism, 190
Non-Proliferation Treaty (NPT), 44, 48
North American Free Trade Agreement (NAFTA), 25, 79, 117–118
North Atlantic Cooperation Council (NACC), 153, 154
North Atlantic Treaty Organization (NATO), 23, 27, 68, 69, 71, 75, 76, 82, 198–201, 206; enlargement of, 50–51, 128–130, 141, 152–160
North Korea, 49, 50, 97, 134, 141, 142, 185, 199, 207, 223
Nuclear Threat Reduction Act, 45
nuclear weapons, 44–45, 46, 47, 48, 49–50, 63–64, 97–98, 141, 197–203, 204, 220–224
Nunn, Sam, 65
Nunn-Lugar program, 45

O

Oakley, Robert, 63, 64
official development assistance, 176–177
Operation Plan (OPLAN) 40104, 73
Operation Provide Hope, 47
Orthodox Church, 51
Oslo Accords, 100, 101
Orthodox Jews, 100, 103–104
Othello Effect, 186
Ottoman Empire, 77

P

Pakistan, 25, 26, 63–64, 79, 83, 84, 202, 206
Palestine, 85–87, 99, 100, 101
Pan Am Flight 103, 191
Partnership for Peace (PFP), 14, 49, 152, 153–156
Patton, 101
peacekeeping, United Nations, 206
People's Liberation Army (PLA), of China, 58, 61
Pepsi-Cola, 36
Persian Gulf War, 55, 93, 95, 135, 212–219
Philippines, 84, 171

Piatelli-Palmarini, Massimo, 186
pivotal states, U.S. foreign policy and, 77–84
Poland, 54, 154, 156, 159, 198, 207
policy of no concessions, as response to terrorism, 190
population growth, 83
Powell, Colin, 213, 215
precision enlargement, military technology and, 133
President's Partnership for Growth and Opportunity in Africa, 89
prosecution, as response to terrorism, 190–191

Q

Qaddafi, Muammar, 82, 193, 195
"Quadrennial Defense Review," 184–188

R

Reagan, Ronald, 66, 97, 98, 116, 190, 191–192
realpolitik, 204
Reform Jews, 101, 103–104
Republican Party: globalization and, 116–117; IMF and, 172
revolution in military affairs (RMAs), technology and, 131–135
Revolutionary Armed Forces of Colombia (FARC), 179, 180, 181
Rezaq, Omar Mohammed, 191
Romania, 207
Rosner, Jeremy, 128–129
Ross, Dennis, 154
Rothenberg, Alan, 104
Rubin, Robert, 117, 170, 173
Rushdie, Salman, 192
Rusk, Dean, 140
Russia, 25, 44–51, 77, 84, 187, 207; arms race and, 197–203; NATO expansion and, 50–51, 154, 158; potential enmity of, 52–56. See also Soviet Union
Rwanda, 77, 95, 109, 204, 206

S

Sachs, Jeffrey, 177
Safire, William, 212
satellite technology, export of, to China, 161–163
Saudi Arabia, 77, 79, 138, 192
Schumpter, Joseph, 26
Schwarzkopf, Norman, 214–215, 216
Scowcroft, Brent, 215
Second Wave, Toffler's theory of the, 8, 132
"second-war capability," "threat-based planning" and, 186

Senate, ratification of expansion of NATO and, 128–130
Serbs, Bosnia and, 72–76
Sese Seko, Mobutu, 98
Shalikashvili, John, 72, 133, 155, 156
Shellum, Brian, 219
Shiite Muslims, 216–217
Singapore, 24
Sixth Amendment, 123
Slovenia, 207
Somalia, 26, 72, 94, 97, 109, 134, 204, 205, 206
Soros, George, 167, 173, 174, 175
South Africa, 79, 83–84, 89, 126–127, 207, 209
South Korea, 23, 24, 49, 50, 77, 171
Soviet Union, 22, 58, 68, 93, 208
Spain, 24, 82
Srebrenica, Bosnia, 76
Sri Lanka, 204, 206, 208
State Department: export of satellite technology to China and, 162; tin cup diplomacy and, 142, 143
Stealth technology, 133
Strategic Arms Limitation Treaties (SALT), 197, 198, 201
Strategic Arms Reduction Treaties (START), 45, 46, 48
Sudan, 204, 206
Suharto, 80
Supreme Court, U.S., 123
Syria, 82, 97, 138, 192, 218

T

Taiwan, 24, 58, 62
Tajikistan, 204
Talbott, Strobe, 154, 157
technology, military, 131–135
10th Mountain Division, 16
terrorism, 98, 138; response options to, 189–196
Tet offensive, 93
Thailand, 171, 172
Thatcher, Margaret, 212, 213
Third Wave, Toffler's theory of the, 132
"threat-based" planning, of Defense Department, 184–188
tin cup diplomacy, 141–143
Toffler, Alvin and Heidi, 132
Trainor, Bernard, 213, 216
treaties, as response to terrorism, 193–194
Truman, Harry, 21, 22–23
Tunisia, 82
Turkey, 77, 79, 82–83, 84, 108, 208
Turkmenistan, 54, 55

U

Ukraine, 45, 48–49
Unabomber, 190
United Jewish Appeal (UJA), 104
United Nations, 61, 201, 204, 206, 208, 209, 213
United States Information Agency (USIA), 142, 143
U.S.–Japan Guidelines for Defense Cooperation of 1997, 57
Uzbekistan, 54

V

Vajpayee, Atal Bihari, 64
Venezuela, 207
Vershbow, Alexander, 153, 158
Vietnam, 23, 72, 77, 93, 94, 95, 134, 140, 208, 218
Vinson, Carl, 21

W

wage levels, globalization and, 113
Walesa, Lech, 153, 159
Walker, Jenonne, 153
Walt Disney Co., 39
Warner, Andrew, 177
Warner, John, 128, 129–130
wars, post–cold war era and, 204–208
Washington, George, 110
Wassenaar Arrangement, 206
welfare reform, globalization and, 113–114
White House Situation Room, 146–151
Wilson, Woodrow, 27
Wohlstetter, Albert, 220
Wolsey, James, 137–138
World Bank, 47, 177
World Trade Center bombing, 191
World Trade Organization (WTO), 25, 174–175
World War II, 22, 66, 71, 94, 111

Y

Yeltsin, Boris, 44, 46, 47–48, 53–54, 55, 197, 198, 200
Yousef, Ramzi, 191
Yugoslavia, 24, 205, 207

Z

Zaire, 79, 98, 141–142, 204
Zionist Organization of America (ZOA), 102

AE Article Review Form

We encourage you to photocopy and use this page as a tool to assess how the articles in **Annual Editions** expand on the information in your textbook. By reflecting on the articles you will gain enhanced text information. You can also access this useful form on a product's book support Web site at **http://www.dushkin.com/online/**.

NAME: _____ DATE: _____

TITLE AND NUMBER OF ARTICLE:
_____

BRIEFLY STATE THE MAIN IDEA OF THIS ARTICLE:
_____

LIST THREE IMPORTANT FACTS THAT THE AUTHOR USES TO SUPPORT THE MAIN IDEA:

_____

WHAT INFORMATION OR IDEAS DISCUSSED IN THIS ARTICLE ARE ALSO DISCUSSED IN YOUR TEXTBOOK OR OTHER READINGS THAT YOU HAVE DONE? LIST THE TEXTBOOK CHAPTERS AND PAGE NUMBERS:

_____

LIST ANY EXAMPLES OF BIAS OR FAULTY REASONING THAT YOU FOUND IN THE ARTICLE:

_____

LIST ANY NEW TERMS/CONCEPTS THAT WERE DISCUSSED IN THE ARTICLE, AND WRITE A SHORT DEFINITION:

_____

We Want Your Advice

ANNUAL EDITIONS revisions depend on two major opinion sources: one is our Advisory Board, listed in the front of this volume, which works with us in scanning the thousands of articles published in the public press each year; the other is you—the person actually using the book. Please help us and the users of the next edition by completing the prepaid article rating form on this page and returning it to us. Thank you for your help!

ANNUAL EDITIONS: American Foreign Policy 99/00

ARTICLE RATING FORM

Here is an opportunity for you to have direct input into the next revision of this volume. We would like you to rate each of the 36 articles listed below, using the following scale:

1. **Excellent: should definitely be retained**
2. **Above average: should probably be retained**
3. **Below average: should probably be deleted**
4. **Poor: should definitely be deleted**

Your ratings will play a vital part in the next revision. So please mail this prepaid form to us just as soon as you complete it. Thanks for your help!

RATING / ARTICLE

1. The Benevolent Empire
2. The Perils of (and for) an Imperial America
3. A New Realism
4. Democracy at Risk: American Culture in a Global Culture
5. The United States and the New Russia: The First Five Years
6. Is Russia Still an Enemy?
7. Testing the United States–Japan Security Alliance
8. South Asian Arms Race: Reviving Dormant Fears of Nuclear War
9. America and Europe: Is the Break Inevitable?
10. Why Are We in Bosnia?
11. Pivotal States and U.S. Strategy
12. The Middle East Peace Process: A Crisis of Partnership
13. Africa, the 'Invisible Land,' Is Gaining Visibility
14. The Common Sense
15. Netanyahu and American Jews
16. On American Principles
17. Globalization: The Great American Non-Debate
18. Against an International Criminal Court
19. Paying Something for Nothing
20. The Senate's Strange Bedfellows
21. Racing toward the Future: The Revolution in Military Affairs
22. Why Spy? The Uses and Misuses of Intelligence
23. Tin Cup Diplomacy
24. Inside the White House Situation Room
25. NATO Expansion: The Anatomy of a Decision
26. The White House Dismissed Warnings on China Satellite Deal
27. Globalization and Its Discontents: Navigating the Dangers of a Tangled World
28. For a New, Progressive IMF
29. Foreign Aid
30. Bogotá Aid: To Fight Drugs or Rebels?
31. Inventing Threats
32. Responding to Terrorism
33. Paring Down the Arsenal
34. The New Arms Race: Light Weapons and International Security
35. Closing the Gate: The Persian Gulf War Revisited
36. Rethinking N+1

(Continued on next page)

ANNUAL EDITIONS: AMERICAN FOREIGN POLICY 99/00

BUSINESS REPLY MAIL
FIRST-CLASS MAIL PERMIT NO. 84 GUILFORD CT
POSTAGE WILL BE PAID BY ADDRESSEE

Dushkin/McGraw-Hill
Sluice Dock
Guilford, CT 06437-9989

NO POSTAGE
NECESSARY
IF MAILED
IN THE
UNITED STATES

ABOUT YOU

Name _____ Date _____

Are you a teacher? ☐   A student? ☐
Your school's name _____

Department _____

Address _____ City _____ State _____ Zip _____

School telephone # _____

YOUR COMMENTS ARE IMPORTANT TO US!

Please fill in the following information:
For which course did you use this book?
_____

Did you use a text with this ANNUAL EDITION?   ☐ yes ☐ no
What was the title of the text?
_____

What are your general reactions to the Annual Editions concept?
_____

Have you read any particular articles recently that you think should be included in the next edition?
_____

Are there any articles you feel should be replaced in the next edition? Why?
_____

Are there any World Wide Web sites you feel should be included in the next edition? Please annotate.
_____

May we contact you for editorial input?   ☐ yes ☐ no
May we quote your comments?   ☐ yes ☐ no